A PRACTICAL APPROACH TO

WORDPERFECT® 5.1

COMPLETE COURSE

(Knights)
Enter
Enter
F2
NHSBUS-F10

Mary Alice Eisch

Office Occupations Instructor
Fox Valley Technical College
Appleton, Wisconsin

SOUTH-WESTERN PUBLISHING CO.

ISBN: 0-538-62834-0

Library of Congress Catalog Number: 93-083285

4 5 6 7 8 9 H 99 98 97 96 95

Printed in the United States of America

Editor-in-Chief: Robert First
Acquisitions Editor: Janie F. Schwark
Senior Developmental Editor: Dave Lafferty
Consulting Editor: Judy Voiers
Coordinating Editor: Lisa McClary
Production Manager: Anne Noschang
Senior Production Editor: June Davidson
Production Editor: Christine M. Kunz
Designers: Nicola M. Jones and Elaine St. John-Lagenaur
Production Artist: Sophia Renieris
Photo Editor/Stylist: Linda Ellis
Marketing Manager: Brian Taylor

PREFACE

WordPerfect®[1] 5.1, A Practical Approach; Complete Course is designed to be a self-teaching guide for users of WordPerfect on IBM®[2] or IBM compatible computers. It is written for the lay person in language that is appropriate for high school and adult students. While the text may be used in the classroom, it is also a good resource for secretaries and managers learning WordPerfect in the home or office.

LEARNING FEATURES

In addition to the hands-on exercises to reinforce learning throughout the lessons, each lesson includes the following features:
* learning objectives
* estimated time for completion
* an explanation of the various features and their use
* a step-by-step guide for using each feature
* written activities to reinforce understanding
* reference questions to acquaint the learner with the WordPerfect documentation

Review exercises are strategically placed to give the learner a break from new material and to reinforce previously learned skills. Command summaries at the end of every few lessons offer the learner an opportunity to review the features learned.

STUDENT HELPS

A study guide, including estimated completion time and a space to check off completed work, is located on page xv. The Quick Reference, listing WordPerfect features, the menu choices, appropriate keystrokes, and lessons where the features are covered, begins on page xi. Also available is a template disk containing a number of the documents in the hands-on exercises. While the actual keying of each exercise greatly enhances learning, the use of prerecorded documents may save keying time for some exercises.

MESSAGE TO THE LEARNER

This book is intended to assist you in learning WordPerfect 5.1. It is designed to be helpful to those of you with limited experience in the use of computers. It assumes that the software has already been installed on your computer, although Appendix C contains instructions for software

---

[1]*WordPerfect is a registered trademark of WordPerfect Corporation.*
[2]*IBM is a registered trademark of International Business Machines Corporation.*

installation. Appendix A contains instructions for formatting a disk, and Appendix B contains the basics of using the mouse with WordPerfect. Appendix D contains a list of commonly used DOS commands.

Unit 1 introduces the basics of text editing using WordPerfect 5.1. Formatting features such as headers and footers, footnotes, tables, and outlines are included in Unit 2. Unit 3 introduces exciting WordPerfect power tools such as Merge, Sort, Macros, Styles, and Document Assembly. Finally, Unit 4 introduces the page layout tools included in WordPerfect such as graphic boxes and lines. Following Lesson 36 is an office simulation where a student may put into practice the skills learned in the textbook lessons. While all of the WordPerfect features are not covered in detail in this book, most features are introduced and explained so that you can proceed more confidently on your own.

The lessons are designed to be completed in sequence; each lesson reinforces skills learned in previous lessons as well as the current lesson. Exercise documents are used a number of times throughout the lessons to eliminate the need for excessive keying. Read thoroughly and follow instructions carefully to make your learning fun and worth your time. As you work through this textbook, you will become increasingly excited about the ease with which you are going to be able to complete your office work or homework using WordPerfect.

MANUAL

The *Manual* contains the following:
- ▸ teaching suggestions for each lessons
- ▸ mastery exercises for additional practice, arranged by lesson
- ▸ two alternate study guides that may be duplicated for class use
- ▸ a solutions section for end-of-lesson activities
- ▸ solutions for documents created in the hands-on exercises
- ▸ two theory tests with solutions
- ▸ five production tests with solutions
- ▸ hard copy illustrating the documents on the template disk

ACKNOWLEDGEMENTS

Many thanks to my consulting editor, Judy Voiers, for her continuing guidance, encouragement, and assistance. Thanks also to Achim, Peter, Sara, Bea, and Chester for their love and support during the development of these materials.

Mary Alice Eisch
Appleton, Wisconsin

CONTENTS

QUICK REFERENCE

Name _____

MOVING THE CURSOR

End . . . . End of the line
Home, Home, ← . . . . Beginning of the line
Home, Home, ↑ . . . . Top of the document (below codes—first character)
Home, Home, Home, ↑ . . . . . . Top of the document (above all codes)
Home, Home, ↓ . . . . Bottom of the document
Page Up . . . . Top of Previous Page
Page Down . . . . Top of Next Page
Keypad Minus Key (-) or Home, ↑ Top of Screen
Keypad Plus Key (+) or Home, ↓ . Bottom of Screen
Ctrl→ . . . . Beginning of next word
Ctrl← . . . . Beginning of previous word
Ctrl-Home, → . . . . To the column at the right
Ctrl-Home, ← . . . . To the column at the left

DELETING TEXT

Backspace . . . . Delete character to the left of the cursor
Delete . . . . Delete character at the cursor
Ctrl-Delete . . . . Delete word at the cursor
Ctrl-Backspace . . . . Delete word at the cursor
Ctrl-End . . . . Deletes from cursor to the end of the line
Ctrl-Page Down . . . . Deletes from the cursor to the end of the page

STUDY GUIDE

Name _____

UNIT 1   WORDPERFECT BASICS

		Score	Date Completed	Instructor
Lesson 1	Introduction to the Course and the IBM PC ½ hour	_____	_____	_____
Lesson 2	Introduction to WordPerfect 1 hour	_____	_____	_____
Lesson 3	The WordPerfect Keyboard ½ hour	_____	_____	_____
Lesson 4	Correcting Text ½ hour	_____	_____	_____
Lesson 5	Saving and Retrieving Documents ½ hour	_____	_____	_____
Lesson 6	File Management 1 hour	_____	_____	_____
Lesson 7	Text Enhancement 1 hour	_____	_____	_____
Lesson 8	Text Entry Features 1 hour	_____	_____	_____
Lesson 9	Editing Features 2 hours	_____	_____	_____
Lesson 10	Speller and Thesaurus 1 hour	_____	_____	_____
Production Test 1		_____	_____	_____

STUDY GUIDE

Name _____

UNIT 2   WORDPERFECT FORMATTING AND EDITING

		Score	Date Completed	Instructor
Lesson 11	Line Spacing, Margins, and Tabs 1½ hours	_____	_____	_____
Lesson 12	More Line Formatting 2 hours	_____	_____	_____
Lesson 13	Block 1 hour	_____	_____	_____
Lesson 14	Page Formatting 1½ hours	_____	_____	_____
Lesson 15	Footnotes and Endnotes 2 hours	_____	_____	_____
Lesson 16	Tables 2 hours	_____	_____	_____
Lesson 17	Text Columns 1½ hours	_____	_____	_____
Lesson 18	Outlining 2 hours	_____	_____	_____
Lesson 19	Review and Practice 3 hours	_____	_____	_____
Production Test 2		_____	_____	_____
Theory Test 1		_____	_____	_____

STUDY GUIDE

Name _____

UNIT 3   WORDPERFECT POWER TOOLS

		Score	Date Completed	Instructor
Lesson 20	Advanced File Management 1½ hours	_____	_____	_____
Lesson 21	Macros 1 hour	_____	_____	_____
Lesson 22	Merge Basics 2 hours	_____	_____	_____
Lesson 23	Putting Merge to Work 1½ hours	_____	_____	_____
Lesson 24	Document Assembly 1½ hours	_____	_____	_____
Lesson 25	Sort 2 hours	_____	_____	_____
Lesson 26	Envelopes and Labels 1 hour	_____	_____	_____
Lesson 27	Styles 2½ hours	_____	_____	_____
Lesson 28	Table of Contents and Index 2 hours	_____	_____	_____
Lesson 29	Feature Bonanza 2¼ hours	_____	_____	_____
Lesson 30	Review and Practice 2¼ hours	_____	_____	_____
Production Test 3		_____	_____	_____
Production Test 4		_____	_____	_____

STUDY GUIDE

Name _____

UNIT 4   WORDPERFECT GRAPHIC TOOLS

		Score	Date Completed	Instructor
Lesson 31	Graphic Boxes 1½ hours	_____	_____	_____
Lesson 32	Graphic Lines 1 hour	_____	_____	_____
Lesson 33	Using Fonts 1 hour	_____	_____	_____
Lesson 34	Graphic Mania 2 hours	_____	_____	_____
Lesson 35	Forms 3 hours	_____	_____	_____
Lesson 36	Review and Practice 3 hours	_____	_____	_____
Production Test 5		_____	_____	_____
Theory Test 2		_____	_____	_____

Unit 1

WordPerfect Basics

LESSON 1
Introduction to the Course and the IBM PC

OBJECTIVES

Upon completion of this lesson, you will be able to discuss:

1. The learning materials for WordPerfect 5.1.
2. The hardware components of the PC.
3. The supplies needed for your training.

Estimated Time: ½ hour

Welcome to WordPerfect! WordPerfect is word processing software for IBM or IBM compatible personal computers. You will learn to use the PC to create and edit documents such as letters, memos, manuscripts, reports with footnotes, tabulations, and newsletters. You will also learn to save documents from the memory of the computer onto a 3½-inch or 5¼-inch floppy disk and retrieve the documents for editing and printing.

This is an individualized self-paced course, which means you will move through the learning materials at your own speed. You don't need to slow down for the student next to you. Neither do you have to keep up with that whiz sitting in front of you. Keep moving, but do it at a pace that's comfortable for you and enhances your learning. Your instructor will provide you with encouragement and technical assistance—in other words, your instructor is there to help you along.

THE TEXTBOOK

This textbook is divided into four units.

Unit 1: WordPerfect Basics

The first unit consists of ten lessons. A production test for this unit is included in the instructor's manual. (The production test is a hands-on test where you will be timed as you prepare and edit a document using WordPerfect.) The unit should take about ten hours to complete. Depending on how your training is scheduled, your instructor may have you omit certain exercises. You should never skip an entire lesson, since each lesson teaches specific concepts to make your word processing operations easy and efficient. In addition, the skills learned in one lesson are expanded and built on in each successive lesson.

Throughout Unit 1 you will find a short exercise or two following the explanation of a concept. Do each exercise carefully. When you leave the exercise to move on, be certain you know what you did and how you did it. If you feel you need extra practice on a particular concept, a number of mastery exercises have been provided in the instructor's manual. The exercises are correlated with the lessons in this book. Ask your instructor whether you may do additional practice to reinforce your learning.

After several lessons, you'll find review exercises. The review exercises will also reinforce what you've learned and help you prepare for the tests. You'll probably find that as you complete the review exercises, you will need to go back into the learning materials to review some features. That's good. It helps you to learn.

Occasionally you'll get stuck! When that happens, make a genuine effort to find a solution using the textbook. However, if you can't solve your problem in a couple of minutes, ask your instructor for help.

Unless you've already had some training or experience with word processing, you'll find some of this learning very frustrating and difficult. That's because there is so much to learn and it is all so new. Knowing that everyone experiences the same frustrations should help you and give you encouragement. It's worth the struggle when you are finally in control of the software and hardware and can use the software to produce a beautifully executed, perfect document.

Unit 2: WordPerfect Formatting and Editing

The second unit consists of nine lessons designed to take about 17 hours. A production test for this unit and a theory test for Units 1 and 2 are included in the instructor's manual. The theory test is much like the end-of-lesson activities that you'll find at the end of each even-numbered lesson and a few of the odd-numbered lessons.

In Unit 2 you will work with some more of the formatting, editing, and layout features that have made word processing indispensable to thousands of office workers, executives, and students. For example, you'll work with multiple-page documents, footnotes, tables, outlines, and columns.

As in Unit 1, there are exercises within the lessons and review exercises at the end of some of the lessons. Additional reinforcement exercises are in the instructor's manual. Some of the lessons in Unit 2 are quite long. Plan to break up your work so it isn't too much in a single sitting. A Review and Practice lesson precedes the production test.

Unit 3: WordPerfect Power Tools

The third unit consists of 11 lessons designed to take about 20 hours. Two production tests for this unit are in the instructor's manual. In Unit 3 you will learn some features that are real time-savers, like Macros, Merge, Sort, Styles, and Document Assembly. You'll also learn how to manage your files in such a way that you can find them when you need them.

Because of the nature of the features in this unit, you will be creating more practice documents than in the previous units. These documents include the exercises within the lessons, the review exercises at the end of some of the lessons, and the Review and Practice lesson at the end of the unit.

Unit 4: WordPerfect Graphic Tools

Unit 4 deals primarily with the graphics capabilities of WordPerfect. You will learn to dress up your documents with graphic images and lines. You will also learn about fonts and how they might be used to create professional-looking documents.

Unit 4 consists of six lessons which will take you about 12 hours to complete. A production test and a theory test are in the instructor's manual to be taken at the end of Unit 4. The final lesson is a Review and Practice lesson to help you prepare for the production test.

Resources

Lesson objectives and the estimated time for completion are included at the beginning of each lesson. That estimated time does not include the time for any of the mastery exercises from the instructor's manual.

A set of true/false and completion questions as well as some reference exercises are included at the end of every two lessons. The true/false and completion questions help you evaluate your comprehension of the material in the lessons. The reference exercises are designed to familiarize you with the documentation that comes with WordPerfect 5.1. As mentioned above, five production tests and two theory tests are available in the instructor's manual for your instructor's use in evaluating your progress. Your instructor will tell you how these exercises and tests will be used in the course.

In all four units, all necessary materials, including exercises, are contained within the lessons. Following the Table of Contents, you will find a Quick Reference listing the commands and a Study Guide to record your progress through the course. Take a moment to look at the Quick Reference and the Study Guide now.

An alternate study guide for recording all exercises as they are completed is also in the instructor's manual, as well as a study guide that includes a place to check off the mastery exercises. Your instructor will tell you which study guide will be used for your learning.

Some students will use what's known as a *template disk* for their training. A number of the learning documents have been prerecorded and are stored on the template disk. If you will be using these prerecorded documents, the documents from the template disk should be copied onto your formatted disk prior to the beginning of the training.

In the lessons where a prerecorded document may be used, you will be directed to retrieve the prerecorded document. Then you will be instructed to follow the steps for that document.

THE HARDWARE

Look at the computer in front of you. It consists of five major hardware components: the disk drives, a video display terminal (VDT), a keyboard, a printer, and a central processing unit (CPU). In addition, you may have a mouse. Can you identify the parts on the hardware illustrations as they are discussed? Find them on your own machine.

1. **The disk drives**. There are a number of possible configurations for the disk drives of the computer you will use for WordPerfect. You might have a computer with two 3½-inch drives, a 3½-inch and a 5¼-inch drive, a hard drive, or any combination of those. If you are working in a networked environment, you might not have any disk drives at all, although that possibility is unlikely.

    Both sizes of floppy drives come in different "densities"—that is, they vary in how densely the information can be packed onto the disks. The 3½-inch drives are suitable for use with either 720K or 1.44MB disks. The 5¼-inch drives are suitable for use with either 360K or 1.2MB disks. If your computer has a lower capacity drive (called double density), you must use the double-density disks. If your computer has a higher capacity drive (called high density), you may use disks of either density. Your instructor will help you determine what kind of drives your computer has and what type of disk you should use for your training.

    If you have never before used a computer, you will want your instructor to give you special instructions regarding the handling of your disks and how to insert them into your computer.

2. **The VDT.** The **video display terminal** (VDT) or monitor looks like a television screen. The purpose of the VDT is to show you what you are doing as you use the computer. It is a window into your work. Look at your VDT. Can you find a power switch and controls for brightness and contrast? You should be familiar with the features of your VDT so that you can adjust the controls for maximum eye comfort.

3. **The keyboard.** Look at the keyboard. In addition to the portion that looks like a typewriter, you should find a set of function keys. The function keys are labeled with "F" and a number, and they may be in a row across the top of the keyboard (there will be 12 of them) or they may be in a double row of five at the left.

   On the right is a series of different keys. You should have a number keypad and some cursor moving keys, including Home, End, Page Down, and others. (The cursor is the little flashing line on the screen that shows where you are working at any time.) You'll get a better introduction to the keyboard in Lesson 3.

4. **The printer.** While there are literally hundreds of printers you might use for printing WordPerfect documents, they all fall into one of three categories with regard to paper handling: printers with sheet feeders, hand-fed printers, and continuous-feed printers.

   a. **Continuous-feed printers.** For some continuous-feed printers, all the paper is connected in one long sheet. It is pushed or pulled through the printer by way of sprocket wheels on each side of the platen area. There are tear strips on each side of the paper with holes that the sprocket pins use to keep the paper straight. Other continuous-feed printers feed cut sheets.

   b. **Hand-fed printers.** A hand-fed printer must have individual sheets fed into it—just like a typewriter.

   c. **Printers with sheet feeders.** Many printers are equipped with a device that feeds individual cut sheets. The sheet feeder often resembles the paper tray of a copy machine and holds a number of sheets of paper. Most printers of this type have a bin that holds completed pages until the operator retrieves them.

5. **The CPU.** The brains or logic center of the computer is housed in the piece of equipment called the **central processing unit** (CPU). Sometimes the CPU sits on your desk under the VDT. In other cases, the CPU might be on the floor beside the desk. In

some situations, WordPerfect 5.1 is installed on the file server of a network. That means that your PC will be running a program stored on a computer in a different part of the room or even in a different room. The disk drives are usually built into the CPU.

The CPU also has a memory area called RAM **(random access memory)** that remembers your work until you save it on your disk. Find the power switch on your CPU. When the power switch is turned off, any text in RAM is lost.

Some system requirements limit which computers can run WordPerfect 5.1. You must have:

- DOS version 2.1 or newer
- two 720K disk drives or a hard drive
- a minimum of 512K RAM with 384K available
- a graphic card

All of this criteria may not have any meaning to you at this time, but it might help you ask some of the right questions if you like WordPerfect 5.1 well enough that you decide to get a computer of your own.

6. **The Mouse.** You may also have a mouse. The mouse is a device used for moving the cursor around in the text and for pointing. If you have never used a mouse, specific instructions in the use of a mouse are included in Appendix B. While all features can be accessed without using the mouse, the mouse is an efficient means of blocking text, positioning the cursor, and accessing features from the pull-down menus.

This has been a rather lengthy introduction to the equipment. If this is your first exposure to a computer used for word processing, you are probably overwhelmed at this point. Becoming familiar with the equipment is necessary for you to use the software efficiently. Don't let the amount of detail in this introduction interfere with learning WordPerfect.

It is recommended that your instructor spend some time with you helping you become familiar with the equipment. If you'd like that kind of help and it is not offered as part of your classroom training, refer to the manuals that came with your computer.

SUPPLIES

You will need several items—besides a willingness to work and learn—to embark on this training. Following is a description of those supplies and a few comments about their sources.

WordPerfect 5.1 for DOS

Obviously, you must have the WordPerfect software to use the program. Your instructor should have already either installed the software on the hard disk or prepared the program disks for your use. You will learn more about this in Lesson 2. (Instructions for installing WordPerfect are in Appendix C.)

A copy or two of the *WordPerfect® Reference*™ and the *WordPerfect Workbook*, published by WordPerfect Corporation and distributed with the software, should be available to share in the classroom. A separate function key template should be available for each computer. A function key template is supplied by WordPerfect Corporation for each computer running a licensed copy of the software. Your own personal function key template is bound in the back of this book. If you use your own template, be sure to put your name on it so it can be returned to you if you accidentally leave it behind.

Other Supplies

In addition to the software, you will need a floppy disk. Your instructor may require you to purchase your own disk.

The disk must be formatted before you can use it. Newer versions of DOS make it easy to give your disk a name when it is being formatted. Appendix A includes instructions for formatting a disk. (Appendix D covers some of the other DOS commands for your learning pleasure!)

CONGRATULATIONS!

You've completed your first lesson. You've learned about the course and a little about the PC. Your goal is to make friends with your PC. In the process, you will find that the PC will be a great help in creating, saving, retrieving, formatting, and editing documents.

LESSON 1 NOTES:

LESSON 2
Introduction to
WordPerfect

OBJECTIVES

Upon completion of this lesson, you will be able to:

1. Start the WordPerfect program.
2. Discuss the WordPerfect working screen.
3. Exit WordPerfect without saving the document.
4. Create and save a document.
5. Discuss the WordPerfect pull-down menus.
6. Access WordPerfect Help.
7. Discuss the WordPerfect default settings.

Estimated Time: 1 hour

ENTERING WORDPERFECT

In order to enter WordPerfect on your computer, you need to follow very specific steps. These steps vary according to whether you have a *dual floppy* system, a *hard disk* system, a *network*, or if you are working from *Windows* or *OS/2*. They also may vary depending on whether a *batch* file has been set up to take you directly into WordPerfect.

Your instructor will probably prefer to give you specific instructions regarding how you should start WordPerfect in your classroom. Outlined below are brief instructions for dual floppy systems, hard disk systems, a network, and Windows. Find the instructions for your system and study them carefully now. You'll get to follow the steps soon.

If you have questions about the computer you will be using, please ask your instructor for help.

Hard or Fixed Disk System

The methods of installing WordPerfect and other software packages on a hard disk vary widely. In some cases the hard disk is set up so that a menu will appear on the screen when the system has finished *booting*. That menu will include WordPerfect along with the other installed programs. In such cases, you may start WordPerfect by simply selecting it from the menu.

In other cases, WordPerfect will be running on a network to which your computer is attached. In still other cases, WordPerfect will be installed into a directory different from the directory described here. You will need to work closely with your instructor as you start WordPerfect the first time to be certain that you are using the right method.

1. If the computer is turned off, check to be sure there is no disk in Drive A, and turn the computer and monitor on. You may need to enter the date and time at the appropriate prompts.

2. If the computer is already turned on and neither the C:\> prompt nor a menu listing WordPerfect is showing on the screen, check with your instructor to see how to proceed.

3. If WordPerfect has been installed in a conventional manner, the program files are probably stored in a directory named WP51. You must change directories from the root directory to use the WordPerfect directory. Changing directories requires the use of the backslash (\) key.

   To change directories, key **cd \wp51** and strike **Enter**. The C:\> prompt will now look like this: **C:\WP51>**.

4. Put your *formatted* data disk into Drive A.

5. Key **wp** at the new prompt and strike **Enter**. The WordPerfect program will start.

Dual Floppy System

1. Boot with a DOS disk or put the **WordPerfect 1** disk in Drive A and a formatted data disk in Drive B. The WordPerfect disk may contain the DOS commands so you don't need a DOS disk.

2. Key the date with numerals and hyphens (for example 1-5-94). Strike **Enter**.

3. Key the time with numerals and a colon (for example 9:30) and strike **Enter**. Computers keep military time. That means that 9:30 p.m. would be 21:30. (Add the afternoon hours to 12 noon to compute military time.)

4. At the **A>** prompt, key **b:** and strike **Enter**. At the **B>** prompt, key **a:wp** and strike **Enter**. All of these instructions tell the computer you will be storing your documents on the data disk in Drive B and doing word processing from the disk in Drive A.

   The computer will respond by loading the program into the computer's memory. It is very important that you follow this step each time you enter WordPerfect. If you don't, your documents will be stored on the software disk instead of the data disk.

5. When the program is finished with the WordPerfect 1 disk, a prompt will tell you to remove the WordPerfect 1 disk and insert the WordPerfect 2 disk.

Windows or OS/2

If you are working with Windows or OS/2, you are working in what's known as a *GUI* (graphical user interface). This consists of *icons* or little pictures that identify the programs on what's known as a *desktop*. In this environment, you can start WordPerfect by pointing with the mouse to the WordPerfect icon and double-clicking the left mouse button.

THE WORDPERFECT SCREEN

When the program has finished loading, a blinking cursor will appear in the upper left corner of a bright blue screen. The status line at the bottom right tells you that you are in Document 1, on Page 1, at Line 1 inch (1"), and at Position 1 inch (1") on the scale.

This information helps you keep track of where your cursor is positioned in a document. It also tells you a number of things about WordPerfect's preset format, which you will learn about soon.

If you are working with a color monitor, the background color on your screen is probably blue and the items listed in the status line are probably white. These colors are restful and comfortable for your eyes.

Lesson 2 Exercise 1

1. Follow the appropriate set of steps above to start WordPerfect on your computer. (If you have a problem, be sure to get some help.)

2. Find the cursor on the screen.

3. Look at the status line in the lower right corner. Do you remember what each part of the status line tells you?

4. With the WordPerfect working screen showing, read on about how to exit from WordPerfect.

EXITING WORDPERFECT

The WordPerfect program requires you to exit WordPerfect at the end of each session. Therefore, it is very important that you learn to exit correctly and do it each time you leave the program.

If you exit improperly, a message will appear the next time you start WordPerfect that says "Are other copies of WordPerfect currently running?" Always answer the Yes/No prompt in this case with **N** for No.

When you exit WordPerfect, you may choose to save or not to save the document showing on the screen. You will learn to exit both ways.

Exiting Without Saving the Document

When you do not wish to save a document, you will follow the steps below. Just READ them for now. The hands-on exercise is below. Exercises are always displayed in a different type.

Choose Exit from the File menu.

1. Strike **F7**, the **Exit** key.

2. The computer will prompt you with: **Save Document? Yes (No)**.

3. Key **N** for **No**.

4. The computer will prompt: **Exit WordPerfect? No (Yes)**.

5. If you wish to reenter WordPerfect with a blank screen, simply key an **N** or strike **Enter**. This will clear the screen and memory of the computer but leave you in WordPerfect.

6. If you wish to exit WordPerfect and leave the system, key **Y**.

   a. On a hard disk system, you will be returned to the **C:\WP51>** prompt, the desktop, or a system start-up menu.

   b. On a dual floppy system, you'll be returned to the **B>** prompt.

   In either case, depending on your instructor's wishes, you may at this point begin some other application or turn off the computer and end the session.

Lesson 2 Exercise 2

1. Follow the steps above to exit WordPerfect without saving whatever may be showing on your screen.

2. Check to see that the correct **B>** or **C:\>** prompt or beginning menu is on the screen. If it is, turn off the computer and go to Exercise 3. If it is not, repeat the steps or ask your instructor for assistance.

Lesson 2 Exercise 3

1. Enter WordPerfect using the instructions at the beginning of this lesson.

2. Look at the working screen. Find the cursor. It follows you as you key, showing your position. Note the status line in the lower right corner.

3. Key the short paragraph shown in Figure 2-1. Don't worry about errors! Key just as you would on a typewriter, but DO NOT strike **Enter** at the end of each line. Allow your text to wrap around to the next line

as you key. Only strike **Enter** at the end of a paragraph or when you purposely want a new line.

4. When you reach the end of the paragraph, strike **Enter** twice and continue reading.

Please note the horizontal lines surrounding Figure 2-1. These lines separate what you are to key from the text of this book. You need not key these lines. They just make it easier for you to recognize material to be keyed. This method of separating material to be keyed from the text will be used throughout this book.

You will also find that even though the font is the same, what you key will look somewhat different from the text in the exercises. The line endings will be different because your WordPerfect line length is preset at 6½ inches.

```
Perhaps more than ever before, American public education is
an issue of national concern.  Major studies have focused on
the weaknesses in our educational system, citing statistics
that appear to reflect a degeneration of teacher and student
performance.
```

Figure 2-1

SAVING A DOCUMENT

When you wish to save the document on which you are working, you must follow these instructions. Keep your document on the screen and just READ the steps for now.

Choose **Exit** from the File menu.

1. Strike **Exit (F7)**.

2. The computer will prompt: **Save Document?** Yes (No).

3. Since you want to *save* the document, Key **Y** or strike **Enter**. (You may strike **Enter** because the cursor is flashing under the **Y** for Yes. WordPerfect is prompting the Yes response. Whenever the response you want is being prompted, you may strike **Enter** instead of the **Y** or **N**.)

4. The computer will prompt: **Document to be Saved:**

   a. **Dual Floppy System**. Key the document name using eight characters or less and strike **Enter**. If you watch, you will see the light on Drive B as your document is saved.

   b. **Hard Disk System**. Your instructor needs to give you some guidance here. If you are one of several students in a classroom situation who use the same computer, your instructor probably does NOT want you to save your documents onto the hard disk. In that case, your instructor has likely set up your software so documents are automatically saved to Drive A. Find out your instructor's preference before saving your first document.

If you are learning WordPerfect on your own and have your own hard disk system (or when you get your own hard drive on the job), the document may be stored onto your hard disk in your own word processing directory.

If you wish to save the document on Drive A, key **a:** and the name of the document. Strike **Enter**. Do not put any spaces in the document name.

5. After saving a document, the computer will prompt you with: **Exit WP?** No (Yes).

a. If you want **No (N)**, simply strike **Enter**. This will clear the screen and memory, and you will remain in WordPerfect.

b. To exit WordPerfect, key **Y** for Yes. This clears the memory buffer and returns floppy disk users to the DOS **B>** prompt. Hard disk users return to the **C:\>** prompt, the start-up menu, or a network menu. Now you have exited WordPerfect.

Later you will be working with documents that have been retrieved from a disk. When that is the case, the name of the disk drive and the document will be displayed as a prompt in the lower left corner of the screen. This may change the steps for saving. You'll learn about that when the situation arises.

Lesson 2 Exercise 4

1. Select the correct set of steps listed above to save your paragraph on your data disk and follow them.

2. Name the document **para.2-3** because it is a paragraph created in Lesson 2, Exercise 3. (The **para** part of the name is not very imaginative. The **2-3** part of the name will be used throughout the course whenever possible to identify the lesson and exercise.)

3. Do NOT exit WordPerfect. (If you exit by accident, follow the steps in Exercise 1 to start WordPerfect again.)

PULL-DOWN MENUS

WordPerfect 5.1 comes complete with nine pull-down menus for people who prefer to work with menus rather than the *function keys*. You do not need a mouse to use the menus, although using a mouse with the menus is more efficient.

There are two ways to display the *menu bar*:

- Click the right mouse button,
- Hold the **Alt** key while you strike the equals (=) key.

With the menu bar displayed, you will see that each menu title and each feature or command is displayed with a bolded letter. (The bolded letter is known as a mnemonic letter because it is a letter that should be easy to remember for that command; e.g., **S** for Save).

You may choose the item from the menu either by striking that bolded letter, by using the arrow keys to move the cursor to the desired feature and choosing it by striking **Enter,** or by pointing to the item with the mouse and clicking the left mouse button.

If you have a menu open and would like to close it without choosing an item, you may do so either by clicking the right mouse button or by striking the space bar two or three times until the menu is cleared.

Some of the items in each menu have an arrow pointing to the right. The arrow signifies that there is a *submenu* for that item. You can access the submenu in the same way that you chose the feature—by using the arrow keys to move the highlight to the item and striking **Enter** or by pointing to it with the mouse and clicking the left mouse button.

Let's look at some of the menus and explore how they work. For now, concentrate on the menu layout and the menu features. We'll discuss what features are in each menu shortly.

Lesson 2 Exercise 5

1. With a clean WordPerfect screen showing, display the menu bar. If you have a mouse, show the menu bar by clicking the right mouse button. If you have no mouse, hold the **Alt** key while you strike the equals (=) key to display the menu bar.

2. Open the **File** menu, either by pointing to it with the mouse and clicking the left mouse button or by striking **F.** It should look much like Figure 2-2.

3. Notice the mnemonic letters that are bolded. Notice the arrows that point to the right indicating that a menu item has a submenu.

File Edit Search Layout Mark To	
Retrieve	Shift-F10
Save	F10
Text In	Ctrl-F5 ▶
Text Out	Ctrl-F5 ▶
Password	Ctrl-F5 ▶
List Files	F5
Summary	
Print	Shift-F7
Setup	Shift-F1 ▶
Go to DOS	Ctrl-F1
Exit	F7

Figure 2-2

4. Move the cursor to the Text In item or point to it with the mouse and click the left button. Look at the submenu that appears. Note that the Spreadsheet item has yet another submenu.

5. Now open the Edit menu by moving the cursor once to the right. With the mouse, point to Edit with the mouse pointer and click the left mouse button to open the menu. The menu should look much like Figure 2-3.

6. Notice that this menu is much like the File menu except that some features are enclosed in brackets. The features enclosed in brackets are not available unless text is highlighted. You will learn about blocking or highlighting text in Lesson 13.

File Edit Search Layout Mark Tools Font Graphi	
[Move (Cut)	Ctrl-Del]
[Copy	Ctrl-Ins]
Paste	
[Append	
Delete	Del
Undelete	F1
Block	Alt-F4
Select	►
Comment	Ctrl-F5 ►
[Convert Case	Shift-F3]
[Protect Block	Shift-F8]
Switch Document	Shift-F3
Window	Ctrl-f3
Reveal Codes	Alt-F3

Figure 2-3

7. Strike the space bar as many times as necessary to close your menus and the menu bar. When you finish, you will be back to your working screen.

The rest of the menus look much the same. As you can see, the menus make it easy for you to find the features you wish to use for your documents. The other way of accessing features is with the function keys. You have already used function keys to exit WordPerfect. You will learn more about the use of the function keys in the next lesson.

As you go through these training materials, the exercise steps will include appropriate function keystrokes to access the WordPerfect features. When a feature can be selected from a menu, a margin note with a picture of a mouse will tell you what menu to access and which item to choose from that menu. In this way, you have the choice of using either the function keys or the pull-down menus to do your work.

Now let's take a brief look at what the menus contain. Open each menu as it is discussed. Note that the features are grouped to help you find what you need when you need it. Most of the features will not be familiar to you yet, but you will work with many of them as you continue your WordPerfect learning.

The File Menu. The File menu is used primarily for any function where the computer or the disk is directly involved. It is your communication tool for your data disk. It is also used for exiting the program.

The Edit Menu. Edit is used for dealing with blocks of text—cutting, pasting, protecting blocks against bad page breaks, etc. It is also the menu where you may choose to reveal your codes to help you edit your documents. If you have a mouse and use it to edit your documents, you will become very familiar with the Edit menu.

The Search Menu. While the Search menu is used primarily for searching for unique strings of text, it is also used for moving around in text in other ways. The Goto function, for example, enables you to move quickly to a particular page of a document.

The Layout Menu. Layout is used for formatting documents. It includes normal formatting features like margins, spacing, and tabs. It is also used for more advanced formats like columns, footnotes, and styles. Most of the Layout features will be covered in this course.

The Mark Menu. The Mark menu is used for automatically creating an index or a table of contents. Most of the features in this menu work only if text is highlighted on the screen.

The Tools Menu. The Tools menu contains such tools as merge, sort, spell, thesaurus, and line draw. You will learn that these features are easy to use. You will become a power user of WordPerfect when you sort names and addresses and combine them with standard documents for bulk mailings, for example. In addition, you can create automatic outlines and check your documents for correct spelling.

The Font Menu. Font is used to change the appearance of the characters when you print your documents. It is from this menu that you select type of different point sizes to make an ordinary document look impressive. The results you may achieve from this menu are heavily dependent on your printer and the fonts that are available on it.

The Graphics Menu. Graphics is used for the features in Word-Perfect that are similar to desktop publishing programs. You can prepare different kinds of boxes with illustrations and text and place them in your documents to prepare newsletters and flyers.

The Help Menu. Last, but certainly not least, is the Help menu. We will take a close look at that menu shortly.

As you can see, the menus contain a wide variety of WordPerfect features. You will learn about these features as you use them in your work and in your lessons.

HELP

The WordPerfect Help feature is designed to help you use the program with a minimum of trouble. Help is accessed when you strike the **F3** key. If you are working on a dual floppy system, you will need to insert a special disk that contains the Help files. Your instructor will tell you where that disk is kept.

The main Help menu tells you that you can request help for features alphabetically or by striking the function keys for the feature with which you need help. Let's take a look at WordPerfect Help.

Lesson 2 Exercise 6

Click **Help** to open the Help menu. Complete the exercise.

1. Strike **F3** for Help and look at the beginning Help screen.

2. Follow the suggestion to strike an alphabetic character. Strike a *C* and look at the list of features available that begin with the letter *C*. Note that in the first column is a description of the function. In the middle column is the word that shows on the keyboard template for that function (you'll learn about the keyboard template soon). In the right column is the keystroke(s) needed to access that function.

3. According to the list of features, the Center feature can be accessed with Shift-F6. Strike **Shift-F6** now and look at the information provided to you about how Center works in WordPerfect.

4. Once you are in Help, you can move from item to item without exiting the feature. For example, strike **S** and look at the list of features beginning with that letter. Choose one about which you would like more information.

5. Spend only a couple of minutes more poking around in the Help feature. Then strike **Enter** to exit Help.

WordPerfect Help is *context sensitive*. That means that if you are working with a feature and strike F3 for help, you will be taken directly to the Help section for the feature with which you're working. You do not need to strike F3 and then an alphabetic character to get help with that particular feature.

Obviously Help will not be the answer to all of your problems, but it certainly can "help" (that's a pun) you with your work. A big limitation to the Help feature right now is that you don't know what you are looking for. You are not yet familiar with the terminology. As you learn about different features, you will find that some of them will be easily remembered. For others, you will find yourself using the Help feature to review how to do a particular thing.

Cancel

One other kind of help that you may need periodically is Cancel. When using a word processing program, it is not at all unusual to strike accidentally an incorrect command or function key. Most programs provide you with a key that allows you to take one giant step backwards and back out of the mistake you made.

In WordPerfect, **F1** is the Cancel key. In those situations where a command puts a prompt in the lower left corner of the screen, it cancels an incorrect command. Let's practice the Cancel key:

Lesson 2 Exercise 7

1. Strike **F7** (Exit). See the prompt in the lower left corner?

2. Whoops! You didn't want to do that. Strike **F1**. Watch the **Exit** prompt go away.

3. Strike **F5** (List Files). See the prompt?

4. Another error. Strike **F1** and watch the **Dir** prompt disappear.

5. Here's one more. Find the **Alt** key. Hold the **Alt** key while you strike **F7**. This brings up the Math menu.

6. You don't want to work with math just yet. Strike **F1** to return to your work area.

The Cancel key provides you with a different kind of help than that provided with F3 Help. It won't work with all incorrect commands, but it gives an indication of what the Cancel key can do.

STANDARD FORMAT

Every word processing program comes with preset formatting known as *default* settings. The better word processing programs anticipate your needs so that you can work with the screen that appears when you start the program. You can then create a good-looking document without worrying about tabs or margins, for example.

WordPerfect is such a program. Figure 2-4 shows an illustration of an 8½- by 11-inch sheet of paper with the most important word processing defaults.

SUMMARY

In this lesson you were introduced to a great many things. For now, probably the most important are the steps for entering and exiting Word-Perfect. You created your first document and you saved that document onto your data disk. You learned about the WordPerfect pull-down menus and the Help facility. Finally, you learned about the WordPerfect default settings.

This has been just an introduction to the program. Don't be bewildered by all the information included in this lesson. In the next few dozen or so lessons you will have an opportunity to review and use most of the material covered in Lesson 2 in a wide variety of ways. Relax and learn!

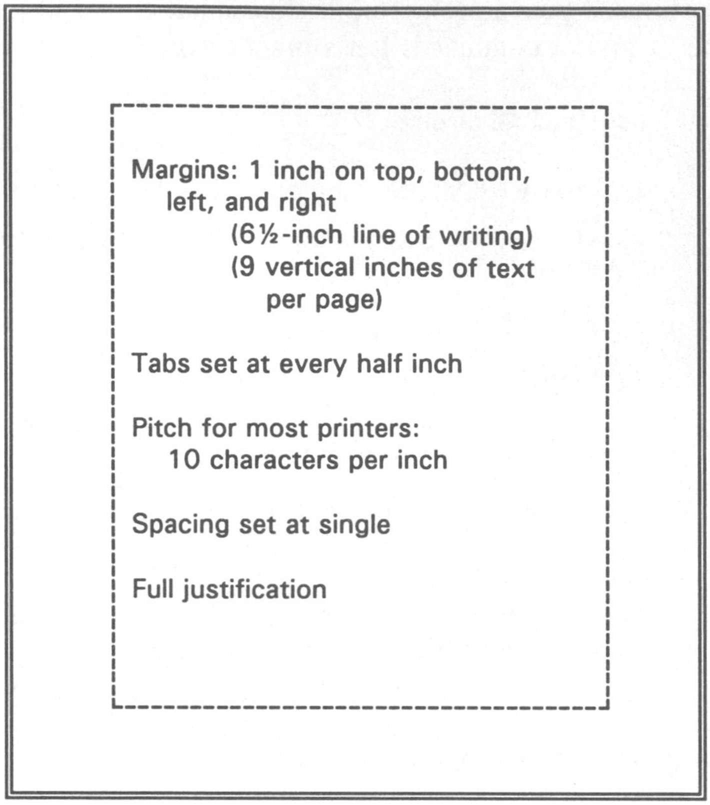

Margins: 1 inch on top, bottom,
    left, and right
            (6½-inch line of writing)
            (9 vertical inches of text
                per page)

Tabs set at every half inch

Pitch for most printers:
    10 characters per inch

Spacing set at single

Full justification

Figure 2-4

LESSON 2 NOTES:

Name _____ Date _____

TRUE/FALSE

Each of the following statements is either true or false. Indicate your choice in the Answers column by circling T for a true statement or F for a false statement.

Answers

1. You must use a series of other books to complete this WordPerfect learning. (Les. 1, Obj. 1) . . . .   1. T F

2. The review exercises at the end of the lessons help reinforce your learning. (Les. 1, Obj. 1) . . . .   2. T F

3. The CPU on your computer looks much like a television screen. (Les. 1, Obj. 2) . . . .   3. T F

4. You don't need to be familiar with the miscellaneous keys on your keyboard, because all you need are the alphabetic keys. (Les. 1, Obj. 2) . . .   4. T F

5. Your WordPerfect program might be installed on a hard drive or it might be on a floppy disk that you will put into Drive A. (Les. 1, Obj. 3) . . . . .   5. T F

6. The four items that show on the status line of the WordPerfect working screen are **Doc**, **Pg**, **Ln**, and **Pos**. (Les. 2, Obj. 2) . . . .   6. T F

7. It is imperative that you strike **Enter** at the end of every line of a paragraph when keying a document in WordPerfect. (Les. 2, Obj. 3) . . . .   7. T F

8. You have just created a new document and wish to exit WordPerfect and save the document. You must name the document. (Les. 2, Obj. 4) . . . .   8. T F

9. You must have a mouse to use the WordPerfect pull-down menus. (Les. 2, Obj. 5) . . . .   9. T F

10. You must set margins before you create a document in WordPerfect. (Les. 2, Obj. 7) . . . .   10. T F

COMPLETION

Indicate the correct answer in the space provided.

Answers

1. How many units are included in the textbook? (Les. 1, Obj. 1) . . . .   1. _____

2. What is the name of the listing at the front of the text of features and their keystrokes? (Les. 1, Obj. 1) . . . .   2. _____

3. What part of the computer is usually used with the pull-down menus? (Les. 1, Obj. 2) . . . .   3. _____

4. In which part of your computer is your work remembered until you save it on your disk? (Les. 1, Obj. 2)   4. _____

5. What must be done to a disk before you can use it for saving your documents? (Les. 1, Obj. 3) . . . .   5. _____

6. If WordPerfect was properly installed on a hard disk system, what is the name of the directory holding the WordPerfect program files? (Les. 2, Obj. 1) . . . . . .   6. _____

7. What is the little blinking light that identifies your position on the WordPerfect screen? (Les. 2, Obj. 2) . . .   7. _____

8. Which function key is used to exit WordPerfect? (Les. 2, Obj. 3) . . . .   8. _____

9. What are the default WordPerfect margins? (Les. 2, Obj. 7) . . . .   9. _____

10. Is your computer a hard disk system or a dual floppy system? . . . .   10. _____

11. How many function keys does your keyboard have? .   11. _____

REFERENCE

Go to the "Getting Started" section of the *WordPerfect Reference* and find the five sources of help provided to the user by WordPerfect. List them.

1._____   4._____

2._____   5._____

3._____

LESSON 3
The WordPerfect Keyboard

OBJECTIVES

Upon completion of this lesson, you will be able to:

1. Locate the function keys on the keyboard.
2. Locate the Shift, Backspace, Tab, and other familiar typewriter keys on the PC keyboard.
3. Locate the Number Keypad and the cursor-moving keys.
4. Recognize from the keyboard template how to use the various function keys.

Estimated Time: ½ hour

Look at the IBM PC or PC-compatible keyboard in front of you. Notice that the major portion of the keyboard is a series of light-colored keys that are similar to those on a typewriter. The positions of these keys are the same as those on a typewriter and should feel comfortable to you. The touch, however, may be a little different. You may need to use a lighter touch.

The other keys on the keyboard are described below. Find each one as you read about it, but don't strike it. Figure 3-1 illustrates the original PC keyboard, and Figure 3-2 illustrates the newer-style keyboard.

Please note that there are a variety of keyboard styles. Locate the keys on your particular keyboard, even if they are not located in the same positions as on the illustrated keyboards. Have your instructor help you if you can't find a key.

MISCELLANEOUS KEYS

Let's look at some of the miscellaneous keys on your keyboard:

1. **Escape.** **Esc** is used in WordPerfect primarily to move the cursor a designated number of keystrokes or lines.

2. **Tab.** The Tab key is located next to the letter *Q*. When struck alone, the cursor moves one tab stop to the right. When struck with either Shift key, the cursor moves one tab stop to the left.

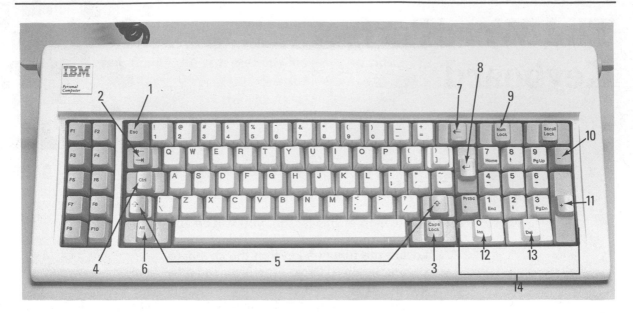

Figure 3-1 (The IBM PC Keyboard)

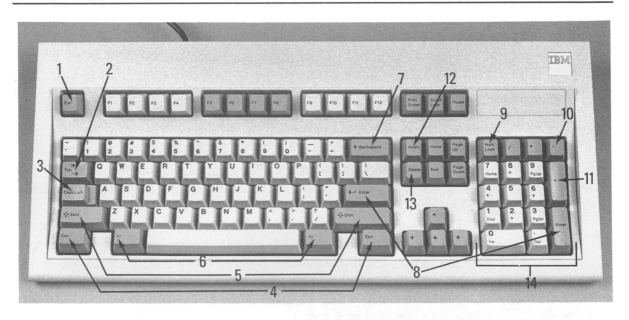

Figure 3-2 (The Enhanced IBM Keyboard)

3. **Caps Lock.** Find the Caps Lock key on your keyboard. It is used to key letter characters in all capitals. It cannot be used for any of the symbols over the numbers or any of the uppercase punctuation marks. When Caps Lock is on and you use one of the Shift keys to capitalize the first letter of a word, you get a lowercase letter, for example, **mARK**.

You can tell Caps Lock is on by looking at the WordPerfect status line at the bottom of the screen. **Pos** will be in all caps, **POS**, when Caps Lock is on. Some keyboards have a light on the Caps Lock key to alert you that it is on. Others have a light elsewhere on the keyboard. Caps Lock is turned off the same way you turned it on so it's known as a *toggle key*. You will find that there are a number of toggle keys on the keyboard. Bold and underline are other commonly used WordPerfect toggle key functions.

4. **Control.** **Ctrl** is located to the left (and on most keyboards also to the right) of the alphabetic keys. Using Ctrl with another key gives you an additional function. You should always press Ctrl first and hold it while you strike the other key, just as you hold Shift to key a capital letter. Don't try to strike them simultaneously. The Control key doesn't do anything by itself.

5. **Shift Keys.** Near the Control key(s) are the Shift keys. Hold Shift to key capital letters and the symbols above the numerals. Like Ctrl, Shift is used in combination with other keys to give those keys additional functions. Always press and hold a Shift key while striking the other key to get the effect you want.

6. **Alternate.** The final miscellaneous key on the left side of the keyboard is the Alternate key, **Alt**. If you study Figure 3-2, you will see that there is an Alt key on either end of the space bar. The Alt key, too, gives the other keys on the keyboard special functions. Like Ctrl and Shift, Alt needs to be struck and held while you strike another key. The Alternate key is used primarily with the function keys, which we will discuss soon.

7. **Backspace.** Backspace is located at the top right of the alphabetic keyboard. It is used to delete characters. Strike Backspace to erase the character or space directly to the left of the cursor. Continue to strike Backspace to erase many characters as the cursor moves to the left. It can also be used to delete a word at a time when used with the Ctrl key.

8. **Enter** or **Return.** Below the Backspace key is a large key that may be marked with a crooked arrow or may say "Enter." It is sometimes known as the "new line" or "return" key (like the carrier return on the typewriter) because it is used when you are entering text and come to the end of a short line.

   When the computer is asking you a question and you strike Enter, it says "Yes" to the question or affirms the response in the prompt line. In your training you may find it referred to either as the return key or as Enter. Look at your keyboard. How many Enter keys do you find?

9. **Number Lock. Num Lock** is used to turn the Number Keypad on and off. When Num Lock is on, you may not use the number keys for cursor movement.

10. **Hyphen**. The hyphen or minus (-) key located all the way to the right of the keyboard on the Number Keypad (not the regular hyphen key) is used to move backwards through your text one screen at a time. You will find this key very useful in reviewing your text.

11. **Plus**. The large plus key (+) below the hyphen or minus key at the extreme right is used to move forward through your text one screen at a time. It, too, is very useful.

12. **Insert**. The Insert key (**Ins** or **Insert**) is a toggle key that puts you in the *typeover* mode. That means that when you place your cursor anywhere in text that has already been keyed and key new words, the new ones will replace the old ones. WordPerfect is usually in the *insert* mode, which means that new text is inserted into the old text, which in turn moves over to make room.

13. **Delete**. The Delete key (**Del** or **Delete**) is used to delete the character or function at the cursor. When held down, Delete erases characters as they scroll in from the right.

14. **The Number Keypad**. The Number Keypad is at the right of the keyboard. These keys are used for several things besides keying numbers. When **Num Lock** is turned off, they may be used as cursor-movement keys. The 8, 4, 6, and 2 keys all have arrows showing you which direction they will move the cursor. Even the 7, 9, 1, and 3 keys have cursor movement functions, which you'll learn about shortly. The only number key that doesn't have another function is the 5.

FUNCTION KEYS

At the extreme left of some keyboards are ten keys numbered F1 to F10. On newer keyboards, they are located across the top of the keyboard, and there may be twelve of them. These keys are referred to as *function keys*. Find the function keys on the keyboards in Figures 3-1 and 3-2 and on your keyboard. These keys are called function keys because they have different functions depending on the program you're using.

WordPerfect assigns four values to each of these keys—more than you can hope to memorize quickly. For that reason, you should have a template that fits onto the keyboard near the function keys to tell you the function of each key. Your own copy of a function key template is bound in the back of this book. If you remove it to use it, be sure to put your name on it so it won't be misplaced. Find the function key template either on your computer or in the back of your book. If you don't have a function key template to use, ask your instructor where you may get one. Note that it is color coded for ease of use.

- Keys that are struck alone are shown in the template in black.
- **Shift** is used for functions in green.
- **Alt** is used for functions in blue.
- **Ctrl** is used for functions in red.

Look at the colored words on the template. Look first at Exit by the F7 key. You've already used this one to save the document you keyed in Lesson 2. Since it is not a colored word, you struck it by itself. If you were to strike the same key while holding down Ctrl, it would give you a footnote function. Striking it with Alt gives you a columns function, and striking it with Shift gives the command to print.

Be careful of your touch when using key combinations. Do not strike and hold both keys. If you do, the command will keep repeating until you release the keys. Press and hold the first key (Ctrl, Alt, or Shift), and then lightly touch the command key that goes with it. You may "park" on the Alt, Ctrl, or Shift keys, but never on the accompanying key.

Look at the remainder of the colored words on the template. You will learn to use most of these functions as your training progresses. Don't be impatient and expect to remember them. Rely on the template until you become an experienced user of WordPerfect. Even then, you'll have to check the template for functions you don't use often.

Elsewhere on the template are some miscellaneous commands, which are also color coded. Check periodically during your training to see which of these you could be using.

When WordPerfect is not in use, your instructor may want you to remove the template from the keyboard. Your instructor will tell you what to do with the keyboard template when you are finished.

If you have a mouse and are using the menus, you will see that the function key for each feature is listed on the menu opposite the feature.

Lesson 3 Exercise 1

This chapter contains a lot of reading about the keyboard. It's time to use it to create another document. This one contains lots of errors.

1. Key the paragraph in Figure 3-3 exactly as shown—with errors. You may make some of your own, if you'd like. Remember to let the words *wrap* at the ends of the lines. Strike **Enter** twice at the end.

Choose Exit from the File menu.

2. When you finish, strike **F7** and answer **Y** to **Save Document?**

3. Key the name of the document, **foreign.3-1**, including **a:** if necessary to be sure the document is saved on your own data disk. Do not exit WordPerfect.

```
An increesing number of American companys are doing busyness
with overseas companies.  Mst Americans are at a
dissadvantage in foreign business negotiations because we
are ignorant of their culchural diffferencees and valu
sustems.  In many cases, forign business pelple have all the
power becuz they have studied our culture and our language.
```

Figure 3-3

SUMMARY

You have had a quick overview of the keyboard. You're not expected to remember all of the above information at this point in your training, but this overview provides a chance to look at the keys and get an introduction to their functions. You may find yourself referring back to this lesson as you progress through your training.

LESSON 3 NOTES:

LESSON 4
Correcting Text

OBJECTIVES

Upon completion of this lesson, you will be able to:

1. Move the cursor using several methods.
2. Delete text using several methods.
3. Use the Reveal Codes feature to help you with your editing.

Estimated Time: ½ hour

Editing in WordPerfect is accomplished by moving the cursor, using the Backspace and Delete keys in a combination of ways, and inserting new material. In this lesson you will learn how to do simple editing, and you'll have several little exercises for practice.

Don't try to learn everything at once. Read the material carefully. Try the exercises. Make a note of the fact that Lesson 4 is a place where you can return for review later when some of these features may have more meaning.

In Lesson 3 you learned about using the arrow keys for cursor movement. In all likelihood, you have two sets of arrow keys—those to the right of the alphabetic keyboard and those on the Number Pad. You may use whichever arrow keys you wish.

Lesson 4 Exercise 1

To get the feel of the various keys and features as you study this lesson, you should have some text on the screen.

1. Key the text shown in Figure 4-1. Strike **Enter** twice following each line to add a blank line between the keyed lines.

2. Number each line consecutively as shown until you come to line 15. When the screen gets full, you will notice that your text begins to disappear from view at the top of the screen. This is called "scrolling."

```
line 1 of practice text

line 2 of practice text

line 3 of practice text

(continue to line 15)
```

Figure 4-1

3. When you finish, leave the exercise on the screen and read on.

THE CURSOR-MOVEMENT KEYS

The Arrow Keys. The up, down, right, and left arrow keys on your keyboard can be used to move the cursor a line or a space at a time. If Num Lock is turned off, the arrow keys move your cursor left and right a space at a time or up and down a line at a time.

If you strike and hold any one of these cursor keys, the cursor movement will continue through the text. You can't, however, move the cursor through something that isn't there. If you are striking the down arrow key, for example, the cursor will stop moving when you get to the end of your document.

Other Cursor-Moving Keys. Another set of keys near the arrow keys include **Page Up (PgUp)**, **Page Down (PgDn)**, **Home**, and **End.** These are also useful for moving the cursor when used alone or when used in combination with the arrow keys. Look at Figure 4-2, which lists some of the more common ways of moving the cursor.

Please note that in some of the commands below, a comma has been placed between some keystrokes. This comma indicates that you release the Home key before striking the next key. In other commands, you will see two commands joined with a hyphen (e.g., **Ctrl-↓**). For those commands, you should hold the first key while you strike the key listed second; then release both keys.

Look over the list briefly. You'll then get to practice the keystrokes.

End	moves to the end of the line	Home, Home, ↑	moves to top of *document*
Home, ←	moves to the beginning of the line	Home, Home, ↓	moves to bottom of *document*
Page Up	moves to top of previous page	Ctrl→	moves one word to the right
Page Down	moves to top of next page	Ctrl←	moves one word to the left
Home, ↑	moves to top of screen or short text	Ctrl-↑	moves the cursor up one paragraph
Home, ↓	moves to bottom of screen or short text	Ctrl-↓	moves the cursor down one paragraph

Lesson 4 Exercise 2

1. Strike **Home, Home, ↑** to move your cursor to the beginning of the text in your document. Watch how the lines at the bottom disappear from the screen.

2. Strike **End** to move your cursor to the end of the first line.

3. Strike **Home, ←** to move your cursor to the beginning of the line.

4. Strike **Ctrl→** to move your cursor to the right one word. Do it again. Now strike **Ctrl←** to move your cursor to the left one word.

5. Strike **Page Down** to move your cursor to the end of your text. (If your document had been more than one page long, Page Down would have moved the cursor to the beginning of the next page.

6. Strike **Ctrl-↑** to move the cursor up one "paragraph." (Since you struck Enter twice between each of the lines, WordPerfect thinks that each is a paragraph.) Do it again.

7. Practice with the other keystrokes in the list in Figure 4-2. When you are finished, move the cursor to the beginning of line 13.

INSERTING TEXT

When using WordPerfect, it is very easy to insert letters, spaces, and words into already-keyed text. To do this, you merely need to position the cursor at the point immediately following the location for the added material and key the new text. Let's try it.

First, check to be sure the word **Typeover** isn't showing at the left in the status line. If it is, turn it off by striking the **Insert** key.

With the cursor under the *l* of *line* at the beginning of line 13, key the words *This is* and space once. Strike the **End** key and put a period at the end of the line. Do the same thing with any two other lines.

That was easy, wasn't it? You can add spaces, text, and punctuation marks anywhere in an existing document, and the old material will automatically move over and make room for the new.

DELETING TEXT

As you learned in Lesson 3, the computer has two kinds of keys to delete text. One of these keys is the Backspace key. The other is in the lower right corner of the keyboard and is labeled "Del." Depending on your keyboard, there might be a second Delete key in the group of keys between the alphabetic and the numeric keypads.

- **Backspace** erases text to the left of the cursor one character or space at a time. Hold down this key to delete several characters quickly. The text to the right of the cursor will shift to the left to close up the space as you press the Backspace key.

- **Delete** and **Del** will delete characters **at** the cursor. Again, if you hold the key down, it will delete several characters as they scroll in from the right.

In addition to the Delete keys, there are three more delete functions you will find useful.

- **Ctrl-Backspace** deletes the word in which the cursor is located. If you hold the Ctrl key and strike Backspace several times, you can delete several consecutive words.

- **Ctrl-End** deletes from the cursor to the end of the line.

- **Ctrl-Page Down** deletes from the cursor to the end of the page. A prompt asks you to confirm a deletion of this size.

Delete Exercise. Try each of the five delete functions above on the lines of text you have showing on the screen. Watch what happens as you use each function. Don't worry about destroying the document. When you finish, strike **F7** and exit from the document without saving it.

Lesson 4 Exercise 3

(Template disk users: Refer to the box on page 33 before beginning.)

1. Key the paragraph in Figure 4-3 exactly as it appears, including the misspelled words. Space twice after the period at the end of each sentence.

2. Correct the errors (there are 12 of them) using the Backspace and the Delete keys. In cases where you need to insert characters, place the cursor under the character or the space **to the right of the point of the insertion** and key the inserted material.

3. When you finish, strike **Page Down** to move the cursor to the end of the paragraph and strike **Enter** twice. Be sure to ask your instructor for help if you run into any kind of problem.

```
More than 600,0000 people are avaiilable fer temporary work
on a daily basis, including routin secretarial, typing,
copuing, and mailing appplicationx.  But many can perform
specialized tasks involving word processsing, statistikal
tuping, legal suport, marketting, and other functions.
```

Figure 4-3

Figure 4-4 illustrates the paragraph again. Each word that contains an error is shown in bold. Did you find all 12 errors? One word has two errors!

TEMPLATE DISK USERS:

1. Retrieve **job.4-3**. Either strike **F5** and then **Enter** to list your files or choose List Files from the File menu and then strike **Enter** to list your files.
2. Use the mouse or the cursor-moving keys to move the highlight to **job.4-3**.
3. Retrieve the document by keying **1**. Correct the errors as directed in the exercise.

More than **600,0000** people are **avaiilable fer** temporary work on a daily basis, including **routin** secretarial, typing, **copuing**, and mailing **appplicationx**. But many can perform specialized tasks involving word **processsing**, **statistikal tuping**, legal **suport**, **marketting**, and other functions.

Figure 4-4

Typeover

While it isn't exactly a delete key, Typeover is used to key new text over existing text. You can turn on typeover by striking **Ins** or **Insert**. (That seems backwards, but remember that the insert mode is the default in WordPerfect.) When you use typeover to replace old text with new, be sure to turn it off again the same way you turned it on. You will practice typeover in Lesson 9.

ADDITIONAL CURSOR-MOVEMENT KEYS

The following is a list of additional cursor-movement keys. You will not use all of them at this time. In fact, you probably won't remember what all of them do until you are much further along in your training. Refer to the condensed list at the end of the Quick Reference regularly to learn quicker ways of getting around in your text.

Locate the keys on the keyboard and try a few of them, if you wish, on the paragraph that is still on your screen from Exercise 3. Don't worry about spoiling the document. You won't be needing it again.

- **Screen Up.** The screen up key is the minus (-) key at the far right of the keyboard. This key moves the cursor backward through the document one screen at a time—usually 24 lines. This feature requires that you have **Num Lock** turned off. If you use your Number Keypad to key numerals, you can accomplish the same thing by striking **Home, ↑**.

- **Screen Down.** The screen down key is the plus (+) key at the far right of the keyboard. This key moves the cursor forward through the document one screen at a time if you have **Num Lock** turned off. If you use the Number Keypad for numerals, you can strike **Home, ↓** for screen down.

- **Escape Key.** The Escape key is used along with the arrow keys, the Page Up key, or the Page Down key. Escape moves you quickly through the text as listed.

Esc, ←	Left 8 spaces	**Esc, ↑**	Up 8 lines
Esc, →	Right 8 spaces	**Esc, ↓**	Down 8 lines

  Remember that the cursor can't move through a screen if nothing is there. If you are at the bottom of your paragraph and you strike **Esc, ↓**, the cursor won't move anywhere!

- **Escape, n, Arrow.** When you strike **Esc**, the message **Repeat Value = 8** appears on the status line. Key the number (**n**) of spaces or lines you wish to move if it is more or less than 8. Then strike the appropriate arrow key. Esc can also be used for repetition of the same keystroke. For example, if you wanted a row of 60 hyphens across the page, you would strike **Esc, 60**, and strike the **hyphen** key once.

- **Escape, n, Page Up or Page Down.** To move forward or backward a certain number of pages, strike **Esc**, key the number of pages you wish to move, and then strike **Page Up** or **Page Down**.

- **Goto Key** combination. When you want WordPerfect to go to a specific page or character, strike **Ctrl-Home**. The message **Goto** will appear on the status line.

  At this point you have several choices. You may "Goto" a page, a character, or move around on the screen.

- **Goto, Page.** Key the page number that you wish to "Goto" and strike **Enter**.

- **Goto, Character.** The cursor will move forward and stop one character to the right of whatever character you key at the **Goto** message.

Lesson 4 Exercise 4

1. Using the paragraph showing on your screen, practice **Screen Up** and **Screen Down**. These will appear to do the same thing as **Page Up** and **Page Down** because your text is so short. If you had a multiple-page document, you would be able to better see the differences between Page Down and Screen Down, for example.

2. Strike **Page Up**. Then try Goto as follows: Strike **Ctrl-Home** and key the letter *y*. The cursor should move to the end of the word *temporary*. Pick out a different unique character and try Goto again.

3. Strike **Page Up** again. This time strike **Esc**, key **3**, and then strike ↓. Your cursor should move down three lines.

4. That's enough for now. Strike **Page Up** one more time and read on.

MOVING THE CURSOR WITH THE MOUSE

You already have learned about an overwhelming number of ways to move the cursor with the keyboard. If you have a mouse, it can be used to reposition the cursor. Simply move the mouse pointer to the desired location and click the left mouse button. If you have a mouse, you can try it. If you don't have a mouse, exit from the document without saving it and skip to Exercise 6.

Lesson 4 Exercise 5

1. Use the mouse and point to the space following the word *applications*. Click the left mouse button. The cursor should move to that position.

2. Now point to the comma in the numeral in the first line. Click the left mouse button. The cursor should move to the comma. If you've never before used a mouse, you might find this a little awkward. You'll find it gets much easier if you use the mouse often.

3. Click to position the cursor at the beginning of the paragraph. Exit from the document without saving it.

Lesson 4 Exercise 6

(Template disk users: Refer to the box below before beginning.)

1. Key the document in Figure 4-5. Remember to space twice after the period following each sentence. Remember also not to strike **Enter** until you reach the end of the paragraph. Your line endings may be different than those shown in Figure 4-5.

2. End the paragraph by striking **Enter** twice.

3. Use **Page Up** to return to the beginning of the paragraph. Then make the corrections in the paragraph as described below Figure 4-5. When you finish, your paragraph will look much like Figure 4-6.

TEMPLATE DISK USERS:

Retrieve **mistakes.4-6** and follow the steps in Exercise 6 to correct the errors.

Usually when you make a mistakes, you feel it. Your right
pinkie should not probably learn the way to the backspace
key by touch to correct that kind of error. however, at the
end of each document you key, you will always go back to to
the beginning and proofread your work and correct all
errors. You may also at this point wish to edit your work.
The section on editing in these learning materials will help
you to get around in your work quickly and efficiently to
make any editing corrections you wish. Get into the habit
of always carefully proofreading your work.

Figure 4-5

- **mistakes**. Strike **Ctrl→** six times to move the cursor to the second *you*. Then strike **←** until the cursor is on the unnecessary *s* in *mistakes* in the first line. Delete it with **Del** or **Delete**. Watch how the other text shifts over to fill up the space of the deleted character.

- **not** (second line). Move the cursor to the word *not*. Then hold **Ctrl** as you strike **Backspace** once. This will delete the word.

- **probably**. Strike **Ctrl-Backspace** once more to delete the word *probably.*

- **small *h* at the beginning of *however*.** Move to the small *h* at the beginning of the next sentence. Do this by using the down arrow key and striking **Ctrl→** or using the mouse to click the cursor on the *h*. Strike the **Insert** or **Ins** key to go into typeover. Note the **Typeover** prompt in the lower left corner of the screen. Key a capital *H*. Insert is a toggle key, so strike it again to turn off typeover.

- **to to**. Move the cursor to either *to*. Delete the word by striking **Ctrl-Backspace**. You also could have positioned the cursor on the *t* of *the* and struck **Home, Backspace** (delete the word to the left of the cursor).

- **Delete the last sentence**. Position the cursor on the *G* of *Get* at the beginning of the last sentence. Strike **Ctrl-Page Down** to delete to the end of the page. You will be asked to confirm the deletion. Strike *Y* for yes.

Usually when you make a mistake, you feel it. Your right
pinkie should learn the way to the backspace key by touch to
correct that kind of error. However, at the end of each
document you key, you will always go back to the beginning
and proofread your work and correct all errors. You may
also at this point wish to edit your work. The section on
editing in these learning materials will help you to get
around in your work quickly and efficiently to make any
editing corrections you wish.

Figure 4-6

4. How does your document compare? Keep the document on the screen. Strike **Page Up** for the next exercise.

In the exercises above, you were directed to use a wide variety of the delete and correct features. As mentioned earlier, you won't remember all of them. You'll soon be comfortable with the use of Backspace and Delete. It's the others you need to train yourself carefully to use:

- **Ctrl-Backspace** to delete the word at the cursor,
- **Ctrl-End** to delete from the cursor to the end of the line,
- **Ctrl-Page Down** to delete from the cursor to the end of the page.

All three of these are big time-savers for you in your work.

THE REVEAL CODES FUNCTION

Hidden behind the characters of any word processing text are function codes for bold, tab changes, center, temporary margins, etc. You can see the entire text, including the codes, with the **Reveal Codes** function. *Codes* are revealed by striking Alt-F3 or F11 or by choosing Reveal Codes from the Edit menu. When your codes are revealed, the screen is split by a ruler across the center as illustrated in Figure 4-7.

```
Usually when you make a mistake, you feel it. Your right pinkie
should learn the way to the backspace key by touch to correct
that kind of error.  However, at the end of each document you
key, you will always go back to the beginning and proofread your
work and correct all errors.  You may also at this point wish to
edit your work.  The section on editing in these learning
materials will help you to get around in your work quickly and
efficiently to make any editing corrections you wish.

                                        Doc 1 Pg 1 Ln 1" Pos 1"
[  ▲     ▲     ▲     ▲     ▲     ▲     ▲     ▲     ▲     ▲     ▲     ▲     )
Usually when you make a mistake, you feel it. Your right pinkie[SRt]
should learn the way to the backspace key by touch to correct[SRt]
that kind of error.  However, at the end of each document you[SRt]
key, you will always go back to the beginning and proofread your[SRt]
work and correct all errors.  You may also at this point wish to[SRt]
edit your work.  The section on editing in these learning[SRt]
materials will help you to get around in your work quickly and[SRt]
efficiently to make any editing corrections you wish.[HRt]
[HRt]

Press Reveal Codes to restore screen.
```

Figure 4-7

The ruler separates the text at the top from a copy of the text at the bottom. The ruler has tepees and braces that show where the margins and tab stops are set. The text below the ruler contains formatting codes, with each code enclosed in brackets.

Unless you are at the top or bottom of your document, the Reveal Codes screen shows three lines of text before the cursor and several lines below the cursor.

You can move the cursor in the Reveal Codes text using the normal cursor-movement functions. For example, you can strike **End** to move the cursor quickly to the end of the line or **Home,** ← to move it quickly to the beginning of the line. You can also use **Ctrl→** and **Ctrl←** to move one word at a time. These functions are more efficient than using the arrow keys to move a character at a time!

The cursor looks different in Reveal Codes than in regular text. Instead of an underline or dash under the character, the cursor in Reveal Codes actually highlights the entire character. The Reveal Codes cursor is always considered to be to the left of (or "in front of") the character or code that is highlighted.

Lesson 4 Exercise 7

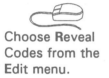

Choose **Reveal** Codes from the Edit menu.

1. Strike **Alt-F3** or **F11** to open the Reveal Codes window.

2. Use the arrow keys to move the cursor to the right a few times. Watch the cursor on both screens as you do this so you can see how the cursor looks. Compare the appearance of the cursor in the document at the top of the screen with its appearance in the Codes window at the bottom of the screen.

3. Look at the ruler separating the text screen from the codes screen. Identify the brackets that mark the left and right margins. Look at the tepees that show where your tabs are set.

4. Look at the [**SRt**] codes at the ends of the lines that are wrapped. These are called *soft returns*.

5. Strike **Page Down**. Strike **Enter** twice to add two hard returns at the end of the paragraph. Look at the two [**HRt**] codes.

6. Begin a list of the codes you've seen in your documents. (So far it has been only the [SRt] and [HRt] codes.) Write the code in one column and a definition of the code in another column. Later, when your list is longer and you have learned how to work with columns in WordPerfect, you will be keying the list as an exercise. Store the list in a safe place (perhaps staple it to the last page of the index in your text).

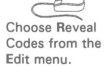

Choose **Reveal** Codes from the Edit menu.

7. Close the Codes screen by striking **Alt-F3** or **F11** again. Exit the document without saving it.

Because the use of Reveal Codes is so important to the editing of your documents, you will be using this feature regularly in this training. A listing of all of the codes can be found in Appendix C of the WordPerfect documentation. Most of the codes are quite easy to figure out. Some of the more commonly used codes are listed for you in Figure 4-8. Make a conscientious effort to learn to work with the codes.

```
[ ]                          Hard space code
                             Normal space
    -                        Hard hyphen
[-]                          Normal hyphen
[BOLD]                       Beginning bold code
[bold]                       Ending bold code
[Center]                     Center code
[Date:]                      Date code
[Flsh Rt]                    Flush right code
[HPg]                        Hard page code
[HRt]                        Hard return code
[->Indent]                   Indent from left code
[->Indent<-]                 Left/Right indent code
[L/R Mar:]                   Left and right margins code
[SPg]                        Soft page code
[SRt]                        Soft return code
[T/B Mar:]                   Top and bottom margin code
[Tab]                        Tab code
[Tab Set:Rel:]               Tab set code with relative tabs
[UND]                        Beginning underline code
[und]                        Ending underline code
```

Figure 4-8

COMMAND SUMMARY

Below is a list of the commands you have learned so far. The list looks small, because the huge amount of material you've already learned about using WordPerfect has been more informational and less functional up to this point.

Lists of this type will be provided for you periodically throughout your training. The list is in alphabetic order, not in the order in which the commands were learned. At the front of your book, near the Study Guide, is a Quick Reference that includes all of the commands covered in the text. In the Quick Reference, you'll find that the features are listed, along with the keystrokes needed for the command, the menu from which the command may be selected, and the lesson in which that command was learned. As you progress with your training, you will find that the Quick Reference will become increasingly useful to you.

Feature	Function	Menu	Lesson
Exit	F7	File, Exit	2
Help	F3	Help	2
Reveal Codes	Alt-F3 or F11	Edit, Reveal Codes	4

SUMMARY

You learned lots of very useful information in this lesson. Most importantly, you learned to edit your document. All of the lesson information supports that editing. For example, you learned:

- a number of different ways to delete big and little chunks of text in your document,
- the use of Reveal Codes to see the formatting in your document,
- a number of different ways to move the cursor from one location to another in your document.

Much of the information covered in this lesson will be quickly forgotten unless you make a point of reviewing periodically. In fact, you will be reminded to return to this lesson for review. Work at increasing your efficiency with the features you learned in this lesson!

LESSON 4 NOTES:

Name _____ Date _____

TRUE/FALSE

Each of the following statements is either true or false. Indicate your choice in the Answers column by circling T for a true statement or F for a false statement.

Answers

1. The Tab key and the Backspace key are in their normal typewriter locations. (Les. 3, Obj. 2) . . . .   1.   T   F

2. The Escape key is used to exit the WordPerfect word processing program. (Les. 3, Obj. 2) . . . .   2.   T   F

3. The only thing the Number Keypad may be used for is entering numbers. (Les. 3, Obj. 3) . . . .   3.   T   F

4. The WordPerfect keyboard template shows the user how to access various WordPerfect features. (Les. 3, Obj. 4) . . . .   4.   T   F

5. Look at the keyboard template. You would have to use **Shift** to access features such as Center, Print, and Retrieve. (Les. 3, Obj. 4) . . . .   5.   T   F

6. The only way to move the cursor around on the screen is to use one of the four arrow keys found on the Number Keypad. (Les. 4, Obj. 1) . . . . . .   6.   T   F

7. The **Esc** key gives you the ability to move quickly through the text a certain number of lines or characters. (Les. 4, Obj. 1) . . . .   7.   T   F

8. **Page Up** takes your cursor to the top of the next page. (Les. 4, Obj. 1) .   8.   T   F

9. **Del** is used to delete characters to the left of the cursor. (Les. 4, Obj. 2)   9.   T   F

10. When your codes are revealed, you cannot move the cursor in your text. (Les. 4, Obj. 3) . . . .   10.   T   F

COMPLETION

Indicate the correct answer in the space provided.

Answers

1. How many function keys are there on the newer keyboards? (Les. 3, Obj. 1) . . . .   1. _____

2. Which two keys are like the Shift key in that they give the other keys additional capabilities? (Les. 3, Obj. 2)   2. _____

3. Can you use Caps Lock to key a dollar sign? (Les. 3, Obj. 2) . . . .   3. _____

4. Which of the keys on the Number Keypad has no extra function in WordPerfect? (Les. 3, Obj. 3) . . . .   4. _____

5. How many function keys does your keyboard have? (Les. 3, Obj. 4) . . . .   5. _____

6. Is it necessary to memorize the information on the template before you can use WordPerfect? (Les. 3, Obj. 4)   6. _____

7. Which three keystrokes used together will move your cursor directly to the end of your text? (Les. 4, Obj. 1)   7. _____

8. What is the quickest way to move the cursor to the beginning of the line? (Les. 4, Obj. 1) . . . .   8. _____

9. Which key is used to delete characters to the right of the cursor? (Les. 4, Obj. 2) . . . .   9. _____

10. Which key is used to delete characters to the left of the cursor? (Les. 4, Obj. 2) . . . .   10. _____

11. Reveal your codes and look at the ruler dividing the page. How many tabs are set between the margins? (Les. 4, Obj. 3) . . . .   11. _____

REFERENCE

Go to Keyboard Layout in the alphabetic section of the *WordPerfect Reference* and discover what key combination is used to access the setup menu where keyboard layout can be changed. What is the combination?

_____

Turn to the Cursor Speed section of the *Reference*. How many times does a key repeat for each second you hold it down? Can the cursor speed be changed? If so, where must you go to change the setting?

_____

Why do you think this might be important for people who do a lot of keying?

_____

LESSON 5
Saving and Retrieving Documents

OBJECTIVES

Upon completion of this lesson, you will be able to:

1. Name a document using conventional naming procedures.
2. Save the document on a disk.
3. Retrieve a document from the disk into the memory buffer of the computer.
4. Add to a document that was previously created.

Estimated Time: ½ hour

NAMING A DOCUMENT

How you name your documents in this course isn't terribly important. Many of these documents don't need to be retrieved, and there aren't as many of them as you would create in an office environment. However, whole books have been written on naming conventions to make it easier to find documents after they have been created and filed.

The names of documents created on your computer have some similarities regardless of what program you use. These characteristics are determined by DOS rules. You probably remember that DOS is the Disk Operating System used by IBM and IBM-compatible PCs. DOS rules specify that:

- The document name (*filename*) may be any number of characters up to a maximum of eight characters.

- The filename may be followed by a period and an *extension* of up to three characters. (In some cases, WordPerfect doesn't allow you to use an extension. For example, in a later lesson you will learn to create a macro. When you name macros, you may not use an extension. WordPerfect automatically supplies the extension WPM to all macros.)

- Document names may NOT contain spaces.

- All of the alphabetic characters and the numbers 0-9 may be used for document names. Most symbols may be used, but some symbols will cause an error message to appear.

- A particular name can be assigned to only one document. If you give a document a name that has already been used for one of the documents on your disk, the second document will take the place of the original one, and the original document will be lost.

Beyond these simple rules, how you name your documents is pretty much up to you. So you need to devise a system whereby your document names have some consistency and meaning. Most of the document names you are given for this training reflect the lesson in which the document was prepared. For example, the first exercise in Lesson 8 would be **job.8-1**, or if a memo was created in the first exercise of Lesson 12, it might be **memo.121**. In some cases, the name of the document reflects what the document is about.

On the job your document name might include the date that the document was created and the initials of the author. That name, created with a combination of numerals and letters, could also appear on the document in the position for the reference initials. If the document is identified in this manner, you can tell at a glance when the document comes back for revision where it is saved and what its name is.

Please note that the words *file* and *document* are used interchangeably in this lesson and throughout the course. A file and a document are the same thing. Become accustomed to both terms.

SAVING A DOCUMENT WITHOUT CLEARING MEMORY (EXITING)

In Lesson 2 you learned how to save a document in a manner that clears the screen and the memory. It is usually preferable to save your document and clear the memory buffer using **F7** or by choosing **Exit** from the **File** menu.

Occasionally, however, you will want to save your document but keep it in the memory buffer and showing on the screen. For example, when you are working on a long document, it is useful to save at the end of every page or two. This practice minimizes your loss in case of a power problem or accidental erasure of your work. Following these instructions will allow you to save frequently but continue to work on the document that is in memory. Since you don't have a document in memory now, just study these easy steps:

1. Strike **F10** to save a document.

2. The message **Document to be Saved:** will appear in the prompt position of the status line. Do one of the following:

a. For a new document, key the name of the document and strike **Enter**. WordPerfect will save the document on your file disk.

b. If you are saving a document that previously has been saved and retrieved, the prompt **Document to be Saved:** will be followed by the drive and the previous name of the file. You have two choices:

   (1) If you would like to save the document with the same name, simply strike **Enter**. A prompt will appear on the status line asking **Replace (filename)?** Key **Y** and the entire new document takes the place of the old document.

   (2) If you'd like to give the document a new name when you save it, key the new name over the old name in the prompt and strike **Enter**. (You don't have to delete the old document name. When you begin to key the new name, the old name disappears.) You will then have the old version of the document saved on your disk as well as the new version of the document.

You will not practice saving with F10 at this time.

THE HARD DISK SYSTEM

Note: If you have a dual floppy system, you should read this section because the information presented here will have future importance to you. However, only those students with hard disk systems should follow the steps in the exercise to change directories.

In Lesson 2 you learned why your instructor may prefer that you save your document on a data disk in Drive A, even though hard disk systems may have a large amount of space available for document storage. This process makes classroom management easier because each student has his or her own disk that can be used in any computer that has WordPerfect installed. But it means that every time a student wishes to save or retrieve a document, the **a:** must be attached to the beginning of the document name. That's how the computer knows it is to go to Drive A, where the student data disk has been inserted.

The designers of WordPerfect have anticipated that users might wish to save documents on disks other than the hard disk. So they made it easy for you to change the default drive. Your instructor has the ability to set up the computer so your documents are automatically saved on your disk in Drive A. If that hasn't been done and you wish to save on the data disk in Drive A, you must make that change each time you start Word-Perfect. The drive to which you change will remain the default drive until the computer is turned off (or until the default is changed again).

The procedure to change the default drive involves only a few simple steps. If you are working on a hard disk system and your instructor wants your documents saved on the data disk in Drive A and the default setting hasn't been changed, check the drive by following the steps in Exercise 1 every time you start WordPerfect.

Lesson 5 Exercise 1

Choose List Files from the File menu.

1. Strike **F5** to list your files. If **Dir a:*.*** appears at the bottom left of the screen, your computer has been set to save automatically on your disk. You may skip the rest of the exercise.

2. If the **C:\WP51*.*** prompt appears, follow the prompt in the lower right corner where you are instructed to strike the equals (=) key to change directories.

3. WordPerfect will ask for the directory to which you would like to change. Key **a:** and strike **Enter**.

4. The prompt will change to a:*.* where you may strike **Enter** if you would like to look at a list of files on the disk in Drive A. Unless you are a template disk user, there's nothing in that list except the memo created in Lesson 2 called **para.2-3** and the **foreign.3-1** paragraph from Lesson 3. Strike the space bar for the list to disappear.

5. Affirm that the change of default drive was made. Strike **F5** followed by **Enter**. Does the Drive A list return? If it doesn't, go through the steps above again. If it does appear, the default has been changed for this session and you're ready to continue with your training.

For the purpose of this training, it will be assumed that hard disk users will be saving their documents onto the disk in Drive A. If you have been told by your instructor to save your documents into a directory on the hard disk, each time you retrieve a document you will see the **C:\WP51*.*** prompt at the bottom of the screen. It will probably include your directory name.

Now let's prepare a document that gives you some keying practice as well as practice in using the Tab key after numerals. It also provides practice in saving a document. Follow the instructions carefully.

Lesson 5 Exercise 2

1. Key the short job description in Figure 5-1. Remember to let your work wrap automatically at the end of the line. Your line endings will probably be different from those shown in the figure.

2. Use **Tab** to indent after each numeral. Remember to strike **Enter** twice at the end of each paragraph, including the last paragraph.

3. Proofread carefully and correct all errors.

Choose **Exit** from the File menu.

4. When you finish the document, strike **F7** to Exit and name the document **job.5-2** (document about a job created in Lesson 5, Exercise 2). Then strike **Enter** to complete the command to save the document.

5. At the **Exit WP? No (Yes)** prompt, strike **Enter** or **N** for No.

An administrative assistant is a competent, well-trained person who performs secretarial duties in an office of a user or users. Some of the responsibilities performed by the administrative assistant are listed below:

1. The administrative assistant is responsible for composing and dictating routine documents to be prepared in the Information Processing Center which will be signed by the user or users. The administrative assistant proofreads work as it comes from the Information Processing Center, and generally interfaces with the Information Processing Center personnel.

2. The administrative assistant receives and screens callers and visitors, makes appointments, and handles telephone duties for the user or users.

Figure 5-1

RETRIEVING A DOCUMENT

You can retrieve a document from a disk in one of two ways.

1. The first method is to use **Shift-F10** (retrieve). When you strike Shift-F10, you will see the prompt **Document to be Retrieved:** on the status line. At the prompt, key the full name of the document and strike **Enter**.

Choose **Retrieve** from the File menu.

2. The second method is to use **F5** to list your files, locate the document in the list, and then retrieve it. Since you may not always remember the exact name of your documents, you will probably prefer this method. Exercise 3 takes you through the steps to retrieve a file from the list of files.

Lesson 5 Exercise 3

1. Strike **F5** and check the prompt in the status line. It should read **Dir A:*.*.** If so, strike **Enter**. (The asterisk-period-asterisk designation is the DOS method of asking for all files.)

2. The directory lists all the files on the data disk in alphabetical order. The cursor is the highlighted bar on the "current" line near the top of

the screen. You can move the cursor from filename to filename with the cursor-moving keys.

3. Move the cursor to **job.5-2** and look at the menu at the bottom of the screen. As you can see, several options are available to you. For now, you are concerned only with the first, **1 Retrieve.** Key **1** now.

4. After a short pause, your document appears on the screen. Check to see that the drive and name of the document are appearing in the lower left corner of the screen.

5. Now strike **F7** to exit the document again. Do NOT save the document and do NOT exit WordPerfect.

Choose **Exit** from the File menu.

When you retrieve a document from the disk, you are really pulling a copy of that document from the disk into the memory of the computer. Once a document is saved on the disk, it is there to stay until you either erase it or store another document using the same name. After retrieving a document, the changes you make to that document on the screen do not become part of the document stored on the disk until you save the document again. When you save it again and give it the same name, the new document takes the place of the old one. If you give it a different name, the original document stays on your disk along with the new one.

You will almost always want to clear the memory before you retrieve a document. If you don't you'll end up with two or more documents in the memory at one time. WordPerfect helps you in this regard by telling you when there is already a document in memory. It does this by showing a prompt at the bottom of the screen that says: **Retrieve into current document? No (Yes).** If you wish to join two or more documents, retrieving a document when another is in memory is a good method.

Unless you are absolutely certain your memory is clear when you retrieve a document, develop the habit of clearing the memory by using **Exit** between documents. Another method is to strike **Home, Home,** ↑ to go to the top of the document screen and check for a document before retrieving. You could also reveal your codes to look for any stray codes that might be lurking there.

Now let's practice retrieving a document again. This time you will add more text to the document and save it with a different name. Follow along carefully.

Lesson 5 Exercise 4

1. Retrieve **foreign.3-1** from your disk.

2. Using the cursor-moving techniques and the correcting techniques you learned in Lesson 4, correct all 13 errors in the paragraph.

3. Proofread the paragraph carefully and correct any additional errors.

4. Key **F7** to save the document again and respond with **Y** at the **Save Document?** prompt. We'll give the document a new name.

5. When the old name of the document is prompted, DO NOT move the cursor. Simply key **foreign.5-4** as the new document name and strike **Enter**. Do not exit WordPerfect.

Now let's add to your paragraph listing the duties of the hardworking administrative assistant.

Lesson 5 Exercise 5

1. Retrieve **job.5-2** from your disk again. Strike **Page Down** to move the cursor to the end of the document.

2. Key the text in Figure 5-2 as the next two items in your list of tasks for an administrative assistant. Remember to use **Tab** to indent after the numerals.

3. Proofread Items 3 and 4 and make any necessary corrections.

4. Key **F7** to save the document again and respond with **Y** at the **Save Document?** prompt.

5. When the old name of the document is prompted, DO NOT move the cursor. Simply key **job.5-5** as the new document name and strike **Enter**.

6. Do not exit WordPerfect.

```
3.   The administrative assistant sets up and coordinates
conferences and meetings and makes necessary travel
arrangements for the user or users.

4.   The administrative assistant establishes and maintains
paper and electronic filing systems to support the user or
users.
```

Figure 5-2

SUMMARY

Most of the material in this lesson has been concerned with saving documents on disks and then retrieving those documents. This is what word processing is all about. You create a document and save it. Then you retrieve that document and revise it and then save it again. Documents can be revised as many times as you wish, and you NEVER have to key a document all over again, unless you can't remember the name you gave it when you saved it!

There are some important things to remember with regard to saving and retrieving documents. Let's review them.

- Choose your document names carefully so you can find the documents when you need them.
- Remember the DOS rules of 8-character filenames and 3-character extensions.
- Make sure your computer memory is clear when you retrieve a document. Even if you can't see the document on the screen, check to see if anything is there before retrieving a document from the disk.

You will find that if you follow these simple rules, you will have little trouble in working with your document disk.

LESSON 5 NOTES:

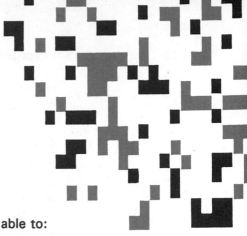

LESSON 6
File Management

OBJECTIVES

Upon completion of this lesson, you will be able to:

1. Delete and rename files and discuss the menu options on the List Files screen.
2. Use your printer to create a hard copy of your documents.

Estimated Time: 1 hour

FILE MANAGEMENT

You learned in Lesson 5 that one way to retrieve documents is by listing the files and selecting the document you need. However, you may not have noticed all the information that is available to you on the List Files screen. Let's look at the List Files screen now and review the various elements of that feature.

Choose List Files from the File menu.

Strike **F5** followed by **Enter**. You should see a screen much like Figure 6-1. Compare it with your own and study the List Files screen as the various options are discussed.

```
04-01-94  11:42a                    Directory A:\*.*
Document size:          0  Free:  725,563 Used:    2467          Files:  5


      .   Current   <Dir>      |   ..   Parent   <Dir>
FOREIGN  .3-1    715 09-10-92 9:40a | FOREIGN  .5-4   762 09-10-92 8:14a
JOB      .5-2    329 09-10-92 9:42a | JOB      .5-5   329 09-10-92 7:42a
PARA     .2-3    332 09-10-92 9:32a |




1 Retrieve; 2 Delete; 3 Move/Rename; 4 Print; 5 Short/Long Display;
6 Look; 7 Other Directory; 8 Copy; 9 Find; N Name Search: 6
```

Figure 6-1

Starting at the top, you can see a section that begins with the date and time. You can see the directory at which you're looking and the ***.*** designation which means ALL files. The directory should be Drive B for dual floppy system users and Drive A for hard disk system users. Also important is the indication of how much disk space is "free." That number tells you how many *bytes* or characters of space are still available on your disk. WordPerfect also tells you how many files are in the directory of the disk you have accessed.

Look at the list of your documents. Unless you are using the template disk, there are not many documents in your list now. The documents are listed by filename in alphabetic order, working across the screen. Notice that in addition to the name and extension of the documents, you can see the size of each document in bytes and the date and time of creation.

Before you can do anything with a file on this list, you must choose that file. A file can be chosen by moving the highlight to that file with either the mouse or the arrow keys. Once the file is selected, you may choose any of the options. A brief description of each of the menu options is listed below.

Read all of the descriptions carefully, trying to get an idea of the purpose of each option. Most of them won't be practiced in this lesson. Some will be practiced later in the course. On the job, these options will become very important to you as you manage your files efficiently.

As mentioned earlier, the words *file* and *document* are used interchangeably throughout this book. Secretaries and information processing people talk about *documents*. Data processors and computer people talk about *files*. Both words refer to a group of keystrokes that say something, such as a letter, a list of names and addresses, or a computing program. This group of keystrokes is given a name and stored on a disk and is called either a file or a document. Don't let the terminology confuse you!

1 Retrieve. To retrieve a file from your disk, move the highlight to the desired file. With the file highlighted, you MUST strike **1** or **R**. You can also retrieve files with the **Shift-F10** combination, but that method requires that you key the exact name of the file.

   You will find that it usually is more convenient to list your files and find the document you wish to retrieve rather than to remember the name of the document and key it.

2 Delete. Striking **2** or **D** will delete a file from your disk. You will be asked to confirm the deletion, just in case you have selected that option accidentally. Once you have keyed **Y**, the file is permanently erased.

3 Move/Rename. Striking **3** or **M** will enable you to rename a file on your disk. Move the cursor to the file you wish to rename and key **3**. Then key the new name of the file.

   As you learned earlier, you may not have two documents with the same name. You'll get an error message if you try to rename a file with a name already in use. In addition to changing a document name, Move/Rename enables you to move a document from one disk or directory to another.

4 Print. With most computer setups, you may print a document saved on a disk from the List Files screen by moving the highlight to the document you wish to print and striking **4** or **P**. This will bring up a prompt asking which page(s) you want to print. This feature doesn't work with hand-fed printers.

Another way of printing a document is to print it from the working screen before the document is saved on the disk. Printing a document in memory is discussed later in this lesson.

5 Short/Long Display. This feature enables you to change the appearance of the List Files screen to accommodate long filenames. The reference question at the end of Lesson 5 introduced you to long filenames. This feature is not covered in this course.

6 Look. This option retrieves a document for you to view only. If you choose **6** or **L** or if you strike **Enter** when a document is highlighted, the document appears, usually unformatted. Across the top of the Look screen you'll see the disk or directory name, the name of the file, and the time and date when the file was last revised. You are allowed only to scroll through the file.

You can close this Look at a file by touching any key other than screen down, Page Down, or the arrow keys.

7 Other Directory. WordPerfect provides you the opportunity to manage your files with a tree-type structure of directories and subdirectories. The Other directory choice (**7** or **O** in this menu) allows you to move from one directory to another. There will be more on this feature in a later lesson.

8 Copy. By selecting **8** or **C**, you can copy the selected file to another file, directory, or drive.

9 Find. This feature allows you to search all the files listed to find those files that contain specific words. After the search, a new directory of files is shown listing only those files containing the word or words for which you searched.

N Name Search. Choosing **N** for Name search enables you to move quickly through the file list for a specific file. You simply key the first letters of the desired filename, and the cursor moves to that file. Then you must strike **Enter** or **Exit** to return to the List Files menu at the bottom of the screen to retrieve, print, or do whatever you wish to do with the file.

That is a brief summary of the List Files functions. You will be using the List Files screen often. Be confident as you work with it.

If you have any questions about the List Files screen (or anything else), ask your instructor now. It is important that you understand the capabilities of WordPerfect that you've learned about up to this point before you continue. List Files is closed by simply striking the space bar.

Let's take a moment to try a few of the options available in the List Files menu.

Lesson 6 Exercise 1

1. Strike the space bar to close List Files. Key the sentence in Figure 6-2.

2. Save the document with **Exit** so the screen and memory are cleared. Name the document **sample**. Do not exit WordPerfect.

Choose List **F**iles from the **F**ile menu.

3. Strike **F5** and **Enter** to list your files. Verify that the document named **sample** is there.

4. Move the highlight to the **sample** document and strike **3**. At the prompt for the new name, key your first name followed by **Enter**. You now have renamed the **sample** document, and your name should appear in the list instead of **sample**.

5. Strike **6**. This gives you an opportunity to look at the document but not to change it. Strike the space bar to return to the List Files screen.

6. You are now finished with this document. Move the highlight to the document that bears your name and strike **2** to delete it. At the prompt verifying that you do, indeed, wish to delete the document, key **Y** and watch the list to see that the document is gone.

7. Strike the space bar to return to the working screen. Later you'll have an opportunity to work with some of the other List Files options.

```
This is a sample exercise to practice using some of the
options available through the List Files screen.
```

Figure 6-2

PRINTING A DOCUMENT

WordPerfect provides you with a number of ways to print a document. One popular way, as you learned above, is to print a document that is saved on your disk. Another way is to print the document as it shows on your screen. When you print a document showing on the screen, you will work with the Print menu. It is from this menu that you control your printer, and it is from this menu that you choose the printer to which your document will be sent. The Print menu is illustrated in Figure 6-3. Look at the illustration. You'll be accessing your Print menu shortly.

If your classroom uses only one printer model, that printer should have been selected when the WordPerfect software was installed. If so, you may simply follow the printing instructions for your kind of printer in the section below to print your documents.

However, if you are in a classroom with several different types of printers, you will always need to check to be sure you are using the correct printer description before you try to print a document. Once you've selected the correct printer, you may print according to the steps below for

Print

1 Full Document
2 Page
3 Document on Disk
4 Control Printer
5 Multiple Pages
6 View Document
7 Initialize Printer

Options

S	Select Printer	**Printer**
B	Binding Offset	**0"**
N	Number of Copies	**1**
U	Multiple Copies Generated by	**WordPerfect**
G	Graphics Quality	**Medium**
T-	Text Quality	**High**

Figure 6-3

your printer. Check to see if your printer description is correct, following the directions in Exercise 2. Then study the information below about your kind of printer so that you can use your printer efficiently and effectively.

Lesson 6 Exercise 2

1. First, look at your printer and determine the brand and model. If several printers are available, find out from your instructor which printer you are to use.

Choose **Print** from the File menu.

2. Strike **Shift-F7** for the Print menu. Look at the **Select Printer** prompt to see if the correct printer has been selected. (Usually once you've affirmed the printer, you can go ahead and print your document.)

3. Choose **S** for Select Printer to get the list of installed printers.

4. Move the highlight to the printer you'll be using. Strike **1** Select or **Enter** to choose the printer. You will be returned to the Print menu.

5. Strike the space bar to return to your working screen. You won't print just yet.

Continuous-Feed Printers

When your printer is ready to print on continuous paper, the perforated top of the page (where it was torn from the previous page) should be directly behind the print head. WordPerfect will automatically give you a one-inch top margin.

In order to get to the right position behind the print head, you may need to adjust the paper position. *To avoid stripping the printer gears, it is VERY important that you turn off the printer power when you turn the printer knob to adjust the paper.*

Some continuous-feed printers have what's called a "back-feed" (push) sprocket, and others have a "front-feed" (pull) arrangement. With front-feed printers, you waste the first sheet of paper because it is used by the sprockets to pull the second sheet into the proper position. With back-feed printers, the first sheet of paper is not wasted.

Once you have chosen the printer description for a continuous-feed printer, you may send documents from the screen to the printer by accessing the Print menu and choosing either Option 1 to print the entire document or Option 2 for a single page.

Hand-Fed Printers

Depending on the kind of hand-fed printer you have, you may find that you can either set the paper behind the platen and push a button or pull a lever and the paper will feed into position. In some cases, the paper will be ready to print. In other cases, you must advance the paper to get the one-inch top margin. You may experiment with this on your own or ask your instructor for help.

Be certain you have selected the printer description for a hand-fed printer. Then follow the steps below to print the document on the screen:

1. Open the Print menu and choose either Option 1 to print the entire document or Option 2 to print the page on which the cursor is located.

2. You may hear a beep that tells you the printer is waiting for you to insert the paper. If you do, return to the Print menu and choose Option 4 (Control Printer).

3. Key **G** for Go. When printing a multipage document, strike **G** after you have inserted your paper for each page.

4. When you have finished printing, strike the space bar to return to the working screen.

If you wish to print a document that is not on your screen, list your files, move the cursor to the document you wish to print, and choose Option 4. You may hear a beep to remind you to insert the paper. Then go to the Print menu and choose Option 4. Strike **G** for Go.

Sheet-Feed Printers

After you have set the printer description for a sheet-feed printer, go to the Print menu and choose either Option 1 for an entire document or

Option 2 for a single page. To print a document that is not on the screen, list your files, move the cursor to the document you wish to print, and choose Option 4. If your document is more than one page long, Word-Perfect will prompt you to enter the numbers of the pages to be printed.

Now, finally, let's print a document!

Lesson 6 Exercise 3

1. Make sure your printer is turned on. Then list your files and retrieve **job.5-2**.

2. Go to the Print menu, strike **1 Full Document**, and follow any steps necessary for your computer to send the document to the printer.

3. Close the document without saving it, and retrieve the *hard copy* (printed copy) of your document from the printer.

4. Look carefully at your printed document. The margin at the top should be one inch deep. The side margins should also be one inch. Is your document correct? If not, the paper should be adjusted in your printer. Have your instructor help you with this.

5. Notice that some of the words seem to be spaced too far apart. That happens when full justification is used with a fixed pitch font like the one you're using. The program spreads out the words on the line so they end evenly at the right margin. You will learn more on that later.

6. This is your first printed document. Now you have something to take home to put on the refrigerator! Congratulations!!

SUMMARY

In this lesson you received a brief introduction to List Files and the capabilities provided by the List Files menu. You'll be using List Files most often to retrieve documents and to print documents. You've already learned how easy it is to delete unwanted files from your disk using the Delete option on the List Files screen. In a much later lesson you will delete more files. You will also work with a number of other List Files options.

Also in this lesson you learned that once you determine which printer you're using and make that selection, printing your documents with WordPerfect is very easy.

WordPerfect is a very printer-dependent program. As you progress through your training and as you use WordPerfect on the job, you'll discover that the only real limits to the capabilities of WordPerfect are the limitations imposed by your printer. You may find that your instructor will need to give you special instructions regarding the use of the printer. On the job, you will want to work closely with your in-house technical support staff, the printer vendor, or the technical support people at Word-Perfect Corporation.

The List Files menu and the Print menu are two of the most useful and powerful WordPerfect tools! They enable you to perform much of what information processing is all about. In fact, this is the backbone of information processing. You have the skills to create a document and save it. You also know how to retrieve that document, edit it, and print it. In learning to do these things, you have learned a number of WordPerfect commands. Let's review.

COMMAND SUMMARY

Feature	Function	Menu	Lesson
Exit	F7	File	2
List Files	F5	File	5 & 6
Print	Shift-F7	File	6
Retrieve	F5 or Shift-F10	File	5 & 6
Reveal Codes	Alt-F3 or F11	Edit, Reveal Codes	4
Save	F10	File	5

REVIEW EXERCISES

Following the End-of-Lesson Activities is a series of review exercises to help you check yourself on what you've learned so far. Be sure to look for review exercises at the end of each lesson as you go through your training.

LESSON 6 NOTES:

Name _____ **Date** _____

TRUE/FALSE

Each of the following statements is either true or false. Indicate your choice in the Answers column by circling T for a true statement or F for a false statement.

                                                                      Answers

1. You must name a document in order to save it on a disk. (Les. 5, Obj. 1)   1   T   F

2. Using F10 (Save) is the only way you can save a document. (Les. 5, Obj. 2) . . . .   2.   T   F

3. It is usually best to clear the memory before retrieving a document from the disk. (Les. 5, Obj. 3) . . . .   3.   T   F

4. When you retrieve a document from the disk, a copy of that document remains on the disk. (Les. 5, Obj. 4) . . . .   4.   T   F

5. Retrieving a document using the List Files screen saves you from having to remember the exact name of a document. (Les. 6, Obj. 1) . . . .   5.   T   F

6. When you view a file with the **6 Look** command in the List Files menu, you may make changes to that file. (Les. 6, Obj. 1) . . . .   6.   T   F

7. You may print a document from the List Files screen. (Les. 6, Obj. 1) .   7.   T   F

8. You should always check your printer selection at the beginning of a work session. (Les. 6, Obj. 2) . . . .   8.   T   F

9. WordPerfect enables you to print using a variety of printer types. (Les. 6, Obj. 2) . . . .   9.   T   F

COMPLETION

Indicate the correct answer in the space provided.

                                                                      Answers

1. What is the maximum number of characters that may be used in the extension of a file name? (Les. 5, Obj. 1)   1. _____

2. What other key besides F10 can be used to save a document? (Les. 5, Obj. 2) . . . .   2. _____

3. What three characters are used to designate a method of asking for a listing of all files? (Les. 5, Obj. 3) . . . .   3. _____

4. What appears in the document name prompt when you resave a document retrieved from your disk? (Les. 5, Obj. 4) . . . .   4. _____

5. Which screen must you access to look at the list of files you have saved? (Les. 6, Obj. 1) . . . .   5. _____

6. After you've moved the cursor to the name of the file you'd like to retrieve, which key do you strike to retrieve that file? (Les. 6, Obj. 1) . . . .   6. _____

7. What key returns you to your working screen from the List Files screen? (Les. 6, Obj. 1) . . . .   7. _____

8. What kind of printer is yours—continuous-feed, hand-fed, or sheet-feed? (Les. 6, Obj. 2) . . . .   9. _____

9. Did your printed document have one-inch top and side margins? (Les. 6, Obj. 2) . . . .   10. _____

REFERENCE

Turn in the *WordPerfect Reference* to the Document Management/Summary portion of the Environment Setup. This section tells about long document names.

What are the maximum number of characters you can use for a long WordPerfect document name? _____

If you choose to use the long document name option, will the document still have a DOS filename? _____

Turn to the Short Display portion of the List Files section of the *Reference* for these questions.

Is the List Files screen that's pictured a sample screen from a hard disk system or a dual floppy system? How can you tell? How many files are listed in that directory?

_____

Turn to the alphabetized list at the beginning of the *Reference* section of the documentation. How many sections begin with the words *Print* or *Printer*? With which three of them have you worked?

_____

Review Exercises

Periodically throughout this course, you'll have an opportunity to complete some review exercises to help you keep track of your progress. There are some major differences between the review exercises and the exercises scattered throughout the lessons. One difference is that in the lesson exercises you are primarily practicing a particular skill. While other skills must be used to do the exercises, emphasis is on the skill being learned. The other difference is that in the review exercises, fewer specific instructions are included. In other words, you have a chance to see what you've learned!

Occasionally as you do the exercises you may get stuck! If this happens, feel free to refer back to the lessons. If you get really stuck, ask your instructor to help you. Don't rely on your instructor, however, to tell you how to get out of every jam. You will learn more if you make an honest effort to solve the problem for yourself before you ask for help. While different students have different tolerance levels when stuck, ten minutes is the absolute maximum time you should devote to trying to solve your problems before asking for help.

REVIEW EXERCISE 1

Choose **Reveal Codes** from the Edit menu.

Key the memo in Figure 6-4. Watch the **Pos** indicator in the status line as you strike the **Tab** key to position Jose Castillo, etc., at **Pos 2"**.

When you have finished, strike **Alt-F3** or **F11** to open the Reveal Codes screen. Look at the [Tab] codes in the document following the headings in the top part of the memo. Add the [Tab] code to the list of codes that you are maintaining. Close Reveal Codes.

Finally, proofread the document and use **Exit** to save it as memo.6-1. Don't exit WordPerfect.

TO: (TAB)(TAB)Jose Castillo

FROM: (TAB) (key your name)

DATE: (key the current date)

RE: Project Development Team

Yesterday's meeting about the new project development team kept me awake last night thinking about the benefits for our organization that might be realized by this idea. Your suggestion that we actively encourage our employees to look for new ways to increase our product line is superb!

I would like to give more thought to this idea and get back to you soon to see how we can implement this plan.

Figure 6-4   DOC CODE

REVIEW EXERCISE 2

DOC CODE

1. Retrieve **job.5-5** from your data disk.

2. Strike **Home**, **Home**, ↓ to move your cursor to the end of the document. Add the items from Figure 6-5 as more job responsibilities for the administrative assistant. Remember to use **Tab** after each numeral.

3. Proofread your work and make all corrections.

4. Finally, use **Exit** to save the document again as **job.5-5**. Clear the screen but do not exit WordPerfect.

---

5.   The administrative assistant takes notes at user meetings and conferences and types confidential, highly complicated documents for the users when necessary.

6.   The administrative assistant is responsible for opening mail, screening it, and routing it for a user or a group of users.

7.   The administrative assistant compiles pertinent facts from files or other sources to aid the user or users in responding to incoming mail.

Figure 6-5

REVIEW EXERCISE 3

Choose **Print** from the File menu.

Choose **Exit** from the File menu.

1. Retrieve **memo.6-1** from your disk.

2. Delete the second paragraph and add the paragraphs in Figure 6-6 at the bottom of the memo. (Reminder: What is the quickest way to delete the last paragraph of anything?)

3. Open the Print menu with **Shift-F7** and choose **1** Full Document to send the memo to the printer.

4. Use **F7** to save the memo as memo.6-3 Clear the screen but don't exit WordPerfect.

I would like to suggest that we begin implementation of this plan by selecting the project team and giving members an orientation session. I have some thoughts about how we will select the team members and the types of information we need

to cover with them. Then we can turn them loose on the
employees in our organization and watch this idea mushroom.

Of course, some caution will have to be exercised with
regard to how we approach the ideas brought to us by the
project development team, but I think that the benefits will
warrant any extra time we must spend in working through the
nuts and bolts of this idea.

Give some thought to how we should choose the team members,
what kind of orientation will be necessary, and how we will
control this whole plan. I would like to meet with you at 9
on Monday morning to discuss your feelings on these points,
and we can begin making our plans for this new project.

Congratulations for your fine idea. I know it will take our
organization along some exciting new avenues.

Figure 6-6

REVIEW EXERCISE 4

The box below illustrates some of the most frequently used proofreader's marks. Study the marks, as they will be used for corrections in your documents.

Then retrieve **job.5-5** from your data disk. Using Figure 6-7, which has corrections marked, edit the document. When you are finished, print a copy. Then use **Exit** to save it with the name **job.6-4**. (Note that the document is shown below with expanded spacing. That makes it easier to read the editing marks. Your document should be single spaced.)

Proofreader's Marks

Change	Mark	Mark in Text	Corrected Text
Capitalize	≡	word processing is fun.	Word processing is fun.
Close up	⌒	Word Perfect	WordPerfect
Delete	ℒ	Your work work is good.	Your work is good.
Insert comma	⋀	apples potatoes and peas	apples, potatoes, and peas
Insert	⋀	Word processing fun.	Word processing is fun.
Insert space	#	Wordprocessing is fun.	Word processing is fun.
Insert period	⊙	Key the memo	Key the memo.
Lowercase	lc	Word Processing is fun.	Word processing is fun.
New paragraph	¶	¶ Please call me next	Please call me next

An administrative assistant is a ~~competent, well-trained~~ person who performs secretarial _and clerical_ duties in an office ~~of a user or users.~~ Some of the responsibilities _of the competent_ ~~performed by the~~ administrative assistant are listed below:

1.   The administrative assistant ~~is responsible for composing~~ _Composes_ and dictat~~ing~~_es_ routine documents to be prepared in the Information Processing Center _for the signature of_ ~~which will be signed by~~ the user or users. The administrative assistant proofreads work as it comes from the Information Processing Center, and generally interfaces with the Information Processing Center personnel.

2.   The administrative assistant receives and screens callers and visitors, makes appointments, and handles telephone duties for the user or users.

3.   The administrative assistant sets up and coordinates conferences and meetings and makes necessary travel arrangements for the user or users.

4.   The administrative assistant _organizes_ ~~establishes~~ and maintains paper and electronic filing systems to support the user or users.

5.   The administrative assistant takes notes at ~~user~~ meetings and conferences and types confidential, highly complicated documents ~~for the users~~ when necessary.

6.   The administrative assistant ~~is responsible for~~ open~~ing~~_s_ mail, screen~~ing~~_s_ it, and rout~~ing~~_es_ it for a user or a group of users.

7.   The administrative assistant compiles pertinent facts from files or other sources to aid the user or users in responding to incoming mail.

Figure 6-7

LESSON 7
Text Enhancement

OBJECTIVES

Upon completion of this lesson, you will be able to:

1. Use bold, underline, italics, and caps to display text attractively.
2. Identify paired codes.
3. Center text on the line of writing.
4. Align text at the right margin with Flush Right.
5. Use tabs to indent text.

Estimated Time: 1 hour

Often when you are creating a document, you need a way to make a word or two or fifteen stand out from the remainder of the text. You must be careful when you do this so that you don't have so many words "standing out" that the formatting is distracting and the text is difficult to read. With that warning in mind, let's look at some of the ways you can enhance the words in your documents to give them emphasis.

CAPS LOCK, BOLD, UNDERLINE

The Caps Lock, bold, and underline keys are more of the toggle keys that you learned about earlier. You strike a toggle key once to turn the format on, key the text to be formatted, and then strike the key again to turn the format off.

Caps Lock

Find the Caps Lock key on your keyboard. When you strike this key, all letters keyed will be capitals. Notice that the **POS** indicator at the bottom of the screen is in all caps when Caps Lock is on. When you strike Caps Lock again, the indicator changes back to **Pos**. Caps Lock only affects alphabetic keys. It won't enable you to key symbols such as $, #, or %.

Caps Exercise. Strike the Caps Lock key and key your name. Notice that **POS** is in all caps. Strike Enter twice, turn off Caps Lock, and key your name again in lowercase letters. Turn on Reveal Codes long enough to see that there is no code for all capital letters. Strike Enter twice again.

Underline

One quick touch of the **F8** key turns on Underline. Look at Underline on your keyboard template. If you are working on a color monitor, the underline will not show. Instead, underlined text will appear in a contrasting color. When Underline is on, the **Pos** indicator in the status line will show in the same contrasting color. If you have a monochrome monitor, underlined text will show in reverse video, or the underline might actually appear on the screen. To stop underlining, strike F8 again.

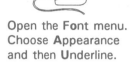

Open the Font menu. Choose Appearance and then Underline.

Underline Exercise. Strike **F8** to turn on Underline and key your name. Strike **Enter** twice. Strike **F8** to turn off Underline again. Turn on Reveal Codes and look at the Underline codes. Turn it off again and strike **Enter** twice.

Bold

The **F6** key turns on Bold. The status line reflects the fact that Bold is turned on by showing the numeral following **Pos** in bold. When Bold is not turned on, the entire status line is bolded—all except the numeral. As with the character formats you've just learned, Bold may be turned off the same way it is turned on.

Open the Font menu. Choose Appearance and then Bold.

Bold Exercise. Strike **F6** and key the words *WordPerfect Word Processing.* Notice that the words show in bold on the screen. Strike **F6** to turn off Bold again. Look at the Bold codes in Reveal Codes. Then strike **Enter** twice and turn off Reveal Codes.

Italics

There is no special function key for italics. Italic type must be chosen from the Font menu accessed by striking **Ctrl-F8**. Strike **Ctrl-F8** now, choose **2 Appearance,** and look at the line menu that appears across the bottom of the screen. The menu will look much like Figure 7-1.

`1 Bold 2 Undln 3 Dbl Und 4 Italc 5 Outln 6 Shadw 7 Sm Cap 8 Redln 9 Stkout:`

Figure 7-1

As you can see, bold and underline are also available from this menu, along with quite a number of other choices for enhancing the text in your document. Some of the choices here are very useful for certain types of work, like double underline, redline, and strikeout. Most of these formatting features will not be covered in your training. To turn off Italics, you may return to the Font menu and choose **3 Normal.** You'll learn another method shortly.

Lesson 7 Exercise 1

Open the **Font** menu.
Choose **A**ppearance
and then **I**talic.

Open the **Font** menu
and choose **N**ormal.

1. Strike **Ctrl-F8** and choose **2 Appearance** and then **4 Italics** to turn on Italics. Key the name of your school.

2. Turn off Italics by striking **Ctrl-F8** and choosing **3 Normal**. Strike **Enter** twice. Your screen now should have samples of regular text as well as bold, underline, and italics.

3. Reveal your codes and look at the smorgasbord of codes. Use the arrow keys to move up and down, if necessary, to see the codes. Add all of the codes to the list of codes you are accumulating. Turn off Reveal Codes.

4. Strike **Shift-F7** and **1 Full** document to send these samples to the printer. You may find that your printer will not support italic type, but underline and bold should print correctly.

5. Exit the document, saving it as **practice.7-1**. Do not exit WordPerfect.

Lesson 7 Exercise 2

1. Key the paragraph illustrated in Figure 7-2. Use caps, bold, italics, and underline as shown.

2. Print the paragraph.

3. Exit the document, saving it as **practice.7-2**. Do not exit WordPerfect.

BUTTE DES MORTS BUSINESS COLLEGE provides all kinds of classes on computers for eager students. One of the more popular areas of training is **word processing** training since **word processing** is becoming widely used in the *Fox River Valley* area. This is a course using the **WORDPERFECT word processing** software program on an IBM or compatible computer. Students are finding that **WORDPERFECT** is <u>easy to learn</u> and easy to use.

Figure 7-2

PAIRED CODES

There are two kinds of codes—paired and open. With the exception of caps (because the use of caps doesn't put any codes in your document), all of the text-enhancement features you've learned so far in this lesson have had paired codes. In other words, in each case an "on" code turns on the feature and an "off" code is used to turn off the feature.

When you turn on a feature that has paired codes, both codes appear in Reveal Codes with the cursor positioned between them. When you turn off the feature, the cursor simply moves past the "off" code. You can do that manually and accomplish the same thing. For example, you could turn off Bold by striking the → key or the **End** key. With Bold, that's not much of a saving of keystrokes because you can turn off Bold by striking **F6**. However, with a feature like Italics, the savings in keystrokes is considerable, especially if you use the feature often. Let's try it.

Lesson 7 Exercise 3

1. Turn on Reveal Codes.

2. Key the paragraph in Figure 7-2 again, using bold, caps, underline, and italics as shown. Watch the codes appear in the Codes screen when you turn on Bold, Underline, and Italics. This time, however, whenever you are ready to turn off Bold, Underline or Italics, strike → to move the cursor past the ending code.

3. When you are comfortable with the "ons" and "offs" of these paired codes, exit the document without saving.

Obviously you have some choices here. Just as you can choose between the function keys and the mouse/menu method in WordPerfect, you can choose to turn off your paired codes the same way you turned them on or cursor past the ending code.

When you make a choice of this kind, you are simply developing your style. Often there isn't a right way or even a best way. It depends on what's comfortable to you. As you progress with your learning, try some of the options and decide what is most efficient for your work.

CENTER, FLUSH RIGHT

In addition to using a change of appearance to enhance portions of your text, the location of the text is often important in how that text is perceived. For example, if you are keying something for display, you might choose to center that text. If you want something aligned at the right margin, Flush Right is the correct choice.

Center

You can automatically center a line of text between the margins. Normally you will give the Center command before you key the line. Look at the keyboard template and note that **Shift-F6** is used for centering. When you strike Shift-F6, your cursor moves to the center of the line and all text keyed is automatically centered. Striking **Enter** ends the centering command.

To center a line that has already been keyed, align the cursor with the first letter in the line to be centered and strike **Shift-F6**. The line must end with **Enter** to be centered in this manner.

Choose **Align** from the **Layout** menu. Then choose **Center**.

Centering Exercise. Strike **Shift-F6** and key the following line. End by striking **Enter**.

```
  This line is perfectly centered!
```

Now key the line again beginning at the left margin and ending with **Enter**. Move the cursor to the capital *T* at the beginning of the line. Strike **Shift-F6** to align this line with the first centered line. Strike **Page Down** to position the cursor for the next exercise.

Flush Right

When you want text to end even with the right margin or *flush right*, strike **Alt-F6**. This will move the cursor to the extreme right of the line. As you key the text, it will "back up" from the right margin. Strike **Enter** to end this command after you have keyed the text.

To flush right material that has already been keyed at the left margin, move your cursor to the beginning of the material to be formatted and strike **Alt-F6**. As with the center command, the line needs to end with **Enter** for the command to work.

Choose **Align** from the **Layout** menu. Then choose **Flush Right**.

Flush Right Exercise. Strike **Alt-F6** and key today's date. Strike **Enter** to return the cursor to the left margin.

Now key the date at the left margin followed by **Enter**. Move the cursor to the beginning of the line and strike **Alt-F6**. Look at the Center and Flush Right codes and add them to your list. Clear the screen. Don't save or print the document and don't exit WordPerfect.

Lesson 7 Exercise 3

1. Key the cast of characters in Figure 7-3. Center the title on the top line using bold and caps. Follow it with a quadruple space. (Strike **Enter** four times for a quadruple space.)

2. Key the name of the character at the left, give the command for Flush Right, and key the name of the actor or actress.

3. Exit and save the document as **fiddler.7-3**.

```
                        CAST

Tevye                                        Tim Riese
Golde                                        Pat Hansen
Tzeitel                                   Rachel Konkel
Hodel                                   Cindy Spaulding
Chava                                         Amy Hart
```

Figure 7-3

---

4. List your files and move the highlight to **fiddler.7-3**. Choose **4 Print** to send the document to the printer. If your paper is properly aligned, the document should have a one-inch top margin.

TABS

The Tab key is located in its usual position next to the letter Q. It can be used to indent text in the usual tab tradition. It can also be used to move existing text back to the previous tab stop if struck together with Shift. That's why the key often has an arrow pointing to the left.

As you know, WordPerfect's preset tabs are at each half inch. Since the WordPerfect default is 10 pitch, there are tabs set at .5 inch, 1.0 inch, 1.5 inches, 2.0 inches, 2.5 inches, or every five spaces. These tab stops can easily be changed. You will learn to do that in a later lesson.

ALWAYS use the Tab key instead of the space bar to indent lines from the left margin. You must do this because the printer recognizes the Tab code as a prescribed amount of space. The printer looks at spaces entered with the space bar as places where the text can be spread or squeezed to make the lines even at the right (full justification). If you indent your paragraphs with the space bar, the printer might adjust the size of those spaces, and your indents might be many different sizes.

You have already used the tab to indent after the numerals in the exercises about the administrative assistant and in the memo exercise. Let's try a little exercise here and then finish the lesson with a big exercise where you'll get to practice most of the skills learned in this lesson.

Lesson 7 Exercise 4

1. Key the alphabet as illustrated in Figure 7-4. Strike the **Tab** key between each of the letters. Stop when a letter wraps around to the next line.

```
a    b    c    d    e    f    g    h    i    etc.
```

Figure 7-4

---

2. When you finish, reveal your codes and look at the letters with [Tab] codes between them. Look at the tepees in the ruler separating the regular text from the Codes screen. Remember that those tepees indicate the locations of your tab stops. Are they aligned with the letters at the top?

3. Counting by fives, how many spaces are available on your writing line?

4. Without keying any spaces, add more letters to the letters you've keyed. How many letters can you add before the "word" drops to the next line?

5. Exit from the document without printing or saving.

Lesson 7 Exercise 5

Key the two-page letter illustrated in Figure 7-5 using the following instructions. You will see a line across the screen somewhere around **Ln 9.8"** as WordPerfect inserts an automatic page break. (This is called a "soft" page break.) Don't worry about the location of the page break or a second page heading. We'll return to this letter later and fix it up.

1. Strike **Enter** six times to give your letter a two-inch top margin. Check the **Ln** indicator in the status line to affirm that two-inch margin. (Six line spaces equals an inch, and WordPerfect automatically gives you a one-inch margin.)

2. Strike Tab as many times as necessary to move the cursor to **Pos 4"** and key the current date. Spell out the date; e.g., April 1, 1994. Follow the date with a quadruple space.

3. **Center** and **bold** the text in the subject line.

4. Use Tab to indent the display material in the body of the letter.

5. Tab to **Pos 4"** for the complimentary closing.

6. Strike **Enter** four times after the complimentary closing and key your name, again at **Pos 4"**.

7. Proofread the letter carefully and print it.

8. Save it on your disk with the name **secure.7-5** and clear the screen. (Are you remembering always to use **Exit** to save your documents?)

```
                              (Use current date)


Ms. Reiko Onodera
Mayfairy Corporation
329 May Building
Milwaukee, WI 54224-1234

Dear Ms. Onodera:

          Subject:  Protecting Vital Information

Thank you for your letter inquiring about the need for protection of
vital information in your organization.  There are a number of different
kinds of disasters that organizations feel could never happen to them.
One recent warning was Hurricane Andrew in 1992 where businesses large
and small in Florida and Louisiana were destroyed.  It is estimated that
of the organizations where massive losses of information occur, 45
percent are out of business within six months.

Listed below are some of the disasters against which the vital records
in your organization need to be protected.
```

(TAB)   <u>Natural Disasters</u>
(TAB) (TAB) Fires
                Floods
                Lightning
                Tornadoes
                Earthquakes
                Hurricanes

(TAB)   <u>Man-made Disasters</u>
(TAB) (TAB) Sabotage
                Theft
                Malfeasance
                Carelessness

These are only the most obvious of the disasters that could destroy your
organization's vital records. Our company has experienced consultants
who will work with your information processing department to protect you
against loss of records in any of these instances. The consultants are
also trained to identify any security problems your organization may
have.

I am enclosing a brochure describing our services and how we have helped
other major corporations protect their information. You may circulate
it to the key members of your staff for consideration.

Please call me at the number on the letterhead to arrange for a
consultation so we can talk about your needs. I can give you a quote,
if you wish, for the price of our service. We would very much like to
work with your organization to make certain that your vital records are
safe.

                Sincerely,

                Your name

Enclosure

Figure 7-5

SUMMARY

As you learned in this lesson, WordPerfect makes it easy for you to
enhance your text in a number of ways. When you want words or letters
or phrases to stand out, you can use all capital letters, bold, underline,
and italics. If your words need more emphasis, you can consider centering and using Flush Right. That's a lot of choices. Use them wisely!

LESSON 7 NOTES:

LESSON 8
Text Entry Features

OBJECTIVES

Upon completion of this lesson, you will be able to:

1. Delete incorrect commands.
2. Use the WordPerfect Indent feature.
3. Align text outside the left margin.
4. Use the hanging indent format.
5. Begin a new page in a document whenever desired.
6. Include the date in your documents automatically.
7. Use a hard space to protect blocks of text.
8. Key different kinds of hyphens.

Estimated time: 1 hour

DELETING COMMANDS

Back in Lesson 2 you learned that if you incorrectly give a command that puts a prompt in the lower left corner of the screen, you can delete it with F1 (Cancel).

Commands like Bold, Italic, Center, or Tab don't cause a prompt to appear in the corner of the screen. Instead, as you know, they put a code into your document. When you give one of these coded commands incorrectly, you can delete it with the Backspace key. Unless you have your codes revealed when you do this, a prompt will appear asking you to strike **Y** to confirm the deletion of the command or **N** to leave the command in the document.

This gives you two ways to correct your mistakes. Let's practice them. Strike each of the command keys in the list in Figure 8-1. Then delete the command with either **F1** or **Backspace**. Jot down which method you used to delete each command.

F6 (Bold) ~~Backspace~~
F5 (List Files) ~~F1~~
Shift-F7 (Print) ~~Backspace~~
F8 (Underline) ~~Backspace~~
F7 (Exit) ~~F1~~

Figure 8-1

INDENT; LEFT/RIGHT INDENT

When creating documents, most PC users work with a variety of indented formats. If the text is entered correctly using the tools provided by the word processing program, formatting is accomplished more easily. What's more, you can save yourself valuable time when the document needs to be edited.

Two of WordPerfect's most useful tools are Indent and Left/Right Indent. Let's learn about these formatting features.

Indent

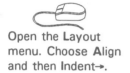

Open the Layout menu. Choose Align and then Indent→.

The **F4** (→Indent) feature causes your text to wrap to a location other than the left margin. Find →Indent on your function key template. A good example of the proper use of Indent is in an enumeration (a numbered list). Look at Figure 8-2. When you strike F4 after the numeral, you don't have to worry about lining up the second line under the first. It happens automatically.

The paragraph above is also formatted with Indent. Note that the second line of that paragraph wrapped to the tab stop, not the left margin. This occurred because F4 was used rather than the Tab key. The paragraph you are reading now was indented with the Tab key so you could compare.

```
1.    This is the first item in an enumeration using F4 to
      indent following the numeral.  I like the way the text
      wraps at the end of each line.

2.    This is the second item in the enumeration that is
      formatted with indent.
```

Figure 8-2

Indent uses tab stops. When you strike **F4**, your text will be indented to the first tab stop. If you wish to indent further than the first tab stop, you may strike F4 more than once. An indent is ended when you strike Enter. The Indent command must be given again if you want another paragraph indented.

Lesson 8 Exercise 1

1. Key the enumeration in Figure 8-2. Strike **F4** following the period after the first numeral. Remember to let the text wrap at the end of each line.

2. At the end of the first item, strike **Enter** twice to leave a double space between items. Remember that Enter turns off the Indent.

3. Strike **F4** following the period after the second numeral. At the end of the exercise, quadruple space before the next exercise.

Left/Right Indent

Open the Layout menu. Choose **Align** and then Indent→←.

In research papers, long quotations are often single spaced and indented five spaces from both sides, as illustrated in this paragraph. To do this, use the →Indent← combination, **Shift-F4**. Find this function on your keyboard template. As with Indent, this command is ended when you strike Enter.

Regardless of the location of the cursor when Shift-F4 is struck, the indentation will begin at the next tab to the right of the cursor and will indent the right side of the text an amount equal to that on the left.

The commands for Indent and Left/Right Indent can be inserted after the paragraphs have been keyed by simply aligning the cursor at the first character of the first line to be indented and striking the proper indent key. Then cursor down and watch the paragraph automatically adjust.

Lesson 8 Exercise 2

1. Repeat Exercise 1. This time, however, use **Shift-F4** following each numeral. Compare the results of this exercise with Exercise 1. Can you see the difference?

2. Reveal your codes and look at the codes inserted with **F4** and **Shift-F4**. Add these codes to the list of codes you are accumulating.

3. Print your samples and exit the document, saving it as **indent.8-2**.

LEFT MARGIN RELEASE

The Left Margin Release allows you to move the cursor to the left of the left margin. This can be done by striking **Shift-Tab**. Try it once. Watch the cursor move to **Pos .5"** even though the default left margin is set at 1 inch. Now strike Tab to return to your left margin at **Pos 1"**.

Obviously, this command is used when you wish to begin left of the margin. It is practical for aligning the Roman numerals in an outline, for example. The default for the left margin is one-half inch because a tab stop is there. This can be changed if you wish.

Lesson 8 Exercise 3

1. Key the sentence in Figure 8-3. Use **Shift-Tab** to begin the sentence one-half inch to the left of the margin.

2. End with a quadruple space to leave space above the next exercise.

```
This sentence begins five spaces to the left of the left margin,
    thanks to WordPerfect's Left Margin Release feature.
```

Figure 8-3

HANGING INDENT

Sometimes you want your text to be formatted in the hanging indent format, illustrated in this paragraph. Hanging Indent looks like the Left Margin Release feature, but instead of beginning outside of the margin, the first line begins AT the left margin. This feature is a combination of the Indent command and Left Margin Release.

To tell WordPerfect you'd like the hanging indent format, first strike **F4** and then **Shift-Tab**. This procedure moves the first line of the paragraph back to the left margin and indents the remainder of the paragraph to the first tab stop.

Lesson 8 Exercise 4

1. Use the procedure outlined above to apply the hanging indent format to the paragraph in Figure 8-4.

2. Key the bold phrases in bold.

3. Reveal your codes and find the Margin Release and Indent codes in the paragraphs on the screen. Record the codes in your list.

4. Save the paragraph with the name **hanging.8-4** and print a copy for your instructor. Do not exit WordPerfect.

```
This is a paragraph keyed to demonstrate that the procedure
    for creating a paragraph with hanging indent format is
    extremely simple.  It involves two easy commands.  These
    are Indent and Left Margin Release. While this format
    isn't commonly used for paragraphs in daily
    correspondence, it is handy for miscellaneous types of
    enumerations and bibliographies.
```

Figure 8-4

NEW PAGE

WordPerfect recognizes a page of text as full when the line counter at the bottom reaches 10 inches. The software starts your document at 1 inch from the top of the paper. That means that unless you change your margins, you will get 9 inches of text on a page. This text is usually measured at 6 lines per inch, just as you are accustomed to on a typewriter, so you get 54 lines of text on a page. When you get to advanced applications where the size of your letters vary, however, you may find it necessary to vary the number of lines of text on each page.

When you have keyed 9 inches of text (a full page), a line of hyphens automatically appears across the screen from side to side to show a page break. This is known as a *soft page* break because if you add or delete text above the break, that page break will move to accommodate the added or deleted text.

You may begin a new page at any point in your text simply by indicating a new page break with the *hard page* command, **Ctrl-Enter**. When you give a hard page break command, the line across the screen will be made up of equals signs. The hard page break will not automatically move when you add or delete text. If you need to change the location of the hard page code, you'll have to delete it by placing the cursor directly above the line of equals signs and striking **Del** or **Delete**.

Whether you create a new page with a soft page break or the hard page command, you'll be able to see the new page number indicated on your status line. When this happens, the line count returns to **Ln 1"**.

Lesson 8 Exercise 5

1. Retrieve job.6-4 from your disk. Strike **Home**, **Home**, ↓ to move the cursor to the end of the document. Note that the line indicator says you are somewhere in the sixth inch from the top of the page.

2. Watching the **Line** prompt in the status line, strike **Enter** as many times as needed until you can see a line of hyphens from side to side on the screen. As you go from 9 inches down the document to 10, you'll see 9", 9.17", 9.33", 9.5", 9.67", 9.83", and then **Pg 2 Ln1"**.

3. Strike ↑ once so the cursor is at the bottom of the first page. Check the status line. Now strike ↓ to return to page 2.

4. Strike **Enter** a few times. Then strike **Ctrl-Enter** for a hard page break. Notice the line of equals signs. Your cursor should now be on page 3.

5. Reveal your codes and use the arrow keys to move around in your document until you see the soft page code [SPg] and the hard page code [HPg]. Add the codes and their descriptions to your list of codes.

6. Move your cursor to the line above the hard page break and delete the code with **Delete**. Clear the screen. Do not save this document.

DATE

Most computers with hard drives have an internal clock that keeps track of the date and time. On other systems you must enter the date and/or time each time you start the computer. While the time isn't of great significance, it's nice to have the date that a document was last revised showing opposite the document name when you list your files.

Having the correct date in the computer can also help you create your documents using the WordPerfect Date feature.

The Date feature inserts the current date at the cursor. Find the word Date on the keyboard template by F5. If you strike **Shift-F5**, you will see a menu of six items at the bottom of the screen. The first three deal with the date: **1** Date Text; **2** Date Code; and **3** Date Format.

Choose Date **Text**
from the **Tools** menu.

- **Date Text.** If you choose **1**, the system will automatically insert the current date at the location of the cursor. This date remains in the file as a permanent part of the text.

Choose Date **Code**
from the **Tools** menu.

- **Date Code.** When you choose **2** from the Date menu, a code will be inserted into the document at the location of the cursor. On screen, the current date will appear. When you retrieve that document at some future date, the NEW current date will appear in the document.

Choose Date **Format**
from the **Tools** menu.

- **Date Format.** You can choose how the date will appear by striking **3** in the Date menu. This choice makes it possible, for example, to change the format to military or European format.

The remaining items in this menu are for outlining. Outlining comes much later in your training.

Dual Floppy Users. If you didn't enter the date when you started WordPerfect, exit WordPerfect now. Replace the WordPerfect 2 disk with the WordPerfect 1 disk. At the **B:\>** prompt, key the word *date*. When prompted, enter the current date using numbers and hyphens. For example, enter January 5, 1995 as 1-5-95, and then restart WordPerfect.

Lesson 8 Exercise 6

1. Strike **Shift-F5**. Choose Option 1 (Date Text) from the menu and watch the date appear. Strike **Enter** twice. Try it again. Easy, isn't it?

2. Strike **Shift-F5** and choose Option 2 (Date Code). Again the date appears on your screen, but it is entered as a hidden code rather than as text. Strike **Enter** twice.

3. Reveal your codes and look at the two dates. Add the appropriate code(s) to your list of codes.

4. Position the date in a number of places as listed below. Position the cursor, strike **Shift-F5**, and choose Option 1. Strike **Enter** twice after each date.
   a. Put the date flush with the right margin.
   b. Center the date on the page.

c. Put the date at **Pos 4"**.

5. Clear the screen. You do not need to save these dates.

6. Retrieve **hanging.8-4** from your disk and use Date Text to insert the date at the top of the document. (When you retrieve a document, the cursor always appears at the very beginning of that document.) After inserting the date, strike **Enter** twice to separate the date from the body of the paragraph.

7. Go to the bottom of the document using **Home, Home, ↓**. Strike **Enter** twice to put some space below the paragraph. Insert a date here using Date Code. The two dates in this document look the same now. Will they look the same tomorrow?

8. Save the document again using the same name.

Lesson 8 Exercise 7

Key the letter in Figure 8-5 according to the instructions on the next page.

```
                        (Current date)


Mr. Paul Weigel
Records Protection Agency
P.O. Box 8760
Beaver Dam, WI 53916-8760

Dear Mr. Weigel:

    Thank you for your reply to my letter about protecting
our vital records.  We would, indeed, like to meet with you
to arrange for your consultants to help us protect our
organization against all those things you listed:

    fires, floods, tornadoes, earthquakes, hurricanes,
    sabotage, malfeasance, carelessness, and others,
    including damage from broken water mains, electrical
    problems, static electricity, and dampness.

    I will call you in the next two days to set up an
appointment.  It will probably be some time in the middle of
next week before I can get free for the meeting.  I am
looking forward to doing business with your organization.

                        Sincerely,


                        Reiko Onodera
```

Figure 8-5

1. Go to **Ln 2"** for the date. Then tab to **Pos 4"** and use Date Text to insert the date automatically. Strike **Enter** four times.

2. Indent the first and third paragraphs with Tab. Use Left/Right Indent for the paragraph in the middle.

3. Tab to **Pos 4"** for each of the closing lines and separate them with a quadruple space.

4. Print a copy of the letter. Then exit the document, saving it as **secure.8-7**.

HYPHEN TYPES

Hyphen Character

When keying words that always contain a hyphen, such as jack-in-a-box or self-esteem, strike the hyphen key in the normal manner. These hyphens are called *hyphen characters* because you put them in as text and they always show as part of the word.

Hard Hyphen

Another kind of hyphen is what WordPerfect calls a *hard hyphen*. It looks like a hyphen, but it is used for keying minus signs in formulas. WordPerfect will not break a line at a hard hyphen as it might with a hyphen character. A hard hyphen is keyed by striking and releasing **Home**, then striking the **hyphen** key.

Hard hyphens are also used for keying dashes. A dash is keyed first with a hard hyphen, then a regular hyphen. The correct keystroking is **Home, hyphen, hyphen.** Strike each key separately. The hard hyphen prevents the hyphens in the dash from being split when the dash falls at the end of the line.

Lesson 8 Exercise 8

1. Key the sentence in Figure 8-6 using the procedure described above for the dash. The two hyphens in the dash will remain together.

2. Reveal your codes and look at the dash. Only the second hyphen should be enclosed in brackets.

3. Strike **Enter** twice.

Please note that the results of this exercise will vary depending on the type of printer you are using. You can see how the sentence will behave when you print it by striking first the **Page Up** key and then the **Page Down** key. The hyphens should still stay together—either at the end of the first line or between the words *gorgeous* and *for* on the second line of the sentence.

```
The sun was shining, the breeze gentle, and the day was
gorgeous--for early autumn, that is.
```

Figure 8-6

HARD SPACE

The *hard space* feature allows you to bind two or more words together with a special kind of space. It prevents you from having awkward breaks at the end of a line. For example, when a date, like January 1, 1994, comes at the end of the line, your keyboarding rules tell you that you may (if you have to) divide that date after the comma but that you should never divide the date between the month and the day. Since that is the case, the space between *January* and *1* should be keyed with a hard space.

The procedure to key a hard space is almost the same as the procedure for the hard hyphen. To key a hard space, strike and release the **Home** key and then strike the **space bar**. The hard space acts like a character and fools the computer into thinking that *January 1* is all one word. When the date falls at the end of the line, the entire "word" will drop to the next line.

Lesson 8 Exercise 9

The sentences in Figure 8-7 are designed so that neither the formula nor the date will fit on the line. If you key the exercise properly, the entire formula will drop to the second line, and part or all of the date will drop to the third line (depending on your printer description).

1. Key the sentences in Figure 8-7. Key every space in the formula portion of the first sentence as hard spaces using **Home, space.** Key the minus sign in the formula as a hard hyphen using **Home, hyphen.** Put a hard space between the month and the day in the date.

2. Reveal your codes to see what hard spaces look like. You document with the codes revealed should roughly resemble Figure 8-8. Add the hard space code to your list.

3. When you finish with the exercise, print the document containing the two exercises and exit from it, saving it as **formula.8-9.**

```
The suggested formula to solve your current problem is
a + b - c = x + y.  The scientist developed this formula on
June 4, 1924.
```

Figure 8-7

You no doubt found that inserting all of those hard spaces and hard hyphens took some concentration, but the result is that you can reformat the text as many different ways as you wish, and the formula and date will both remain intact.

```
The suggested formula to solve your current problem is[SRt]
a[ ]+[ ]b[ ]-[ ]c[ ]=[ ]x[ ]+[ ]y.  The scientist developed
this formula on[SRt]June[ ]4, 1924.
```

Figure 8-8

SUMMARY

You learned a number of small but very important text-entry features in this lesson. Some of them, like the Date feature, are nice, but you could manage OK without them. Others, like Indent and hard hyphens, are critically important to your work.

Some of the lesson was strictly informational, although it will be very important to you as you create documents using WordPerfect. For example, you learned that some incorrect commands can be deleted with F1 and others must be deleted with Backspace. You learned about hard page and soft page breaks.

If you are feeling a little overwhelmed at this point, don't despair. Instead, try to be optimistic about it. Maybe you can't remember everything you've learned, but think about how much you HAVE learned in eight short lessons!

It is a good idea to periodically go back through the lessons you've completed and briefly review the features covered in those lessons. This will give you a good reminder of the features you've forgotten are available. Don't use class time to do this. Instead, do it while you sit in front of the TV or use it as bedtime reading. (What a wonderful way to fall asleep!) At any rate, keep learning!

LESSON 8 NOTES:

Keep together - home space
page (Home Space) 15
Dash = hypen, hyphen
He won a prize ← Home Hyphen Home Hyphen a new car.

TRUE/FALSE

Each of the following statements is either true or false. Indicate your choice in the Answers column by circling T for a true statement or F for a false statement.

Answers

1. The Caps Lock key is a toggle key. (Les. 7, Obj. 1) . . . .   1.   T   F

2. When you view underlined text on a color monitor, it shows in a contrasting color. (Les. 7, Obj. 1) . . . .   2.   T   F

3. The use of italics puts paired codes into your document. (Les. 7, Obj. 2.)   3.   T   F

4. It is possible to go back and center a line without rekeying the line. (Les. 7, Obj. 3) . . . .   4.   T   F

5. Preset tabs cannot be changed. (Les. 7, Obj. 5) . . . .   5.   T   F

6. You can delete a formatting command with the Backspace key. (Les. 8, Obj. 1) . . . .   6.   T   F

7. The Indent command ends when you strike Enter. (Les. 8, Obj. 2) . . . .   7.   T   F

8. Hanging indent is a paragraph format used regularly in daily correspondence. (Les. 8, Obj. 4) . . . .   8.   T   F

9. The status line always tells the number of the page on which you're working. (Les. 8, Obj. 5) . . . .   9.   T   F

10. A hard space is entered by striking first the Enter key and then the space bar. (Les. 8, Obj. 7) . . . .   10.   T   F

11. Hard spaces are useful in keeping word wrap from affecting critical units of text such as dates, formulas, etc. (Les. 8, Obj. 7) . . . .   11.   T   F

COMPLETION

Indicate the correct answer in the space provided.

Answers

1. Which key is used to turn on Underlining? (Les. 7, Obj. 1) . . . .   1. _____

2. What happens to the Pos indicator in the status line of a color monitor when Bold is on? (Les. 7, Obj. 1) . . .   2. _____

3. What do the two Bold codes look like? (Les. 7, Obj. 2)   3. _____

4. What is the term used to refer to a portion of text that is aligned at the right margin? (Les. 7, Obj. 4) . . . . . .   4. _____

5. What is the significance of the left arrow on the Tab key? (Les. 7, Obj. 5) . . . .   5. _____

6. Which feature is used to indent a series of lines from the left margin? (Les. 8, Obj. 2) . . . .   6. _____

7. What key combination is used for a hard page break? (Les. 8, Obj. 5) . . . .   7. _____

8. What key combination automatically inserts the Date Text into your document? (Les. 8, Obj. 6) . . . .   8. _____

9. What is the name of the feature used for a minus sign? (Les. 8, Obj. 8) . . . .   9. _____

10. Of all the features learned in this lesson, which one do you think you like the best? . . . .   10. _____

REFERENCE

Check the alphabetic listing in the reference section of the *WordPerfect Reference*.

Can you find a specific section about Italics? If so, what is the section called?

_____

If there isn't a specific section about Italics, turn to the Index of the *Reference* and look up Italics. Under what section do you find it?

_____

Turn to the section on Hyphenation in the *Reference*.

Find the discussion of the two types of hyphens you've just learned about plus one more. What is the third type of hyphen? What does it do?

_____

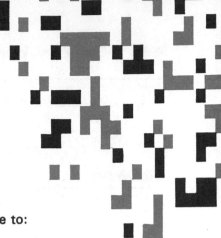

LESSON 9
Editing Features

OBJECTIVES

Upon completion of this lesson, you will be able to:

1. Add or delete format codes to edit formatted text.
2. Rewrite text after editing.
3. Use the typeover mode.
4. Delete text to the end of a line.
5. Delete text to the end of a page.
6. Delete text a word at a time.
7. Search for unique strings of text.
8. Use Replace as well as Global Search and Replace.

Estimated Time: 2 hours

EDITING FORMATTED TEXT

By now you are probably pretty comfortable with formatting codes and the way they look when you reveal your codes. These codes can be deleted easily to change the appearance of your documents. Formatting codes can be deleted either with the codes revealed or with the codes turned off. Mostly you'll prefer to reveal your codes when you work with formatting codes. It's much easier when you can see what you're doing.

Function codes may be deleted with codes revealed using these steps:

1. Move the cursor to the code to be deleted.
2. If the cursor is to the right of the unwanted code, strike **Back-space**. If the cursor is on the code, strike **Delete**.

With paired codes like Bold and Underline, delete either of the pair. When you do this, both of the codes in the pair will disappear.

Lesson 9 Exercise 1

Key the paragraph in Figure 9-1 as follows:

1. Strike **Enter** six times so your paragraph will be two inches from the top of the page. Then strike **F4** once at the beginning to indent the entire paragraph and **Tab** once to indent the first line of the paragraph.

2. Key the word *Information* at the beginning of the second sentence in bold.

3. Strike **Enter** twice at the end of the paragraph.

The 1980s have been proclaimed as the beginning of the "Information Age." **Information** has become the leading topic in magazines, at conferences and seminars, and in daily office operations.

Figure 9-1

4. Move the cursor back to the *T* at the beginning of the paragraph. Reveal your codes. Find the Reveal Codes cursor, the [→Indent] code and the [Tab] code at the beginning of the paragraph.

5. Delete the Tab code; you may use **Backspace** because the code is to the left of the cursor. Delete the →Indent the same way. (Are you watching the text reformat at the top of the screen as you do this? You may need to strike ↓ to see the document reformat.)

6. Delete either of the Bold codes that surround the word *Information*.

7. Return to the top of the document. Delete [HRt] codes until your paragraph is only 1½ inches from the top of the page. (How many codes must you delete?)

8. Keep the document on the screen for the next exercise.

REWRITE

As you probably noticed in the above exercise, WordPerfect provides automatic rewrite. In other words, whenever you add or delete text or make big changes to the format, simply striking an arrow key or Page Down will usually cause the text to rewrite so that all lines are filled to the margin.

WordPerfect also has a Rewrite feature that is helpful when automatic rewrite doesn't work. You can select it with **Ctrl-F3**, Option **3**. You don't need to practice here, because your automatic rewrite has probably been working just fine. You'll probably find it more useful when you get to more complicated documents. Remember to use, Ctrl-F3, Option 3 for Rewrite.

Lesson 9 Exercise 2

1. Use the same paragraph you created for the first exercise and experiment with it by adding and deleting indents and tabs.

2. Reformat the paragraph each time you do something with it by striking ↓ or **Page Down**.

3. Use Reveal Codes, if you'd like to look at the codes after they are inserted. Note that [→Indent] is an open code, so there are no ending indent codes.

4. Close the document without saving.

Lesson 9 Exercise 3

1. Retrieve **job.6-4**.

2. Reveal your codes so you can watch as you delete all of the Tab codes following the numerals and replace them with →Indent codes. Watch your document rewrite.

3. Print the revised document and exit from it, closing it with the name **job.9-3**.

TYPEOVER

You have learned that if you place the cursor within an already-keyed body of text and begin keying, the new words will be inserted and the rest of the text will move to the right. No words or characters are lost. This is called the *insert mode*, and it is the default in WordPerfect.

Sometimes, however, you will want to replace the characters of the text with new characters. You learned in Lesson 3 about the Insert key (**Ins** or **Insert**) that's located near Delete. This toggle key changes Word-Perfect from the insert to the typeover mode.

When you strike **Insert**, the word **Typeover** appears in the prompt position in the lower left corner of the screen. When you strike **Insert** again, you return to the insert mode and the word **Typeover** disappears. It is highly recommended that you use the typeover mode only for specific corrections and then return to the default setting. Don't leave typeover on when you are formatting your documents. You may get some results quite different from what you expect when you forget to turn off the typeover mode.

Typeover Exercise. Key the following sentence:

`The dog jumped over the moon and the cat laughed.`

Position the cursor on the *d* in dog. Strike **Insert** and key *cow*. Move the cursor to the *c* in *cat* and key *dog*. Strike **Insert** to return to the insert mode. Close the practice without saving.

Lesson 9 Exercise 4

1. Key the paragraphs in Figure 9-2. Be certain to key the dash properly.

2. Proofread and correct all errors. Use **F10** to save the paragraphs as **phones.94a** and print a copy.

3. Use **Insert** to change to the typeover mode and replace the second paragraph with the sentence in Figure 9-3. Some of the words from the original paragraph will remain. Delete them.

4. Use Exit to save the document as **phones.94b** and print a copy.

```
Some of the security problems created for its customers by
the breakup of the Bell System several years ago are only
now beginning to become obvious.  These relate to such
things as restoring equipment or service after a flood or
other disaster--and providing a reliable electrical power
supply to the new PABX facilities that have been installed
in many organizations.

When equipment has been purchased outright from other
sources, the vendor is under no obligation to aid in
recovery and may lack the ability to help.
```

Figure 9-2

```
Responsibility for the maintenance of most leased on-
premises telephone equipment has been divided since the AT&T
divestiture.
```

Figure 9-3

DELETE LINE, PAGE, WORD

So far you have been deleting unwanted characters and codes with the Backspace and Delete keys. You learned in Lesson 4 that you can also delete from the point of the cursor to the end of the line or from the cursor to the end of the page. Let's review these processes.

- **Delete to End of Line.** Use **Ctrl-End** to erase the material from the cursor to the end of the line.

- **Delete to End of Page.** Use **Ctrl-Page Down** to erase the material from the cursor to the end of the page. WordPerfect will ask you to confirm the deletion. **Y** will confirm that deletion, while **N** will give you the opportunity to change your mind.

- **Delete Word.** You may delete a word at a time by positioning the cursor anywhere in the word and striking **Ctrl-Backspace**. By continuing to strike this key combination, you may proceed to delete words as they scroll in from the right. The **Ctrl-Delete** combination also deletes the word at the cursor.

- **Home, Backspace** deletes the word to the left of the cursor. This command is different from the one above because you strike **Home** first, release it, and then strike **Backspace**.

Lesson 9 Exercise 5

(Template disk users: Refer to the box below before beginning.)

1. Key the paragraphs in Figure 9-4. Use **F10** to save it on your disk as **job.9-5**.

2. Try deleting a word, deleting to the end of the line, and deleting to the end of the page. Strike **Y** when you are asked to confirm a deletion.

3. Clear the screen without saving the revised document and retrieve the original document again if needed in order to provide more paragraphs with which to practice.

4. When you are comfortable with these delete functions, exit the document without saving.

TEMPLATE DISK USERS:

1. Retrieve **copiers.9-5** from the template disk files.
2. Follow the directions in the exercise to practice the use of the delete features.

```
Office reprographic operations are moving toward a quiet
revolution.  New equipment now enables company personnel to
create increasingly sophisticated graphic output with a
minimum of effort and time--material that may once have been
reserved for the special skills of the print shop.  Leading
the change in office printing is the intelligent
copier/printer (IC/P).

Several different product technologies and terms fall under
the IC/P umbrella.  Companies looking into IC/Ps may find
them referred to as non-impact printers, color printers,
page printers, laser printers, or electronic printing
systems.
```

Figure 9-4

SEARCH

Searching is the term in word processing that refers to the computer looking through the text on the screen—either forward or backward—to locate certain words, numbers, functions, or misspelled words.

Choose **Forward** from the **Search** menu.

- **Forward Search** Striking **F2** enables you to search forward through the text.

Choose **Backward** from the **Search** menu.

- **Reverse Search**. Striking **Shift-F2** enables you to search backward through the text.

When you search forward, the **→Srch:** message will appear on the status line. When you search backward, you'll see the message **←Srch:**. At the colon, key the word or character string for which you wish to search and strike **F2** again. The system will then search forward (or backward) through the text and move the cursor to the end of the target word. Be careful not to strike Enter after keying the word for which you're searching.

To search forward, the cursor should be at the top of the document or above the text to be searched. To begin a backward search, the cursor should be at the end of the document or below the text through which you're searching. If you wish to change the direction of a search after you have started the Search procedure, you can strike **↑** to search backward or **↓** to search forward.

The computer searches for a unique string of characters. If you wish to search for a certain word as a word instead of a group of letters, place a space after the word. The computer will then search for that word with the space. However, if the word appears with punctuation, a hyphen, or any character following it, the computer will not locate it. For example, if you were to search for the word *the* and you did not put a space after it, the computer would stop after all words containing the *the* combination, such as *theater, these, them, weather, they,* etc. You can edit the character string in Search like any other text.

The computer will prompt you with the last word for which you searched when you strike either of the search keys. If you wish to search for a different word or character string, simply key the new characters.

There are a couple of miscellaneous things you should know about Search:

- If WordPerfect can't find the unique string of characters for which you are searching, the message *** Not Found *** will appear in the prompt position at the bottom of the screen.

- If you search for a word and then wish to search for the next occurrence of the word, strike **F2** twice. The search will then move on to the word later in the document. You can cancel the Search command with **F1**.

- Search can also be used to find codes in your text. After you've struck **F2** for Search, key the command in the normal manner. The code will appear at the Search prompt in bold, much like it appears in Reveal Codes. When you strike **F2** again, WordPerfect will move your cursor to the first occurrence of the code.

- You can only search for one character string at a time.

- WordPerfect Search will match lowercase letters with both upper-
  and lowercase letters. It will match uppercase letters only with
  uppercase letters. For example, if you told WordPerfect to search
  for *services*, it would find *Services* and *services*. If you told it to
  search for *Services*, it would only find the occurrences of *Services*
  with a capital *S* at the beginning.

Lesson 9 Exercise 6

Choose **Forward** from
the **S**earch menu.

Retrieve **job.5-2** from your disk.

1. From the beginning of the document, search for the word
   administrative as follows: Strike **F2**, key *administrative*, and then strike
   F2 again. Each time the computer finds the word, strike **F2** twice so
   it searches for the next occurrence of *administrative*.

2. Return to the top of the document with **Page Up** and search for the
   word *responsible*.

3. Go to the end of the text with **Page Down** and do a Reverse Search for
   the word *user* as follows: Strike **Shift-F2**, key *user*, and then strike **F2**
   again. You will need to strike **Shift-F2** for each occurrence. How many
   times do you find the word *user*?

4. Search forward from the beginning for a normal hyphen. Notice how
   the code looks on the prompt line when you tell Search that you would
   like to search for the hyphen. This is a quick way to move to a
   particular point in your text.

5. Keep the document open for the next exercise.

REPLACE

This feature is sometimes called Global Search and Replace. It helps
you replace every occurrence or certain specified occurrences of a word,
phrase, or WordPerfect code in the document on the screen and in the
memory with a different word, phrase, or code. Read carefully the steps
that tell you how to use Search and Replace.

Choose **R**eplace from
the **S**earch menu.

1. Give the Replace command, **Alt-F2**.

2. Strike **Y** if you want to confirm each replacement or **N** if you
   want WordPerfect to make all replacements automatically. If you
   choose *yes*, WordPerfect will stop at every occurrence and give
   you a chance to say *yes* or *no* to the replacement.

3. Key the string of characters and/or strike the function key(s) for
   which you wish to search. Put a space after whole words to be
   replaced so you don't get portions of larger words. Be sure not to

strike Enter after keying the words. Be careful of upper- and lowercase letters. (This means that Search is known as *case sensitive*.)

4. Strike **F2**. You'll be prompted to key the words you'd like to have as the replacement.

5. Key in the replacement words. Again put a space after whole words. Be careful of uppercase and lowercase letters. Do not strike Enter.

6. Strike **F2** again. WordPerfect will begin the Search and Replace and, if you asked for it in Step 2, prompt you at each occurrence.

It is important that you can choose between confirming the replacements or not because some occurrences of words should NOT be replaced. For example, if you had a long document containing the names Mary Christensen and Harry Christianson, and you keyed every one of them as *Christensen*, you could use Search with confirmation and replace only the misspelled occurrences of Harry's name and leave Mary's name alone. Let's try the Replace feature.

Lesson 9 Exercise 7

Choose **R**eplace from the **S**earch menu.

You already have **job.5-2** on the screen. You'll use this document for the exercise.

1. Return the cursor to the beginning of the document. Strike **Alt-F2**.

2. Strike **Y** to tell WordPerfect that you wish to confirm each occurrence as the words are replaced.

3. The computer will prompt you to key the string of characters or the word for which you wish to search. Key *administrative assistant*. Spell it correctly!

4. Strike **F2** and you will be prompted to key the replacement words.

5. Key *secretary* and strike **F2** one more time to begin the replacement.

6. The cursor will stop at the end of the words *administrative assistant* and ask for confirmation of the replacement. Strike **Y** for Yes. Continue though the entire document in this manner.

You have searched out all occurrences of *administrative assistant* and replaced them with *secretary*. It is tedious to confirm each replacement when you know you would like the words changed in every instance.

There is a better way. Let's reverse the process and change *secretary* back to *administrative assistant*. This time you will do a Global Search and Replace—that is, you will not confirm the replacements.

Choose **R**eplace from the **S**earch menu.

Lesson 9 Exercise 8

1. Return the cursor to the top of the document and strike **Alt-F2**.

2. At the " **Confirm? No (Yes)**" prompt, strike **Enter** for No. You don't wish to confirm the replacements.

3. Key *secretary* and strike **F2**.

4. Key *administrative assistant* and strike **F2**. Look carefully at your document and see if all occurrences of *secretary* have been replaced with *administrative assistant*. If you'd like more practice, try Search and Replace to change the word *user* to *author* and *users* to *authors*.

5. Close the document without saving.

Lesson 9 Exercise 9

(Template disk users: Refer to the box below before beginning.)

1. Key the text in Figure 9-5 as shown. Strike **Enter** twice between paragraphs.

2. Strike either **Tab** or **F4** (Indent) before each numeral. Strike **F4** AFTER each numeral so the text is automatically indented as in the figure.

3. Print the document and save it as **telecom.9-9**.

TEMPLATE DISK USERS:

1.   Retrieve **telecom.9-9**.
2.   Remove the tab following each numeral and replace it with an Indent command (F4).
3.   Save and print the document as directed in Exercise 9.

(Tab) The problem of traffic congestion is constantly increasing on the highways and streets of America's cities. One solution to this problem is to arrange with your boss to "telecommute." When a worker has a job where he or she may telecommute, a computer and other electronic equipment are used in the home to send work between the office and the home workplace. DS

(Tab) Working from the home is not practical for all kinds of jobs. Nor is it possible in many kinds of businesses. Often the person who telecommutes must go to the office at least two or three days each month for meetings. Workers who telecommute immediately realize a number of benefits:

DS

(Tab) 1. F4 Less time is wasted sitting in an auto breathing
noxious fumes, and less stress occurs from the
aggravation of the commute. Both factors result
in better health.

   2.   Less money is spent on clothing appropriate for
         the office and on food for lunches or lunches out.
         Less money is spent on automobiles, auto repairs,
         and insurance.

   3.   There are fewer interruptions during the workday,
         resulting in better concentration and increased
         productivity.

(Tab) In some companies and with some kinds of employment,
the workers must appear at the office each day. Many bosses
fail to see any reason why they should have workers who work
away from the office. Those bosses, however, that employ
workers who telecommute often notice some very important
benefits:

(Tab) 1. PF Less expensive square footage in the office needs
         to be devoted to worker offices. Fewer parking
         spaces are required in places where parking places
         are at a premium.

   2.   Greater productivity is realized (an increase of
         20 percent is not uncommon), giving the worker a
         higher sense of accomplishment and higher morale.

   3.   Companies who participate in telecommute programs
         receive public recognition for their efforts in
         eliminating some of the problems with auto
         pollution.

Figure 9-5   DOC CODE
_____

Lesson 9 Exercise 10

Figure 9-6 illustrates the document you just created with corrections
marked. It is shown with expanded spacing to make room for the editing
marks. Do not change the spacing of your document. Edit it as follows.

1. Retrieve **telecom.9-9**. Go through the document making the corrections
   as marked.

2. Return to the beginning of the document. Use Replace to replace each
   occurrence of the word *worker* with the word *employee*. When
   starting the search, don't space when you key *worker* at the →**Srch**
   prompt. Then both *worker* and *workers* (singular and plural) will be
   replaced.

3. Return to the beginning of the document. Use Replace to replace each occurrence of the word *boss* with *employer*. In this case, since the plural of *boss* is more than just the *s*, strike the space bar once after *boss* and after *employer*.

4. When you finish, proofread, fix the replacement that didn't work, and print your document again. Save it as **telecom.910**. (Do you know why you still had to fix one occurrence of *boss*?)

The problem of traffic congestion is constantly
increasing on the highways and streets of America's cities.
One solution to this problem is to ∧arrange∧ *make* *ments* with your boss to
"telecommute." When a worker has a job where he or she may
telecommute, a̶ computer∧ *s* and other electronic equipment are
used in the home to send work between the office and the
home workplace.

Working from the home is not practical for all kinds of
jobs. Nor is it possible in many kinds of businesses.
Often the person who telecommutes must go to the office ~~at~~
~~least two or three~~ *several* days each month for meetings. ~~Workers~~
~~who telecommute immediately realize~~ a number of benefits. *are*
realized by both the worker and the boss.
1.   Less time is wasted sitting in an auto breathing

noxious fumes, and less stress occurs from the

aggravation of the commute. Both factors result

in better health *for the worker.*
The worker spends
2.   ∧Less money ~~is spent~~ on clothing appropriate for
   lc

the office and on food for lunches, ~~or lunches out.~~

Less money is spent on automobiles, auto repairs,

and insurance.

3. ~~There are~~ *The worker has* fewer interruptions during the workday,

resulting in better concentration and increased

productivity.

In some companies and with some kinds of employment,

the workers must appear at the office each day. Many bosses

fail to see any reason why they should have workers who work

away from the office. Those bosses, however, that employ

workers who telecommute often notice some very important

benefits:

4 *1.* *The company may devote less money to* ~~Less~~ expensive square footage in the ~~office needs~~ *workplace for*

~~to be devoted to~~ worker offices. Fewer parking

spaces are required in ~~places~~ *locations* where parking ~~places~~ *is often*

~~are~~ at a premium.

5 *2.* Greater productivity is realized *by the company* (an increase of

20 percent is not uncommon), giving the worker a

higher sense of accomplishment and higher morale.

6 *3.* Companies who participate in telecommute programs

receive public recognition for their efforts in

eliminating some of the problems with auto

pollution.

Figure 9-6

SUMMARY

Let's review before going on. This lengthy lesson, like some of the previous ones, contains an incredible amount of information.

- You learned about taking advantage of Reveal Codes to see what you're doing when you delete formatting codes.
- You also reviewed ways to delete chunks of text larger than individual letters, such as words, lines, and the remainder of a page.

- You learned that when you make major changes in the text, WordPerfect usually rearranges the words on the line so that all lines are filled completely.
- You learned to use the typeover mode so that you can save yourself some keystrokes by keying new text over the old.
- Finally you learned to use the Search and Replace features to find particular places in your text and to make sweeping changes in it.

All of the things you learned in this lesson are time-savers—some more than others. Search and Replace, for example, will save you hours of frustration in scrolling through documents to get to the point of a needed correction. As you use WordPerfect to do your work, take advantage of the features available to you so you have more time for "play."

Here is another list that includes all of the new commands you have learned in Lessons 7, 8, and 9. It is an impressive list!

The list is in alphabetic order, not in the order in which the commands were learned. Take a few minutes now to turn to the front of your book near the Study Guide and look at the Quick Reference, which includes all of the commands covered in the text. Take a pencil and lightly mark the commands you've already learned.

Review the cursor movement section at the end of the Quick Reference. Are there some things you aren't remembering to do as you work with your documents?

COMMAND SUMMARY

Feature	Function	Menu	Lesson
Backward Search	Shift-F2	Search	9
Bold	F6	Font, Appearance	7
Cancel	F1	—	8
Center	Shift-F6	Layout, Align	7
Date Code	Shift-F5, C	Tools	9
Date Text	Shift-F5, T	Tools	9
Flush Right	Alt-F6	Layout, Align	7
Hard Hyphen	Home, Hyphen	—	8
Hard Space	Home, Space	—	8
Indent	F4	—	8
Italics	Ctrl-F8, A	Font, Appearance	7
Left/Right Indent	Shift-F4	—	8
Left Margin Release	Shift-Tab	—	8
Replace	Alt-F2	Search	9
Rewrite	Ctrl-F3	—	9
Search	F2	Search	9
Typeover	Ins or Insert	—	9
Underline	F8	Font, Appearance	7

LESSON 9 NOTES:

LESSON 10
Speller and Thesaurus

OBJECTIVES

Upon completion of this lesson, you will be able to:

1. Check your work using the WordPerfect Speller.
2. Choose the correct word using the WordPerfect Thesaurus.

Estimated Time: 1 hour

SPELL

WordPerfect has a speller that helps you proofread a document while it is in the memory of your computer. It does this by comparing each word of the document with a list of correctly spelled words (a dictionary). WordPerfect will even help you determine the correct spelling of words the speller identifies as being incorrectly spelled.

In addition to checking your words against WordPerfect's dictionary of over 120,000 words, WordPerfect helps you build supplemental dictionaries to fill specific needs.

Perhaps the best way to get a feel for the speller is to try it on a document containing errors. After using the speller, some of the features, cautions, and peculiarities of the speller will be discussed.

Lesson 10 Exercise 1

(Template disk users: Refer to the box below before beginning.)

1. Key the two paragraphs in Figure 10-1 exactly as shown. Insert your name and your school name where requested.

2. After keying the paragraphs, save them on your disk as **errors.101**, in case you wish to retrieve them again to practice with the speller. Carefully follow the steps after Figure 10-1 to use the speller to correct the document.

TEMPLATE DISK USERS:

1. Retrieve **errors.101** from the template disk files.
2. Use the steps following Figure 10-1 to check the spelling of your document.

This is a document craeted by (insert your full name) to try
out the speller which comes with WordPerfect. The purpose
of this exercise is to creat a document filled with erors
and run the speller, trying the different options availabel
to deal with each mispelled word.

AFter completing this excercise, (insert your full name)
should be relativly cOmfortable in using the the speller to
check the accuracey of a document created in class at
(insert the name of your school) or on the job using
WordPerfect.

Figure 10-1

Dual Floppy Users: With the document still showing on the screen, remove the data disk from Drive B and insert the speller disk. (Leave the WordPerfect 2 disk in Drive A.)

Hard Disk Users: The speller has been installed on your hard disk. Go ahead with the exercise.

Choose Spell from the
Tools menu.

1. Activate the speller by striking **Ctrl-F2**. You'll see the menu illustrated in Figure 10-2 on one line across the bottom of the screen.

Check: 1 Word; 2 Page; 3 Document; 4 New Sup. Dictionary; 5 Look Up;
6 Count: 0

Figure 10-2

2. Choose **3** Document to start the speller. Handle the prompts for the "errors" WordPerfect finds as follows:

craeted   Look at the screen. A ruler divides the text at the top from a menu and list of possible alternatives at the bottom. Note that each word choice is identified by a letter. Key the letter opposite the correct spelling of the word *created*.

(your name) Depending on your name, Spell may highlight part or none of it. Choose **2** to skip it always because you've most likely spelled it correctly and you'd like the speller to recognize it for the rest of this document as a correct word. If you choose **1** Skip Once, your name will be highlighted when the speller encounters it in paragraph 2.

creat, erors, availabel, mispelled   Choose the correctly spelled words from the list for each of these misspelled words.

AFter   The menu now gives you some choices regarding what it calls "irregular case." Your choice from this menu changes depending on the word and its position in the sentence. In this situation, you can choose **3** Replace, and WordPerfect will fix it as the first word of a sentence.

excercise, relativly   Fix these words appropriately.

cOmfortable   In this irregular-case situation, you must edit. None of the other options will automatically fix the error. Strike **4** to edit, fix the error, and strike **F7** to return to the speller.

the the   A "double word" menu appears. Sometimes you will need to edit to correct the double word. At other times the double words will be correct. You'll need to evaluate the surrounding text to determine how to deal with this type of error. In this case, you have an extra word so you can choose **3** to delete the second occurrence of the word.

accuracey   Finally, choose the correct spelling of this word.

3. When the speller is finished, it will give you a word count. You may strike any key to exit the speller.

4. Print the document and exit from it, saving it this time as **errors.fix**. (Dual floppy users: Remove the speller disk and replace it with your data disk so you save it on your data disk, not the speller disk.) The copy with the misspelled words will remain on your disk in case you want to practice the speller again. Do not exit WordPerfect.

The document in Exercise 1 was filled with foolishly misspelled words that you could have caught and corrected if you had been asked to proofread. But many times, even if you've proofread, it's a good idea to run the speller to be certain.

You didn't use all the choices in the menu when repairing this document. The following options are used when you aren't selecting a word from the list to replace the misspelled word.

1 **Skip Once.** This option might be chosen when you'd like the speller to stop at each occurrence of a particular word.

2 **Skip.** You used this for your name in Exercise 1. This option is for a word that is spelled correctly but isn't in the dictionary and you don't wish to add it to the dictionary. If your name was highlighted and you chose **2** Skip in the first line, your name was skipped the second time it appeared.

3 **Add Word.** This option saves the word in your personal supplementary dictionary. Since software and training materials may be shared by a number of students, it is best not to change the dictionary. The Add Word option won't be used at all in this training. More information on this option is in the *Reference* section of the documentation. It is very useful in office situations.

4 **Edit.** If the speller highlights a word and doesn't provide the correctly spelled word in the list below the ruler, choosing Edit will remove the highlight and allow you to fix the word yourself. You used this option to fix one of the capitalization errors.

5 **Look Up.** This option allows you to give the computer a word pattern. You can do this by substituting a question mark (?) in place of a single character you're not sure of or an asterisk (*) in place of zero or more characters in succession. Then the speller will retrieve a list of possible words with that word pattern.

For example, if WordPerfect hadn't prompted you with the correct spelling of *exercise*, you could have chosen **5 Look Up** and keyed *exer**. All words beginning with *exer* would be listed.

6 **Ignore Numbers.** WordPerfect will highlight numbers that have text attached, such as 22nd and 8th. If you are working with text containing a number of these kinds of references, you may find it more efficient to tell the speller to ignore numbers.

Lesson 10 Exercise 2

Retrieve **job.5-2** and use the speller to check it. Then resave it with the same name. A quick summary of using the speller is given below.

1. The document to be spell-checked should be in the memory of the computer. You should be able to see it on the screen.

2. Dual floppy system users must remove the file disk from Drive B and replace it with the spell disk. Leave WordPerfect 2 in Drive A.

3. Access the speller by striking **Ctrl-F2**. View the first Spell menu:

   a. **1 Word.** This option is chosen when you are keying and run into a word you don't know how to spell. It's like using a dictionary, but it saves you the steps.

   b. **2 Page.** This option is for checking shorter documents or for checking a longer document a page at a time.

   c. **3 Document.** This option is for checking an entire document.

   d. **4 New Sup. Dictionary.** This option is for using specialized dictionaries you may need to create for your work.

   e. **5 Look Up.** This option allows you to look up a particular word, as mentioned earlier, without going into the complete speller.

Miscellaneous Notes About Spell

Here is some additional information about the WordPerfect speller.

• While the speller is checking, *** Please Wait *** appears in the lower left corner of the screen. Be patient! It doesn't take long, and there is nothing you can do as long as the message is there.

• Any time you wish to get out of the speller or back out of any of the Spell menus, strike **F1** as many times as necessary.

- Spell doesn't recognize a word placed incorrectly if the word is spelled correctly. It can't distinguish, for example, between the correct usage of *house* and *horse*. This means *you must proofread your work carefully*, even when you use the speller.

- You can check a block of text by first highlighting the text to be checked in the usual manner and then following the steps for the speller. You will learn to work with blocks of text shortly.

- **Dual Floppy Users:** Always be sure to remove the spell disk before you save the revised document or you will save it on the spell disk. You may want to have your instructor demonstrate how to put a protective tab on the notch of your spell disk so you can't accidentally save a document onto the incorrect disk.

The WordPerfect speller can help you produce error-free documents. Don't be afraid to use it.

THESAURUS

In addition to the spell utility, WordPerfect also provides a thesaurus. This utility helps you find just the right word when you're unsure how to say something. It does this by providing a list of synonyms (words that have the same meaning). Let's try the thesaurus on the corrected document you used for the speller.

Lesson 10 Exercise 3

Retrieve **errors.fix** from your file disk. Follow the steps below to practice using the thesaurus.

Dual Floppy Users. Replace your file disk with the thesaurus disk.

Hard Disk System Users. When your document is on the screen, you are ready to use the thesaurus. It has been installed on your hard disk.

1. Move your cursor to the word *created* in the first line.

Choose Thesaurus from the Tools menu.

2. Start the thesaurus by striking **Alt-F1**. Note that a list of verbs that might replace the word *create* is shown in the first column and continues into the second column. Some of the words have a bullet (dot) in front of them. These are called *headwords* (words that are further referenced in the thesaurus). The word *produce* is one of the words in the list of synonyms showing. Since *produce* is a headword, let's explore it further.

3. Strike → once. Notice that the capital letters that preceded the left column of words have now moved to the middle column. Find the word *produce* in the list and select it by striking the alphabetic character in front of *produce*.

    a. The word *produce* appears at the top of the second column followed by a column and a half of synonyms for that word.

    b. The highlighted capital letters have moved to the list of synonyms for *produce*.

    c. The first column of the *create* list has disappeared to make room for *produce*. You can use the arrow keys to move to the right or left to access any word that shows on the screen.

4. The word *compose* is in the first column for *produce*, and you would like to see a list of synonyms for *compose*. Strike the correct letter to choose *compose*. (If you choose additional headwords to see more synonyms, they will appear in the third column.)

5. Let's replace the word *created* with the word *compose* from the second column. Use an arrow key to return to the middle column. Choose **1** to replace a word. At the prompt, key the identification letter for *compose*. The thesaurus will close automatically. When the new word is in the text, change it to past tense by adding a *d*.

6. Save the document with the same name and clear the screen. Dual floppy users: Replace the thesaurus disk with your file disk before saving.

      If you choose not to replace a word, you may exit the thesaurus with the space bar or with F7.

      You probably noticed that the part of speech (v for verb, n for noun, etc.) is given opposite the groups of words displayed in the thesaurus lists. You will also find some antonyms (words of the opposite meaning) for many of the words in the thesaurus.

SUMMARY

      The WordPerfect speller is a very useful tool in your document creation. Remember that it does NOT take the place of careful proofreading! And, of course, you must remember to use it.

      The thesaurus, on the other hand, is not particularly useful unless you are creating original documents. When you write, use the thesaurus to help you find exactly the right word. No matter how sophisticated your vocabulary is, your writing can always be improved upon by using a new word or two.

LESSON 10 NOTES:

TRUE/FALSE

Each of the following statements is either true or false. Indicate your choice in the Answers column by circling T for a true statement or F for a false statement.

Answers

1. When you tell WordPerfect to center or underline your text, hidden codes that can later be deleted are put into your document. (Les. 9, Obj. 1) . . .   1.   T   F

2. Typeover mode allows newly keyed characters to take the place of characters already on the screen. (Les. 9, Obj. 3) . . . .   2.   T   F

3. When you use Ctrl-End to delete text from the cursor to the end of the line, WordPerfect asks you to confirm the deletion. (Les. 9, Obj. 4) . . . . . .   3.   T   F

4. To delete a word at a time with Ctrl-Backspace or Ctrl-Delete, the cursor must be at the end of the word. (Les. 9, Obj. 6) . . . .   4.   T   F

5. You can search for codes (such as centering) as well as unique words with the Search feature. (Les. 9, Obj. 7) . . . .   5.   T   F

6. The document must be on the screen and in the computer memory for you to use Search or Replace. (Les. 9, Obj. 7&8) . . . .   6.   T   F

7. A word processing package with a spell-checking utility eliminates the need for you to proofread your work. (Les. 10, Obj. 1) . . . .   7.   T   F

8. If you were on the job and the speller highlighted a word you use frequently, you could add it to a dictionary. (Les. 10, Obj. 1) . . . .   8.   T   F

9. The WordPerfect thesaurus helps you find a word when you're writing by providing a list of synonyms. (Les. 10, Obj. 2) . . . .   9.   T   F

10. You must identify the word for which you'd like synonyms before you can use the thesaurus. (Les. 10, Obj. 2) . . . .   10.   T   F

COMPLETION

Indicate the correct answer in the space provided.

Answers

1. Which two keys are most useful for deleting unwanted codes? (Les. 9, Obj. 1) . . . .   1. _____

2. What appears on the status line when you are in the typeover mode? (Les. 9, Obj. 3) . . . .   2. _____

3. What key combination enables you to delete from the cursor to the end of the page? (Les. 9, Obj. 5) . . . .   3. _____

4. How many unique strings of text can you search for at one time? (Les. 9, Obj. 7) . . . .   4. _____

5. Are some common names included in the speller dictionary? (Les. 10, Obj. 1) . . . .   5. _____

6. Rather than keying the correct word from the list below the divider, how can you tell WordPerfect the word you've chosen from the speller list? (Les. 10, Obj. 1)   6. _____

7. How are headwords marked in the list of synonyms? (Les. 10, Obj. 2) . . . .   7. _____

8. When you finish a document, which will you do first—use the speller or proofread the document? . . . . . .   8. _____

9. Why? _____

10. Give an example or two of work you do where the WordPerfect thesaurus would be useful.

REFERENCE

Turn in the *WordPerfect Reference* to the Delete Codes section. In the notes portion it explains why you are sometimes NOT asked for a confirmation when deleting codes. Why do some deletions not require confirmation? What are some examples?

In the Replace portion of the *Reference,* a suggestion is made about protecting your document before using Replace due to the many changes an unconfirmed Replace might make. What is that suggestion? _____

Turn to the section on the Speller and read about the dictionary. What is the name of the main dictionary? Where are the words saved when you add words? If you want to create your own dictionary, what must you choose from the menu before spell checking?

Review Exercises

This series of review exercises will help prepare you for your first production test, which follows this lesson. It also will provide you with practice in using the features you've learned. Some of these exercises will be used again in the next few lessons.

REVIEW EXERCISE 1

Create the memo illustrated in Figure 10-3. Tab to **Pos 2"** for the information following the headings in the opening lines. Proofread carefully and use the speller to double-check your accuracy. Close the memo, saving it as **qualty10.r1**. Do not print the document.

[handwritten: 1inch top margin Pos 3"]

TO: Juan Hernandez

FROM: (key your name) *[handwritten: DS]*

DATE: (use the Date Text feature) *[handwritten: Shift+F5]*

RE: Quality Training

You have been scheduled for Phase 2 of your quality training. The class you will attend meets for six weeks on Mondays from 9 to 10:30 a.m. in Room A116.

There is no assignment for this first class session. Please be prompt.

Figure 10-3   *[handwritten: DOC CODE]*

REVIEW EXERCISE 2

Key the half-page document illustrated in Figure 10-4. Flush Right your name and the Date Code at the top of the document. Center the title on **Ln 2"** and key it in caps. Follow the title with a quadruple space.

Use bold and italics as shown. Indent the second paragraph with the Left/Right Indent feature. When you finish, proofread and spell-check the document, making any necessary corrections.

Print a copy of the document. On the bottom of the printed page, make a list of all of the codes in the document. Tell what each of the codes does in the document. Finally, exit the document, saving it as **online10.r2**.

online 10.r2   *Flush Rt. cttre*

(Your Name)
(Current Date)

LINE 2" COMMUNICATIONS ONLINE

QS

The issue of free speech on computer networks is a new concern for the online services available to computer users. Online services have become a popular way for subscribers to shop and to communicate with one another. However, the providers of online services don't control the contents of the newsletters and other communications available through their services. Some services screen messages for obscene language.

DS

Online providers have a contract with subscribers that outlines the rights and responsibilities of both the service and the subscriber. If the rules are broken, subscribers receive a warning. Rarely are a subscriber's privileges suspended.

Shft F4 BOLD

As the use of online services increases, the problems are apt to increase. Eventually it will be up to the courts to decide what is reasonable in the area of _free speech_ and _full exchange of ideas_.

Figure 10-4   *Italics*   *DOC CODE*

REVIEW EXERCISE 3

Key the half-page document illustrated in Figure 10-5. Flush Right your name and the Date Code at the top of the document. Center the title on **Ln 2"** and key it in caps. Follow the title with a quadruple space. Strike **F4** after each numeral in the enumeration. Underline as shown.

Proofread and spell-check the document, making any necessary corrections. Print a copy of the document and close it, saving it as **dsktp10.r3**.

(Your Name)
(Current Date)

LINE 2" DESKTOP PUBLISHING

QS

The term "desktop publishing" seems to be synonymous with computers today. Everyone who has ever used a computer thinks he or she is destined to be a great desktop

publisher. "Just give me a computer and some desktop
publishing software, and I'll create great newsletters and
brochures," seems to be the common cry.

Unfortunately, not everyone has the ability to produce
great-looking newsletters and brochures. Besides having a
good understanding of the computer, there are some other,
more artistic prerequisites to good desktop publishing.
These knowledge areas include:

1. F4 <u>Graphics</u>. Boxes, charts, drawings, rules, and
      illustrations can easily be added to documents.
      Sometimes it's so easy that the "artist" gets carried
      away with too much junk on the page.

2. F4 <u>Layout</u>. Page layout skill comes from much trial and
      error and learning from the experts.

3. F4 <u>Typography</u>. An understanding of typefaces and fonts
      and how they may be used together to draw attention to
      the integrated page is imperative.

4. F4 <u>Well-written material</u>. The effect of a masterpiece can
      be completely ruined by poorly written material with
      spelling or grammatical errors. Skill with word
      processing to create the basic document is also
      important.

Figure 10-5

REVIEW EXERCISE 4

Retrieve **qualty10.r1** and make the corrections illustrated in Figure 10-5.
Proofread and spell-check the document, making any necessary corrections.
Print a copy of the revised document and close it, saving it again with the
same name.

TO: Juan Hernandez

FROM: (key your name)

DATE: (use the Date Text feature)

RE: Quality Training

You have been scheduled for Phase 2 of your quality
training. The class you will attend meets for six weeks on
~~Mondays~~ from ~~9 to 10:30 a.m.~~ in ~~Room A116.~~
Tuesdays   10:30 to noon   Conference Room A.

~~There is no assignment for this first class session. Please~~ ﹖
~~be prompt.~~ ﹖
Attached is an article that will be discussed at the first class session.
Read the article and make a list of comments and questions to bring
for the discussion. Also, be on the lookout for magazine and/or
newspaper articles dealing with the aspect of quality discussed
in the attached article.

Please be prompt.

Attachment

Figure 10-5

REVIEW EXERCISE 5

Retrieve **online10.r2**. Delete your name and the date from the top of the document. Make any adjustments necessary to assure that the title is still two inches from the top of the page.

Delete the Bold, Italics, and Left/Right Indent codes. Check the document for appropriate spacing. Print a copy. Then exit the document, saving it this time as **online10.r5**.

REVIEW EXERCISE 6

Key a short paragraph or two, telling how you feel about your training in WordPerfect so far. Which features do you like the best? Which do you like the least? With which features do you have the most problems?

Use any of the formatting features you have learned thus far. When you finish your paragraph, proofread it carefully. Then check the spelling with the WordPerfect speller.

Finally, print a copy of your work for your instructor. Exit the document, saving it as **opnion10.r6**.

EVALUATION

This is the end of Unit 1. A production test follows this unit. It involves creating a short document with formatting such as indent, bold, underline, dashes and hard spaces, and centering. After creating, proofreading, spell-checking, and printing the document, you will revise it and submit a perfect corrected copy. Good luck!

Unit 2

WordPerfect Formatting and Editing

LESSON 11
Line Spacing, Margins, and Tabs

OBJECTIVES

Upon completion of this lesson, you will be able to:

1. Discuss default formats.
2. Change from single to double spacing and back again.
3. Change the margin settings.
4. Use scrolling to move around in your documents.
5. Change the tab settings and use tabs.

Estimated Time: 1½ hours

You learned in your keyboarding or typing class to change the appearance of your documents with line spacing, margins, and tab stops. You've probably become quite adept at making those changes. So far you haven't had to worry about formatting changes in the documents you've created using WordPerfect. That's because the defaults for WordPerfect, which you learned about in Lesson 2, have been set to give you a good-looking document without much interference.

FORMATTING DEFAULTS

The defaults with which we will be working in this lesson are set as follows:

1. **Line Spacing:** set to single spacing.

2. **Margins:** set so that you will have equal one-inch side margins and one-inch top and bottom margins. (We will work only with the side margins in this lesson.)

3. **Tab Stops:** set with a tab stop at each half inch.

All of these settings can be changed very easily to format your documents so that they look exactly as you'd like. Here are some general guidelines with regard to changing formats.

- The default formats were determined by someone who knew what a document should look like. Most of the time you will use them. If you find after using WordPerfect for a while that you are repeatedly changing the formats for your documents, you should consider changing the defaults.

- Format changes that affect an entire document should be inserted at the top of the document. While the Search function can be used to find the codes inserted in your document for format changes, having a standard placement point will make your work easier.

- If you make a format change within a document, the text above the change will be unaffected. In other words, a format change only affects the text forward from the point of the change. The default setting is in effect prior to the change.

- Formatting changes remain in effect until you make another formatting change that overrides the previous one.

- Use Reveal Codes to locate and delete any unnecessary codes. They "garbage up" your documents and sometimes cause strange things to happen when you print. Keep your documents clean!

- Format changes made within the body of a document should be placed at the beginning of a line (at the left margin) unless there is a very good reason not to do so.

- Format codes become a permanent part of a document and are saved with the document when you save it. Saving a document properly using **F7 (Exit)** clears the memory of all Format codes, and the memory is returned to the default settings.

The Format Menu

All of the formatting changes you will learn about in this lesson and the next one come from the Line Format menu. The Line Format menu is only a portion of the larger format menu. We will take a moment now and look at the Format menu so you will be familiar with it when we really begin using it.

Strike **Shift-F8** and look at the menu that appears. It should look much like Figure 11-1. (You'll learn the mouse and menu choices in Exercise 1.)

Notice that the Format menu is divided into four sections:
1   **Line Format**
2   **Page Format**
3   **Document Format**
4   **Other**

So that you never have to wonder which menu you need to use to make a formatting change, all of the topics covered in each menu are listed on this first menu screen. As you look over the topics here, you will see some that are familiar and some that are new to you. For now, we'll begin with the Line Format menu and learn about the features one at a time.

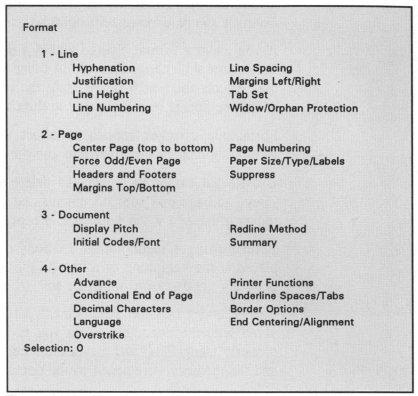

Format

1 - Line

Hyphenation	Line Spacing
Justification	Margins Left/Right
Line Height	Tab Set
Line Numbering	Widow/Orphan Protection

2 - Page

Center Page (top to bottom)	Page Numbering
Force Odd/Even Page	Paper Size/Type/Labels
Headers and Footers	Suppress
Margins Top/Bottom	

3 - Document

Display Pitch	Redline Method
Initial Codes/Font	Summary

4 - Other

Advance	Printer Functions
Conditional End of Page	Underline Spaces/Tabs
Decimal Characters	Border Options
Language	End Centering/Alignment
Overstrike	

Selection: 0

Figure 11-1   The Format Menu

LINE SPACING

So far everything you have keyed has been single spaced. There will be many times when you want all or part of a document keyed using spacing other than single spacing. WordPerfect enables you to set double, triple, quadruple spacing, etc. You may also set half spacing. For example, you could set the spacing at 1.5.

It is very important when you want a format other than single spacing that you change the spacing by inserting a code rather than by striking Enter twice at the end of each line. Not only do those hard returns make it impossible for WordPerfect to give you fully justified text, but they make quite a mess when you decide to edit the text. Setting double spacing is very easy. We'll try the spacing feature in the next exercise.

Lesson 11 Exercise 1

The Format menu should still be showing on your screen. If it isn't, open it again now with **Shift-F8**.

Choose **L**ine and then **S**pacing from the Layout menu.

1. Choose the Line Format menu by striking **1** or **L** in the Format menu. Here in menu form you will see the Line Format features. Notice that as with other menus, each feature may be chosen with a numeral or a letter. Your Line Format menu should look like Figure 11-2.

2. Notice that Line Spacing is **6** or **S** on the menu. Strike **6** or **S** and notice that the cursor moves to the **1**, which tells you that your work is being single spaced.

3. Key **2** to change to double spacing.

4. Strike **Enter** three times or **F7** twice to exit the menu and return to your working screen. Reveal your codes and look at the Line Spacing code. Add it to the list of codes you're keeping.

5. Key the short paragraph in Figure 11-3 and watch how the text is automatically double spaced on the screen. Be sure to let the text wrap around at the end of each line. Do NOT strike **Enter** until the last line.

```
Format: Line

   1 - Hyphenation                      No

   2 - Hyphenation Zone - Left          10%
                          Right         4%

   3 - Justification                    Full

   4 - Line Height                      Auto

   5 - Line Numbering                   No

   6 - Line Spacing                     1

   7 - Margins - Left                   1"
                 Right                  1"

   8 - Tab Set            Rel; -1", every 0.5"

   9 - Widow/Orphan Protection          No

Selection: 0
```

Figure 11-2   The Line Format Menu

A record is any form of recorded information. The medium on which it is recorded may be paper, film, or magnetic media (such as a computer tape or disk). In other words, virtually any information created or communicated within an organization is a record.

Figure 11-3

6. When you are finished, use **Page Up** to return to the beginning of the paragraph and reveal your codes. Delete the code that causes your paragraph to be double spaced. Look at the paragraph now!

7. Turn off Reveal Codes. With your cursor still on the first character of the paragraph, follow Steps 1 through 4 above to change the paragraph back to double spacing. (In order to change this

paragraph to double spacing, your cursor MUST be positioned at the beginning of the paragraph!)

8. When you are finished, use **F10** to save the document as **record.111** so it remains on your screen. Then print it. (Note that we now have to make a change in exercise numbering because the lesson numbers have two digits—hence, Lesson 11, Exercise 1 is 111.)

Lesson 11 Exercise 2

1. Edit the paragraph from Exercise 1 as illustrated in Figure 11-4. If you did the first exercise correctly, the changes you make will simply cause the lines to readjust and wrap differently.

2. Print the exercise and use Exit to save it again, this time as **record.112.**

A record is any ~~form~~ kind of recorded information. The medium on which it is recorded may be paper, film, ~~or~~ magnetic media or laser (such as optical disk or CD-ROM). (such as a computer tape or disk). In other words, virtually any information created, or communicated, or saved within an organization is a record.

Figure 11-4

Lesson 11 Exercise 3

(Template disk users: Refer to the box below before beginning.)

1. Key the two-page letter in Figure 11-5. Use the Date Text feature to insert the date at **Pos 4"** two inches from the top of the page. Follow the date with a quadruple space.

2. Change to double spacing just before you key **1**. Change to single spacing at the beginning of the paragraph following the enumeration. Remember to use →Indent following each of the numerals.

TEMPLATE DISK USERS:

1.   Retrieve **furnitur.113** from the template disk.
2.   Format and save the letter as directed in Exercise 3.

---

3. Begin each of the closing lines at **Pos 4"** with a quadruple space between them.

4. If you prepare the letter correctly, it will have a terrible page break. We'll deal with that shortly. Exit from the letter, saving it as furnitur.113. Do not print it.

(Current date)

Mr. Thomas Zeander
Zeander, Incorporated
2425 Seminole Street
Menasha, WI 54952-7890

Dear Mr. Zeander:

Thank you for your recent inquiry about our line of modular office furniture. As you well know, ergonomically designed workstations can increase efficiency by a whopping 25 percent. When you consider the cost of salaries today, no one can afford to have uncomfortable employees in business offices.

I am enclosing a brochure containing all of the specifications for the type of modular furniture in which you are interested. The components included are:

1. A flat, light-colored work surface measuring 24 by 60

    inches. The work surface should be finished with a dull

    finish to eliminate the glare from any overhead lighting.

2. Acoustically treated sound barriers to separate one

    worker from another. These barriers need to be large

    enough so the workers have semiprivate office areas but

    not so large that the workers feel claustrophobic.

3. An overhead shelf the same width as the workstation for

    reference materials and paper organizers. Also included

    are under-counter filing and storage areas, all within

    easy reach of the worker.

4. A task light attached to the underside of the overhead

    shelving unit.

As you know, of course, the most important element in any office is the chair. Our company handles a full line of ergonomically designed office chairs that you can mix and match with the other components of the work station.

Please contact me if you would like to discuss your needs further.

Sincerely,

(your name)

Figure 11-5

MARGIN SET

The Line Format menu is also used for setting new side margins. As discussed earlier, the default margins are one inch on each side of your text. The default paper size is 8½ inches. That means that you have a default line length of 6½ inches.

Side margins are easy to change. There are, however, some restrictions you need to keep in mind when you change the settings.

- Most printers will not print all the way to the edges of the paper. The "no print zone" varies by printer and ranges from ¼ to ½ inch on all sides of the paper.

- WordPerfect 5.1 thinks of a standard page as 8½ inches wide. If you want something different, you must change the paper size. You'll learn to do that in a later lesson.

Here is the procedure for changing from the default margin settings.

Choose **Line** and then **Margins** from the Layout menu.

1. Strike **Shift-F8** for the Format menu and choose **1 Line** for the Line Format menu.

2. Choose **7 Margins**. The cursor will move to the spot for you to key the measurement for the left margin.

3. Key the size of the desired margin in inches and tenths of an inch. Then strike **Enter**. The cursor will move to the spot for you to key the measurement for the right margin.

4. After keying the size of the right margin, strike **Enter** until you are returned to your working screen.

When you set margins, only the text following the change will be affected. You may change the margins in your document as many times as you wish. If you have two Margin Set codes in the same place, the second one overrides the first. Use Reveal Codes to see the Margin codes and delete any extra ones. Remember to keep your document clean!

Margin changes become part of the document. When you save the document, the Margin Set codes will be saved with the document. When you clear the screen with Exit, all changes, including margin settings, are deleted from memory and default settings are restored. This prepares your screen for a new document.

Lesson 11 Exercise 4

Choose **Line** and then **Margins** from the Layout menu.

1. Strike **Shift-F8** for the Format menu and choose **1 Line** for the Line Format menu.

2. Choose **7 Margins** and set the margins at two inches. Then key the paragraph in Figure 11-6. Use a hard space to separate the whole number from the keyed fraction in the first sentence.

3. Move the cursor back to the beginning of the paragraph. Look at the Margin Set code with codes revealed. Add the code to your list.

4. Delete the Margin Set code and watch the document reformat. Then reset the margins at two inches again. (Remember that in order for the setting to affect the document, the code must be above the paragraph.) You may need to strike ↓ to see the new margins take effect.

5. Try setting other line lengths. Then use Reveal Codes to find and delete all Margin codes. Reset the margins at two inches and read on.

```
The line length for this paragraph is about 4 1/2 inches.
Because of that, this paragraph will be like a column in the
middle of the page.  The lines may be spaced strangely if
the paragraph is printed, because justification evens all
line endings by adding extra space between words.
```

Figure 11-6

SCROLLING

In Lesson 4 you learned about getting around quickly on the line. But you may have forgotten some of the commands. Study Figure 11-7.

Home, ← . . . . Beginning of text line	Home, ↓ . . . Bottom of current screen
End . . . . End of text line	Home, ↑ . . . Top of current screen
Home, Home, ↑ . Beginning of text, after opening codes	Page Down . . Top of next page (or on the last page, bottom of text)
Home, Home, ↓ . Bottom of document	
Page Up . . . . Top of previous page, before all codes (or on the first page of the document, top of document—before all codes)	
Home, Home, Home, ↑ . Beginning of text, before all codes	

Figure 11-7

Lesson 11 Exercise 5

1. Practice these cursor-moving functions on the paragraph you created in Exercise 4. Notice the difference between the results of **Home**, **Home, ↑** and **Page Up**. **Page Up** should move your cursor BEFORE the Margin Set code while **Home, Home, ↑** positions it at the beginning of the paragraph.

2. Clear the screen without saving. Then retrieve **furnitur.113** and practice moving the cursor in that two-page document. Especially compare the **Home, ↑** and **Home, ↓** functions with **Page Up and Page Down**.

3. When you are comfortable with moving the cursor in your document (*scrolling*), exit the letter without saving.

TAB SET AND CLEAR

Tabs are a very important part of any word processing program. Tabs help you indent items efficiently and help the items hold their position when changes are made in the document.

The WordPerfect default for tab settings is a tab every half inch. Since your margin is set at one inch, there is a tab one-half inch to the left of the left margin. You used that tab stop when you used the Left Margin Release in Lesson 8. There is a tab stop at the margin and another one every half inch to the right all the way across the scale. Let's look at how changes can be made in tab settings.

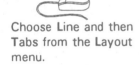

Choose Line and then Tabs from the Layout menu.

Tab Exercise. Follow these steps to open the tab ruler.

1. Access the Format menu with **Shift-F8**. Choose **1 Line Format**.

2. Choose Tabs with either **T** or **8**. Look at the ruler that appears. It should look much like Figure 11-8. Note the **L** where each tab is set. Read on to see what you can do with this ruler.

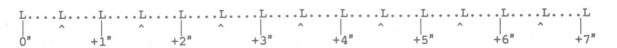

```
L....L....L....L....L....L....L....L....L....L....L....L....L....L....L
|    ^    |    ^    |    ^    |    ^    |    ^    |    ^    |    ^    |
0"       +1"      +2"      +3"      +4"      +5"      +6"      +7"

Ctrl-End (clear tabs); Enter Number (set tab); Del (clear tab);
Type; Left; Center; Right; Decimal; .= Dot Leader; Press Exit when done
```

Figure 11-8

With this ruler on the screen, you can do the following things:

• **Erase All Tabs.** Strike **Ctrl-End**. This will erase all tabs from the cursor forward to the end of the line. You should use this procedure to get rid of unwanted tabs each time you reset tab stops.

- **Move the Cursor.** The left and right arrows are used to move the cursor one space at a time. The up and down arrows are used to move the cursor a tab stop at a time.

- **Erase One Tab.** Key the number at which you would like the tab to be erased and strike **Enter** to move the cursor to that location. Then strike **Delete**. If you wish, for example, to erase the tab stop at two inches, you would key **2, Enter, Delete**. You can also use the arrow keys to move to the tab you wish to delete and strike **Delete**.

- **Set a Tab.** Key the number where you wish to set a tab and strike **Enter.** You may also move the cursor to the spot for a desired tab and strike **Tab** or key a lowercase *l*. It will appear as a capital *L*.

- **Reset Tabs Evenly Spaced Across the Page.** If you have deleted all of the default tab stops, you can reset them if you wish. First strike **Home, ←** and clear all tabs with **Ctrl-End.** Then key **0,.5** and strike **Enter,** which tells WordPerfect to set the first tab at **0** and another one every half inch (**.5**) across the scale. You can insert evenly spaced tabs at any interval using this method.

When you finish setting tabs, follow the prompt to exit the tab ruler with **F7 Exit.** Tabs may be set and reset as many times as you'd like in a document. Each time you change tab settings, the text from that point forward is affected—up to the next time you change the tab settings. When you save your document, the tab settings become a part of that document and are saved with it.

When you exit to clear your screen, all tabs return to the default settings so your screen is ready for you to begin a new document. The defaults can be changed if you consistently use different margins and tabs. The WordPerfect documentation gives instructions for changing defaults.

Relative Tabs

With the tab ruler showing on the screen, the first choice in the menu at the bottom is **Type.** WordPerfect provides you with two types of tabs. These are *absolute tabs* and *relative tabs*. Relative tabs are relative to the margin. They move when the margin settings are changed. Relative tabs are the default.

Because the tabs are relative to the margin, tabs are measured beginning at -1.0" at the left edge of the paper. In the ruler, the left margin setting is 0", no matter where the margin is set. A tab stop one inch from the left margin would be set at +1".

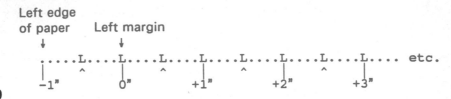

Left edge
of paper   Left margin
   ↓   ↓
.....L....L....L....L....L....L....L....L.... etc.
   | ^ | ^ | ^ | ^ |
   -1"   0"   +1"   +2"   +3"

Figure 11-9

Lesson 11 Exercise 6

1. Strike **Home, Home, ←** to move the cursor back to the left edge of the "paper." Your scale should look much like Figure 11-9. Study it and then strike **F7** to return to your working screen. Use **F7** again to clear your screen of any unwanted codes.

2. Strike **Shift-F8** for the Format menu. Then choose **1 Line** and **8 Tab** to open the tab ruler. You cursor will be at the left edge of the ruler (at zero). The scale should look much like the illustration in Figure 11-8.

3. Strike **Ctrl-End** to clear all of the existing tabs.

4. Key **1.1** and strike **Enter**. You have set your first tab at +1.1" (1.1 inches to the right of the left margin). Follow the same procedure to set tabs at **+2.2, +3.3,** and **+4.4.** Strike **F7** until you return to your working screen.

5. Reveal your codes and look at the Tab Set code. It starts with **Rel** because you are setting tabs that are relative to the left margin. Add the Tab code to your list of codes. Then turn Reveal Codes off.

6. Key the columns in Figure 11-10 with the first column beginning at the left margin. Working across, use the Tab key to jump from column to column. Strike **Enter** at the end of each line, including the last.

7. Save the document as **colors.116** and clear the screen.

```
red          blue         yellow       green        pink
gray         white        black        orange       chartreuse
brown        tan          gold         teal         mauve
```

Figure 11-10

Lesson 11 Exercise 7

1. Look at Figure 11-11. Center the title in bold caps positioned two inches from the top of the page. Quadruple space after the title.

2. Go to the tab ruler and clear all tabs.

3. Key **0,.4** and strike **Enter**. (That looks strange, but it is a zero and a comma followed by a period and finally a four. It sets the first tab at zero and succeeding tabs each four spaces across the ruler.)

4. Set the line spacing for double.

   Please note that both the settings for the tab stops and the line spacing are made at the beginning of the section to be formatted. This is a good "rule" for you to remember: When you add formatting to a document, position the formatting codes at the location where the formatting takes place.

5. Key the "outline" in Figure 11-11. Use Tab or Indent to indent after each numeral and letter at the beginnings of the lines. (If the lines were long enough to wrap around to the next line, it would be imperative that you use Indent. Because the lines are short, it is OK to use Tab to indent.)

6. Proofread, spell-check, and look over the document for layout. Then print it, and exit it, saving it as **systems.117**. Remember that when you save the document, the tab settings and line spacing codes are saved with the document. The defaults are reset on your screen for the next document.

INFORMATION PROCESSING

A.   Categories of Information Processing Equipment

    1.   Electronic Typewriters

    2.   Stand-alone Display Word Processors

    3.   Multiterminal Information Processing Systems

        a.   Shared Logic Systems (dumb terminals)

        b.   Shared Resource Systems (smart terminals)

B.   Computer-Based Systems

    1.   Microcomputers

    2.   Minicomputers

    3.   Mainframe (host) Systems

    4.   Time-Shared Systems

Figure 11-11

Tab Types

WordPerfect gives you some choices about the kinds of tabs you may set. In the exercises above, you used left tabs (**L** on the tab scale). There are actually four kinds of tabs. These tabs are listed in a menu at the bottom of the tab ruler. Turn back to Figure 11-7 and look at the four kinds: Left, Center, Right, and Decimal tabs. Next to the decimal tab is yet another kind—dot leaders—which we'll learn about shortly.

The sample in Figure 11-12 shows how you could use all four kinds of tabs.

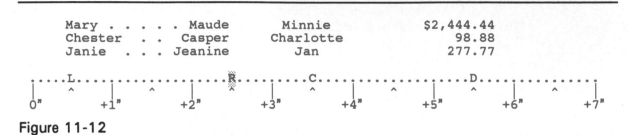

Figure 11-12

Let's discuss the different kinds of tabs, one at a time, and see how they can be used.

- Left. The Left tab is used to align text at the left. This is the most commonly used kind of tab. Mary, Chester, and Janie are lined up with a Left tab at +0.5" in the scale in Figure 11-12.

- Right. When a Right tab is set on the scale, anything keyed at that tab will back up from the tab. In other words, the copy will end up where the tab is set. As you can see, the Right tab is set at +2.5" on the scale.

  The **R** at +2.5" is shaded with gray because a period was keyed over the **R** when the tab was set. This tells WordPerfect that dot leaders should be inserted in the space between the columns. When you key the period over a tab to set dot leaders, the character will appear in a contrasting color. You'll have an opportunity to try this in a minute. In the meantime, notice that the dot leaders were, indeed, inserted between the columns of names.

- Center Tab. The Center tab tells WordPerfect to center everything keyed in that column. All you have to do when keying the text is tab to that column and key the material. The sample in Figure 11-12 isn't very large, but Minnie, Charlotte, and Jan are centered over one another at +3.5" on the scale.

- Decimal Tab. This feature enables you to key numbers—such as dollars and cents—without having to worry about getting the numbers properly aligned at the decimal. As with the Center tab, once the **D** is positioned on the scale, all you have to do is tab to the column and key the text.

Let's key the exercise in Figure 11-12. Follow along carefully.

Lesson 11 Exercise 8

1. Go to the tab ruler and clear all tabs.

2. Set the tabs illustrated in Figure 11-12 as follows: Key the number of the location for a tab and strike **Enter**.

   In the cases where you want something other than a Left tab, change the **L** to a different setting by keying the appropriate letter. For example, in the case of the Center tab, key a *c* (it does NOT have to be keyed in uppercase). For the Right tab with dot leaders, key the number, strike **Enter**, key *r*, and then key a period.

3. When the tabs are set, strike **F7** to return to your working screen and key the columns. Be sure to strike Tab before each of the names in the first column, since they are not to be keyed at the left margin.

4. When you finish, proofread and print the exercise. Then exit from it, saving it as **chester.118**.

Moving Tabs

With WordPerfect 5.1, you can watch as you adjust the tabs after the document has been keyed. In this way, if you don't figure the locations of the tabs correctly the first time, you can realign them by eye later. Let's try it.

Lesson 11   Exercise 9

1. Retrieve **chester.118**. Your cursor will be at the top of the document.

2. Reveal your codes and position the cursor so it is just to the right of the Tab Set code. [Tab] will be highlighted. Then go to tab ruler.

3. Strike ↑ three times so the cursor is on the **C** for the Center tab.

4. Hold **Ctrl** while you strike → two or three times. Watch as Minnie, Charlotte, and Jan move to the right. Using the right and left arrow keys, reposition the column until it looks like it is better centered between the other columns. Exit the tab ruler.

5. Look at the two Tab Set codes. The one to the right is the one formatting your columns. Move the cursor so that the second code is highlighted. Then strike Backspace once to delete the original code.

6. Save the document again with the same name. You don't need to print it again.

Just a word about moving tabs is needed here. The position of the cursor when you do this is critically important. It must be positioned to the right of the existing Tab Set code but before the beginning of the text to be affected. Also, it is a good idea to delete any extra codes. It falls into the category of "keeping your documents clean"!

SUMMARY

This lesson is a long one and contains quite a number of very useful skills for information processing, including:

- reviewing some of the WordPerfect default settings,
- changing between single and double spacing,
- changing the side margins,
- reviewing methods of moving the cursor in your text, and
- setting and clearing tabs as well as using different kinds of tabs.

Again, you should be reminded that in order to use a word processing program efficiently, you should take advantage of the features that are available to you. That includes changing margins and tabs. It especially includes changing line spacing, because if you want something double spaced and you don't change the line spacing, the only alternative is to strike Enter twice at the end of each line. That can cause such a terrible mess in your document if you need to make some changes! Develop the habit of thinking through an application before beginning and planning how you can use the tools available to enhance the results of your work.

LESSON 11 NOTES:

LESSON 12
More Line Formatting

OBJECTIVES

Upon completion of this lesson, you will be able to:

1. Preview your documents before printing.
2. Work with the four kinds of WordPerfect justification.
3. Use hyphenation to improve the appearance of your documents.
4. Use dot leaders to improve readability.
5. Use widow/orphan protection for better page endings.

Estimated Time: 2 hours

PRINT PREVIEW

Unless you are working with a large-screen monitor, you can only see about 25 lines of your page at one time. That portion is adequate for checking the accuracy of your work, but it does not enable you to check the layout of your document on the page.

After you've gained considerable experience in working with a word processing program, you can judge pretty well the placement of document parts in simple documents. To help you with more complicated formats, WordPerfect provides you with a feature called Print Preview that enables you to look at the WHOLE page before printing. Using Print Preview will save you much in terms of printing time and supplies.

To preview a document before printing, the document must be showing on the screen. Strike **Shift-F7** and **6** View Document. A miniature of the document will appear with several view options. Let's try it.

Lesson 12 Exercise 1

1. Open **systems.117**. Look at it.

Choose **Print** from the File menu. Then choose **6** View Document.

2. Strike **Shift-F7** and then **6** View Document to see what this document will look like when printed. It should resemble the document in the thumbnail illustration here.

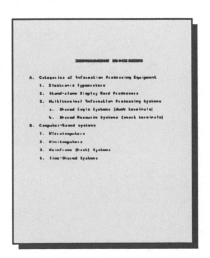

3. Look at the menu of choices at the bottom of the screen. You can look at the document at 100%, 200%, and full page. You can also look at the document with facing pages.

4. Exit from Print Preview by striking **F7**. Exit from your document without saving.

You will find it wise to check the appearance of your documents before printing. This is especially important for those documents with lots of formatting and for those documents with formats you can't see on the working screen, like headers, footers, page numbers, etc. You'll learn about those kinds of formats in Lesson 14.

JUSTIFICATION

One of the common kinds of formatting for documents is justification. WordPerfect has four different kinds of justification, as illustrated in the four sample paragraphs of text in this thumbnail document.

- **Full**—All lines begin and end exactly at the margins (Paragraph 1).
- **Center**—All lines are centered between the margins (Paragraph 2).
- **Left**—All lines begin evenly at the left margin but are ragged at the right (Paragraph 3).
- **Right**—All lines are ragged at the left margin but aligned evenly at the right (Paragraph 4).

The default setting for justification is Full. Full justification and Left justification are most often used for the paragraphs of a document. Center justification is more often used for display purposes. Use Right justification only for special kinds of documents.

When you select one kind of justification, that setting will remain in effect until you select one of the other kinds. This saves you time that you would have spent on individual centering, for example, if you have a number of consecutive lines that need to be centered.

Justification is also chosen from the Line Format menu. When you choose **3 J**ustification, the following one-line menu appears:

```
Justification: 1 Left; 2 Center; 3 Right; 4 Full:
```

Then all you need to do is choose the correct setting and key your document. Let's work briefly with the different kinds of justification.

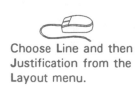

Choose **Line** and then
Justification from the
Layout menu.

Lesson 12   Exercise 2

1.   Strike **Shift-F8** and choose **1 Line**. Choose **3 Justification**.

2. Choose **2** Center. Then strike F7 to return to your working screen and key your name three times, striking **Enter** at the end of each. Reveal your codes and look at the Center Justification code. Add it to your list of codes.

3. Now return to the Justification menu and choose **3 Right**. Strike **F7** and again key your name three times, each time ending with **Enter**. Strike **Enter** twice after the third keying of your name.

4. Retrieve **record.112**. (Since you already have text on the screen, you will need to respond with **Y** to the question about whether you wish to "Retrieve into Current Document?") Look at the paragraph. It should be Right justified, because that is the last setting you used.

5. With your cursor positioned at the beginning of the paragraph, change the justification from Right to Left.

6. While you are in the Line Format menu, change the margins to two inches on each side. Strike **F7** to return to your document. Then strike **Page Down** and strike **Enter** twice.

7. Retrieve **record.112** again. Because of the existing settings, this paragraph will also have two-inch side margins and left justification.

8. With the cursor positioned at the beginning of the new paragraph, change the justification to Full. It will look the same on the screen as the previous one because full justification never shows on the screen.

9. Strike **Shift-F7** and **6** View Document to preview your document before printing. NOW you can see the full justification!

10. Print everything that is showing on your screen. Save the document as **practice.122** and clear the screen. Look at your hard copy of the document. Which do you like best—the left-justified paragraph or the full-justified paragraph?

As you can see, we could spend all day "fiddling" with a document, working for just the right look. But wait! There's more!!

HYPHENATION

When you work with short line lengths, you've probably noticed that big spaces follow some words because the next word has wrapped to the next line. WordPerfect's Hyphenation feature can help with that problem.

Hyphenation may be chosen from the Line Format menu; when that option is chosen, WordPerfect looks through your text and places hyphens in some of those long words. Usually the placement of the hyphens will be OK according to word division rules. In other cases, you may wish to turn off Hyphenation and then remove or move the offending hyphens. We'll try a quick exercise with hyphenation to see how it works.

Lesson 12 Exercise 3

1. Open **practice.122**. With the cursor positioned at the top of the document, choose Line from the Format menu.

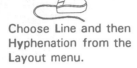

Choose Line and then Hyphenation from the Layout menu.

2. Choose **1** Hyphenation. Note that the prompt is **No**. Choose **Y** for Yes. Return to your document.

3. Use the cursor keys to move down through your document. Notice that the six lines containing your name aren't affected. Look at the left-justified and full-justified paragraphs. They may be hyphenated differently. The placement of the hyphens will vary depending on the printer you are using.

4. Print your document and compare it with the copy from Exercise 2. The hyphens changed the appearance of your document, didn't they?

5. Save the document again, this time as **practice.123**, and close it.

Hyphenation is one of those features that you may use on a regular basis or you may choose not to use at all. In most documents, hyphenation won't make a great deal of difference, especially if you work with something other than a fixed-pitch font like the 10cpi Courier. (You'll learn about fonts in a later lesson.) The documents where you will find hyphenation to be most useful are those documents with especially short line lengths, like the one we worked with here, or with columns.

DOT LEADERS

In Lesson 11 you learned how to insert a period over a tab stop in the tab ruler when you wanted dot leaders to join two columns. You can also insert dot leaders without any special kind of tab by simply giving the Flush Right command twice in succession.

Dot Leader Exercise. Try it. Strike **Alt-F6** twice. A line of dots should appear across your screen—from the left margin to the right. That was pretty easy, wasn't it? Look at your codes. How many Flush Right codes are there? Backspace once. What happened?

Dot leaders are very useful in drawing your attention from one side of the page to the other. They are often used in financial statements and programs. They can be added to existing documents where you already used Flush Right. Let's add them to a document created in Lesson 7.

Lesson 12 Exercise 4

1. Retrieve **fiddler.7-3**. Position the cursor directly on the *T* of *Tim*.

2. Strike **Alt-F6** and watch the dot leaders appear.

3. Move the cursor to the *P* of *Pat*. Proceed to add leaders to each line of the exercise. Print the exercise and exit it, saving it as **fiddler.124**.

In this exercise, you only needed to give the Flush Right command once because one Flush Right command already existed between your columns. If you were keying a fresh document, you'd have to give the command twice to get the dot leaders.

WIDOW/ORPHAN PROTECTION

One last item in the Line Format menu is widow/orphan protection. It is a good practice to avoid having a single line of a paragraph printed by itself either at the top of a page or at the bottom of a page. These single lines are called *widows* and *orphans*. Widow/Orphan protection should be chosen at the top of the first page of a multiple-page document.

The procedure for protecting your documents against this kind of bad page break is simple. Choose Line from the Format menu and then choose **9 Widow/Orphan Protection**. As you can see, the default is **No**. Choose **Y** to turn on this option.

Lesson 12 Exercise 5

1. Retrieve **furnitur.113**. If you remember, the second page of this letter begins with the first line of a paragraph. Use **Home, ↓** three times and look at that bad page break.

2. Strike **Home, Home, ↑** to return to the top of the document.

3. Strike **Shift-F8**, followed by **1 Line**, and then **9 Widow/Orphan**. Change the prompt to **Y** and return to your document. Move down the page again and see if the problem has been corrected.

4. Position your cursor somewhere on the first page of the document. Then use Print Preview to see what the bottom margin of that page will look like. It will appear to be large because the first line of the paragraph was moved to the next page.

5. Strike **Page Down** to see what the second page of the letter looks like. If you would like to return to the first page, strike **Page Up**.

6. Close the document again, saving it with the same name.

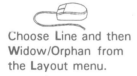

Choose Line and then Widow/Orphan from the Layout menu.

Since the bottom margin can't be violated, WordPerfect's procedure for dealing with a situation like this is to move the offending line to the next page. If the problem was a paragraph on the first page with only a single line on the next, WordPerfect would move an additional line to the next page.

SUMMARY

In this lesson you learned to preview your documents before printing. You also learned about three more features in the line format menu:
- justification,
- hyphenation, and
- widow/orphan protection.

In addition, you learned about an odd feature that doesn't come from any menu—dot leaders. All of these features are easy to use and are useful for fine-tuning your documents. Feel free to use them whenever you wish!

LESSON 12 NOTES:

TRUE/FALSE

Each of the following statements is either true or false. Indicate your choice in the Answers column by circling T for a true statement or F for a false statement.

Answers

1. You may go back into previously keyed material and change the spacing. (Les. 11, Obj. 2) . . . .   1. T F

2. If two spacing codes are together in a document, the one that appears first will be the one to affect the document. (Les. 11, Obj. 2) . . . .   2. T F

3. In order to change the left margin, you must also change the right margin. (Les. 11, Obj. 3) . . . .   3. T F

4. Striking the End key will take your cursor quickly to the extreme right of the line. (Les. 11, Obj. 4) . . . .   4. T F

5. Default tab settings have a tab stop every four spaces. (Les. 11, Obj. 5) .   5. T F

6. You can look at a miniature of your document to check formatting before printing it. (Les. 12, Obj. 1) . . . .   6. T F

7. Full justification evens the line endings by putting extra spaces between words. (Les. 12, Obj. 2) . . . .   7. T F

8. Even when your document has full justification, it appears on the screen to be left justified. (Les. 12, Obj. 2) . . . .   8. T F

9. Hyphenation helps eliminate big spaces between words in text that is prepared with Full justification. (Les. 12, Obj. 3) . . . .   9. T F

10. Dot leaders can be inserted with the Flush Right command. (Les. 12, Obj. 4) . . . .   10. T F

11. Widow/orphan protection is especially important in one-page documents. (Les. 12, Obj. 5) . . . .   11. T F

COMPLETION

Indicate the correct answer in the space provided.

Answers

1. Which choice in the Line Format menu gives you the opportunity to change the spacing? (Les. 11, Obj. 2) .

    1. _____

2. How many times may you change margins within a document? (Les. 11, Obj. 3) . . . .

    2. _____

3. Which combination of keys enables you to erase all of the tab stops at one time? (Les. 11, Obj. 5) . . . . . .

    3. _____

4. What would you key in the Tab menu to reset all tabs with the first tab at **0** and the rest of them spaced evenly at every half inch? (Les. 11, Obj. 5) . . . .

    4. _____

5. Which feature must you use to see your text with full justification before printing? (Les. 12, Obj. 1) . . . . .

    5. _____

6. When justification is set at Left, how will the right margin appear? (Les. 12, Obj. 2) . . . .

    6. _____

7. What kinds of words would be hyphenated if you use hyphenation in a document with all short words? (Les. 12, Obj. 3) . . . .

    7. _____

8. Can WordPerfect dot leaders be added to a document after it has been keyed? (Les. 12, Obj. 4) . . . .

    8. _____

9. Through which format menu is the Widow/Orphan feature accessed? (Les. 12, Obj. 5) . . . .

    9. _____

REFERENCE

Turn to the Line Spacing section of the *WordPerfect Reference*. What is the word used to refer to the amount of space added to the height of characters in a line of text?

_____

Turn to the Widow/Orphan section of the *WordPerfect Reference* and read about the other two features that protect text from being split by page breaks. What are those features?

_____

Review Exercises

Here are a few exercises for you to practice all of the line formatting features you've learned in Lessons 11 and 12.

REVIEW EXERCISE 1

(Template disk users: Refer to the box below before beginning.)

Key the document illustrated in Figure 12-1. Format it according to the instructions below. When you finish, the first page should look much like this thumbnail illustration.

1. Begin with the Widow/Orphan Protection feature. Place this code at the beginning of the document, before any returns, enters, or characters.

2. Set each of the side margins at 1.5 inches.   *L+R*

3. Position the title 2 inches from the top of the page. Center the title and follow it with a quadruple space.

4. At the beginning of the text (the start of the first paragraph), set justification at Left.

5. Key the document using double spacing. It is shown with single spacing and an extra blank line between paragraphs. When you double space a document, you should not put any extra space between paragraphs.

6. Format the third paragraph with single spacing, and use Left/Right Indent to indent it a half-inch from both side margins.   *Sh F4*

7. Single space the items in the list of "excuses." Leave a double space before the list and following it. Use Indent following the hyphen for each "excuse."   *Tab — F4*

8. When you finish, proofread carefully and view the document with Print Preview to check the formatting.

9. Finally, spell-check the document and print it. Then exit from it, saving it as **license1.12r**.   *DOC CODE*

2nd page
1 inch margin
Double Space

TEMPLATE DISK USERS:

Retrieve **license.12r** from the template disk. Format it as directed in the exercise.

LEGAL SOFTWARE

The problem of violations of copyright laws relating to computer software continues to plague software developers. Some companies buy one or two copies of a software program and install that software on ten or twenty computers. This procedure is a federal crime. Penalties may run as high as $100,000 per violation and/or up to 5 years in jail.

While software is a relatively new medium of "intellectual property" (compared with books, records, magazines, and film), the same rules apply.

Software companies liken the piracy of their software to the actual theft of more "material" goods. For example, if a company manufactures $300 bicycles and each person who pays for one bicycle takes 2, 3, or 5 of them from the warehouse, the manufacturer probably won't be in business for long.

Many people who violate the copyright laws by copying software don't understand licensing procedures. Other people justify their actions with excuses like
- "I can't afford to buy the software."
- "Everyone else is doing it."
- "I'm just <u>one</u> person with <u>one</u> copy of the software."
- "The boss told me to do it."
None of these excuses would stand up in court.

Software development companies have joined together in an effort to keep the use of their products legal. The Software Publishers Association, based in Washington, D.C., works to educate the public regarding what is and what is not legal. This organization also works with litigation cases involving companies who are in violation of the law.

Licensing agreements may vary from one software house to another. The smart consumer will know what is legal for each software program used and will abide by those agreements. The customer should also be certain to send in the necessary registration cards when purchasing new software so the licensing process is complete.

Figure 12-1

REVIEW EXERCISE 2

Create a memo format that you can use for your memos as follows. When you finish, your format will look much like this thumbnail illustration.

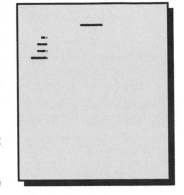

1. Center the word *MEMORANDUM* in bold capital letters at the top of the screen. Quadruple space.

2. Go to the tab ruler and delete the tab at 0.5".

3. Add a Right tab at 0.8" and exit from the tab ruler.

4. Tab once and key *TO*: in bold capital letters. Turn off Bold, tab once, and strike **Enter** twice.

5. Tab once and key *FROM*: in bold capital letters. Turn off Bold, tab once, and strike **Enter** twice.

6. Tab once and key *DATE*: in bold capital letters. Turn off Bold.

7. Strike **Tab** again and enter the Date Code (so that each time you open this document the current date will appear). Strike **Enter** twice.

8. Tab once and key *SUBJECT*: in bold capital letters. Turn off Bold, tab once, and strike **Enter** twice.

9. Use **F10** to save your document as **memo.frm**. (You used F10 to save because you will be using the form for the next exercise.)

REVIEW EXERCISE 3

Key the document illustrated in Figure 12-2. Format it as directed below. When you finish, it should look much like this thumbnail illustration.

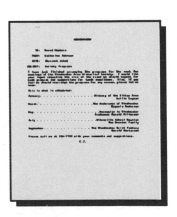

1. Position the cursor on the **TO:** line and strike **End** where you will fill in the correct information.

2. Move the cursor to the **FROM:** line and follow the same procedure.

3. Continue filling in the heading section.

4. Key the body of the memo.

5. For the listing, key *January*. Then give the Flush Right command twice and key the topic for the January program. Strike **Enter**, give the Flush Right command once, and key the name of the person presenting the program.

6. Follow the same procedure for the rest of the programs.

7. Key Ms. Johnson's initials a double space below the last line of the memo, beginning at **Pos 4"**.

8. Proofread carefully, preview the document to check the format, print the document, and exit from it, saving it as **programs.12r**.

MEMORANDUM

TO: Winchester Historical Society Executive Board

FROM: Catherine Johnson, Program Chairperson

DATE: (Current date)

SUBJECT: Upcoming Programs

I have finally finished scheduling the programs for the first part of next year. The topics for the programs are listed below, along with the names of the presenters.

Please study the list carefully, making notes of your thoughts regarding how we can make each program special. Also include suggestions for lunch committee members so we can get the committees set up early in the year.

January . . . . Settling the Zittau Area
                                           Eugenia Layman

March . . . . The Christensens of Winchester
                                         Samuel Christensen

May . . . . The Norwegian Language in Winnebago County
                                           Olaf Svenson

July . . . . Mikesville School Reunion
                                         The Breaker Family

September . . . . The Winchester Brick Factory
                                         Gustaf Mortarson

I will see you at the Board meeting the first Tuesday of next month. If you have any questions or suggestions prior to that time, please call me at 555-7789.

DCC CODE

Figure 12-2

REVIEW EXERCISE 4

1. Retrieve **license1.12r**.

2. Find the Margin Set code at the beginning of the document and delete it, returning your document to the 1-inch default margins.

3. Then find the Left Justification code at the beginning of the first paragraph and delete it, returning your document to full justification.

4. Return to the top of the document and turn on Hyphenation. Look through the document and see how many words were hyphenated and whether you like the hyphenation decisions WordPerfect made in your document.

5. Print the document and exit from it, saving it this time as **license4.12r**.

REVIEW EXERCISE 5

1. Retrieve **memo.frm**. Fill in the top information as follows:

   TO: The Winning Team

   FROM: Terrell, Your Captain

   SUBJECT: Fun Day Fines

2. Key the body of the memo as illustrated in Figure 12-3. For the tabulation portion of the memo, set Left tabs at +0.5" and +3.75". Set Decimal tabs at +2.5" and +5.75". You may add a period to the Decimal tab settings, if you'd like, so dot leaders are included within the columns. Work across the screen when you key the columns, using the Tab key to move from item to item.

3. You may key the closing initials at the left margin (or they will be preceded by dot leaders!), or you may get extra practice in setting tabs by clearing all tabs and setting a new one at center for the closing initials.

4. Proofread your document carefully, paying special attention to the dollar amounts. Spell-check the document, if you'd like, although the speller will probably stop at the majority of the names in the list.

5. Preview the document to see if the format looks correct.

6. Print the document and exit from it, saving it as **fun-day.12r**.

Congratulations on your spectacular Fun Day win! Each of you
deserves a medal for outstanding performance.

Some of you have not yet paid your penalty fines for the day.
I have listed the names and amounts of the overdue fines
below. Please pay this week so we can get the books in order.

For those of you who are paid up, thanks for your promptness.
You have my permission to harass the members listed below
until they, too, have paid their fines!

Robert	$2.50	Monica	$4.75
Arletta	3.75	Samuel	2.00
Andre	4.00	Kitrick	1.75
Ben	2.25	Naomi	1.00

As you know, our group is in charge of the next Fun Day. I
will be in touch with you soon with a date for the first
planning meeting.

mmm. DOC CODE

Figure 12-3

REVIEW EXERCISE 6

Create a document of your own that includes making adjustments in at
least four of the features that you've learned about in Lessons 11 and 12. A
list of features follows this paragraph. You might want to prepare a list of
telephone numbers for people you call frequently. Perhaps you need to prepare
the minutes of a meeting or a financial report for a group to which you belong.
Whatever you choose, try to make it something that is useful for you!

Line Spacing
Margins
Tabs
Justification
Hyphenation
Dot Leaders
Widow/Orphan Protection

When you finish the document, preview it to check the format, proofread
it carefully, and print a copy for your instructor. Then save it on your disk. You
may give it any name you'd like. Be careful to choose a name that will help
you identify the document at a later date.

On the back of the printed copy of the document, write the features that
you used so your instructor can see how you formatted your document.

LESSON 13
Block

OBJECTIVES

Upon completion of this lesson, you will be able to:

1. Use Block to select text.
2. Delete, restore, and format blocked text.
3. Rearrange blocks of text.
4. Use the Document 2 screen.

Estimated Time: 1 hour

By now you have become adept at correcting your errors by using the Delete and Backspace keys and rekeying the material correctly. Sometimes, however, the incorrect text is too big to delete a character, a word, or even a line at a time. Or sometimes the words are in the incorrect place. It's frustrating to have to rekey the text. There's a better way!

BLOCKING TEXT

WordPerfect Block enables you to mark or select a chunk (block) of text. Once that text is highlighted or *blocked*, you can do a variety of things with it. You can move or copy it to a different location, bold it, print it, underline it, or add it to the end of a file on your disk.

There are a couple of ways to block text. One of them is with the mouse. Another is by turning on Block and using the arrow keys to select your block. If you have a mouse and are comfortable with the use of it, that is usually the quickest way to block your text. Otherwise you can do a great job of blocking text from the keyboard. Let's get some text on the screen and practice blocking text. We'll start with the mouse. If you do not have a mouse, retrieve **license1.12r** and skip to Exercise 2.

Lesson 13 Exercise 1

1. Retrieve **license1.12r**.

2. Move your mouse so the pointer is beside the *S* of the word *Software* in the third paragraph. Press the left mouse button and hold it while you drag the mouse down the left side of the paragraph to block the entire paragraph. Release the mouse button when the entire paragraph is blocked.

   Block On will flash in the lower left corner of the screen. You have blocked the paragraph. Click somewhere in the margin to remove the highlighting from the paragraph.

3. Now start in the same place and drag the mouse diagonally toward the period in the second line that marks the end of the first sentence. Include the spaces following the period so if you delete the sentence, you won't have leftover spaces hanging there. Click somewhere in the margin to remove the highlighting.

4. Starting with *Other people . . .* block that sentence, the entire list of excuses, and the sentence following the excuses. Click in the margin to turn off Block.

5. Spend a moment choosing groups of words or sentences or even paragraphs and blocking them by dragging the mouse pointer over them. Click outside of the block to remove the highlighting.

6. Now put your mouse aside and use the keyboard to practice blocking.

Lesson 13 Exercise 2

Choose **Block** from the **E**dit menu.

1. Position the cursor on the *S* of the word *Software* in the third paragraph. Strike **Alt-F4** or **F12** to turn on Block. (**Block On** will flash in the lower left corner of the screen.)

2. Strike ↓ until you get to the beginning of the last line of the paragraph. Then strike **End** to move the cursor to the end of the line. You have blocked the paragraph.
   Turn off Block by striking **Alt-F4** or **F12** again. (Obviously F12 is easier to use because it requires only one keystroke, but the choice is yours regarding which command you wish to use for turning Block on and off from the keyboard.)

Choose **Block** from the **E**dit menu.

3. Return the cursor to the *S* of *Software*. Turn on Block. Strike **Enter** to advance the cursor to the end of the paragraph, blocking the text along the way. (Block searches for the hard return.) Turn off Block.

4. Turn on Block at the beginning of the same sentence. Key a period to advance the cursor to the end of the sentence, again blocking the text. (Block searches for the period.) Turn off Block.

5. Move the cursor to *Other people . . .* in the paragraph before the excuses. Turn on Block and cursor down until the sentence preceding the excuses, the excuses, and the following sentence are blocked. Turn off Block.

6. Choose groups of words or sentences or even paragraphs and block them by positioning the cursor, turning on Block, and moving the cursor through the text to be blocked. Each time, turn off Block. Keep the document open for the next exercise.

DELETE, RESTORE, AND FORMAT

Now that you know how to select a block of text, there are a number of things you can do with that blocked text. For example, you could give the Print command, and only the blocked text would go to the printer. Or you could choose to save the block of text, and WordPerfect would ask you what you'd like to name the block before saving it on your disk.

Let's practice working with blocked text. If you have a mouse, you may block the text from the keyboard or with the mouse.

Delete

With the text blocked, you can remove it from your document by striking either the Delete key or the Backspace key. You will be asked to confirm the deletion.

Lesson 13 Exercise 3

1. The document you have on the screen is a practice document. In practicing Block, we will destroy much of the screen copy of the document. Don't worry. The original is still on your disk.

2. Block the *Penalties* sentence at the end of the first paragraph. Strike either **Backspace** or **Delete** to delete it. Confirm by keying **Y**.

3. Block any six words in the final paragraph and delete them. Keep the cursor in position and read on.

Restore

WordPerfect remembers the last three things you've deleted, so if you make a big mistake in deleting text and realize it right away, you can fix that big mistake by striking **F1** (Cancel). WordPerfect will then show the text you deleted last. You may strike **1** to **R**estore the text into your document, or you may strike **2 P**revious Deletion to look at the other two most recent deletions. When you find the text you wish to restore, strike **1 R**estore. Let's practice.

Lesson 13 Exercise 4

1. Strike **F1** and **1** Restore and watch the six words you just deleted return to the last paragraph.

2. Position the cursor at the end of the first paragraph. Strike **F1** and then **2** Previous. The *Penalties* sentence should appear because that was the second-from-last piece of text you deleted. Strike **1** to restore the sentence.

3. Block the fifth paragraph—the one about the Software Publishers Association. Include the blank line following the paragraph in your block by extending the block until your cursor rests at the beginning of the first line of the next paragraph. Delete the block.

4. Strike **Page Up** to move your cursor to the beginning of the document. Strike **F1** and **1** to restore the paragraph to the new location.

5. Try that again on your own. Block a sentence or a group of words, delete them, and then restore them—either in the same location or a different location. WordPerfect will restore the text at the cursor location when you give the Restore command.

Format

You can add formatting to blocked text. When you were learning the Bold, Underline, and Italics features, you probably wished there was some way to go back and add one of those formats without having to rekey the text. There is a way—you can block the text to be formatted and simply give the formatting command.

Lesson 13 Exercise 5

1. Block *Software Publishers Association* in the first paragraph. Go to the Appearance portion of the Font menu and choose Italics. Your text will appear in the italic "color," and the block will be turned off.

2. Block the sentence near the end of the second paragraph that talks about a federal crime. Format that sentence with Bold.

3. Choose two or three words or phrases elsewhere in the document to be underlined. One at a time, block them and give the Underline command. This document probably is quite a mess. Close it without saving it.

MOVE AND COPY

In the Delete and Restore section, you learned one way to move text from one location in your document to another. You can do the same thing with Move (**Ctrl-F4**). When you block text and choose Move, you will see a short line menu:

```
Move: 1 Block; 2 Tabular Column; 3 Rectangle: 0
```

For now we will concentrate on the first choice—Block. When you choose **1 Block**, you will see another short line menu:

```
1 Move; 2 Copy; 3 Delete; 4 Append: 0
```

When you choose **1 Move**, the blocked text will be deleted from its original location and moved to whatever new location you specify. When you choose **2 Copy**, the blocked text will remain in the original location, and you may insert a copy of that text in whatever new location you specify. Either way, you must complete the transaction immediately; otherwise the text may be lost. This is because the text is held in a temporary buffer area while WordPerfect waits for you to decide where you would like it inserted. The buffer holds only one piece of text.

The **3 Delete** choice is just another way to remove text from your document. The final choice in this menu, **4 Append**, enables you to add the blocked text to a document on your disk. We won't practice this, but you merely need to name the file. The blocked text is added to the end of the document. You can rearrange that document later, if you'd like.

Lesson 13 Exercise 6

In this practice exercise, you are going to rearrange the items in a list. There is no logical order for these items, but the numbers help you to keep track of what you're doing. Follow these steps carefully.

1. Retrieve **job.9-3**. Position the cursor just to the left of the *2* for the second item in the list and turn on Block.

2. Block the item, extending it until the cursor is just to the left of the *3* for the third item.

Choose **M**ove from the **E**dit menu.

Choose **P**aste from the **E**dit menu.

3. Strike **Ctrl-F4**, choose **1 Block** and **1 Move**. Item 2 will disappear from your document, and the rest of the document will move up to fill in the space. Notice that at the bottom of the screen you are told to position the cursor where the blocked text should be inserted and strike **Enter**.

4. Move the cursor so that it is just to the left of Item 1 in the list and strike **Enter**. The blocked text will be inserted there.

5. Correct the numbers so the items are listed in numeric order.

6. Now, on your own, move Item 3 so that it becomes Item 6 and fix the numerals.

Choose **C**opy and then **P**aste from the **E**dit menu.

7. Now follow the same procedure with Item 2 except that you will choose **2 Copy**. The copy should be positioned ahead of Item 7. When you fix the numbering, you'll find that you have eight items in the list!

8. Finally, just for practice, move Item 4 so it becomes the last item. You may need to add a hard return or two at the bottom of the list in order for the spacing to be correct.

9. Practice moving items in the list until you are comfortable. Try moving a sentence or a few words from one place to another. Each time, do any necessary repairs to the spacing surrounding the text. You'll find that if you get good at moving the appropriate spaces within the text, little adjusting will be necessary. Finally, exit from this messed-up document without saving.

Column Move

Moving columns within a document is similar to what you have been doing. Block the text to be moved, "cut it," and retrieve it at a new location. To use this feature, the columns must have been created with tabs between the columns and hard returns at the ends of the lines.

Let's try an exercise with some text created earlier. You will learn about the steps for this feature as you complete them.

Lesson 13 Exercise 7

1. Retrieve **colors.116**. Position the cursor on the *b* of *blue*. Turn on Block. Strike ↓ and → until the block ends with the *n* of *tan*. (Everything across the columns between *blue* and *tan* will be highlighted.)

2. Strike **Ctrl-F4** and choose **2 Tabular Column**. Now the block showing on the screen will change so that only the column to be moved and the spaces to the left of that column are highlighted.

3. Choose **1 Move**. Note that the column to be moved disappears and the others fill in the space.

4. Move the cursor to the *p* of *pink*. You will insert the "blue" column in front of the "pink" column. Strike **Enter** to retrieve the column.

5. You may practice more with moving columns, if you'd like. Then print the exercise and save it as **colors.137**.

If you work much with columns of numbers, you will find this tool to be very valuable. There are, however, some things you should know about moving columns.

• When blocking the column to be moved, you must begin with the cursor somewhere in the first word or numeral of the column you wish to move and end with the cursor somewhere in the last word or numeral of that same column.

• In the blocking step, remember that the entire text will be highlighted from the beginning of the block to the end of the block. It will stay that way until you choose **2 Tabular Column**.

• Column move will not work unless the columns are separated by tabs or indents. Columns separated with spaces keyed on the space bar or other vertical chunks of text cannot be moved.

• Since the first column of **colors.116** was keyed at the left margin and not preceded by a tab, you cannot move that column. Nor can you insert a different column in front of it. To move that column or insert another column in front of it, you must first set a tab for that column and tab or indent each item from the left margin.

SWITCH

When using WordPerfect, you can have two documents active at one time. You may remember that the first item in the status line tells you that you are in Document 1. You can switch between the Document 1 screen and the Document 2 screen by striking **Shift-F3**. Once on the Document 2 screen, you can retrieve documents, edit them, and do anything that you are able to do on the Document 1 screen.

The best thing about having the Document 2 screen is that you can move blocks of text from the document on one screen to the document open on the other screen.

Lesson 13 Exercise 8

Choose **S**witch Document from the Edit menu.

Choose **S**witch Document from the Edit menu.

1. Open **license1.12r**. Move your cursor to the beginning of the first paragraph. Block the paragraph and choose **2 Copy**.

2. Strike **Shift-F3** to switch to the Doc 2 screen. Strike **Enter** to retrieve the paragraph. Is the paragraph on the Doc 2 screen single spaced or double spaced? Is the paragraph indented or not?

3. Strike **Shift-F3** to return to the Doc 1 screen and reveal your codes. Obviously if you want the formatting to go along when you copy or move a chunk of text from one place to another, you have to be sure to include the formatting codes in the block.

4. Return to the Doc 2 screen. Exit the document without saving. Note that this time you are asked if you wish to **Exit Doc 2?** instead of whether you would like to **Exit WordPerfect?** Respond with **Y**.

5. Copy the first paragraph to the Doc 2 screen again, this time taking the double spacing code and the Tab code along.

6. Practice moving paragraphs or sentences or groups of words from one screen to the other until you are comfortable with the procedure. Then exit from the documents on both screens without saving. Be sure you end up on the Doc 1 screen.

Split Screen

Rather than having a complete Document 1 screen and a complete Document 2 screen, you can split the screen so that parts of both documents show at the same time. This is done with the **Ctrl-F3** (Screen) command. When you strike **Ctrl-F3** and choose **1** Window, WordPerfect will prompt **Number of lines in this window? 24**. You may make the windows the same size, or you may have one larger than the other.

Once the window is split, you can use **Shift-F3** like you did in the exercise above to move your cursor from Doc 1 to Doc 2 and back. Let's split the screen in a short exercise.

Lesson 13 Exercise 9

Choose **Window** from the **Edit** menu.

1. On a clear WordPerfect screen, strike **Ctrl-F3** and choose **1 Window**. At the "Number of . . ." prompt, key *12* and strike **Enter**.

Choose **Switch Document** from the **Edit** menu.

2. Immediately your screen will split, and the familiar ruler will separate the two documents. Use **Shift-F3** to move the cursor from one document to the other, ending with the cursor in Doc 1.

Choose **Window** from the **Edit** menu.

3. Strike **Ctrl-F3** and choose **1 Window** again. At the "Number of . . ." prompt, key *24*. The Doc 2 window will close and you will be returned to the full Doc 1 window.

Whether you split the screen or use the full-sized Document 2 screen, WordPerfect won't allow you to lose a document that may be forgotten on the Doc 2 screen. When you exit WordPerfect and clear the Doc 1 screen, the Doc 2 screen will appear and ask if you'd like to save the document there.

SUMMARY

In this lesson you learned to block a section of text and to do a number of things to the text once it has been highlighted.
- Delete the block of text.
- Restore deleted text (the last three deletions are available).
- Format the text with Block, Underline, or Italics (or any of the other character appearance attributes in the Appearance menu).
- Move or copy the text from one place in your document to another or to a different document.
- Exchange the columns in a tabular document.
- Access the Document 2 screen and use it to move blocked text from one document to another.
- Split the screen so you can see Doc 1 and Doc 2 at the same time.

The Block feature is one of the most important word processing editing tools. You should be good at it! It is recommended that you reread the information in this lesson one more time before you leave it so you have this skill well in hand.

LESSON 13 NOTES:

LESSON 14
Page Formatting

OBJECTIVES

Upon completion of this lesson, you will be able to:

1. Format pages using headers and footers.
2. Number the pages of your documents automatically.
3. Use miscellaneous page numbering features such as Suppress and New Page Number.
4. Center text from top to bottom on the page.
5. Adjust the top and bottom margins of your document.

Estimated Time: 1 ½ hours

PAGE FORMATTING

Look at the book in front of you. Turn to a page that isn't the first page of a lesson and notice the information included at the tops of the pages. These pieces of information are known as *headers*.

The left-hand page is *always* the even-numbered page. In this book, the header includes a page number set all the way to the left. Next to the page number is the name and number of the unit. This is an even-numbered page header, and you will find that the same format is used throughout the book on the left-hand pages.

The right-hand page is *always* the odd-numbered page. Here you will find a header that includes the page number, all the way to the right, preceded by the lesson number and name.

Much of the work you do when you create multiple-page documents will be formatted differently from what you see here because most business documents aren't printed with facing pages. Instead, the documents are printed on one side of a page and fastened together at the left. Therefore, you will have little need for odd and even headers.

Page Formatting in WordPerfect

WordPerfect provides many options for how a page will print. All of the options presented in this lesson have default settings that the software developers thought would be most practical. In most cases you can use those settings. We'll work with most of the Page Format features.

Choose **Page** from the Layout menu.

Strike **Shift-F8** and then **2 Page** to display the Page Format menu. It should look much like Figure 14-1. We will jump around in this list of features. When you've studied the items in the menu, strike the space bar to close the menu.

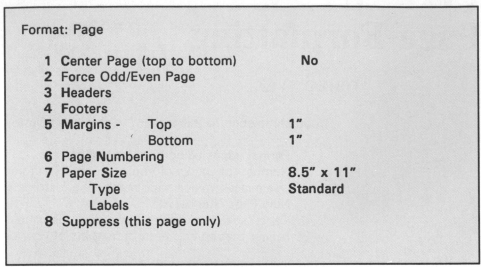

Figure 14-1

HEADERS AND FOOTERS

Headers are the text that appears at the top of pages to tie a document together. The headers may identify the page, document, chapter, etc. Footers are similar text printed at the bottom of the pages. Here are some important miscellaneous facts about WordPerfect headers and footers.

- Two headers and two footers (a total of four) may be defined in one document.

- After selecting **3 H**eader from the Page Format menu, you'll work through a couple of levels of menus. The first looks like this:

  `1 Header A; 2 Header B: 0`

  Normally you will have only one header, so you'll probably select **1** for Header A. That will bring up a new menu:

  `1 Discontinue; 2 Every Page; 3 Odd Pages; 4 Even Pages; 5 Edit: 0`

  These menu items are pretty obvious. In this lesson, you will be working primarily with choice **2** Every **P**age. However, you will no doubt want to edit your header. To do that, you must choose **5 E**dit from the Page Format menu.

  The procedure for footers is the same except that you'll choose **4** Footer, and the footer will go at the bottom of the page.

- When you choose to define a new header or footer, the screen is cleared so you may enter the text. When you have finished keying each header or footer, you must strike **F7** to return to the Page

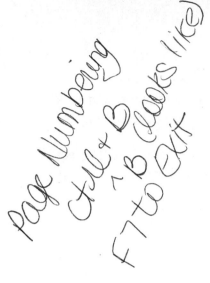

Format menu. From there you may exit to the working screen using Enter, F7, or the space bar.

- Many WordPerfect functions such as Margin Set, Center, Font changes, and Flush Right may be used in headers and footers.

- A header or footer may exceed one line in length. The first line of a header will print one inch from the top of the page. The last line of a footer will print one inch from the bottom of the page.

- WordPerfect automatically adjusts the number of lines of text on a page to make room for headers and footers. Both headers and footers are automatically separated from the text by 0.16 of an inch. (This is the equivalent of one blank line.) A one-line header plus the blank line following it decreases the number of text lines on the page by two.

- To take effect on the first page, header and footer functions must be entered at the beginning of the page. They MUST be before any letters, numbers, spaces, or returns. Develop the habit of striking Page Up before entering your headers and footers, even though your cursor appears to be at the top of the page.

- In the instances where you don't want the header or footer to appear on the first page, you will use Suppress on the first page. You'll do this later in the lesson.

- You can add automatic page numbering to documents from within the Header/Footer menu by moving the cursor to the desired location and striking **Ctrl-B**. In your document, it will look like this: **^B**. Although page numbering can be added independently from the Header or Footer feature, adding your page numbering to a header or footer enables you to include text with the page number. For example, you could key **Section A, Page ^B**; and on page 4 of your document, it would print **Section A, Page 4**.

- Headers and footers are spell-checked along with your document.

- Headers and titles are two entirely different things. Here are definitions of each. Do not confuse them.

A *title* is the name of the document. It appears only on the first page of the document, where it is usually keyed two inches from the top of the page. Normally the title is keyed in all capital letters and separated from the text by a quadruple space. The title is considered to be part of the text.

A *header* may use the same words as the title of the document, but headers rarely appear on the first page of a document. (You'll learn soon how to suppress the header on the first page.) The header appears instead on other pages of the document, and it is normally keyed in lowercase letters with the first letter of important words capitalized.

You enter the header information only once, and it will affect all of the pages of the document. Create your headers using the procedures outlined in this lesson.

Now let's apply what you've learned about headers and footers in a short exercise.

Lesson 14 Exercise 1

Choose **Page** from the Layout menu.

1. Strike **Shift-F8** and choose **2** Page to open the Page Format menu.

2. Choose **3** Header, then **1** Header **A**, and then **2** Every **Page**. You will see a blank Header screen that prompts you to **Exit** when you are finished. It is on this screen that you will key your header.

3. Beginning at the left margin, key *Church Council Meeting*.

4. Give the Flush Right command and use the Date Text feature to insert the date. Follow the prompt to strike **F7** to return to your document. THE HEADER WILL NOT SHOW!

5. Return to the Page Format menu and choose **4** Footer, **1** Footer **A**, and then **2** Every **Page**. You are now on a screen that looks just like the Header screen with the **Exit** prompt at the bottom.

6. Center the following two lines:

    For Discussion Purposes Only
    CONFIDENTIAL

7. Strike **F7** to return to your document. THE FOOTER WILL NOT SHOW!

8. Reveal your codes and look at the Header and Footer codes. Add them to your list of codes.

9. Use Print Preview to see the header and footer in your document.

Congratulations! You have created your first header and footer for a document that doesn't yet exist. Let's add some text to this document. Then we'll try another exercise where you will add a header that includes a page number to one of the documents you created in Lesson 12. Follow along carefully (and have fun doing it!!).

Lesson 14 Exercise 2

(Template disk users: Refer to the box below before beginning.)

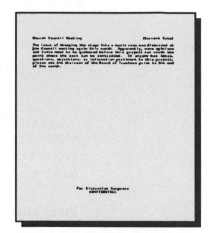

1. Check to be sure your cursor is *below* the Header and Footer codes. Then key the text in Figure 14-2.

2. Preview your document. It should look much like the thumbnail illustration shown here.

3. Use the speller to check the document. Proofread it carefully.

4. Print the document and exit from it, saving it as **council.142**.

TEMPLATE DISK USERS:

Retrieve only the paragraph for this exercise from the template disk. It is named **council**. Position your cursor ABOVE the paragraph to add the header and footer.

The issue of changing the stage into a music room was discussed at the Council meeting again this month. Apparently, more opinions and facts need to be gathered before this project can reach the point where the work can be contracted. If anyone has ideas, questions, objections, or information pertinent to this project, please see the chairman of the Board of Trustees prior to the end of the month.

Figure 14-2

Lesson 14 Exercise 3

1. Retrieve **license4.12r**. This review exercise from Lesson 12 has a title and is primarily double spaced. It is two pages long.

2. Reveal your codes to assure that your cursor is at the top of the document. (You can position the cursor above the codes by striking Page Up, even when your cursor appears to be at the top of the document.)

Choose **Page** from the Layout menu.

3. Choose Page from the Format menu and then Headers A and Every Page. On the header screen, key *Software Licensing*.

4. Give the Flush Right command and hold **Ctrl** while you strike **B**. The Page Numbering code ^B should appear.

5. Strike **F7** to return to your working screen. Use Print Preview to look at the document with the header. (You will first see page 1 because your cursor is on page 1.)

6. Strike **Page Down** to look at the second page of the document.

7. Use **F10** to save the document as **license.143**, but keep it open on the screen.

You may have noticed that the second page of the document looked pretty good with the header. The first page looked awful! That's because you are unaccustomed to seeing a header used like this. Normally headers don't appear on the first page.

You're doing well. Read on to find out how to make the first page more attractive.

SUPPRESS

Sometimes you won't want your headers or page numbers to appear on certain pages. The exercise you just completed is a good example. You may turn off the page numbering on those pages by placing the cursor at the top of the page(s) to be suppressed and choosing Option 8 in the Page Format menu.

The Suppress command only affects the page on which you place the code. This is different from headers and footers, where one header or footer affects the entire document.

When you strike **8** Suppress from the Page Format menu, you will see the menu illustrated in Figure 14-3.

```
Format: Suppress (this page only)

    1  Suppress All Page Numbering, Headers and Footers
    2  Suppress Headers and Footers
    3  Print Page Number at Bottom Center          No
    4  Suppress Page Numbering                      No
    5  Suppress Header A                            No
    6  Suppress Header B                            No
    7  Suppress Footer A                            No
    8  Suppress Footer B                            No
```

Figure 14-3

Normally the first choice—Suppress All Page Numbering, Headers and Footers—will work best for your work in this course. If you wish to try other choices, feel free to experiment. Let's use Suppress in the Legal Software document.

Lesson 14 Exercise 4

1. With **license.143** showing on the screen, check to be sure your cursor is at the top. (It may be before or directly after the Header code.)

2. Go to the Page Format menu and open the Suppress menu. Choose **1** Suppress All . . . .

3. Strike **Enter** or the **space bar** to return to your document. Use Print Preview to see if the header no longer appears at the top of the first page. Strike **Page Down**. Is it still on the second page?

4. Return to the top of your document on the working screen and look at the Suppress code. Add it to your list.

5. Use **F10** to save the document as **license.144**. Do not print it just yet. Keep it on the screen for the next exercise.

Headers and footers can easily be edited. The procedure is simply to return to the header or footer and make the desired changes. Let's practice on the document you have on the screen.

Lesson 14 Exercise 5

1. Return to the header by going to the Page Format menu. Choose Header, Header A, and, instead of choosing **2** for Every Page, choose **5** for Edit.

2. Change the header so it reads *Legal Software*.

3. Preview and print your document with the edited header. Then exit from it, saving it as **license.145**.

PAGE NUMBERING

Page numbering can be included in your document without the use of headers or footers. This is done with **6** Page Numbering from the Page Format menu. You will see a menu that looks much like Figure 14-4.

```
Format: Page Numbering

   1  New Page Number          1
   2  Page Number Style        ^B
   3  Insert Page Number
   4  Page Number Position      No page numbering
```

Figure 14-4

Choice **4** gives you a smorgasbord of choices for the location of the page number and opens a menu that looks much like Figure 14-5.

Choose **Page** from the Layout menu.

Go to the Page Format menu now and choose **6 Page Numbering**. Then select **4 Page Number Position** and study the menu. When you finish, strike **F7** to close the menu without changing the settings.

If you choose **3**, your page number will always appear at the top right. If you choose **6**, your page number will always be centered at the bottom of the page. If you have facing pages, where printing is on both sides of a page, you may wish to choose **4** for the numbers at the top or **8** for the numbers at the bottom, etc. Let's practice.

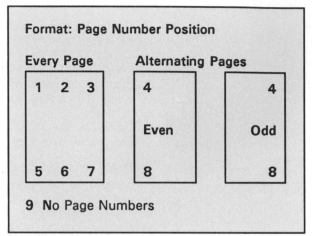

Figure 14-5

Lesson 14 Exercise 6

1. Again, open **license4.12r**.

2. With your cursor at the top of the document, go to the Page Format menu. Choose Page Number and then Page Number Position.

3. Key **6** to center the page number at the bottom of each page.

4. Return to your document and use Print Preview to see your centered page numbers.

5. Record the code in your list. Then print the document and exit from it, saving it as **license.146**.

As you can see, it is not difficult to add page numbers to your documents. No matter how long a document is, WordPerfect is able to number the pages according to your needs.

NEW PAGE NUMBER

The New Page Number feature is a useful one for renumbering the pages in your documents. If you have the chapters of a multiple-page document in separate files, you can put a New Page Number code at the top of Chapter 2 that gives the continuing page number for your document. For example, if Chapter 1 is 18 pages long, you could use the New Page Number feature to begin numbering Chapter 2 on page 19.

Every time you open the Page Number menu, a New Page Number code is inserted into your document. You might want to use Search to look for a stray New Page Number code when your pages aren't numbering correctly.

CENTER PAGE (Top to Bottom)

The first item in the Page Format menu enables you to give a short document even top and bottom margins. If you have display material or text that you would like centered vertically on the page, you will select this function.

Like Headers, Footers, and Suppress, this code must be placed above any characters, numbers, etc., that are keyed on the page. Otherwise WordPerfect will ignore the command. Even a hard return or a space will prevent the command from working.

You can verify that this option has been chosen by using print preview to look at your document. When you print, if the paper is properly aligned in the printer, your text will have even top and bottom margins.

Lesson 14 Exercise 7

1. Go to the Page Format menu and change the setting for Center Page to Yes. Reveal your codes and look at the code. Add it to your list.

2. Key the short paragraph in Figure 14-6.

3. When you finish, use Print Preview to see how your paragraph looks centered on the page. Then print it and exit it, saving it as **center.147**.

```
This is a paragraph to be centered on the page from top to
bottom.  The user of WordPerfect will have to select the
page format menu to get the computer to perform this
centering.  This option should be set before the user begins
to key the paragraph.  In order to see if it works, the user
will then have to use print preview or print the paragraph.
The paragraph will not appear to be vertically centered on
the screen.
```

Figure 14-6

Now let's try a more practical exercise using the Center Page feature. Again, we will use the *Legal Software* document. This time we'll use the version of it to which you added a header earlier in the lesson. We'll also include a New Page Number code in this document.

Lesson 14 Exercise 8

1. Retrieve **license.145**.

2. Strike **Page Up** so your cursor is above all codes in the document and strike **Ctrl-Enter** for a hard page break.

3. Strike ↑ to move your cursor above the page break.

4. Go to the Page Format menu and give the Center Page (top to bottom) command. Then key the information included in Figure 14-7. Strike **Enter** as desired between the items so they are attractively spaced.

5. When you are finished, proofread carefully. Then use Print Preview to see how your title page looks. Strike **Page Down** and look at the **Pg** prompt in the status line. WordPerfect now thinks the first page of your text is page 2 of the document. This is incorrect because the title page of a document should not be counted with the others.

6. Reveal your codes and position the cursor below the hard page break on either side of the Header code.

7. Go to the Page Format menu and choose Page Numbering and then New Page Number. The feature is prompting you that you are on page 1. That's fine. Strike **Enter** and return to your document. Now you have a three-page document where the third page is actually page 2. Are you confused?

8. Print your document. Then exit from it, saving it as **license.148**.

```
                    LEGAL SOFTWARE



                         by

                   (your name)



                  (current date)

                Word Processing 1
              (your instructor's name)
```

Figure 14-7

TOP AND BOTTOM MARGINS

The final feature for this lesson is Top and Bottom margins. Occasionally, as in Exercise 5 where you centered the page number at the bottom, you might want a smaller bottom margin. Let's practice.

Lesson 14 Exercise 9

1. Open **license.146**. Strike **Page Up** to reposition the cursor above the codes.

2. Go to the Page Format menu and choose **5 Margins**. Your cursor will be moved to the setting for the top margin. Strike **Enter** to leave that setting at one inch.

3. With your cursor at the setting for the bottom margin, key **.5** for a half-inch and strike **Enter**.

4. Return to your working screen and preview the document. Then print only the first page of the document. Do this by positioning the cursor on page 1 and striking **Shift-F7**. Instead of striking **1** for the full document, strike **2** for the current page.

5. Exit from the document saving it as **license.149**.

SUMMARY

What a lesson! You learned many good things about formatting multiple-page documents in this lesson, such as:

- headers
- footers
- page numbering
- the Suppress feature
- top and bottom margins

You will have an opportunity to review most of these features in the review exercise that follows the end-of-lesson activities. The only really important feature from this menu that you didn't learn is the Paper Size/Type feature. Lesson 26 is mostly devoted to working with paper of different sizes. You'll be there soon!

COMMAND SUMMARY

Now let's review your commands. You have learned many of them since the last review at the end of Lesson 9. Go through the list and see if it includes any features you need to review.

Feature	Function	Menu	Lesson
Block	Alt-F4 or F12	Edit	13
Center page	Shift-F8, P	Layout, Page	14
Copy	Ctrl-F4	Edit, Copy	13
Dot Leaders	Alt-F6, Alt-F6	—	12
Footers	Shift-F8, P	Layout, Page	14
Headers	Shift-F8, P	Layout, Page	14
Hyphenation	Shift-F8, P	Layout, Line	12
Justification	Shift-F8, L	Layout, Line	12
Left/Right Margins	Shift-F8, L	Layout, Line	11
Line Spacing	Shift-F8, L	Layout, Line	11
Move	Ctrl-F4	Edit, Move	13
New Page Number	Shift-F8, P	Layout, Page	14
Page Format	Shift-F8, P	Layout, Page	14
Page Number	Ctrl-B	Layout, Page	14
Print Preview	Shift-F7, V	File, Print	12
Restore	F1	Edit	13
Speller	Ctrl-F2	Tools	10
Suppress	Shift-F8, P	Layout, Page	14
Switch	Ctrl-F3	Edit	13
Tab Set	Shift-F8, L	Layout, Line	11
Thesaurus	Alt-F1	Tools	10
Top/Bottom Margins	Shift-F8, P	Layout, Page	14
Widow/Orphan Prot.	Shift-F8, L	Layout, Line	12

LESSON 14 NOTES:

Name _____ Date _____

TRUE/FALSE

Each of the following statements is either true or false. Indicate your choice in the Answers column by circling T for a true statement or F for a false statement.

Answers

1. The words **Blocked Text** will flash on the status line when you have the Block function turned on. (Les. 13, Obj. 1) . . . .   1. T F

2. After Block is turned on, the block of text can be defined by striking a unique character. (Les. 13, Obj. 1) . . . .   2. T F

3. When you have blocked a word or several, you can add a format like bold or underline to that text. (Les. 13, Obj. 2) . . . .   3. T F

4. You can "cut and paste" your document using the Move function. (Les. 13, Obj. 3) . . . .   4. T F

5. Both the Switch and Screen features make the Document 2 screen available to you. (Les. 13, Obj. 4) . . . .   5. T F

6. Most page formatting changes should be made with the cursor in the upper left corner of the document. (Les. 14, Obj. 1) . . . .   6. T F

7. Headers and footers may be edited after they are keyed. (Les. 14, Obj. 1)   7. T F

8. WordPerfect will automatically print numbers on the pages of a multiple-page document. (Les. 14, Obj. 2) . . . .   8. T F

9. You can tell WordPerfect not to number certain pages of your documents. (Les. 14, Obj. 3) . . . .   9. T F

10. In WordPerfect, the default top and bottom margins are set at one-half inch. (Les. 14, Obj. 5) . . . .   10. T F

COMPLETION

Indicate the correct answer in the space provided.

Answers

1. How does a blocked section of text appear on the screen? (Les. 13, Obj. 1) . . . .   1. _____

2. What is the limit to the size of the block of text you can select? (Les. 13, Obj. 1) . . . .   2. _____

3. What must you give a block of text if you wish to save it as a document? (Les. 13, Obj. 2) . . . .   3. _____

4. Which would you select, Move or Copy, if you wanted to transfer a section of text from one place in a document to another? (Les. 13, Obj. 3) . . . .   4. _____

5. How do you tell WordPerfect how large you'd like the Doc 1 split screen to be? (Les. 13, Obj. 4) . . . .   5. _____

6. Which key combination accesses the Page Format menu? (Les. 14, Obj. 1) . . . .   6. _____

7. A total of how many headers and footers may be defined for one document? (Les. 14, Obj. 3) . . . .   7. _____

8. What is the key combination that will put automatic page numbering into a header or footer? (Les. 14, Obj. 3) .   8. _____

9. What feature would you use to change the page number on the third page of a document to Page 1? (Les. 14, Obj. 3) . . . .   9. _____

10. What happens to the top and bottom margins of a short document when you use the Center Page command? (Les. 14, Obj. 4) . . . .   10. _____

REFERENCE

Turn to the Block section of the *WordPerfect Reference* and learn about another method of moving text. What three kinds of text are automatically blocked by WordPerfect AFTER you strike **Ctrl-F4**?

_____

How many characters of a Header or Footer may be viewed using Reveal Codes?

_____

Review Exercise

(Template disk users: Refer to the box below before beginning.)

1. Key the document in Figure 14-8 in manuscript format. That includes the following formatting:

    a. One-inch margins on all sides of all pages. (The default margin settings are fine.) The exception is the first page, where you should strike **Enter** six times to give the document a 2-inch top margin.

    b. Quadruple space following the title.

    c. Five-space paragraph indents. (The default tab settings are fine.)

    d. Double spacing throughout.

    e. Side headings at the left and displayed in bold.

2. Save the document with the name **pc-care.14r**, but keep it on the **screen** for the revisions that follow the figure.

TEMPLATE DISK USERS:

1. Retrieve **pc-care**.

2. Add the title and the formatting in the steps both above and below Figure 14-8.

3. Save and print the document as directed.

Enter 6 X S

2 in CARING FOR YOUR PC

Congratulations! It has finally arrived! That new computer you've been eagerly (and apprehensively) awaiting has just been installed! The software is loaded, and you're all ready to start creating documents and "crunching" numbers.

Today's personal computer (PC) enables us to perform many of our office tasks efficiently and with great ease. In many ways, we're much better off now than when we were using typewriters and calculators for those tasks. PCs, however, are sometimes a curse as well as a blessing. Who, for example, appreciates his or her computer when it breaks down in the middle of a critical job?

While it's impossible to foresee and eliminate all disasters due to PC breakdowns, there are some things you can do to protect your computer and your data.

Equalize the Power

Fluctuations in electricity cause many problems with electronic equipment. Even our lights vary in intensity, although we often don't notice it. A surge suppressor between your PC and the outlet will equalize the power coming to your PC and give it some protection.

Surge suppressors come in all sizes and prices. They don't have to be costly to be effective, although the more expensive the device, the more protection it will provide. Some cost as little as $20.

Keep Your PC Clean

Avoid eating or drinking around your PC. Food crumbs and liquid spills are damaging to the keyboard. Even ordinary dust has a way of gumming up the works, although most computers can handle an average amount of dust without too much trouble.

The disks that you insert into your computer should also be kept clean. While today's 3.5-inch disks are protected from dirty fingers, anything that you put into that central processing unit can carry dirt into the computer.

Prevent Burn-in

If your computer is on all day, the pixels in certain parts of the window are constantly lit. After several months, you may notice an annoying image of those words, letters, or symbols even when those words or images aren't displayed.

Commercial screen savers can be set to blank the screen after a set number of minutes that the computer is idle. In the absence of a screen saver program, you can turn down the brightness and intensity of your screen when you are going to be away from the PC for a time.

Defuse Static Electricity

Take precautions against the damaging effects of static electricity. When you "zap" a filing cabinet, doorknob, or other metal object, you're carrying as much as 15,000 volts of electricity. The delicate microcircuitry of your PC is no match for that kind of abuse.

Antistatic carpeting and furniture, proper grounding, carefully monitored air humidity, and good common sense will all help eliminate PC problems caused by static electricity.

Make Backups

Finally, when you've exhausted the list of precautions to prevent PC breakdown, know that computers, like most kinds of equipment, do break down. Protect yourself by backing up critical data.

Make backups of the programs you use. Make backups of the documents prepared using those programs. Make backups of the utility files that keep your computer working the way you want it to work. Personalized files like *config.sys* and *autoexec.bat* are often overlooked in the backup process and are difficult and time consuming for the average PC user to recreate.

Keep an extra set of backups in a safe off-site location to protect important company data against loss due to fire, tornadoes, earthquakes, flooding, monsoons, and hurricanes (depending on your geographic region).

Summary

Utilize every opportunity to learn about your computer and the different ways it can help you work. Take classes, read magazines, and join groups of other computer users where you can share your knowledge and learn from others. As a whole, you will find that with proper use and proper care, your PC will give you years of trouble-free service and enjoyment.

Figure 14-8

1. Add a header and page numbering to the document. (Remember to go to the top of the first page to do this.)

   a. The header should say *PC Care*, and it should be positioned at the left.

   b. The page number should be in the upper right corner. It may be part of the header, or you may insert the page number using the Numbering feature.

2. Suppress the header and the page number on the first page. Protect your document against widows and orphans.

3. Spell-check your document. Then proofread it thoroughly for any errors the speller might have missed.

4. Print the document. Save it with the name **pc-care.14r** and close the document.

LESSON 15
Footnotes and Endnotes

OBJECTIVES

Upon completion of this lesson, you will be able to:

1. Include footnotes in your documents.
2. Include endnotes in your documents.
3. Edit your footnotes or endnotes.
4. Discuss footnote and endnote options.

Estimated Time: 2 hours

In technical writing, footnotes and endnotes are used to identify some of the sources of the information used in a report. Footnotes are usually numbered consecutively, and each footnote appears on the bottom of the page where the resource is referenced. Footnotes are completely different from footers, where the same text appears at the bottom of each page of a document.

WordPerfect helps you create footnotes simply and accurately. If you have ever keyed a document with footnotes and struggled to get them just right (with the correct note on the correct page with the proper spacing everywhere), you will appreciate this feature in WordPerfect. Footnote numbering is automatic, footnotes are properly placed, and endnotes can even be placed in your document—either in place of footnotes or in addition to them.

FOOTNOTES

Choose Footnote from the Layout menu.

Begin with **Ctrl-F7** to open the Footnote menu. Your first choice will appear as follows: **1** Footnotes; **2** Endnotes; **3** Endnote **P**lacement. Choose **1** Footnote. The following menu gives you four choices:

    1 Create; 2 Edit; 3 New Number; 4 Options

When you choose **1** Create, the Footnote screen appears for you to key the footnote. Only the footnote number shows when you first access the screen. The Footnote screen is much like the blank Header/Footer screen with which you worked in Lesson 14. Until you key the footnote, it is empty except for the number.

After keying the footnote, strike **F7** to return to your document. You will notice that a number automatically is inserted in your document at the location of the cursor. Since the footnote number will be inserted at the cursor when you choose Create Footnote, remember to consider the following:

- WordPerfect automatically inserts the footnote numbers. Do not key the footnote number in the text or in the footnote.
- If you want the reference number in the manuscript to appear tight against the preceding text in the proper manner, DON'T SPACE before choosing Footnote and Create.
- Since WordPerfect knows you want the first line of each of your footnotes to be indented one-half inch, you don't need to worry about that. It is automatically taken care of.
- Footnotes generally appear with a superscript number—the number a half space above the line. WordPerfect sends this instruction to the printer, and most printers are able to comply.
- Do not strike Enter at the end of a footnote. WordPerfect automatically inserts one blank line between footnotes.

When keying a footnote, you can do most of the things you do with regular word processing. For example, you can use Italic, Underline, and Bold, and you can edit as usual. The computer will sound a warning if you try to do something that is not allowed.

When preparing a document containing footnotes, you cannot see the footnotes in the document. Reveal Codes will show you a portion of each footnote; however, you can't do anything with the footnotes or endnotes in Reveal Codes except see that they are there or delete them. You CAN see your footnotes in Print Preview.

In most cases, it is best to insert the footnotes as you key the document. In other words, key to the point where the reference number is to appear. Then create a footnote at that position. The number will automatically be inserted. You may also key the document and then go back and insert the notes. Let's try a simple footnote exercise.

Lesson 15 Exercise 1

1. Key the short paragraph in Figure 15-1. Set double spacing at the beginning of the document. Remember that line endings will vary according to the printer chosen.

2. When you come to the footnote reference number, don't key the numeral. Instead, create a footnote using these steps.

    a. Strike **Ctrl-F7**. Then choose **1 Footnote** and **1 Create**.

    b. Key the text of the footnote on the special Footnote screen. You do not need to key either the reference number in the text or the footnote number. Key the name of the book in italics.

    c. Follow the prompt to strike **F7** to return to your document. Finish keying the paragraph.

3. Use Print Preview to see how your document looks with a footnote.

Choose **Footnote** from the **Layout** menu.

4. Turn on Reveal Codes and look at the Footnote code. Add it to your list of codes.

5. Print your short document. Then save it with the name **footnote.151**, keeping it on the screen for the next exercise.

This is a paragraph that contains a footnote. The footnote number is here.[1] This is the sentence that follows the footnote. It is a thrill to discover how easy footnotes can be!

(Here is the text for the footnote:)

[1]Mary Makebelieve. *Practice Footnotes*, (Larsen: Ann Street Press, 1992), p. 85.

Figure 15-1

EDITING FOOTNOTES

You can return to the Footnote menu and choose **2 Edit** to edit a previously keyed footnote. When you choose Edit, a prompt asks you for the number of the footnote you wish to edit. WordPerfect will take you to the Footnote screen. When you finish editing in the normal manner, use Exit to return to your document.

Lesson 15 Exercise 2

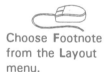

Choose Footnote from the Layout menu.

1. Strike **Ctrl-F7** and choose **1 Footnote** and then **2 Edit**. If the Footnote Number prompt shows any number except **1**, key **1** and strike **Enter**.

2. When the footnote appears on the screen, change the page number to **25**. Change *Mary* to *Maria*.

3. Strike **F7** to exit the footnote. View your document (with the footnote) using Print Preview.

4. Print a copy of the revised document. Exit from the document, saving it with the name **footnote.152**.

Now that you know how easy it is to create and edit footnotes, let's try a real exercise.

Lesson 15 Exercise 3

Key the document in Figure 15-2. Format the report as follows:

1. Key *Electronic Documents* (no italics!) as the header to appear on all pages except the first. Number the pages at the top right. Turn on Widow/Orphan protection.

2. Using Caps Lock and Center, key the title two inches from the top of the paper followed by a quadruple space.

3. Key the document using double spacing.

4. Create a footnote wherever a number appears. The footnote text is displayed for you at the bottom of the document.

5. Use Print Preview to check your document with footnotes before printing. Check to make sure the header and footnotes are correct.

6. Proofread your document and check your work with Spell. Then print the document and exit from it, saving it as **telemail.153**.

ELECTRONIC DOCUMENT DISTRIBUTION

In the same way that telecommuting provides a working alternative to millions of Americans and bulletin board access to millions more, the capability of our computers to communicate via telephone lines has provided an alternative in terms of document distribution.[1] Letters and other documents that once had to be sent by mail or by private courier service now can be sent instantly from one location to another anywhere in the world via telecommunications.

The result is instant delivery rather than a two- or three-day delay. The cost of telecommunications is higher than ordinary mail services unless the communication takes place at night, when the phone rates are considerably lower. Most computers can be programmed to send and receive at night, while the boss and the workers are partying or at home sleeping.

Document distribution by telecommunication is not a new and novel idea. Television, newspapers, and magazines have used wire service communications for a number of years.[2] Indeed, computers of all sizes have been technically equipped for electronic communications for quite some time. What's different in the '90s is that the capabilities of the networks to carry these communications have been improved greatly, making telecommunications available to anyone with the right equipment.

For an individual or a company to telecommunicate by computer, the right equipment includes modems to change the computer's digital signal to analog (for the telephone) and back again. In the near future, with the advent of the Integrated Services Digital Network (ISDN), modems will no longer be necessary because telephone networks will be digital rather than analog. Communications software is also needed. It is the communications software that enables you to tell your computer to dial a telephone number, to send, and to receive electronic documents.

Telecommunication networks vary from large, high-priced services where the incentive is primarily profit, down to smaller, low-priced services located in individual homes where the incentive is more altruistic.[3] Businesses usually subscribe to the larger, world-wide networks.

(The Footnotes)

[1]Dana Tracy, "Telecommunications—More Than Good English," *Floor Avenue Report*, January 6, 1992, p. 14.

[2]"Digital Communications in the '90s," *Timely Technology*, July, 1992, p. 24.

[3]Chuck Tomasen, "Bulletin Board Mania," *Home Computing Journal*, December, 1991, p. 44.

Figure 15-2

ENDNOTES

Endnotes are created like footnotes. The major difference between endnotes and footnotes is their location. Footnotes are placed by Word-Perfect at the bottom of the page on which the note number occurs. Endnotes come at the end of a document, usually on a separate page.

If you want the endnotes on a separate page at the end of the document, you must put a hard page break (Ctrl-Enter) after the last paragraph of the document. You will probably want to format that page with the word *ENDNOTES* about two inches from the top of the paper, followed by a quadruple space.

The creation of endnotes is handled almost exactly like the creation of footnotes. When you are ready to place an endnote in your document, position the cursor at the location for the endnote and follow these steps.

Choose Endnote from the Layout menu.

- Strike **Ctrl-F7** and choose **2** Endnote. Then choose **1 Create**. The endnote number will appear followed by a period.
- To indent the text of the endnote, strike **F4**. Then key the text of the endnote.

As in the case of footnotes, the text screen is cleared while you key the endnote. Strike **F7** to return to your document. Endnotes are edited in exactly the same manner as footnotes.

Now let's add endnotes to the document about the care and feeding of PCs that you created at the end of Lesson 14.

Lesson 15 Exercise 4

1. Open **pc-care.14r**. Add endnotes to the document by positioning the cursor for the endnote, then following the steps above for endnote

creation. The endnotes are illustrated in Figure 15-3, and the locations for those endnotes are shown below.

a. Endnote 1 at the end of the first paragraph in the section about *Equalizing the Power*.

b. Endnote 2 following the sentence about *commercial screen savers* in the second paragraph of *Prevent Burn-in*.

c. Endnote 3 following the sentence telling about the *15,000 volts*.

d. Endnote 4 following the second paragraph under *Make Backups*.

---

1. Freddy Keelowatt, "Power Up," *PC Prognostigators*, April 1991, p. 42.

2. "Pixel Protectors," *Timely Technology*, July 1990, p. 61.

3. Keelowatt, *Op. Cit.* p. 37.

4. Hiam Halpa, "Better Backups," *Timely Technology*, January 1992, p. 61.

Figure 15-3

---

2. After the final paragraph, insert a hard page break followed by the word *ENDNOTES* which you should capitalize and center approximately two inches from the top of the page. Change from double spacing to single spacing so your endnotes aren't double spaced like the manuscript. Leave a quadruple space after the heading.

3. Strike **Ctrl-F7** and choose Endnote Placement. At the prompt about restarting numbering, key **Y** for Yes. A message about the amount of space the endnotes will occupy will appear. You may ignore it.

   Use Reveal Codes to find and delete the Hard Page code at the bottom of the document below the endnote placement message; otherwise an extra blank page will print. The Endnote Placement code tells WordPerfect where to print the endnotes, so it should always be positioned where you want your endnotes listed.

4. With your cursor on the endnotes page, use Print Preview to see how the page will look when printed.

5. Proofread, save the document as **pc-care.154**, and print it. You may leave it on the screen for the next exercise. Check over your hard copy over carefully to see that all of your formatting is done correctly.

FOOTNOTE AND ENDNOTE OPTIONS

The footnotes and endnotes in the documents you prepared in this lesson were pretty straightforward. Most footnotes and endnotes are. Sometimes, however, you may want to format your footnotes a little differently. So WordPerfect gives you some alternate choices.

New Number. Footnotes and endnotes are usually numbered consecutively. However, there are times when you might wish to change the numbering. For example, you may have one document broken into two different files. Or you might want to restart footnote numbering for each chapter in a book.

Simply position the cursor to the left of the footnote or endnote number you wish to change. Choose New Number from the Footnote or Endnote menu. Then key the new note number at the prompt.

Other Options. In the Options menu for footnotes or endnotes you can change the character, the dividing line between the footnote and the text on the page, and a host of other variables. The menu is simple to use for formatting footnotes and endnotes according to your needs.

OTHER FOOTNOTE AND ENDNOTE INFORMATION

Some other general information about footnotes and endnotes should be of interest to you.

- If you wish to delete a footnote or an endnote, simply move the cursor to the note number in your text and delete it. WordPerfect will delete the footnote number and text for that number and will automatically renumber the remaining footnotes or endnotes.

- Sometimes your editing involves a text move that affects the numbering of footnotes. This happens when you delete or move text or when you add notes. WordPerfect will automatically renumber the notes. However, if you've used Latin terms such as *Ibid.* or *Op.Cit.*, you will want to check to be certain that the content and order of the notes are correct.

- Since your footnotes and endnotes don't show on the screen as you are keying your document, it is often easy to overlook errors in them until the document is printed. The obvious solution is to make an extra effort to proofread each footnote or endnote as you key it—before you leave the Note screen. You could also use Spell to check the note.

Lesson 15 Exercise 5

Follow the steps below to edit Endnote 3 of **pc-care.154**.

1. Choose Edit from the Endnote menu.

2. You will be asked which endnote you would like to edit. Key **3** and strike **Enter**. On the Endnote screen, change the page number to page **73**. Exit from the editing screen.

3. Print only the page with the error by positioning the cursor on the page with endnotes and choosing **2 Page** in the Print menu.

4. Save the document as pc-care.155 and exit from it.

Lesson 15 Exercise 6

In this exercise you will prepare a cover page for CARING FOR YOUR PC similar to the one you prepared for the software licensing exercise in Lesson 14. Follow these additional steps for your cover page.

1. Retrieve **pc-care.154.** Position the cursor at the top of the document above all codes. (You can do this by positioning the cursor on the first page and striking **Page Up**. You may want to use Reveal Codes to be absolutely certain the cursor is above everything.)

2. Strike **Ctrl-Enter** to insert a hard page break. Move the cursor to the left of (above) the Hard Page code.

3. Prepare the cover page as directed in Exercise 8 of Lesson 14. Include the correct name of the new document and the current date. Don't forget to put the New Page Number code at the top of the first page of the text so the pages are numbered correctly.

4. Resave the document as **pc-care.156** and close it.

SUMMARY

This lesson was full of practice with some of the WordPerfect features that make manuscript preparation so easy. In this lesson you did the following:

- Created footnotes and endnotes in new documents as well as added them to old documents
- Edited footnotes and endnotes
- Printed individual pages of a multiple-page document
- Reviewed headers and page numbering and learned to use the New Page Number feature

All of these features should be highly useful to you as you prepare reports and papers for your other classes.

LESSON 15 NOTES:

LESSON 16
Tables

OBJECTIVES

Upon completion of this lesson, you will be able to:

1. Discuss table terminology.
2. Create a table using the WordPerfect 5.1 Tables feature.
3. Format a WordPerfect table.
4. Import a Lotus spreadsheet into a WordPerfect table.

Estimated Time: 2 hours

Now let's learn about a WordPerfect feature called Tables. The Tables feature helps you place your information into columns using graphic lines to divide the information. The first table you will create in this lesson will end up looking much like Figure 16-1. Isn't it pretty?

EMPLOYEES BY DEPARTMENT		
Personnel	Accounting	Marketing
Mai Xiong	Brenda Smith	Emily Jones
Cornelius Karlton	Esther Franklyn	Alfonzo Allen
Josie Jackson	William McCabe	Su Chung
Diane Dirk	Kathy Kushman	Valerie Mitchell
Sheila Sorenson	Frank Lorenzo	Jonathan Verkuilen

Figure 16-1

TABLE TERMINOLOGY

A table looks much like a spreadsheet. The terminology is similar. Here are some terms peculiar to the use of spreadsheets.

Columns. Vertical collections of information are called *columns*. Columns are labeled with letters (e.g., A, B, C).

Rows. Information is arranged horizontally into *rows*. Rows are labeled with numbers.

Cells. The point at which a row meets a column is called a *cell*. Each cell is said to have an *address* that identifies the row and the column where that cell is located. Cell addresses help refer to a particular cell. For example, the cell where Row 3 meets Column B is called B3.

When working with a table, the cursor becomes as large as the size of the cell in which it is located. Also, an additional piece of information is added to the status line telling the address of the cursor at a given time.

CREATE A TABLE

Let's practice as you learn. We'll begin by creating a simple table and putting some text into the columns.

Lesson 16 Exercise 1

Create a table.

Choose Tables from the Layout menu.

1. Strike **Alt-F7** for the Columns, Tables, Math menu. From that menu, choose **2 Tables** and then **1 Create**.

2. You will be prompted to enter the number of columns desired in your table. The default is **3**. That is OK, so strike **Enter**.

3. You will be prompted to enter the number of rows desired in your table. The default is **1**. Change that number to **5** and strike **Enter**.

4. Your first table will appear on the screen. Actually it is a simple grid containing three columns and five rows that looks like Figure 16-2 (without the identification for the rows and columns). The address in the status line says your cursor is in **Cell A1**. Note that the cursor is quite large—in fact, it fills the entire cell.

	A	B	C
1	▓▓▓▓▓▓▓		
2			
3			
4			
5			

Figure 16-2

5. Study the menu at the bottom of the screen.
   When you create a table, you enter what's known as the *table editor*. While in the table editor, you may make changes to the table using the features in the menu at the bottom of the screen. You cannot key anything into the table while in the table editor, but you can change the sizes of the cells, put headers in the cells, do math, or

reformat the cells in any number of ways. The table editor is illustrated in Figure 16-3.

```
Table Edit: Press Exit when done     Cell A1 Doc 1 Pg 1 Ln 1.14" Pos 1.12"
--------------------------------------------------------------------------
Ctrl-Arrows Column Widths; Ins Insert; Del Delete; Move Move/Copy;
1 Size; 2 Format; 3 Lines; 4 Header; 5 Math; 6 Options; 7 Join; 8 Split:
```

Figure 16-3

6. Use the arrow keys to move the cursor around in your table. Use Tab and Shift-Tab to move the cursor. Move the cursor back to cell A1.

7. Strike **F7** to exit the table editor. Your cursor will remain in Cell A1, but it looks like a normal cursor.

Lesson 16 Exercise 2

Add text to the table.

1. To add text to the table, key *Mai Xiong* and strike the **Tab** key once. Key *Brenda Smith* and tab once. Key *Emily Jones* and tab once. Do NOT strike Enter at the end of a row. If you strike Enter, it will make the cell bigger. Use Backspace to delete hard returns keyed in error.

2. Continue keying the names in Figure 16-4 until you have all the names keyed, each in a different cell of the table.

Mai Xiong	Brenda Smith	Emily Jones
Cornelius Karlton	Esther Franklyn	Alfonzo Allen
Josie Jackson	William McCabe	Su Chung
Diane Dirk	Kathy Kushman	Valerie Mitchell
Sheila Sorenson	Frank Lorenzo	Jonathan Verkuilen

Figure 16-4

3. Your table now includes text. Reveal your codes and move around in the table. Find the Table Definition code. Add it to your list. Note that the items in your table are separated with [Cell] codes rather than Tab codes and that there is a [Row] code at the beginning of each row.

4. Use **F10** to save your table. Use the name **table2** (because it's from Exercise 2). You will be recalling this table for a later exercise.

Setting up that table was easy, wasn't it? The best part was that you didn't have to do any figuring. The columns were automatically set up. In this first table, the columns were set up evenly. You can easily change the sizes of columns. You can also decide if you want the table to extend to the margins and whether there should be lines around the cells.

Before we make any of the changes mentioned above, let's take this table a couple of steps further by adding headings.

Lesson 16 Exercise 3

In the next couple of exercises, you will be adding to the table and formatting it. These steps will take you through quite a number of menus in the table editor. Look at some of the other options in the editor as you go.

Add rows and key the headings.

1. First, we'll add two rows. Move your cursor to Cell A1. Strike **Alt-F7**. This time you were taken directly into the table editor because your cursor is in the table. Press **Ins** or **Insert**. WordPerfect will ask if you wish to insert **1** Rows or **2** Columns. Strike **1** Rows.

2. You will be asked how many rows you wish to add. Respond with **2** since we will add column headings and a main heading to this table. Strike **Enter**. Note that what was once Row 1 is now Row 3.
   The rows are added at the cursor. If you wanted to add rows elsewhere in the table, you would begin by positioning the cursor at the location where you wished to add the rows.

3. Move your cursor to Cell A2. Strike **F7** to exit the table editor. Key *Personnel*. Then tab to the other cells and key *Accounting* and *Marketing* as the other column headings.

4. Move your cursor to Cell A1. Strike **Alt-F7** to return to the table editor. Turn on Block and strike **End** to block all of Row 1.

5. Strike **7** Join to join all three cells into one. Key **Y** to confirm.

6. Exit the table editor. Be sure the cursor is in Row 1. Key *EMPLOYEES BY DEPARTMENT* in caps.

7. Your table should look much like Figure 16-5. Save it as **table3**, but keep it open on the screen.

EMPLOYEES BY DEPARTMENT		
Personnel	Accounting	Marketing
Mai Xiong	Brenda Smith	Emily Jones
Cornelius Karlton	Esther Franklyn	Alfonzo Allen
Josie Jackson	William McCabe	Su Chung
Diane Dirk	Kathy Kushman	Valerie Mitchell
Sheila Sorenson	Frank Lonzo	Jonathan Verkuilen

Figure 16-5

FORMAT A TABLE

In the next portion of this long table exercise, you will be making many formatting changes to your table. Most of the formatting will be done from within the table editor. You have learned to position your cursor somewhere in the table before striking **Alt-F7** to enter the table editor and to strike **F7** to exit the table editor. You will be doing this often, because you must exit the editor to work with the text, to look at your table with Print Preview, and to save your table.

Lesson 16 Exercise 4

Adust the column sizes and center the table horizontally.

1. Move the cursor to Cell A2 and return to the table editor. Hold the **Ctrl** key while you strike ← twice to make the first column smaller.

2. Tab to Column B and follow the same procedure to adjust the column size. You can make this column a few spaces smaller than the first because there are no long names.

3. Finally, adjust Column C. Be careful not to go too far. If *Verkuilen* drops to the next line, use **Ctrl** → to make it larger again. The longest name in each column should fit comfortably within that column when you finish adjusting column sizes.

4. Choose **6** Options from the menu at the bottom. In the menu that appears, choose **3** to adjust the position of the table. From the line menu at the bottom of the screen, choose **3** Center.

5. Return to your working screen and use Print Preview to look at your table. Is it centered horizontally between the side margins?

6. Do an interim save of your table as **table4**.

Lesson 16 Exercise 5

Center the headings and change the table lines.

1. Return to the table editor and block the first two rows (the heading rows) of the table. You may do it with the mouse or by positioning the cursor in Row 1, turning on Block, and striking ↓ once.

2. From the menu, choose **2** Format, then **1** Cell, and then **3** Justify. Choose **2** Center to center the text in both rows within their cells.

3. Block the entire table. Choose **3** Lines and **6** Outside. At the choice of lines, choose **6** Thick. Your lines will look strange on the screen!

4. Block Row 2 (column headings). Choose **3** Lines, **3** Top, and **6** Thick.

5. Exit from the table editor. Block the main heading. Strike **Ctrl-F8** for Font. Choose **1** Size and **7** Ext Large.

6. Use Print Preview to look at your table. Does it look like Figure 16-1? Print your table. Exit from it, saving it as **table.165**.

TABLE MATH

Now let's change the table in a different way. Turn to Figure 16-11 and study it. It shows the first quarter, second quarter, and mid-year sales figures for the five top salespersons in the company. That's what the table will look like when you finish with it.

We could start from scratch with a new table, but it is good practice for you to manipulate the size of a table. We'll begin by keeping only the names in the first column. Then we'll add numerical amounts for those people and figure a total using the Math feature. Finally, we'll add headings to the table and to the columns. There are a lot of steps. Follow along carefully.

Lesson 16 Exercise 6

Change table size and structure and add text.

1. Retrieve **table2**, move the cursor into the table, and enter the table editor.

2. Move the cursor to Cell B1. Block all of Columns B and C. Delete them by striking **Del** or **Delete**. You will have to confirm the deletion of columns. Your table should look like Figure 16-6.

| Mai Xiong |
| Cornelius Karlton |
| Josie Jackson |
| Diane Dirk |
| Sheila Sorenson |

Figure 16-6

3. Move your cursor to Cell A1. Hold the **Ctrl** key while you strike → as many times as necessary to make the column the full width of the page. (When you reach maximum size, the column will stop growing.)

4. Now we'll split the one remaining column into four columns. Block the entire table. Then tell WordPerfect you would like to split the table into four columns: Choose **8** Split, **2** Columns, and key **4**. Strike **Enter**. You'll notice that the columns are separated with double lines rather than single lines. You will also notice that some of the names take two lines because they are too long for the first column.

5. Move your cursor to somewhere in the first column. Hold **Ctrl** while you strike →. Stop when all of the names are back on one line.

6. Just in case you mess up, exit the editor and do an interim save of your table. Call it **table2.6**. Your screen will look like Figure 16-7.

7. Return to the table editor. Change the double lines between columns to single lines by blocking the entire table. Then choose **3 Lines, 5 Inside, 2 Single**. Save your table, again calling it **table2.6**.

Mai Xiong			
Cornelius Karlton			
Josie Jackson			
Diane Dirk			
Sheila Sorenson			

Figure 16-7

Lesson 16 Exercise 7

Add dollar amounts, format them, and total them.

1. Figure 16-8 shows this same list of five names with amounts entered for the first and second quarterly sales. Exit from the table editor and key the numbers into Columns B and C. Do an interim save of your table, calling it **table2.7**. (It should look like Figure 16-8.)

Mai Xiong	550.00	385.90	
Cornelius Karlton	625.75	431.80	
Josie Jackson	499.25	1,605.50	
Diane Dirk	379.80	275.60	
Sheila Sorenson	495.40	540.00	

Figure 16-8

2. Those money figures look awful when positioned at the left of the cell. We'll decimal justify them so they are more attractive. Column D will also contain money figures, so we'll decimal justify that column, too.
    Use **Alt-F7** to return to the table editor. Place the cursor in Cell B1. Block all of columns B, C, and D.

3. Choose **2 Format**. Then select **1 Cell, 3 Justify** from the menu at the bottom of the screen, and **5 Decimal Align**. All of your numbers should be aligned at the decimal. Do an interim save, again calling it **table2.7**.

4. Now we'll total the sales for Mai Xiong. Use **Alt-F7** to return to the table editor. Move the cursor to Cell D1. Select **5 Math** and **2 Formula** to enter a formula in this cell. Key the formula **b+c** and strike **Enter**. The numbers should be added. (The amount in Column D will align correctly because you set that at Decimal Justification earlier.)

5. Copy that formula to the other cells in Column D by selecting **5 Math** and **3 Copy formula**. Then select **2 Down**. You will be asked how many times you would like to copy the formula. Key in **4** and strike **Enter** since there are four more cells in Column D.

6. In order to give emphasis to the column with the mid-year totals, let's shade the entire column. Block Column D. Then select **3 Lines** followed by **8 Shade** and **1 On**. You won't be able to see the shading on the screen.

7. Use print view to look at the table. It should look like Figure 16-9. Do an interim save of the table, once more calling it **table2.7**.

Mai Xiong	550.00	385.90	935.90
Cornelius Karlton	625.75	431.80	1,057.55
Josie Jackson	499.25	1,605.50	2,104.75
Diane Dirk	379.80	275.60	655.40
Sheila Sorenson	495.40	540.00	1,035.40

Figure 16-9

Your table is taking shape, but it's not finished yet. Let's make it look pretty before we add a row for the totals and give it some headings.

Lesson 16 Exercise 8

Adjust the column size and center the table.

1. Position your cursor in Column D1. Use **Ctrl ←** to make the column narrower so that the numbers are snugly contained.

2. Make Columns B and C approximately the same width as Column D.

3. Choose **6 Options** and center the table.

Lesson 16 Exercise 9

Add rows for headings and totals.

Now practice what you learned in earlier exercises. This table of sales representatives needs headings, and those headings should be created in additional rows at the top of the table.

1. Add two rows to the top of the table for headings, like you did in Exercise 3. Both rows will appear with 0.00 because of the totals in Column D. Exit the table editor and delete those figures.

2. Join the cells in Row 1 to center the main heading there. Center the column headings in Row 2. Figure 16-10 shows the headings to use.

3. With the cursor in Row 1, choose **3 Lines**, **6 Outside**, and **1 None** to remove the lines around the title. Exit the table editor and move the cursor to the end of the title. Strike **Enter** to add some space below it.

QUARTERLY AND HALF-YEAR SALES EARNINGS

| Salesperson | First | Second | Mid-Year |

Figure 16-10

4. Position the cursor in the bottom row of the table and enter the editor. You will add one more row for totals, and this procedure is different.

5. Choose **1 Size** and **1 Rows**. Change the prompt to **8** and strike **Enter**. (When you adjust the size of a table with Size, the rows are added at the bottom.)

6. In the Cell A8 (beneath Sheila), key *Totals*.

7. Position the cursor in Cell B8. Choose **5 Math** and then **4** or **+** to add the numbers in Column B. Add Columns C and D the same way. Because the columns are decimal aligned, the totals are affected, too.

8. Does your table look like Figure 16-11? Save it as **table2.9**.

QUARTERLY AND HALF-YEAR SALES EARNINGS

Salesperson	First	Second	Mid-Year
Mai Xiong	550.00	385.90	935.90
Cornelius Karlton	625.75	431.80	1,057.55
Josie Jackson	499.25	1,605.50	2,104.75
Diane Dirk	379.80	275.60	655.40
Sheila Sorenson	495.40	540.00	1,035.40
Totals	2,550.20	3,238.80	5,789.00

Figure 16-11

Think about what you've accomplished in this table. You probably don't remember all the steps, but the Table Editor menu is very helpful. If you needed to do the same things again, you might be able to do most of it without having to look back at the steps for each procedure.

But wait! When checking your work, you find that an error has been made. Diane Dirk's second quarter sales should have been 375.60 instead of 275.60. That change will have to be made and the totals adjusted.

Lesson 16 Exercise 10

Amend the table.

1. Move the cursor to Cell C6 and change the amount to 375.60.

2. Enter the table editor and choose **5 Math** and **1 Calculate**. Watch the mid-year and second quarter totals adjust. Are you impressed?

3. Save your finished table as **table16.10** and print it.

Lesson 16 Exercise 11

Look at Figure 16-12. This is what the table you just prepared would look like if you prepared it on a typewriter. If you want to fool your boss into thinking you slaved over the typewriter, you can remove all of the lines from your table, add an extra Enter here and there for vertical spacing, remove the shading, and add some underlining (with Cell Formatting).

You know enough about tables to do most of those things without help. There are two sticky steps in converting **table16.10** to this format. Look below the figure for some help with formatting.

QUARTERLY AND HALF-YEAR SALES EARNINGS

Salesperson	First	Second	Mid-Year
Mai Xiong	550.00	385.90	935.90
Cornelius Karlton	625.75	431.80	1,057.55
Josie Jackson	499.25	1,605.50	2,104.75
Diane Dirk	379.80	375.60	755.40
Sheila Sorenson	495.40	540.00	1,035.40
Totals	2,550.20	3,338.80	5,889.00

Figure 16-12

• To add the underlines in the column headings and the columns above the totals, choose the Underline feature as follows: **2 Format**, **1 Cell**, **2 Attributes**, **2 Appearance**, **2 Undrln**.

  Then exit from the table editor, position the cursor under the *4 of 495.40* in Column B, and strike the space bar twice to get the underline the same length as the total. Do the same for Column C. The line length for Column D is OK.

- Block the entire table and set all lines at none. When you do this, the table will appear to be double spaced. Choose **6 O**ptions and change the Top portion of the Spacing to 0".

Play with the table until it looks like Figure 16-12. Then save your "typewriter-appearing" table as **table16.11** and print a copy. You should be getting VERY good at tables by now. Close the document.

There are times when you want to convert something that has already been keyed in columns into a table. WordPerfect provides you with that capability. Let's try it with the list of colors you created in Lesson 11.

Lesson 16 Exercise 12

1. Retrieve **colors.116**.

2. Block the entire document. Then strike **Alt-F7** and choose **2 T**ables and **1 C**reate. You will be asked if you wish to create the table from tabular columns or from parallel columns. Choose **1 T**abular Columns.

3. Voila! Your colors are now in a table. If you had a hard return at the bottom of the document, your table will have an extra row. You can position the cursor in that row and delete it. Don't save the document.

Lesson 16 Exercise 13

Create a table of your own choosing. Perhaps you'd like to make a list of phone numbers for your friends and family. Or you could make a list of the courses you're taking and the grades you'd like to earn in those courses. Then you can study the list daily for inspiration. Could you use the Tables feature to prepare your weekly or monthly budget?

Give your table some special formatting. Remember that shading and a variety of lines add emphasis to parts of your table. Your production test at the end of this unit will include a small table. In it you will be expected to use formatting that will make the table attractive. Any practice you get before the test will help you on the test.

SPREADSHEETS

WordPerfect has made it possible for you to import worksheets prepared in the popular spreadsheet programs like Excel, Lotus 1-2-3™ and Quattro Pro™. To import a spreadsheet into WordPerfect 5.1, simply retrieve the spreadsheet. It will enter your WordPerfect document in table format. From there you can reformat the worksheet to meet your needs.

A worksheet named **calories.wk1** is on the template disk. If you are using the template disk or if you have other worksheets you've prepared, you might wish to experiment with opening a worksheet in WordPerfect.

MORE MATH

The math you used in the tables in this lesson involved only simple addition. Formulas can be more complicated. You won't work with them here, but it is good to know that you can figure extensions, for example, by multiplying the quantity times the price. With the proper formula, you can also figure sales tax and add that to your total.

The following operators are used for totalling columns:

+ Subtotals the numbers above it
= Totals the subtotals
* Provides a grand total

The following functions are used in formulas:

+ Add
- Subtract
* Multiply
/ Divide

The Table, Math section of the *WordPerfect Reference* covers that topic thoroughly. An exercise is also included in the *WordPerfect Workbook*. If you discover that you need to work with math, you will find this feature very useful.

SUMMARY

While it seems like you MUST have learned everything there is to know about tables, you've barely scratched the surface. You have learned to create tables, increase the size of a table, enter text and numerals into a table, add the numbers in columns and rows, adjust the size of the cells, format a table with shading, create a table from tabular columns, and make a table look like it was prepared on a typewriter. (That last one is a questionable achievement!)

Look for opportunities to use tables in your work. You will find that the Tables feature will enhance the appearance of your documents and will make your work much easier.

LESSON 16 NOTES:

TRUE/FALSE

Each of the following statements is either true or false. Indicate your choice in the Answers column by circling T for a true statement or F for a false statement.

Answers

1. WordPerfect automatically numbers footnotes. (Les. 15, Obj. 1) . . . . . .   1. T   F

2. Footnote text does not appear on the screen with the document. (Les. 15, Obj. 1) . . . .   2. T   F

3. Endnotes are created in a manner similar to that used to create footnotes. (Les. 15, Obj. 2) . . . .   3. T   F

4. You may edit your footnotes in Reveal Codes. (Les. 15, Obj. 3) . . . . .   4. T   F

5. Footnotes may be numbered with letters or other symbols. (Les. 15, Obj. 4) . . . .   5. T   F

6. A row is a vertical collection of information in a WordPerfect table. (Les. 16, Obj. 1) . . . .   6. T   F

7. You have the option of determining how many columns and rows will be in the table when you create it. (Les. 16, Obj. 2) . . . .   7. T   F

8. Once your table is established, it is not possible to add rows or columns to that table. (Les. 16, Obj. 3) . . . .   8. T   F

9. If you wish to center a table horizontally, you must choose Table Options. (Les. 16, Obj. 3) . . . .   9. T   F

10. You may use Math in a WordPerfect table. (Les. 16, Obj. 4) . . . .   10. T   F

COMPLETION

Indicate the correct answer in the space provided.

Answers

1. What is the key combination that tells WordPerfect you wish to create a footnote? (Les. 15, Obj. 1) . . . . . .   1. _____

2. What happens to the screen when you indicate that you are ready to key a footnote? (Les. 15, Obj. 1) . . . . .   2. _____

3. Do the endnotes automatically print on a page by themselves following the manuscript? (Les. 15, Obj. 2) . .   3. _____

4. What key do you strike when you have finished editing a footnote? (Les. 15, Obj. 3) . . . .   4. _____

5. Do you need to change a default to get the footnotes to print at the bottom of the page? (Les. 15, Obj. 4) . . .   5. _____

6. What is the term used to name the place where a column meets a row? (Les. 16, Obj. 1) . . . .   6. _____

7. What portion of your working screen identifies the address of your cursor when you are working on a table? (Les. 16, Obj. 2) . . . .   7. _____

8. How do you adjust the size of a column in a WordPerfect table? (Les. 16, Obj. 3) . . . .   8. _____

9. Which item must you choose from the menu of the table editor to change the kind of lines surrounding the cells in a table? (Les. 16, Obj. 3) . . . .   9. _____

10. What was the result of the simple formula (b+c) used in the table in the lesson? (Les. 16, Obj. 4) . . . .   10. _____

REFERENCE

Turn in the *WordPerfect Reference* to the section about Footnotes. How do Footnotes affect the amount of Text Space on a page?

_____

_____

Look through the Tables, Create section of the *Reference* until you come to the part about placing tables in Columns. How can you put a table in either a newspaper or a parallel column?

_____

Ctrl Enter

Spanish 54 → 3 type Lesson 3

LESSON 17
Text Columns

OBJECTIVES

Upon completion of this lesson, you will be able to:

1. Format documents using newspaper columns.
2. Format documents using parallel columns.

Estimated Time: 1½ hours

You learned in Lesson 16 that the WordPerfect Tables feature is an excellent way to arrange your tabular material into columns. You will use Tables to prepare much of what you will key into columns. There are a number of other ways to arrange work into columns. You can:

- figure and set tabs as you would on a typewriter
- use newspaper columns for text
- use parallel columns for text or numeric data

Newspaper and parallel columns are lumped together in WordPerfect under the Columns heading, a feature that is accessed with Alt-F7 or by choosing Columns from the Layout pull-down menu. On some jobs there is little use for WordPerfect columns. On others, columns are an important part of the work to be done. Let's learn about them, one at a time.

NEWSPAPER COLUMNS

Newspaper columns are side-by-side columns of text that flow from one column to the next. When you finish formatting a document with newspaper columns, your document will resemble a page of a very small newspaper, as shown in the illustration here. WordPerfect does all the work for you and allows you as many as 24 columns.

Lesson 17 Exercise 1

(Template disk users: Refer to the box on page 190 before beginning.)

1. Key the paragraphs in Figure 17-1. Strike **Home, Home, ↑** to return to the beginning of the document.

One of the features that has made WordPerfect such a popular text editor is the columns feature. The WordPerfect columns feature enables you to create as many as 24 side-by-side columns.

One kind of WordPerfect column is the newspaper column, where the text snakes (wraps) from the bottom of one column to the top of the next. The other kind of WordPerfect column is known as a parallel column, where related sections of text can be printed side by side across the page.

With both kinds of columns, WordPerfect assumes equal column sizes and figures the column margins within whatever text margins are set. The default settings allow a half-inch space called a "gutter" between columns. Text can be added to or deleted from that in the columns, and the integrity of the columns is not destroyed.

Figure 17-1

Choose **Columns** from the **Layout** menu.

2. Open the Define Columns dialog box by striking **Alt-F7** and choosing **1 Columns**. Then choose **3 Define**.

3. This opens the Columns Define menu that looks much like Figure 17-2. For now, the defaults are acceptable. We'll discuss the menu later.

4. Strike **Enter** to leave the menu and display three choices at the bottom of the screen. Choose **1 Column On**.

5. Notice that **Col 1** has been added to the status line. Reveal your codes and look at the [Col Def] and the [Col On] codes. These codes must be at the beginning of the text to be formatted into columns.

Text Column Definition

			Column	Left Right
1 Type		**Newspaper**		
2 Number of Columns		**2**		
3 Distance Between Columns				
4 Margins				
Column	Left	Right	Column	Left Right
1:	1"	4"	13:	
2:	4.5"	7.5"	14:	
3:			15:	

Figure 17-2

TEMPLATE DISK USERS:

1.   Open **columns.171** and study it.
2.   Follow the steps of the exercise, excluding keying the document.

As you can see, any text can be converted to columns quite simply. Making it look good is also a simple process, and you'll find that there are a number of things you can to do enhance the look of columnar text.

Lesson 17 Exercise 2

1. Look at your long column aligned at the left margin. If the document had been longer than a column, it would have filled the first column and "snaked" to the second column. If you'd like your column evenly divided into side-by-side columns, you must tell WordPerfect where to divide it.

2. This column is 31 lines long. That means you need to divide it at the beginning of the sixteenth or seventeenth line. (Normally you will need to count the lines yourself.)

3. Position your cursor at the left of the ninth line of the second paragraph and strike **Ctrl-Enter**. Watch your text format into evenly spaced side-by-side newspaper columns.

4. Obviously, because of the short line length, there are big spaces between words. With the cursor at the beginning of the document, go to the Line Format menu and change Justification from Full to Left. Does that look better?

5. Return to the Line Format menu and turn on hyphenation. This should fill out the lines so it looks even better!

6. Print your lovely two-column document. Then exit from it, saving it as **columns.172**.

That was pretty easy, wasn't it? When you wish to move your cursor from one column to the other column, use **Goto (Ctrl-Home)** and then strike the right or left arrow key. For example, if you are in the left column and wish to move the cursor to the right column, you'd strike **Ctrl-Home** followed by →. If you have a mouse, you can move the pointer to the desired column and click the left mouse button.

Now let's go back to the Column Define menu and see what else you can do with your newspaper-style columns. We'll work with a longer document created in Lesson 14 and revised in Lesson 15.

Lesson 17 Exercise 3

Choose **C**olumns from the **L**ayout menu.

1. Open **pc-care.155** and move the cursor to the left margin, opposite the first line of the first paragraph. Find and delete the Double Space code.

2. Strike **Alt-F7** and choose **1** Columns and then **3** Define to open the Column Define menu. Note that the first choice enables you to set the column type. We'll work with that later in the lesson.

3. Item 2 deals with the number of columns. Choose that item and key **3** for the number of columns. When you strike **Enter**, the column margins are inserted automatically for three evenly-spaced columns.

4. Strike **Enter** to exit the menu. Choose **1 On** to turn on the Columns. You will be returned to the document. You may need to strike ↓ once to cause the document to be formatted into columns. Look at your three-column document.

Obviously, this practice format doesn't look very good for this document. Let's make some changes in the format of this document using the Column Define menu. We'll change the margins so you'll have two unevenly spaced columns and decrease the size of the gutter.

Lesson 17   Exercise 4

1. Reveal your codes and position the cursor just to the right of the Column Define code. Return to the Column Define menu and change the number of columns to **2**.

2. Choose **4 Margins** and strike **Enter** for the left margin of the first column. It is at the left margin, and that's OK.

3. Key **5** for the right margin of the first column and strike **Enter**.

4. Key **5.3** for the left margin of the second column and strike **Enter**. Strike **Enter** one more time to leave the right margin of the second at the margin.

5. Return to the document and adjust the hyphenation and justification, if you wish. Also, reveal your codes and delete the [Col Def] code on the left. That one is no longer needed.

6. Go to the last page of the text and find the right place to add a hard page break to even up the columns on the page. (If you don't do it exactly right, you can remove the [HPg] code and put it in a different place.)

7. Move the cursor to the end of the last paragraph. Remember to use **Ctrl-Home** followed by an arrow key to move from one column to another.

Choose **C**olumns from the **L**ayout menu.

8. Strike **Alt-F7** and **1 C**olumns. Turn Columns **2 O**ff. (If you don't do this, your endnotes will try to print in columns, too!)

9. Use Print Preview to check all pages of your document. Then print it. Exit from it, saving it as **pc-care.174**.

Let's try one more little exercise to see how well you understand the setup and manipulation of newspaper columns. You're pretty much on your own with this exercise. Can you make it beautiful?

Lesson 17 Exercise 5

1. Open **foreign.5-4**. Set it up with two newspaper columns, the left column two inches wide and the right column four inches wide. There will be a half-inch between columns.

2. Use hyphenation and left justification to enhance the appearance of the text.

3. Because the text is so short, you'll need to add a hard page break to split the columns. This will take some guesswork and probably some trial and error because the columns are not the same size. Remember that if you position the hard page break in the wrong place, you can remove it and add it in a different location.

4. When your little document is beautiful, with two evenly divided columns, print it and exit from it, saving it as **foreign.175**.

That's enough about newspaper columns for now. As you can see, you have great flexibility regarding the formatting of your documents in columns. You will get a better feel for what you can do with newspaper columns when you work with them. Now let's learn about a new kind of column—parallel columns.

PARALLEL COLUMNS

Parallel columns are used to prepare groups of information of varying lengths that are kept side by side on the page. Parallel columns might be used for scripts, inventories, itineraries, or other kinds of listings.

These are some characteristics of parallel columns that will help you set them apart from other kinds of columns.

- Column widths can be any size, as long as they fit on the paper. The column widths may be equal or unequal.
- You may have as many as 24 columns across the page.
- You must key an entire segment at a time. (A segment is all the text about a topic, for example the Employee Advancement Plan in Figure 17-3.) The information in that segment may be keyed continuously while the text wraps around within the column.
- Parallel columns may be set with or without Block Protect. Block Protect keeps segments from being broken from page to page.
- You may key column headings as if they were document segments, and they can be centered over the columns.
- In many cases, a document could be prepared more easily with Tables than with Parallel Columns.

Look at Figure 17-3. We will learn about parallel columns as we prepare this simple document.

Document	Description	Author
Employee Protection Plan	This document was prepared for the purpose of telling about the new employee protection plan devised for all employees of the organization. It was created on January 14, 1986.	Margaret Jones
Employee Assistance Plan	This document tells all about the Employee Assistance Plan put into effect to help employees in trouble. It was created on June 11, 1988.	Maria Rafferty
Employee Advancement Plan	This document is a guide to employees who wish to move up in the organization. It includes suggestions on how to grow enough for promotion and some cautions regarding how NOT to go about working for advancement. It was created on December 7, 1985.	Hermanson Hulk

Figure 17-3

Lesson 17 Exercise 6

1. Beginning on a clear screen, go to the Column Define menu and choose **1 Type**. Then choose **2 Parallel**.

2. Set the number of columns at **3**. Do not adjust the column margins just yet. (Your document will not look like Figure 17-3 when you key it because the column margins will be different. You'll fix that later.)

3. Exit from the Column Define menu and turn on Columns.

4. Give the center command, turn on Underline, and key *Document*. Turn off Underline, and strike **Ctrl-Enter** for a hard page break. Repeat the same procedure for *Description* and *Author*. The Hard Page command after *Author* will move your cursor to the left margin, a double space below the column headings. The headings should be centered over three evenly spaced columns.

5. Key *Employee Protection Plan* allowing the text to wrap to the next line when the line is filled. Strike **Ctrl-Enter**. Key all of the information under *Description* about the Employee Protection Plan. Strike **Ctrl-Enter**. Key *Margaret Jones* and strike **Ctrl-Enter**.

Choose **C**olumns from the Layout menu.

6. Continue keying chunks of text separated by Ctrl-Enter until the document is finished. Then strike **Alt-F7**, choose **1 Columns**, and turn off Columns.

7. Do an interim save of your document. Call it **parallel.176**, but keep it open for some more formatting.

In the newspaper column exercise, you adjusted the size of the columns by keying new column margins. We'll again adjust the size of the columns in this document to make the document more attractive.

Lesson 17 Exercise 7

1. Move your cursor back to the top of the document. Position the cursor just to the right of the Column Define code and go to the Column Define menu.

2. Change the column margins so the menu looks like the portion illustrated in Figure 17-4.

3. Use hyphenation and left justification to enhance the appearance of the document.

4. Return to your document screen. Make up a title for the document. Be sure to position the title ABOVE all column codes. Adjust the top margin so the document is attractive.

Text Column Definition

1 Type		**Parallel**
2 Number of Columns		**3**
3 Distance Between Columns		
4 Margins		

Column	Left	Right
1:	1.0"	2.17"
2:	2.5"	6.0"
3:	6.25"	7.5"

Figure 17-4

5. Visually check your document, and look at it using Print Preview. If it looks good, print it.

6. Exit from the exercise, saving it as **parallel.177**.

Lesson 17 Exercise 8

Now prepare the same exercise using the Tables feature instead of Parallel Columns. Remove all of the lines from the table except the underlines under the column headings.

See if you can make the two exercises look exactly alike. Print the exercise. Label the two exercises so your instructor will know which was prepared using Parallel Columns and which was prepared using the Tables feature.

One of the things you didn't encounter in your parallel columns exercises was spreading of words in narrow columns. If you choose to leave Justification set at Full, shorter words like *Maria* or *Employee* in Exercise 6 may spread across the width of the column when the text wraps from one line to the next. You can remedy this by striking **Enter** after those short words. This forces the words to the next line, and the problem of spreading is eliminated.

SUMMARY

This has been a quick introduction to text columns. You've learned to format text in newspaper and parallel columns. You've also learned to adjust the size of the columns to fit the needs of the application and to use hyphenation to improve the appearance of short lines of text.

As with so many of the other WordPerfect features about which you've learned, this sample should give you a good enough background so that you can explore and learn more about text columns when you need them in your work.

LESSON 17 NOTES:

Review Exercise

The document listing cruises in Figure 17-5 is the final exercise for this lesson. You may prepare it using Parallel Columns or using the Tables feature. Either way, make the document attractive. When you finish, print it and save it as **cruise.17r**.

This exercise includes some challenges you haven't encountered in your previous exercises. These challenges depend on whether you create the document as a table or as a parallel column exercise.

A list of some of the challenges and possible solutions follows the text for the exercise on page 198.

VACATION GETAWAYS

Dates	Description	Price[1]
October 4-8	Sail aboard the luxurious *Sunny Seasons* cruise ship from Miami to Freeport, Nassau, and St. Thomas. Enjoy white sand beaches, water sports, shopping, palm-fringed golf courses, and casinos.	$500
November 10-14	A West Coast mini-cruise from Los Angeles to Vancouver or Victoria. Limited port calls. Relaxation and fun aboard the *Pacific Rover* includes movies, cocktail parties, revue shows and musical entertainment, swimming, food galore, and exercise classes.	$550
January 3-7	See the Dome of the Rock in Jerusalem and Egypt's sphinx and pyramids on this 4-day Mediterranean mini-cruise. Sail aboard the spacious *Mediterranean Queen* through Port Said at the western tip of the Suez Canal.	$950 (includes airfare)
August 7-23	Board the *Atlantic Wayfarer* in St. Petersburg and cross the Atlantic with stops in Oslo, Copenhagen, Stockholm, Helsinki, Lisbon, and Barcelona. Return airfare from Genoa included.	$1450
January 19-25	Spend a week enjoying the benefits of the sea-going fitness center on the luxurious *Exersea*. Cruise from San Diego to Acapulco includes state-of-the-art fitness and exercise equipment, massages, whirlpool, health and beauty treatments, and daily fitness consultations. Return home looking and feeling revitalized!	$900

---

[1]Starting prices are based on double occupancy.

Figure 17-5

As a Table

- You can remove all lines and underline the column headings in the normal manner.
- Use the Footnote feature to give the starting prices information.
- You may format the first and third columns with Centering.

As Parallel Columns

- The footnote will have to be inserted, instead, as a footer. Key an asterisk (*) after the word *Price* and start the footer with another asterisk to match it. You can't put footnotes in parallel columns.
- You may wish to center each price and each date to make those columns look neat. Those will have to be handled individually.

LESSON 18
Outlining

OBJECTIVES

Upon completion of this lesson, you will be able to:

1. Use the WordPerfect Outline feature for outlines.
2. Use Outline for bulleted lists.
3. Use Outline for paragraph numbering.
4. Edit outlines of all types.

Estimated Time: 2 hours

As you know, WordPerfect has quite a number of features designed to make your work easier. You have already learned many of them. The feature covered in this lesson is automatic outlining. It can be a big help to you in the preparation of outlines.

> • This is an item in a bulleted list.
> • This is another item in the bulleted list.
> • This is item 3 in the list.

Bulleted List

The WordPerfect Outline feature does more for you than just make the creation of formal outlines easier. You can also use the feature for numbered paragraphs and bulleted lists. All three are illustrated here. Study the examples so you are familiar with their names and types. You will learn to create each of them.

In addition to the three types of outlines included in this lesson, the Outline feature can also be used to number paragraphs using a legal format. You will see the Legal option in the Outline Define menu, but it won't be practiced in this lesson.

After you've learned to create outlines, you will learn how easy it is to revise an outline by moving parts of the outline or by adding text to the outline or by deleting information from the outline. As you work with outlines, reveal your codes occasionally to see the WordPerfect codes for the different kinds of outlines.

> 1. This is level one, the first item in the numbered paragraphs.
>   a. This is level two, an item under the first item.
>   b. Another item at level two.
> 2. This is another first-level item in the numbered paragraph list.

Paragraph Numbering

AUTOMATIC OUTLINING

Outlines are commonly used to organize listed information and to present it in a straightforward manner. Outlines usually include several levels of information, as illustrated here.

Look at Figure 18-1. It is the outline you will prepare in Exercise 1, and it has three levels of information. The default settings of a tab stop every half inch will be used. Follow the steps in the exercise for this little outline. When working with outlines containing several levels, you must remember three basic rules.

```
I.    This is level one.
      A.   This is level two.
      B.   This is a second item in level
           two.
           1.   This is level three.
                a.   This is level four.
                b.   This is a second
                     item at the fourth
                     level.
```

Outline

- Always use **F4** to indent the text following a numeral.
- To change to a lower outline level, (e.g., from III. to A. or from B. to 1), strike **Tab**.
- To return to a higher outline level, strike **Shift-Tab**.

If you make an error in the levels when creating an outline, backspace to the end of the line above the error and begin again at that point.

```
I.    This is level one of the outline.  It is the first item
      at this level.  Note that it wraps automatically.

II.   This is the second item at the first level.

III.  This is the third item.

      A.   This is a level two item.
      B.   This is the second item at Level 2, the first
           indented level.
           1.   This is Level 3.  It, too, will wrap
                automatically because I used F4 to indent.
           2.   This is the last line that is indented. Now I
                will strike Enter and then Shift-Tab twice to
                return to Level 1 to put in the final item.

IV.   This is the final item of the outline.  Note that this
      outline has double spacing before and after the first
      level lines and single spacing elsewhere.  This is the
      customary spacing for outlines.
```

Figure 18-1

Lesson 18 Exercise 1

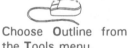

Choose **O**utline from the **T**ools menu.

1. Strike **Shift-F5** to open the menu you used for the Date feature. Note that the last three choices are as follows:

    4 Outline; **5** Para Num; **6** Define

2. For this first outline, the default definition is acceptable. Choose **4** Outline and then **1** On. The word **Outline** will appear in the lower left corner of your screen.

3. Strike **Enter**. The first numeral will appear.

4. Indent with **F4** and key the information for the first item in the outline in Figure 18-1.

5. Strike **Enter**. The second Roman numeral will appear. Strike **Enter** again to leave a blank line. Then strike **F4** and key the information for the second Roman numeral. Follow the same procedure for the third Roman numeral and then strike **Enter** twice.

6. Strike **Tab** once to change *IV* to *A*. Strike **F4** to indent and key the text in the figure. Continue to indent and key sections *A* and *B*. Tab once to indent to the next level for *1* and *2* and key those sections. Strike **Enter** twice following the text for *2*.

7. Strike **Shift-Tab** twice to change from *3* to *IV* and key the final section of the outline.

Choose **O**utline from the **T**ools menu.

8. Strike **Shift-F5** and choose **4** Outline. Choose **2** Off to turn off outlining. The word **Outline** should disappear from the lower corner of the screen. Reveal your codes and look through the outline at all of the codes included. Add the Outline codes to your list of codes.

9. Proofread your outline, save it as **outline.181**, and keep it showing on the screen.

Notice that the Roman numerals are not aligned at the period. This format is not especially attractive, and you'd be in trouble if the outline extended to item VIII because the numeral wouldn't fit. Let's align those numerals so that the periods following them are vertically aligned.

Lesson 18 Exercise 2

1. Move your cursor so it's at the beginning of Roman numeral *II*. Strike **Shift-Tab** to move the numeral back to the tab stop that's located halfway between the left edge of the paper and the left margin. (Remember, those tab stops are five spaces apart when you work with the 10-pitch default.)

2. Strike the space bar 4 times. (By tabbing backward 5 spaces and spacing forward 4 spaces, you've moved your numeral one space to the left.) The numeral is now aligned with the numeral above it.

3. Position the cursor at the beginning of the *III*. Repeat the same procedure, except this time only space forward three times. Are the numerals aligned?

4. Finally, align Roman numeral *IV*. How many times must you space forward to align this one?

```
I.   This is level
II.  This is the
III. This is the
```

5. Position the cursor at the top of the document above all codes and title it *MY FIRST OUTLINE*. Add returns so the title is two inches from the top of the page and is followed by a quadruple space. Print your outline and exit from it, saving it as **outline.182**.

BULLETED LIST

Bulleted lists are used for casual listings of items that don't need to be in any particular order. Bullets can be added to any WordPerfect document, which you'll learn about in a later lesson. In the bulleted list, however, they are inserted automatically.

To create a bulleted list using the WordPerfect Outline feature, you must define the list as a bulleted list. That choice is made by choosing **6 D**efine from the menu that appears when you strike **Shift-F5**. This opens a menu that looks much like Figure 18-2.

Paragraph Number Definition

1 - **Starting Paragraph Number**   1
   (in legal style)

	Levels							
	1	2	3	4	5	6	7	8
2 - Paragraph	1.	a.	i.	(1)	(a)	(i)	1)	a)
3 - Outline	I.	A.	1.	a.	(1)	(a)	i)	a)
4 - Legal (1.1.1)	1	.1	.1	.1	.1	.1	.1	.1
5 - Bullets	•	o	-	_	*	+	•	x
6 - User-defined								
Current Definition	I.	A.	1.	a.	(1)	(a)	i)	a)
Attach Previous Level		No	No	No	No	No	No	No

7 - **Enter Inserts Paragraph Number**   **Yes**

8 - **Automatically Adjust to Current Level**   **Yes**

9 - **Outline Style Name**

Figure 18-2

The menu is really quite simple. Note that in the figure the Current Definition is obviously set for an outline. You know that's true anyhow because you created an outline without changing any settings. When you select one of the other definitions, the listing in the Current Definition location will change to match the setting you choose. For now, the rest of the menu can be ignored. Let's try an exercise where you must change the definition. Look at Figure 18-3. It is a bulleted list of issues to be addressed in international business education. You'll change the definition and then key the list, much like you keyed the outline in Exercise 1.

Lesson 18 Exercise 3

Choose **O**utline from the **T**ools menu.

1. Strike **Shift-F5** and choose **6** Define to open the Define Paragraph Numbering menu.

2. Watch the Current Definition line as you key **5** or **B** to choose the Bullet definition. The numerals change quickly to a variety of bullets.

3. Strike **Enter** to close the menu. (The Shift-F5 line menu will remain on the screen.)

4. Choose **4** Outline from the menu and then **1** On to turn on your bulleted list style. The word **Outline** will appear in the lower left corner in its usual position because you are still working with an outline—just a different style.

5. Strike **Enter** for the first bullet to appear. Strike **F4** to indent following the bullet, and key the first item in Figure 18-3.

6. Continue keying the items in Figure 18-3. After keying the final item, turn off Outlining.

7. Proofread your list, print it, and exit from it, saving it as **global.183**.

- A knowledge of time zones.
- An understanding of major trade regions of the world.
- An understanding of the impact of geography on world trade.
- A knowledge of different monetary units and exchange rates.
- An understanding of the economics involved in the exporting and importing of goods.
- A knowledge of the metric system.
- An understanding of customs and the cultural differences between countries of the world.
- An appreciation of the different languages spoken in various countries.
- A general knowledge of the earth's continents and the countries located on those continents.

Figure 18-3

PARAGRAPH NUMBERING

Bullets were appropriate for the preceding list because the items don't need to be in any particular order. In other situations, however, it may be important for the items to be listed in a set order. For example, if the numbered steps in Exercise 4 were mixed up, you certainly would end up with some unexpected results!

Paragraph numbering is as easy as the bulleted list. We'll try a paragraph numbering exercise by keying the five steps in Exercise 4 as the text for the exercise. The numerals will be aligned at the left margin. You'll get lots of practice with Bold. Read through the entire exercise. (Remember, the exercise is the text you will be keying.) Then follow along carefully.

Lesson 18 Exercise 4

1. Open the Define Paragraph Numbering menu. Choose **2 Paragraph** to change to the paragraph numbering style. Watch the Current Definition line change.

2. Close the menu and turn on Outline. Strike **Enter** for the first numeral.

3. Strike **F4** to indent after the numeral and key the instruction for the first step above followed by a double space.

4. Continue keying until all five steps have been keyed. They should be separated by one blank line. Turn off Outlining.

5. Proofread your numbered items, print the document, and exit from it, saving it as **paranum.184**.

GENERAL NOTES

There are some general things to keep in mind as you work with outlines. Some of the information below is review; some is new information.

- You can begin the numbering in your outline with a number other than 1 or I by changing the number at the top of the Define Paragraph Numbering menu. Otherwise the number is always 1.

- A [Par Num Def:] code is placed in your document each time you open the menu and exit from it. This will cause a new number 1 in the middle of any outline or list. Randomly placed paragraph Define codes can give you some quirky results in your outline. (Keep your documents clean of unneeded codes!)

- You can interrupt an outline for any kind of text inserted between outline parts. Then you can resume the outline with the numbering continuing from above the interruption. Simply turn off Outline before the interruption and turn on Outline after it.

- Turn off Outline when the outline is complete. Otherwise you will continue to get numbers or bullets each time you strike Enter.

EDITING OUTLINES

One of the benefits of using WordPerfect automatic outlines is that they are easily edited. You can add information to your outlines as well as delete items and move items around. When you do, the outline will automatically renumber. That means you don't ever have to repair the numbering after revising the outline.

You may have noticed when you were turning Outlining on or off that the menu included some references to "family." The menu looked much like Figure 18-4.

```
Outline: 1 On; 2 Off; 3 Move Family; 4 Copy Family; 5 Delete Family:
```
Figure 18-4

Look at Figure 18-1. In this outline the text with *I* is a family. The text with *II* is a different family. Everything included under *III* is also a family. If you wanted to be more specific with the text under *III*, *A* is a family and so is *B*. Once you are comfortable with what is considered a family, you can do bulk editing of your outline. Let's practice.

Lesson 18 Exercise 5

1. Open **outline.181**. Position the cursor somewhere in the first Roman numeral section.

Choose **O**utline from the **T**ools menu.

2. Strike **Shift-F5**, choose **4** Outline, and then choose **3** Move Family. The entire text for the first Roman numeral will be highlighted.

3. Strike ↓ twice. Watch as the first section moves down in the outline. Although it is still highlighted, it is now section three, and the numerals are correctly reporting that fact. Strike **Enter** to accept the new placement of the first section. The highlighting will disappear. Move up through the outline and look at the result of your change.

4. Now, on your own, return the first section to the top of the outline by following the same procedure, except use ↑ to move the text up.

Choose **O**utline from the **T**ools menu.

5. Position your cursor somewhere in the first line of the third section. Strike **Shift-F5**. Then choose **4** Outline and **4** Copy Family. The entire section will be highlighted and copied immediately, so there will be two of them alike, one above the other. The numbers will also be adjusted, so your outline now has five items.

6. Strike ↑ twice and strike **Enter**. Check the numerals. You now have five items in your outline, and the first and fourth are the same. The difference between moving and copying a family is quite clear, and you

can see what WordPerfect considers a family. If you had positioned the cursor in the *A* line of Item III, only that individual line would have moved.

7. Now, with the cursor positioned in that renegade first item, return to the Outline menu and choose **5 D**elete Family to delete the entire extra item from your outline.

Sometimes when you are moving, copying, or deleting families of text from your outlines, sailing isn't quite so smooth. You need to know how to get yourself out of trouble when working with outlines. Whenever you're in the area of text between the Outline On code and the Outline Off code and you haven't given the command to move or copy text, striking **Enter** will add a numeral to your outline. Usually you can backspace to delete that numeral, and the remainder of the outline will be corrected. Let's see if we can cause ourselves some trouble with this outline.

Lesson 18 Exercise 6

1. Strike **Page Down** and reveal your codes to see how many hard returns follow the last item in the outline. If more than one are there, delete them. The only thing following the fourth item in your outline should be one [HRt] code and the [Outline Off] code.

2. Return your cursor to somewhere in the first item and go to the Outline menu, choosing **4 C**opy Family.

3. Strike ↓ four times, so the first item is copied to the bottom of the outline. Strike **Enter** to accept the copy. Move the cursor up a line and notice that the fourth and fifth items need a blank line between them.

4. Position your cursor at the beginning of that last item and strike **Enter** to add the blank line. You'll also get an extra numeral. Reveal your codes and look at the two [Para Num:Auto] codes in a row. You can delete either numeral with the Backspace key to fix your numbering.
   Had you revealed your codes and positioned the cursor immediately to the right of the [Para Num:Auto] code before striking Enter to add the extra blank line, the extra number wouldn't have appeared. It wasn't so difficult to correct, however.

5. Spend a few extra minutes moving, copying, and deleting parts of this outline. Watch what happens, for example, when you position the cursor in the *A* line and move it up! Feel quite free to mess up the outline, but pay attention to what you're doing and how you're doing it so that when you finish, you understand editing outlines.

6. Exit from the document without saving it.

In the same way that you can delete items from an automatically prepared outline, you can add items, and the numbering will take care of itself. How many times have you keyed a long numbered list, for example, and gotten to the bottom only to realize you forgot an item near the top? The solution is to position the cursor at the end of the item directly above where you need to add information and strike **Enter**. The new number will appear, the other items will renumber, and you can key the added information. Let's try it.

Lesson 18 Exercise 7

1. Retrieve **paranum.184**. We'll add your name as the second item in this numbered list.

2. Position the cursor at the end of the first step in the exercise (just to the right of the period).

3. Strike **Enter** twice (once to add the numeral and once for the blank line). A new number *2* should appear, and the remainder of the items in the list should renumber.

4. Strike **F4** to indent and key your name. Look at your new listing. Are you impressed?

5. Print the amended exercise. Exit from it, saving it as **paranum.187**.

SUMMARY

Well, that's what outlining and paragraph numbering are all about. By now you are probably pretty good at striking the Tab, Shift-Tab, and F4 keys in all the right places. You've created an outline and a bulleted list, and numbered your paragraphs, all using WordPerfect's Outline feature. What's more, you edited those outlines with a minimum of trouble. Congratulations!

You'll get a little more practice with outlining in Lesson 19, the review lesson that comes next. The review lesson contains a variety of exercises with which you will brush up on the skills you've been accumulating. Lesson 19 will be followed by a theory test and a production test.

Lesson 19 is also the end of the first half of your training. If you are in one long course, you will continue into Lesson 20 after your testing. If you are taking a series of two courses, Lesson 20 marks the beginning of the second course. Your instructor will explain the procedure for your continued training.

There are many exciting features in the next 17 lessons. They include working with Macros, Merge, and Sort. You will also learn to prepare envelopes and labels, and you'll have a whole section using the graphic features of WordPerfect. The material you've learned up to this point will be very important in the following lessons. You now have the basics, so you can move forward and have some real fun using WordPerfect to create your documents. Good luck!

COMMAND SUMMARY

Feature	Function	Menu	Lesson
Bulleted List	Shift-F5, D	Tools	18
Endnotes	Ctrl-F7, E	Layout	15
Footnotes	Ctrl-F7, F	Layout	15
Outline	Shift-F5, O	Tools	18
Paragraph Numbering	Shift-F5, P	Tools	18
Table Editor	Alt-F7, T	Layout	16
Table	Alt-F7, T	Layout	16

LESSON 18 NOTES:

Name _____ **Date** _____

TRUE/FALSE

Each of the following statements is either true or false. Indicate your choice in the Answers column by circling T for a true statement or F for a false statement.

Answers

1. WordPerfect allows you up to 36 newspaper columns at one time. (Les. 17, Obj. 1) . . . . 1. T F

2. To format a document using columns, you must turn on the Columns feature. (Les. 17, Obj. 1) . . . . 2. T F

3. If your text is long enough, newspaper columns "snake" from one column to the next. (Les. 17, Obj. 1) . . . . 3. T F

4. WordPerfect automatically figures the margins if you select evenly spaced columns. (Les. 17, Obj. 1) . . . . 4. T F

5. When keying parallel columns, you must key one line at a time all the way across the numerous columns. (Les. 17, Obj. 2) . . . . 5. T F

6. When preparing a WordPerfect Outline, you must manually key every numeral in the outline. (Les. 18, Obj. 1) . . . . 6. T F

7. The default numbering for Outline is bullets. (Les. 18, Obj. 1) . . . . . . 7. T F

8. You can number your paragraphs using the WordPerfect Outline feature. (Les. 18, Obj. 3) . . . . 8. T F

9. WordPerfect helps you revise your outline by enabling you to move all related segments at one time. (Les. 18, Obj. 4) . . . . 9. T F

10. If you add text in the middle of an outline that has already been keyed, you must manually change all of the numbering from the added material to the end of the outline. (Les. 18, Obj. 4) . . . . 10. T F

COMPLETION

Indicate the correct answer in the space provided.

Answers

1. What is the default for the distance between WordPerfect columns? (Les. 17, Obj. 1) . . . . 1. _____

2. How can you change the size of your column margins?
   (Les. 17, Obj. 1) . . . .   2. _____

3. How do you change from columns to a full-line text
   format? (Les. 17, Obj. 1) . . . .   3. _____

4. With which kind of columns do you key your text in a
   single long column? (Les. 17, Obj. 1) . . . .   4. _____

5. When keying text in columns, which command is used to
   end one column and move the cursor to the next one?
   (Les. 17, Obj. 2) . . . .   5. _____

6. Can the Center command be used to center headings over
   parallel columns? (Les. 17, Obj. 2) . . . .   6. _____

7. What kind of numerals are the default for WordPerfect
   Outlining? (Les. 18, Obj. 1) . . . .   7. _____

8. How do you key the bullets for a bulleted list? (Les. 18,
   Obj. 2) . . . .   8. _____

9. What happens to the numbering in an outline if you
   delete a section in the middle? (Les. 18, Obj. 4) . . .   9. _____

10. Name two or three uses that you can think of for the Columns and/or Outline features
    you've learned about in Lessons 17 and 18.

    _____

    _____

REFERENCE

In the Columns, Parallel section of the *WordPerfect Reference*, a comparison is made between
Parallel Columns and Parallel Columns with Block Protect. What is the example given for each
of these styles?

_____

Look in the *Reference* under Outline. What are the three sections of the *Reference* devoted
entirely to outlining?

_____

LESSON 19
Review and Practice

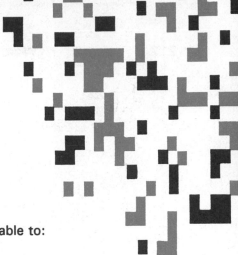

OBJECTIVES

Upon completion of this lesson, you will be able to:

1. Key, format, and edit a memo.
2. Key, format, and edit a letter.
3. Key a recipe.
4. Key, format, and edit a report.
5. Prepare a table.
6. Prepare a report with numbered paragraphs.
7. Prepare a document using columns.

Estimated Time: 3 hours

This lesson contains exercises that will reinforce what you have been learning in the previous lessons. It contains only a few documents that you will create, format, and revise. This practice will help you to prepare for Production Test 2.

If you have documents of your own that you would like to prepare in class, your instructor will probably encourage that activity. Whether you use the documents in this lesson or some of your own, you will be practicing your word processing skills using WordPerfect.

Try to work efficiently as you prepare these documents. Do as much as you can without referring back to earlier lessons. When you need help, look first at the resources in this book. Then, if necessary, ask your instructor. The Quick Reference Sheet can help you find information you need quickly. WordPerfect Help may also provide some assistance.

Always use Print Preview to check the format of your documents before printing. This will save you time and resources.

CREATING THE DOCUMENTS

You will create five documents—a memo, letter, recipe, report, and table.

Lesson 19 Exercise 1

(Template disk users: Refer to the box on page 212 before beginning.)

1. Use your memo form (memo.frm) to prepare the memo in Figure 19-1.

print all

2. Single space the body of the memo and double space between paragraphs. Begin the author's initials at **Pos 4"** followed by a double space and the enclosure notation.

3. When you finish, return to the top of the memo and turn on Hyphenation to even the lines.

4. Proofread, spell check, and print the memo. Save it as **manual.191**.

TEMPLATE DISK USERS:

Exercise 1: Use **memo.frm** to prepare the opening lines of the memo as directed. Then retrieve **manual**, which contains the body of the memo. Key the closing lines, print, and save as directed.

memo.frm

MEMORANDUM

TO: All Personnel
FROM: J. R. Jones
DATE: (current)
SUBJECT: Procedures

Attached are revised pages to be inserted into your departmental procedures manual. Please study each page carefully before inserting it in your manual.

You will notice that some pages are replacement pages and others are to be added to the end of an existing section. All new pages are appropriately numbered.

As you know, the company is fully committed to procedures manuals and feels that keeping them up to date contributes to the efficiency with which the company functions.

If you have any questions with these revised pages or the procedures manual in general, please call me at Ext. 247.

DOC CODE

Enclosure

Figure 19-1

Lesson 19 Exercise 2

(Template disk users: Refer to the box below before beginning.)

1. Key the letter in Figure 19-2. Since it is such a short letter, use a 5½-inch line. This means changing the margins to 1.5 inches from each side.

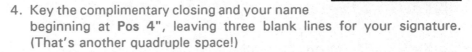

2. Position the date two inches from the top of the page at **Pos 4"**. Use the Date Text feature. Follow the date with a quadruple space.

3. Double space above and below the salutation. Single space the text and double space between paragraphs.

4. Key the complimentary closing and your name beginning at **Pos 4"**, leaving three blank lines for your signature. (That's another quadruple space!)

5. Add the enclosure notation a double space below your name. Position it at the left margin. Then print the letter and save it as **berry.192**.

TEMPLATE DISK USERS:

Exercise 2: Key the opening lines of the letter as directed. The body of the letter (berry) may be retrieved from the template disk. Key the closing lines, print, and save the letter as directed in the exercise.

Lesson 19 Exercise 3

(Template disk users: Refer to the box below Figure 19-2 before beginning.)

1. Key the report in Figure 19-3 in manuscript style. Center the title two inches from the top of the page followed by a quadruple space.

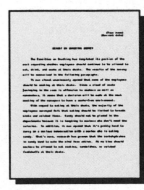

2. Double space the body of the report with no extra spaces between paragraphs.

3. Include a header, *Snacking Survey*, that appears with the page number at the top of all pages except the first.

4. Use the Table feature to center the columnar information between the last two paragraphs. Format the percent columns with right justification. Remove all lines from the table and underline column headings.

5. Print the report and save it as **food.193**.

(current date)

↓4 in

Mrs. Susan Sanderfoot
3346 Quiet Road
Olsonville, WI 53333-0124

Dear Mrs. Sanderfoot:

Thank you for the invitation to speak at the Olsonville Strawberry Festival. It is an honor to be asked.

It is with regret that I must inform you that I will be out of town during the entire Strawberry Festival, so I must decline the invitation. As you are well aware, strawberries are my favorite, and I am enclosing my favorite strawberry recipe which you may share with others at the festival.

My best wishes to you for an outstanding Strawberry Festival. Perhaps I can be with you next year.

Sincerely,

4 in

(your name)

Enclosure

Figure 19-2

NO DOC CODE

TEMPLATE DISK USERS:

Exercise 3: The body of this report (food) is saved on the template disk. Retrieve it and add all of the formatting in the exercise, including the table between the last two paragraphs. Print and save the completed exercise as directed.

CreateHeader
FL. Rt.
Alt F6

SNACKING SURVEY — ^B

SUPPRESS PG 1

REPORT ON SNACKING SURVEY

The Committee on Snacking has completed its portion of the work regarding whether employees should continue to be allowed to eat, drink, and smoke at their desks. The results of the survey will be summarized in the following paragraphs.

It was almost unanimously agreed that none of the employees should be smoking at their desks. Since a cloud of smoke hanging in the room is offensive to smokers as well as nonsmokers, it seems that a decision will be made at the next meeting of the managers to have a smoke-free environment.

With regard to eating at their desks, the majority of the employees surveyed felt that eating should be limited to breath mints and related items. Candy should not be placed in the departments because it is tempting to workers who don't need the calories. In addition, it was agreed that it's pretty hard to carry on a serious conversation with a worker who is eating candy. What's more, research has proven that the carbohydrates in candy tend to make the mind less active. At no time should workers be allowed to eat cookies, sandwiches, or related foodstuffs at their desks.

The survey concluded that drinking at desks was a little different. Many employees felt that a cup of coffee or a can of soda did not present a threat to the efficiency of the workers in the office and should be allowed as long as it is done discreetly. It was emphasized that care should be taken not to spill the beverages either at the workplace or in getting them to the workplace.

Here is a breakdown of the results:

create a table

	Yes	No	?
Food	5%	93%	2%
Smoking	1%	98%	1%
Drinking	75%	20%	5%

The bottom line of this report is that the survey only presented the workers' point of view with regard to this matter. Company policy will be determined when the Board has had a chance to review the results of the survey and discuss the matter at the next board meeting on Monday. We shall all look forward to the decisions.

DOC CODE

Figure 19-3

Lesson 19 Exercise 4

1. Key the recipe in Figure 19-4 using two-inch side margins.

2. Use the Center Page (from top to bottom) feature to center the recipe on the page.

3. Center and underline the name of the recipe as shown.

4. Clear all tab stops and set tabs at 0.4" and 0.8" for the ingredients.

5. Print a copy of the recipe and save it as recipe.194.

<u>Strawberry Pizza</u>

Spread 1 pkg. refrigerator cookie dough on two 9" round tins or one 13-14" pizza pan for crust. Bake and cool.

Whip together and spread on crust:

    1 8-oz. pkg. cream cheese
    1 c. sour cream
    1 c. powdered sugar

Arrange strawberries, cut in half, on top of cream mixture. Top with glaze. Garnish with whipped cream if desired.

Glaze: 2 c. water
        1 1/4 c. sugar
        1/4 c. cornstarch

Mix together and boil until clear. Stir in:

    1 small box strawberry gelatin

Cool and pour over strawberries.

Note: This recipe can be adapted to include any desired fresh fruit. When using fruit other than strawberries, use lemon gelatin for the glaze.

Figure 19-4

Lesson 19 Exercise 5

1. Choose about two dozen of the codes from the list you have been keeping throughout the course and prepare a two-column table. The

code will be in the left column and a description of what the code does in your document will be at the right.

2. Format the table and position it on the page in an attractive manner.

3. Print the table and save it as **codes.195**.

REVISING THE DOCUMENTS

In this section, you will revise three of the four documents you just created. Some of the revisions will be made to improve the appearance of the documents. Others will change the text. Work carefully and efficiently!

Lesson 19 Exercise 6

Figure 19-5 is a double-spaced copy of the memo with corrections.

1. Retrieve **manual.191** and make the corrections indicated. Do not change the memo to double spacing.

2. In moving the third paragraph, block the paragraph and move it as you learned in Lesson 13. Do NOT delete it and rekey it in the new location. (Remember to check spacing after moving the text.)

3. Add a postscript. Follow the P.S. with Indent so the second line is aligned with the first.

4. Print the document and save it again, this time as **manual.196**.

Lesson 19 Exercise 7

The letter from Exercise 2 looks good, but it still needs some changes. Retrieve **berry.192** and revise it as follows:

1. Change the margins back to the default. (The best way to do this is to move the cursor to the top of the document, reveal your codes, and delete the Margin Set code with either Delete or Backspace.)

2. Tab to indent the first line of each paragraph.

3. Go to the top of the document and change justification to left. Full justification is too formal for this letter.

4. Print the revised letter and save it again, this time as **berry.197**.

Lesson 19 Exercise 8

Finally, some changes need to be made in **food.193**. Make the changes indicated in Figure 19-6. Print the document and save it again as **food.198**.

MEMORANDUM

TO: All Personnel

FROM: J. R. Jones

DATE: (Current date)

SUBJECT: Procedures

Attached are revised pages to be inserted into your departmental procedures manual. Please study each page carefully before inserting it in your manual.

You will notice that some pages are replacement pages and others are to be added to the end of an existing section. All new pages are appropriately numbered.

As you know, the company is fully committed to ^the use of^ procedures manuals and feels that keeping them up to date contributes to the efficiency with which ^our employees work.^ ~~the company functions.~~

If you have any questions ~~with~~ ^about^ these revised ~~pages~~ ^ions^ or the procedures manual in general, please call me at Ext. 247.

DOC ~~CODE~~   ~~JRJ~~.

Enclosure

P.S. We are always looking for suggestions about ways to improve our manual. Do you have any?

Figure 19-5

REPORT ON SNACKING SURVEY

(add footnote)

The Committee on Snacking has completed its portion of the work regarding whether employees should continue to be allowed to eat, drink, and smoke at their desks. The results of the survey will be summarized in the following paragraphs.[1]

It was almost unanimously agreed that none of the employees should be smoking ~~at their desks.~~ *in the office.* Since a cloud of smoke hanging in the room is offensive to smokers as well as nonsmokers, it seems that a decision will be made at the next meeting of the managers to *change to* ~~have~~ a smoke-free environment.

With regard to eating at their desks, the majority of the employees surveyed felt that eating should be limited to breath mints and related items. Candy should not be ~~placed~~ *made available* in the *office* ~~departments~~ because it is tempting to workers who don't need the calories. In addition, it was agreed that it's pretty hard to carry on a serious conversation with a worker who is eating candy. What's more, research has proven that the carbohydrates in candy tend to make the mind less active. At no time should workers be allowed to eat cookies, sandwiches, *candy bars,* or related foodstuffs at their desks.

The survey concluded that drinking at desks was a little different. Many employees felt that a cup of coffee or a can of soda did not present a threat to the efficiency of the workers in the office and should be allowed as long as it is done discreetly. It was emphasized that care should be taken not to spill the beverages either at the work~~place~~ *station* or in getting them to the work~~place~~ *station*.

Here is a breakdown of the results:

	Yes	No	?
Food	5%	93%	2%
Smoking	1%	98%	1%
Drinking	75%	20%	5%

The bottom line of this report is that the survey only presented the workers' point of view with regard to this matter. Company policy will be determined when the Board has had a chance to review the results of the survey and discuss the matter at the next board meeting on Monday. We shall all look forward to the *Board's* decisions.

¹*Snacking survey conducted by the Employee Relations Committee in April, 1993.*

Figure 19-6

Lesson 19 Exercise 9

1. Key the text illustrated in Figure 19-7. Allow a two-inch top margin and a quadruple space following the title. When you finish, end with two hard returns and retrieve **global.183** into the document.

2. Reveal your codes to help you position your cursor between the [Para Num:Auto] code and the [Outline On] code. Go to the Define Paragraph Numbering menu. Choose **2 Paragraph style**.

3. Return to your document and move the cursor down through the listing. Watch the bullets change to numerals.

4. Rearrange the items in the list so the two about geography are at the top of the list, followed by major trade regions, economics, time zones, monetary units, culture, language, and the metric system.

5. Add a new Item 5: *An understanding of the major laws governing international trade*.

6. Align Item 10 like you aligned your Roman numerals in the outline—strike **Shift-Tab** to move it into the left margin and strike the space bar 4 times to "bulldoze" the numeral into place.

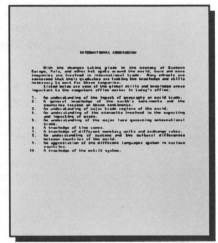

Figure 19-8

7. When you finish, check your work. The document should look much like Figure 19-8. Then print it and close it, saving it as **global.199**.

INTERNATIONAL STUDIES

   With the changes taking place in the economy of Eastern Europe, Asia, and other hot spots around the world, more and more companies are involved in international trade. Many schools are concerned that their graduates are lacking the knowledge and skills necessary to work for those companies.
   Listed below are some of the global skills and knowledge areas important to the competent office worker in today's office.

Figure 19-7

Lesson 19 Exercise 10

1. Retrieve **license.149**. Make the revisions listed below. When you finish, the document should look much like Figure 19-9.

2. Find the [Ln Spacing:2] code near the beginning of the first paragraph. Remove that code and the [Hyph On] code.

3. Go through the document and remove all other spacing codes. Add an extra hard return between paragraphs so the paragraphs are separated by one blank line.

4. Delete the Indent code at the beginning of the third paragraph and indent the paragraph with Tab so it looks like the other paragraphs.

5. Set Justification at Left.

6. Delete the tab before each of the hyphens introducing the list of excuses.

7. At the beginning of the first paragraph, insert the necessary codes to format this document with two evenly spaced newspaper columns.

8. Insert a hard page break dividing the document into columns that are nearly equal, as illustrated.

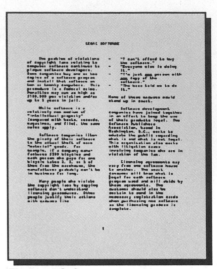

Figure 19-9

9. Make any other changes that you think would make the document look good. You may turn Hyphenation back on if you wish. Finally, print a copy and save it as **license.190**.

SUMMARY

You have already finished Unit 2! What an accomplishment! In this lesson you reviewed nearly everything you've learned about WordPerfect 5.1. Production Test 2 and Theory Test 1 comes next. If you have some extra time, you may wish to practice with headers and moving blocks of text. Good luck!

Unit 3

WordPerfect Power Tools

LESSON 20
Advanced File Management

SKIP

OBJECTIVES

Upon completion of this lesson, you will be able to:

1. Describe methods of organizing files.
2. Describe methods of naming files.
3. Manage files by using proper backup procedures, purging, and archiving.
4. Organize files using directories and subdirectories.
5. Convert files from other formats.
6. Lock your files.
7. Work with the Print menu

Estimated Time: 1 ½ hours

ORGANIZING FILES

Visualize an office with no organized paper filing system. When you open the file drawers, you find letters, memos, manuscripts, and reports just piled into the drawers. Imagine trying to find a specific document.

The same thing can happen when you store files (documents) on disks and have no plan for what is stored on which disk (or with hard disk storage, *where* on the disk the documents are stored). File management is as important for computerized files as it is for paper files—maybe even more so because you can't see what's on a disk simply by looking at it. You must access each document, unless it is very clearly named, to see what that document is about. That is a time-consuming and frustrating task when you need to find a document in a hurry.

Whether you work on a dual floppy system or a hard disk system, the issue of file management is critical. In this lesson we will learn about organizing files on both kinds of systems since the same principles apply. Then we will study some other critical aspects of file management.

Dual Floppy System. As you know, the usual procedure on a dual floppy system is to put the software disk in Drive A and the data disk in Drive B. If you start WordPerfect properly, all documents are saved on the data disk in Drive B. With that in mind, let's look at some basic information about managing files.

One of the first things you can do to eliminate filing problems is to be organized about what you put on each disk. Think of your disks as file folders in the drawers of a filing cabinet. Organize your work so that you can access your documents as quickly and efficiently as you would be able to access a paper document from the proper file folder in the proper drawer of the proper four-drawer filing cabinet.

Plan ahead and have enough disks so that you can group types of documents. For example, you might want to have a disk for all clients whose names begin with letters A through C. Perhaps one disk might be designated for mailing lists. Or, if you do a lot of mailings, perhaps a certain type of mailing would go on one disk and a different type of mailing on another. If you do work for several bosses, you might have a disk for each boss.

Of course, in each office the way files are saved on disks will vary because each office and its function is unique. Careful planning, however, will enable you to arrange your documents on disks so your retrieval time is cut to a minimum.

Hard Disk System. As you learned earlier, with a hard disk system both the software files and your files are stored on the same hard disk. With everything stored on one disk, it is especially important to set up a system of organizing files so you can find them when you need them.

With a hard disk system, you can't separate the types of files onto individual disks, so you must instead group the documents into directories. You'll learn about creating and using directories shortly.

Your employer will probably have a system set up regarding how your directories are to be organized. For example, you might have a directory for each client. Or all of your correspondence about a particular product might be grouped together in a directory.

NAMING FILES

You learned earlier that a file name may consist of eight characters plus a three-letter extension after the period. You've been given the document names throughout your training. Each name usually has included something about the document as well as the lesson and exercise number.

It is important to devise a naming convention that is comfortable for you. You might use the extension **.ltr** for each letter you save or **.rpt** for each report. The surname of a person to receive a letter might be used in the filename with a numeral to keep track of the file (i.e., jones1.ltr or jones2.ltr). It would be a waste of filename space to use the current date in the first part of the file name because when you list your files, DOS includes the date the file was stored.

Whatever method you choose, be sure that it is indeed a method—not just a haphazard naming of documents. When you need a file, you need to know exactly "which drawer to open and which file folder to retrieve."

MAKING BACKUP FILES

One of the most important things you must do when you are filing documents on disks is to make backup files on a regular basis. This prevents loss of important documents due to disk damage or problems with the computer. Proper backup procedures also protect your company from theft and natural disaster. Backup disks may be stored in a fireproof vault or at a different location.

Backing up your files may simply include copying all the documents created during one working day from the file disk you were using that day onto another disk. This gives you two copies of everything you save.

The Disk Operating System (DOS) Copy and Backup commands are usually the most efficient methods of making your backup copies. Consult a good DOS manual for instructions regarding making backups on both dual floppy and hard disk systems.

The method of backup your company uses might determine how you name your files. The ease of backup will be affected by how your files are grouped. In any case, it is important that you back up your work with regularity and store your backup disks in a safe place.

PURGING FILES

Regular paper filing cabinets must be cleaned out occasionally. A good records management program mandates the disposal of documents that are old or no longer needed. Disk files need to be cleaned out on a regular basis, too. Time should be set aside each week or preferably each day to go through the files on your disks and "clean house." The Look feature in the List Files menu of WordPerfect will help to preview documents when you can't immediately remember from the document name what is stored in that location. By limiting the documents stored on your disks to those currently needed, your retrieval time for accessing documents will be improved.

Some documents can simply be discarded when they have no further value to you or your company. You can do that with the Delete option when you are on the List Files screen. Other documents may have value but may be used only once every several months. Those documents that are not needed on a regular basis might need to be archived.

Archiving refers to storing seldom-used documents in a safe but out-of-the-way place. By copying these seldom-used documents to a special disk and deleting them from your working disks, you can improve your retrieval time. In addition, your working disks will have more room for your current work. You will want to have some system for archiving documents so that you can find them when you need them.

DISK CAPACITY

DOS places some limits on what you can store on a disk. Obviously, the total bytes available on a disk limits you. (A *byte* is equal to a character.) Here are some disk limits, although the manufacturers keep making it possible to squeeze more onto disks:

5¼-inch disks	double density (DD)	360,000	(360K)
	high density (HD)	1,200,000	(1.2M)
3½-inch disks	double density (DD)	720,000	(720K)
	high density (HD)	1,440,000	(1.44M)

The label on a disk usually identifies it as either a double-density or high-density disk. Use disks that are compatible with your computer drive. Double-density disks can be used in high-density drives, but high-density disks should not be used in double-density drives.

You shouldn't fill a disk too full. Regardless of disk capacity, you should use a new disk or purge some files when about 50,000 bytes remain. Of course, the full-disk guideline can vary depending on the size of your documents and the type of work that you do. You are told how many bytes remain each time you access your List Files screen.

Another restriction DOS puts on your filing is that you are limited to 112 files in the directory on a double-density disk and 224 files on a high-density disk. If you reach that limit, even if your disk isn't nearly full, an error message will appear when you try to print or save another document. Pay attention to the number of files you have stored. That number is displayed each time you list your files.

In this training, you have been asked to save some documents that have no future importance so that you will get experience saving and retrieving documents. It is possible, especially if you are using the template disk, that you will exceed the 112-file limit before you finish the course. Now would be a good time to practice purging files and making room on your disk for the remainder of your training.

Lesson 20 Exercise 1

Figure 20-1 contains a list of documents you created in this course that you will no longer need. This list is in alphabetic order, as are the documents in the list on your disk. You could delete them one at a time. Instead, follow the steps below to delete them all at once.

1. List your files. Look at the top right of the screen to see the number of documents on your disk.

2. Move the cursor to each of the documents in the list in Figure 20-1 and "mark" that document with an asterisk (*). You may use the shift of the 8 key or the asterisk in the Number Keypad.

3. Look through the list for any documents you may have created on your own that are no longer needed and mark those in the same way. If you accidentally mark a file for deletion that you don't wish to delete, you can unmark it by highlighting it and keying another asterisk.

4. When you have marked all the files to be deleted, strike **2 Delete** to remove them from your disk. You will need to confirm the deletion—not once but twice!

5. Check the number at the top right again. You should now have lots of room on your disk for the next part of the course!

berry.172	formula.8-9	memo.6-1	record.111
center.147	fun-day.12r	memo.6-3	record.112
chester.120	hanging.8-4	online10.r2	secure.7-5
colors.137	indent.8-2	opnion10.rr6	secure.8-7
council.142	job.5-2	para.2-3	systems.117
errors.1-1	job.5-5	parallel.174	table2
errors.fix	job.6-4	phones.94a	table2.6
fiddler.124	job.9-5	phones.94b	table2.7
fiddler.7-3	license.143	practice.122	table2.9
food.173	license.144	practice.123	table3
footnote.151	license.146	practice.7-1	table4
footnote.152	license.148	practice.7-2	telecom.9-9
foreign.3-1	license1.12r	programs.12r	
foreign.5-3	manual.171	quality10.r1	

Figure 20-1

DIRECTORIES

Whether you work on a dual floppy system or a hard disk system, you can organize your documents into groups of files called directories. A *directory* is like a file folder in a file drawer. Study Figure 20-2. Think of the *root* directory as the drawer. Up to this point, you have been just throwing your documents into the drawer in no particular order.

The boxes labeled *John*, *Miguel*, *Sally*, *Sasha*, and *Keu Ye* are like the file folders in the drawer. They are sometimes called subdirectories, although in computerese you don't have to worry about the "sub" part of that. You can just call them directories.

Each directory can contain any kind of document. What's more, you can even give two documents the same name if they are in different directories! You can probably think of smarter ways to divide your work rather than giving directories the names of people.

You can easily create a directory on your disk when you are on the List Files screen. We will do that now, so you can learn to work with directories and use them to organize your work.

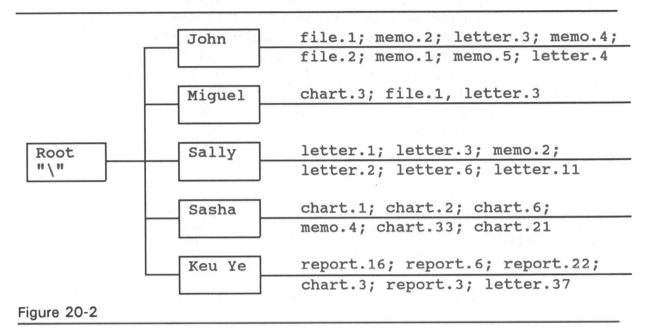

John	file.1; memo.2; letter.3; memo.4; file.2; memo.1; memo.5; letter.4
Miguel	chart.3; file.1, letter.3
Sally	letter.1; letter.3; memo.2; letter.2; letter.6; letter.11
Sasha	chart.1; chart.2; chart.6; memo.4; chart.33; chart.21
Keu Ye	report.16; report.6; report.22; chart.3; report.3; letter.37

Figure 20-2

Lesson 20 Exercise 2

1. List your files. Strike **7 Other** directory. WordPerfect will prompt you with **New Directory =**, and the name of your current directory will be listed (either *a:* or *b:*).

2. Key *Sasha* and strike **Enter**. WordPerfect will ask **Create Sasha?** Strike **Y** for Yes.

3. Your List Files screen will return and you will see **Sasha <dir>** at the top left. You now have a directory named Sasha! Easy, isn't it?

4. Move the highlight so the Sasha directory is highlighted and strike **Enter** twice. (Watch the prompts at the bottom of the screen!)

5. The Sasha directory should open. (Look at the directory designation at the top of the List Files screen to see that you are in the Sasha directory. Notice that this directory contains no files.) Finally, strike the space bar to close List Files.

You have some choices regarding how you can work with your different directories. For example, if you wished to retrieve something from the Sasha directory, you'd list your files, move the highlight to the Sasha directory, and strike Enter twice. The list of files in the Sasha directory would appear, and you could retrieve the file in the normal way.

If you occasionally wish to save a file in the Sasha directory, you could key the directory name before the name of the document when naming it for storage. (For example, to save *filename.11* in the Sasha directory on the disk in Drive A, at the **Document to be Saved:** prompt you'd key *sasha\filename.11*.)

That takes some extra keying. If you are doing lots of work that should be saved in or retrieved from the Sasha directory, it would be smarter and more efficient to make a temporary change to that directory. You can make that change by again using the **7 Other** directory choice. Simply move the cursor to the desired directory, strike **7** for the Other Directory, strike **Enter** twice, and return to your working screen as usual. Now, when you save documents or list your files, you will automatically be in the directory you chose. Let's practice it both ways.

Lesson 20 Exercise 3

1. Key the words *This is a sample document.*

2. Strike **F7** to save the document and affirm saving the document.

3. At the **Document to be Saved:** prompt, key *\sasha\sample* and strike Enter. (Use backslashes.) Don't exit WordPerfect.

4. Now list your files again. Move the highlight to the Sasha directory and strike **Enter** twice. The *sample* document should be there. Is it? You could retrieve it in the normal manner, if you wished.

5. Strike the space bar to close List Files.

So far each time you've opened List Files, you've been in the root directory and had to open the Sasha directory to see that one file. Now we'll make a more permanent move to the Sasha directory.

Lesson 20 Exercise 4

1. List your files. Move the highlight to the Sasha directory.

2. Strike **7** Other directory to tell WordPerfect you want to make a directory change. Then strike **Enter** twice. Because your cursor was on the Sasha directory, WordPerfect knows that's the one to which you wish to switch. You should now be in the Sasha directory.

3. Strike the space bar to close List Files.

4. List your files again. Are you in the Sasha directory? If not, you'd better try it again!

5. Strike the space bar to close List Files.

OK. Now that you're there, let's assume you're finished with whatever work you wished to do in the Sasha directory and you'd like to reset List Files so it accesses the root or main directory. If you looked at the headings above the two columns of directories, you saw the words *Current <Dir>* and *Parent <Dir>*. Until now, that wasn't important.

In the situation with which we're working, the Sasha directory is the current directory and the root directory is known as the parent directory. You can return to the root temporarily by moving the highlight to *Parent <Dir>* and striking Enter twice. You can return to the root permanently by moving the highlight to *Parent <Dir>* and striking **7** Other Directory before striking Enter twice.

Lesson 20 Exercise 5

1. List your files. Move the highlight to *Parent <Dir>* and strike **Enter** twice. Are you in your root directory? If so, good, but remember that it's not permanent.

2. Strike the space bar to close List Files. Then list your files again. Are you still in the Sasha directory? You should be.

3. Move the highlight to *Parent <Dir>*. Strike **7** Other directory, and then strike **Enter** twice. You are back to the root directory. Strike the space bar to close List Files.

4. List your files one more time. You should be in the root directory.

Are you getting the hang of it? It's really not difficult. When you've worked with directories a little, moving from one directory to another (both temporarily and permanently) will become second nature.

COPY

Now let's try an exercise in moving documents from one place on your disk to another. We will put all of the exercises created in Unit 1 into a Unit 1 directory. We will put all of the exercises created in Unit 2 into a Unit 2 directory. Then we will make a Unit 3 directory for your work in this unit. Finally, we'll remove the Sasha directory. We are finished with her! Follow the exercise steps carefully so you don't get lost!

Lesson 20 Exercise 6

1. List your files. (The root directory should appear.) Create a directory named **unit-1**. (If you need to review, return to Exercise 2 where you created a directory.)

2. Create another directory named **unit-2**.

3. Go through the remaining approximately 30 files on your disk and mark (with an asterisk) all of the documents you created in the first 10 lessons. That means they will have extensions like **.9-3** or **.810**, and there's even one named **dsktop10.r3**.

Don't be confused by the documents from Lesson 11. The document names may look like exercises created in Lesson 1, but you didn't create any documents in Lesson 1.

4. With the files marked, strike **8** Copy from the menu at the bottom. You will be asked to verify that you wish to copy the files, and then you'll be prompted to give the destination.

5. Key *a:\unit-1* and strike **Enter**. The files will be copied from the root to the Unit 1 directory, and you will remain in List Files. In addition, the files you copied are still marked.

6. Choose **2** Delete to delete these files from the root directory. Remember that you must confirm the deletion two times.

7. Move the highlight to the **unit-1** directory and strike **Enter** twice. Are the Unit 1 files in the Unit 1 directory?

8. Move the highlight to *Parent <Dir>* and strike **Enter** twice to return to the root directory.

Lesson 20 Exercise 7

1. Now mark all of the documents created in Unit 2. That includes Lessons 11 through 19. About all you'll have left in the root directory is the **memo.frm** document. (If you use the template disk files, a set of documents from the template disk will also remain.)

2. Following the procedure in Exercise 6, copy all of those marked files to the Unit 2 directory. Then delete them from the root directory.

3. Open the Unit 2 directory to see if your files are there. Then return to the root directory.

4. Move the cursor to the Sasha directory. Strike **Enter** twice to open it. Mark the **sample** document and delete it.

5. Move the cursor to *Parent <Dir>* and return to the root directory. Your cursor will still be on *Sasha <Dir>*.

6. Strike **2** Delete to remove the Sasha directory from your disk. Then strike the space bar to return to your document screen.

A few things need to be mentioned at this point.

• You can't delete a directory that has anything in it. All files from the directory must be deleted before the directory can be removed from the disk.

• If you wish to delete all of the files in a directory, you can save some time by striking **Alt-F5** to mark ALL FILES. This places an asterisk by each of the files in the directory.

• If you mark a file by mistake, you can "unmark" it by striking the asterisk again. The asterisk will be removed. If you wanted to delete or copy almost all files in a directory, you could mark them all with Alt-F5 and then go through the list and unmark the few files you wished to leave in place.

- When you retrieve a file from a directory other than the root, the entire *filepath* appears in the prompt at the bottom of the screen. The filepath includes the drive, the name of the directory, and the name of the document. If you use directories, you will become accustomed to seeing that larger group of information in the prompt.

- The methods used above for changing directories work fine as long as you remain on the same disk drive. When you need to switch from one drive to another, you must use a different method. Again, before making this change, you must decide if you want a temporary change or a more permanent one so you can choose the best method.

  For a *temporary* change of drive, strike **F5** like you are going to list your files, but before striking Enter, key the name of the desired drive (i.e., **c:**). Then strike **Enter**. This example will take you to the root directory on Drive C. The next time you list your files, however, the list that appears will be the one you were in before making the change.

  For a more *permanent* change of drive, list your files in the normal manner. Then strike **7 O**ther Directory. Key the name of the drive to which you wish to switch (i.e., **c:**) and strike **Enter** twice. This takes you to the new drive. The next time you list your files, the new drive file list will be the one that appears.

TEXT CONVERSION

One of the more troublesome problems in many offices is the transfer of documents from one word processing program to another. More than a few gray hairs have sprouted when a company gets a new word processing program and has a large number of documents that were saved using the old program. Or documents might be received on disk from a client who uses one of the other word processing programs such as *XyWrite* or *Displaywrite*. The good news is that there are some solutions.

Each successive version of WordPerfect is better at converting to WordPerfect format documents prepared in other programs. Sometimes the transfers can be made by simply retrieving the document into Word-Perfect and making a few quick changes to the format.

Another way to deal with documents created in other formats is to transfer them to what's known as *DOS text format* before bringing them into WordPerfect. Documents that are in DOS text format are referred to as *ASCII* files. ASCII stands for the American Standard Code for Information Interchange, and it means that a document has been stripped of any formatting codes that would be confusing to another program. Instead of Tab and Centering codes, for example, spaces are inserted. Many DOS text files have hard returns at the end of each line. In ASCII language, each hard return tells the printer to advance the paper one line and return the printer to the beginning of the line.

Text In/Out

Ctrl-F5 is used for text-in and text-out functions. When you strike this key combination, you will see the following menu:

```
1 DOS Text; 2 Password; 3 Save As; 4 Comment; 5 Spreadsheet
```

The choice with which we are concerned obviously is the first one. When you choose **1 Dos Text**, you will see this line menu:

```
1 Save; 2 Retrieve (CR/LF to [HRt]); 3 Retrieve (CR/LF to
[SRt] in HZone): 0
```

The first choice saves the document you currently have on the screen in DOS format, which is a format the Disk Operating System can understand. The second choice in this menu tells WordPerfect to put hard returns at the end of each line (CR/LF means Carrier Return, Line Feed). The third choice puts a soft return at the end of each line that falls in the hyphenation zone (an area at the end of the line where WordPerfect looks for places to divide words). Let's begin with Save.

Lesson 20 Exercise 8

Choose Text **Out** from the File menu.

1. Retrieve **colors.116**. Strike **Ctrl-F5**. Then choose **1 DOS Text** and **1 Save**. At the prompt for the name of the document, key **colors.dos** and strike **Enter**. The document will be saved on your disk but will remain on the screen.

2. Strike **Page Down** to move the cursor below the document and strike **Enter** a couple of times to add some space.

3. Now retrieve **colors.dos** into the document you have open. The two documents look the same, right?

4. Reveal your codes and compare the two documents. Note that in the second document, not only have the tabs between columns been converted to spaces, but the Tab Set code is missing. In fact, all codes are missing except the [HRt] codes at the ends of the lines.

5. Close the document without saving.

It would be a big pain to revise the ASCII version of the document. For a document that's simple and short, you probably wouldn't even try.

You'd rekey it. But if your document were longer and didn't need much revision, you could save rekeying time using the Text Conversion feature.

The other part of the Text In/Out feature deals with retrieving documents saved in other formats. Success with this again depends on what must be done with the document after you've retrieved it.

The following documents created using other word processing programs are saved on your template disk:

ecol.1	ASCII text file
ecol.2	Microsoft Word v. 2
ecol.3	Word for Windows v. 2.0
ecol.4	WordPerfect 5.1 for Windows

If you have the template files, follow the steps in Exercise 9 to see how much trouble it would be for you to work with them in WordPerfect 5.1. If you don't have the template files, you will have to skip this exercise. Ask your instructor if you are unsure.

Lesson 20 Exercise 9

1. Strike **Ctrl-F5**. Then choose **1 DOS Text** and **2 Retrieve**.

2. At the name of document prompt, key *ecol.1*.

3. Use the arrow keys to move through the document and look at the indented formats and the tabulation near the end. It looks pretty good, doesn't it? It would probably print nicely.

4. Reveal your codes and check the indented formats and the tabulation. Again, you will see the absence of codes. Spaces have been inserted to align the indented text. As with the **colors** document, that's OK until you try to revise it. Then you could run into some problems. Close the document without saving.

5. One at a time, use Text In/Out to look at the others in the list. You will find some code at the top of **ecol.2** and **ecol.3**, and the formatting will be different. The only one you can't retrieve using Text In/Out is **ecol.4**. That one must be retrieved into WordPerfect 5.1 like a regular WordPerfect document because WordPerfect 5.1 and WordPerfect 5.1 for Windows are completely compatible.

6. When you are finished, close all documents.

LOCKED DOCUMENTS

WordPerfect provides a feature that enables you to give a document a password so that no one else may access or print that document. This feature is also in the Text In/Out menu. When you strike **Ctrl-F5** and choose **2 Password**, you will see the following menu:

`Password 1 Add/Change; 2 Remove`

Let's try an exercise to learn how to use the Password feature.

Lesson 20 Exercise 10

1. Retrieve **colors.116** again. Strike **Ctrl-F5**. Then choose **2 Password** and choose **1 Add**.

2. At the password prompt, key your initials. Key carefully. The password will not show on the screen as you key it because you don't want someone looking over your shoulder to learn your password.

3. When you've keyed the password, strike **Enter**. You will be asked to key the password again, just to be sure. Key it again and strike **Enter**.

4. Exit from the document, saving it on your disk in the normal way.

5. List your files and retrieve **colors.116** again. You will be asked for the password. Key your initials.

6. Remove the password from the document by striking **Ctrl-F5** again. This time choose **2 Remove**.

7. Exit from the document, closing it again. You MUST save the document again after you've removed the password, or else the locked copy will remain on your disk.

That was pretty simple, wasn't it? You probably won't need to lock most of your documents unless you share a computer with someone who might mess them up for you. Or perhaps you might work with highly confidential documents that should be locked for safekeeping.

PRINTING OPTIONS

In Lesson 6 you learned to choose your printer driver. You also learned to print your documents by striking **Shift-F7** and choosing **1 Full**. In Lesson 15 you learned to print a single page of a document by positioning the cursor on the desired page and choosing **2 Page** from the Print menu. You have consistently used **6 View** to preview your documents before printing. The Print menu, however, holds the key to many more capabilities when you are working in WordPerfect 5.1.

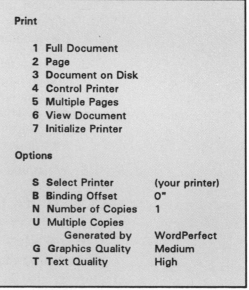

```
Print

   1  Full Document
   2  Page
   3  Document on Disk
   4  Control Printer
   5  Multiple Pages
   6  View Document
   7  Initialize Printer

Options

   S  Select Printer          (your printer)
   B  Binding Offset          0"
   N  Number of Copies        1
   U  Multiple Copies
         Generated by         WordPerfect
   G  Graphics Quality        Medium
   T  Text Quality            High
```

Figure 20-3

Strike **Shift-F7** and look at your Print menu. Compare it with Figure 20-3. Let's analyze the other choices you may make while in the Print menu. We'll begin with the bottom section.

- **S**elect Printer is the portion of the Print menu from which you select your *printer driver* or the program that enables your computer to communicate with your printer. A printer must be listed here, or you cannot print your documents. The printer that you choose must exactly match the printer you are using. If you choose the incorrect printer, you may get some unexpected results when you print.

  If you have only one printer available, you won't change this option often. If you need to be switching from one printer to another because of the kinds of work you do, it is a good idea to choose the correct printer driver before you begin the document. The choice of printer driver will affect how your document is formatted.

- **B**inding Offset enables you to tell WordPerfect to print facing pages with a larger margin on the inside so words won't get lost in the binding.

- **N**umber of Copies enables you to print multiple copies of a document without having to send the document to the printer a number of times. The next choice tells you that WordPerfect will take care of printing as many copies as you have requested.

- **G**raphics Quality and **T**ext Quality affect how your document will look when it comes from the printer. The higher the quality, the better the document will look. However, high quality printing takes more time on most printers and uses more toner or ribbon or whatever causes the images to show on your paper. This is a nice feature because you can set both Graphics and Text Quality to **D**raft for documents that don't need to be lovely, and you'll save time and resources.

The choices you've used most frequently are at the top of the menu. Let's look at some of the other choices.

- **3 D**ocument on Disk enables you to print a document without opening it. When you choose this option, WordPerfect will ask you for the name of the document you wish to print. After you key the name, a **Page(s): (All)** prompt asks you to list the pages to be printed. If you want all pages to print, simply strike **Enter**. If you want to print only selected pages, you may key those page numbers. WordPerfect is incredibly intuitive regarding how you key the page numbers. If you want pages 2 through 5, key **2-5** or

2,3,4,5. If your document is about 9 pages long (and you can't remember exactly how long it is), and you want all of the pages after page 7 to print, key **7-15.** The pages will print beginning at page 7 and going to the end of the document. You will enjoy working with this option!

• **4** Control Printer brings up a menu that resembles Figure 20-4. Open this menu and study it while you read about its features.

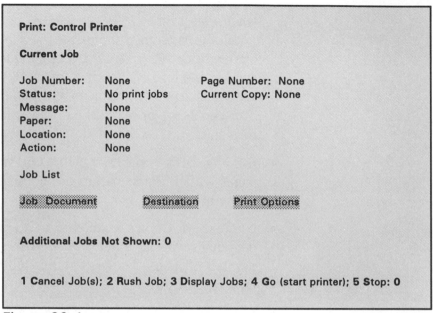

Figure 20-4

This is an important menu because this is where you can cancel print jobs, look at the list of jobs to be printed, check for prompts regarding why a job isn't printing, and tell WordPerfect that you would like to **R**ush a job. Not only can you move a job from the bottom of the list (the *print queue*) to the top, but you can tell WordPerfect to interrupt the job currently printing if you're really in a rush!

WordPerfect does what's called *background printing*. That means you can send a job to the printer and while it's printing begin your next job. That's useful because you never need to wait around for the printer. If a document doesn't print, you shouldn't send it again until you open the Control Printer menu to see what the problem might be. The Message portion of this menu might tell you that the printer isn't accepting your text. The Action portion of the menu might tell you to turn on the printer or check the cables connecting the printer to your CPU. It might tell you that your printer is out of paper.

If you accidentally send a document to the printer, quick action in opening the Control Printer menu might enable you to cancel the print job before it is sent to the printer. How successful you'll be in canceling an incorrect print job will depend on how fast your computer is and how much memory is in your printer. On some equipment, you can send a five-page document to the printer and come immediately to the Control Printer menu, only to find it empty. Your computer was so powerful that it already sent the document to the memory of the printer. In other cases, you can access the Control Printer menu, choose **1** Cancel, and key the job number to cancel the job.

If a lot of jobs are queued to the printer, you can choose **3** Display Jobs and see an entire list of documents waiting to be printed. Then you can choose the one you want to cancel by number. Print jobs number beginning when you turn on the computer in the morning and continuing until the computer is turned off. In a busy day's work, that number might become quite large.

An added benefit of the Control Printer menu is that you can actually monitor the work being sent to your printer. The top portion of the menu reports the name or number of the job printing and the page number currently being printed. Strike your space bar to return to the Print menu.

- **5** Multiple Pages is the choice you will make in the Print menu to print only a portion of a document that is open on your screen. With a five-page document showing, you can choose this option and tell WordPerfect to print pages 2-4 or 2,4 depending on whether you want to include page 3.

- **7** Initialize Printer is the final choice in the Print menu. If you are using downloadable fonts for your printer, you may need to make this choice. Use the *WordPerfect Reference* if you need more information about initializing your printer.

Strike the space bar once to close the Print menu. This pretty well wraps up this short discussion of some of your printer capabilities. You will want to try some of them when you have a document to be printed. It is important that you are familiar with the printer options discussed in this portion of the lesson so you don't waste extra time and resources by using inefficient printing methods.

SUMMARY

This lesson required a lot of reading. But it is very important reading. How well you manage your files could make a difference in whether you can find what you need when you need it.

It is recommended that you review this lesson an extra time. Even if all of your exercises worked when you did them, take your book home and use this lesson for bedtime reading so you're sure you understand it!

LESSON 20 NOTES:

Name _____ Date _____

TRUE/FALSE

Each of the following statements is either true or false. Indicate your choice in the Answers column by circling T for a true statement or F for a false statement.

Answers

1. One way to organize your files is to divide them among several disks or directories, each containing a particular type of file. (Obj. 1) . . . .   1.   T   F

2. A good method for naming files is to use your own name in the first part of the file name. (Obj. 2) . . . .   2.   T   F

3. It is usually adequate to back up important files at the end of each work-week. (Obj. 3) . . . .   3.   T   F

4. Backup copies of files are made to protect the company against illegal aliens. (Obj. 3) . . . .   4.   T   F

5. Purging your files once or twice a year should be adequate. (Obj. 3) . . .   5.   T   F

6. Directories are like file folders—the purpose of storing documents in them is to separate unrelated documents. (Obj. 4) . . . .   6.   T   F

7. Your must rekey all documents that were created using a different word processing program. (Obj. 5) . . . .   7.   T   F

8. ASCII stands for A Simple Command Is Issued. (Obj. 5) . . . .   8.   T   F

9. You must key the password twice to lock a document. (Obj. 6) . . . . . .   9.   T   F

COMPLETION

Indicate the correct answer in the space provided.

Answers

1. Would **jefferson.ltr** be an appropriate name for a letter to a client named Jefferson? (Obj. 2) . . . .   1. _____

2. What term refers to storing seldom-used documents in a safe but out-of-the-way place? (Obj. 3) . . . .   2. _____

3. What term refers to erasing from your disk files that no longer have value to your company? (Obj. 3) . . . . .   3. _____

4. What symbol is the designation for the root directory?
    (Obj. 4) . . . .   4. _____

5. Which choice in the List Files menu must you choose to
    change directories or create a new directory? (Obj. 4)   5. _____

6. If you were in the root directory of the disk in Drive A
    and wished to save a document named **mailing** directly
    into an existing directory called **labels**, what would you
    key at the file name prompt after striking F7? (Obj. 4)   6. _____

7. What must you do with the documents in a directory
    before you can delete that directory? (Obj. 4) . . . . .   7. _____

8. What takes the place of [Tab] codes and [Indent] codes
    in a document retrieved in ASCII format? (Obj. 5) . .   8. _____

9. Documents retrieved from other programs often look
    pretty good and print well. When do you most often run
    into trouble with imported files? (Obj. 5) . . . .   9. _____

10. What must you choose from the Print menu if you wish
    to cancel a print request? (Obj. 7) . . . .   10. _____

11. What is the word used to describe the list of jobs sent to
    the printer? (Obj. 7) . . . .   11. _____

12. What is meant by the term *background printing*? (Obj. 7)

_____

13. List an example from your own experience that would be a good reason to lock some or
    all of your documents.

_____

REFERENCE

Turn in the *WordPerfect Reference* to the Text In/Out section. It discusses using Ctrl-F5 and 3
Save As to save WordPerfect 5.1 documents in previous WordPerfect formats. What two
WordPerfect formats can you choose to save your documents? What is the third choice in that
menu? (You may have to try it on your computer to find the answer to the second question.)

_____

LESSON 21
Macros

SKIP

OBJECTIVES

Upon completion of this lesson, you will be able to:

1. Explain why macros are useful.
2. Create and use a macro.
3. Edit a macro.
4. Chain macros.

Estimated Time: 1 hour

In most jobs there are some sets of keystrokes that are very repetitive. You key the same thing over and over and wish there were some way to streamline the task. Word processing programs provide you with that way. A function called a *macro* enables you to save a series of keystrokes to be used over and over, as many times as needed.

WordPerfect macros are used to store frequently used phrases, paragraphs, or complicated formats to be retrieved with a few keystrokes.

Before you begin this section on macros, you need to be sure your macros will be saved on your data disk so that they don't become mixed with macros created by other students. You are well enough trained in WordPerfect now so that you can go to the Setup menu to check this yourself. Follow along carefully.

Lesson 21 Exercise 1

Open the File menu. Choose Setup and then Location of Files.

1. Strike **Shift-F1** for the Setup menu. Then choose **6** Location of Files.

2. This opens a list of types of files that are saved in WordPerfect. Look at **2** Keyboard/Macro files. Does the setting there reflect the location of your data disk? (Hard disk and network users should be set at **a:**.)

3. If the drive where you have your data disk is not entered opposite choice **2**, strike **2** and key your drive designation so your macros will save onto your data disk automatically (e.g., **a:** or **b:**).

4. Look at some of the other items in the menu. This menu has affected your work throughout your training. For example, **7** Documents should be set for the drive where your data disk is located—**a:** or **b:**, depending on whether you are working with a hard disk system, a networked system, or a dual floppy system.

5. Strike **F7** to return to your working screen.

Let's begin by creating a quick macro and testing it. After the exercise we'll analyze what you did and discuss macro rules.

Lesson 21 Exercise 2

Open the **T**ools menu. Choose **M**acro and then **D**efine.

1. Strike **Ctrl-F10** to tell WordPerfect you would like to create a macro.

2. At the **Define Macro:** prompt, key *bbc* and strike **Enter**. Strike **Enter** again to bypass the **Description** prompt. **Macro def** will begin flashing in the lower left corner of your screen, telling you that your keystrokes are being recorded.

3. Turn on Bold and key *Butte des Morts Business College*. Do not put a period or a space at the end.

4. Turn off Bold.

5. End the macro by striking **Ctrl-F10** again. Then use Exit to clear your screen.

Open the **T**ools menu. Choose **M**acro and then **E**xecute.

6. Key the paragraph in Figure 21-1. Each time you come to the name of the organization (Butte des Morts Business College), strike **Alt-F10** and key *bbc*. Strike **Enter**. The words in your macro should automatically appear in bold on the screen!

7. Print your little paragraph and close it, saving it as **macro.212**.

```
The faculty and administration of Butte des Morts Business
College are pleased to welcome you as a new student at Butte
des Morts Business College.  Your fellow students here at
Butte des Morts Business College are happy that you have
selected Butte des Morts Business College to get the
training necessary for you to acquire the job you have
always desired.  If there is anything that we at Butte des
Morts Business College can do for you, please be sure to let
any member of the staff at Butte des Morts Business College
know about it.
```

Figure 21-1

Wasn't that fun? Already you know most of what you need to know to use macros, and we've barely begun the lesson!

CREATING A MACRO

Three steps are involved in creating a macro: naming the macro, capturing the keystrokes, and ending the macro. Study the steps below to learn more about creating a macro.

Naming the Macro

Open the **Tools** menu. Choose **Macro** and then **Define**.

1. Begin by striking **Ctrl-F10** to define the macro. **Define macro:** appears on the prompt line, waiting for you to name your macro.

2. Enter a name for your macro. The macro name may be two to eight characters with no extension. **Description:** appears on the prompt line waiting for you to give the macro a description. It is not necessary to give the macro a description.

3. **Macro def** begins to blink on the prompt line. It will continue to blink until you end the macro.

Capturing the Keystrokes

4. Key the material you want saved in your macro. Try to work accurately because WordPerfect includes every key you touch in the macro, including Backspace, the arrows, and Delete.

Ending the Macro

5. Strike **Ctrl-F10** again to end the macro. **Macro Def** should stop flashing in the prompt line, and the macro is saved on your disk.

USING A MACRO

Open the **Tools** menu. Choose **Macro** and then **Execute**.

When you are ready to use a macro, strike **Alt-F10** and key the name of the macro. The keystrokes that you saved in the macro will be played out on your screen.

Now that you know how to create and use a macro, let's put that knowledge into practice.

Lesson 21 Exercise 3

Open the **Tools** menu. Choose **Macro** and then **Define**.

1. Be sure you are on a clear screen. Then strike **Ctrl-F10** to tell WordPerfect you'd like to create another macro. Use your initials as the name of the macro.

2. At the **Description** prompt, key *Letter Closing Lines* and strike **Enter**.

3. Strike **Tab** six times or until your cursor is at **Pos 4"**. Key the word *Sincerely,* and strike **Enter** five times.

4. Strike **Tab** six times again and key your full name. Strike **Enter**.

5. Strike **Tab** six times and key the title you would like to have on your job. (Maybe you'd like to be boss!) Strike **Enter** once.

6. Strike **Ctrl-F10** to end the macro. Now let's try it.

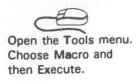

Open the **Tools** menu.
Choose **Macro** and
then **Execute**.

7. Use **F7** to clear your screen.

8. Strike **Alt-F10** and key your initials followed by **Enter**. Did your closing lines appear, each line beginning at approximately center? Keep this work on the screen while you read on.

INFORMATION ABOUT MACROS

Here are some important things you should know about macros.

- There are several kinds of macros. The two most popular kinds are *named macros* and *Alt* macros.

  ▶ A *named macro* is named by keying eight or fewer characters, as we did in Exercise 2. To run a named macro, strike **Alt-F10** and key the name of the macro followed by **Enter**.

  ▶ An *Alt* macro is named with an alphabetic character to be struck with the **Alt** key. For example, if you want a macro to send the document on the screen to the printer, you could use **Alt-P** for the macro. To define the macro, you would start with **Ctrl-F10**. At the macro name prompt, you'd strike **Alt-P** and key the strokes you want in the macro before ending it with **Ctrl-F10**. To run the macro, start it by keying **Alt-P**.

- Macros are saved on your disk similar to a document except that WordPerfect assigns **.wpm** as the extension. If you were to look at your list of files right now, the **bbc.wpm** macro would be in the "b" section.

- Macros cannot be accessed from the disk like a regular document. You cannot list your files, move the highlight to the macro, and retrieve it into your document.

- If you have a hard disk system on the job, the macro is saved on the hard disk and is always available. If you save the macro on a data disk, it will be available only on the disks to which you've copied it.

- You can repeat a macro a specific number of times using **Esc**. If you wanted a macro to repeat five times, you would strike **Esc**, key **5**, and run the macro.

- WordPerfect enables you to chain two or more macros together. When one macro is finished, the next one automatically begins.

- If you make a mistake when creating a macro, you may redo or edit it. When you define the macro and give it the same name as a macro already on your disk, a menu will appear that asks if you would like to **1** Replace or **2** Edit the existing macro.

Now let's try a simple Alt macro. This one can be used to clear your screen without saving whatever is there. It will then return you to a clear working screen.

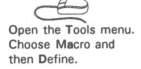

Open the **T**ools menu. Choose **M**acro and then **D**efine.

Lesson 21 Exercise 4

1. Strike **Ctrl-F10** and then strike **Alt-x** to name the macro.

2. At the **Description** prompt, key *Clear screen without saving* and strike **Enter**.

3. Strike the keys used to clear the screen: **F7** followed by **N** for No and another **N** for No.

4. End the macro by striking **Ctrl-F10** again. The closing lines you had on the screen should now be cleared.

5. Key some garbage. Then strike **Alt-x**. Did the garbage disappear? Congratulations!

Lesson 21 Exercise 5

In this exercise, you will create a named macro that sends your document to the printer. Follow along carefully.

1. Tell WordPerfect you would like to create a macro called *print*. For the description, key *print and save the document*.

2. When **Macro def** begins flashing, strike **Shift-F7** and then **1** to send the document to the printer.

3. End your macro.

That was for practice. It's almost easier to give the Print command as you have been doing throughout the course than to use this macro. But we'll put it to good use in a later exercise.

Lesson 21 Exercise 6

Now that you're so good with macros, you're on your own as you create an Alt macro attached to the letter *i*. You will be able to use it whenever you wish to key something in italics. The same macro will turn Italics on and off.

To review, you must strike **Ctrl-F8** for Font, **2** Appearance, and **4** Italc to turn on Italics. These keystrokes are needed in your macro.

When you finish creating your macro, Italics will be turned on. Use Exit to clear your screen. Then key your entire name with just the middle name in italics. You'll need to strike **Alt-i** once to turn on Italics before you key your middle name and again to turn off Italics before the space separating your middle and last names. Reveal your codes to check to be sure the Italics codes are there.

MACRO EDITING

WordPerfect provides you with a macro editor that enables you to make changes in your macros rather than rekeying them. The macro editor is accessed by telling WordPerfect you'd like to create a macro and then naming the macro you wish to edit. A prompt appears asking if you wish to replace or edit the macro. To edit, of course, you would choose the Edit option. When you do this, the macro editor is opened and the keystrokes are displayed, ready for you to make changes.

Let's practice. We are going to revise the closing lines you saved as a macro with your initials. There is one extra blank line between the complimentary closing and your name.

Lesson 21   Exercise 7

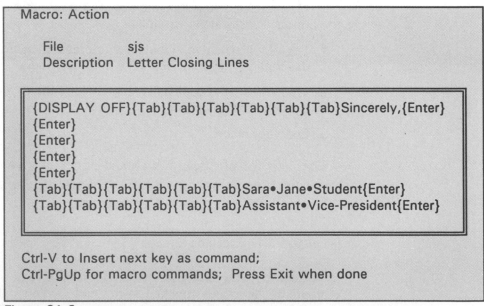

Open the **Tools** menu. Choose **Macro** and then **Define**.

1. Strike **Ctrl-F10** and key your initials. At the replace/edit choice, choose **2 Edit**.

2. Look at the macro editor. It will look much like Figure 21-2.

```
Macro: Action

    File          sjs
    Description   Letter Closing Lines

  ┌─────────────────────────────────────────────────────────┐
  │ {DISPLAY OFF}{Tab}{Tab}{Tab}{Tab}{Tab}{Tab}Sincerely,{Enter}│
  │ {Enter}                                                   │
  │ {Enter}                                                   │
  │ {Enter}                                                   │
  │ {Enter}                                                   │
  │ {Tab}{Tab}{Tab}{Tab}{Tab}{Tab}Sara•Jane•Student{Enter}   │
  │ {Tab}{Tab}{Tab}{Tab}{Tab}{Tab}Assistant•Vice-President{Enter}│
  └─────────────────────────────────────────────────────────┘

Ctrl-V to Insert next key as command;
Ctrl-PgUp for macro commands;  Press Exit when done
```

Figure 21-2

3. Position your cursor beside one of the {Enter} codes and delete it. Then delete the blank line so the text closes up. Pretty easy, huh?

It's not always so easy to make a correction. Removing commands is easier than adding commands. The first message below the macro editor tells you to use **Ctrl-V** to add certain commands. Tab and Enter are two of the commands for which you must use Ctrl-V. You won't know which commands require Ctrl-V until you try to add one and it doesn't work. Then you can go back and do it right! Let's practice adding a command to your macro.

Lesson 21 Exercise 8

1. Position the cursor somewhere among the {Enter} codes between "Sincerely," and your name.

2. Strike **Enter** once. As you can see, a blank line was added (which doesn't do anything), but the Enter code was not inserted.

3. Without moving the cursor, strike **Ctrl-V** and then strike **Enter**. Now you've added an Enter code to the document. In fact, you're back up to four blank lines where you only wanted three. Take out one of the Enter codes as well as the blank line. (This was just practice.)

4. Look at your macro in the editor. Is it clean like the one in Figure 21-2? Did you make some mistakes and corrections when keying your closing lines? If you have extra codes like {Backspace} or {Left}, remove them along with the incorrect material. The cleaner your macro, the more quickly it will run when you want to use it.

5. Finally, strike **F7** to return to your working screen. You might wish to use **Alt-F10** to test your macro to make sure you didn't mess it up.

This was just a brief introduction to macro editing. You'll use the macro editor in the next exercise. If you use macros a lot (and they certainly can save you time), there will be times when you'll find it easier to fix a macro than to redo it. Don't be afraid of the macro editor.

MACRO CHAINING

The term *macro chaining* refers to a number of features available in WordPerfect. The simplest macro chain is one in which one macro is imbedded in another macro so that the second macro is automatically called up by the first. In fact, you can include several macros in a chain to accomplish a particular task.

A very simple macro chain can be built with the macros you have already created in this lesson. Let's assume that every time you add your closing lines to a document, you are ready to send that document to the printer. We'll chain the print macro to the closing macro you created in Exercise 3. Follow along carefully.

Lesson 21 Exercise 9

Open the **T**ools menu. Choose **M**acro and then Define.

1. Strike **Ctrl-F10** and key your initials for your macro with the closing lines. Choose **2** Edit because you will be editing it again.

2. Move the cursor to the end of the macro on the line below your title.

3. Strike **Ctrl-Page Up.** A list of macro commands will appear. You can move quickly to a particular part of the list by keying the first letter of the command you want. Strike *C*.

4. Use ↓ until you come to the command called {chain}macroname~. Strike **Enter** to place that command into your macro. Only {chain} appears.

5. Following {chain}, key the word *print* to enter your print macro, and then key a tilde (~). (The tilde is on the shift of the key next to 1.)

6. Strike **F7** to resave your macro and exit from it.

7. Make sure your computer is connected to the printer. Strike **Alt-F10** and key your initials to run the macro. Your closing lines should go directly to the printer. Obviously, if you run this macro at the end of a letter, you'd want to proofread first. Then the entire letter is printed.

8. Finally, since you will want to use your closing macro for a variety of tasks, return to the macro editor for this macro and remove the {chain} command you just added to your macro. You've had practice with chaining, and you could do it again, if necessary.

SUMMARY

This lesson has been just a teaser in the way you can use macros to make your work easier. In addition to the things you've learned here, you can chain a macro to itself so it repeats until there is nothing left to format. You can set up a macro so it pauses while you key something on the keyboard and then starts up again when you strike Enter. You can use Esc to repeat a macro a given number of times. The list is nearly endless. In fact, WordPerfect's Macro feature is a programming language in itself.

Many people don't need all of those fancy features to get good use from WordPerfect macros. The biggest thing with macros is that you need to remember to use them. Whenever you find yourself doing something repetitive, question whether you could do it more efficiently with a macro. If so, go ahead and make one.

One important aspect of macros is remembering what macros you have created and what they are named. **Your final exercise** in this lesson is to make a list of the macros you've created in this lesson. List the name of each macro and a brief description of the purpose of the macro. Include this list in the exercises you show your instructor for this lesson.

LESSON 21 NOTES:

LESSON 22
Merge Basics

OBJECTIVES

Upon completion of this lesson, you will be able to:

1. Define the terms related to the merge process.
2. Create a secondary file.
3. Create a primary file.
4. Merge the secondary file with the primary file.
5. Merge from the keyboard.

Estimated Time: 2 hours

One of WordPerfect's most useful applications is the ability to merge a list of names and addresses with a standard document. This feature is sometimes referred to as "mail-merge" because it is commonly used to mass-produce personalized form letters and mailing labels. The Merge in WordPerfect can be used for much more. Contracts, boilerplates, phone lists, and memos are just a few of the documents that WordPerfect helps people prepare daily.

Every merge must start with a *primary file*. This is the main form containing the Text and Merge codes. A primary file can merge with information from the keyboard or a secondary file (such as an address list), or a combination of these.

Once you have created the primary and secondary files, the merge process is simple: choose the merge command, identify the primary file, and identify the secondary file. WordPerfect does the rest by preparing your multiple documents.

MERGE TERMINOLOGY

Before using Merge, you should know some merge terminology.

- Merge Codes. There are dozens of codes that can be used for WordPerfect merges. They look a little strange when you put them in your documents because they are enclosed in braces. Once you begin to work with them, however, they will become a comfortable part of your merge documents.

  A few of the most commonly used Merge codes are available in a line menu that appears when you strike **Shift-F9**. That menu is illustrated in Figure 22-1. The last choice, **6 More** opens an even larger list of WordPerfect Merge codes. We'll work with a few of those codes later in the lesson.

Choose Merge Codes from the **T**ools menu.

1 Field; 2 End Record; 3 Input; 4 Page Off; 5 Next Record; 6 More: 0

Figure 22-1

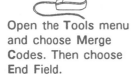

Open the **Tools** menu and choose Merge Codes. Then choose End Record.

- **Record.** A record is one complete entry in the list. For example, if you have a list of names, addresses, and telephone numbers for a group of people, the complete information for one person is a record. An **{END RECORD}** code identifies the end of a record.

  End Record codes are inserted by striking **Shift-F9** and then **2 End Record.** Each End Record code includes a hard page break.

- **Field.** A field is one piece of data included in a record. Depending on your merge needs, each of the following could be a field:

  Name
  Street Address
  City, State, Zip Code
  Telephone

  There is no limit to the number of lines in a field. Therefore, the first three lines in the list above could be considered one field, and the telephone number could be considered a second field. Including smaller chunks of information in a field involves more keying, but it makes your secondary file more versatile.

  An **{END FIELD}** code marks the end of a field. It is always accompanied by a hard return. Both the End Field code and the hard return are inserted by striking **F9**.

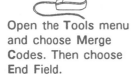

Open the **Tools** menu and choose Merge Codes. Then choose End Field.

- **Primary File.** This is the name given to the document prepared to be merged with the lists. Sometimes it is called the "shell document." Often it is a letter or memo to be sent to a number of people, although there are no restrictions on the format you might choose to use for a primary file.

- **Secondary File.** The secondary file is generally made up of some kind of list containing a number of records, as mentioned earlier. The number of records in a secondary file is unlimited.

You will be able to see the End Field and End Record codes on the screen when you are preparing your secondary files. The codes do not show in the completed documents after the merge has taken place. Neither do they show if you print your primary or secondary documents.

Fields may be referenced by name or by number. Numbered fields are fine for simple secondary files. More complicated secondary files are easier to handle with named fields. You will have an opportunity to work with both in this lesson.

CREATING A PRIMARY FILE

We'll prepare a primary file and a secondary file as examples while you are learning about Merge. It doesn't matter which is prepared first. However, you do need to PLAN your merge. Study Figures 22-2 and 22-4 before doing Exercise 1 so you can see how the primary file (Figure 22-2) will fit together with the secondary file (Figures 22-3 and 22-4).

The primary file for this merge is a letter. In the letter you will ask for the information from the secondary file in the appropriate places. In this particular letter, the telephone number in Field 2 isn't used.

Lesson 22 Exercise 1

(Template disk users: Refer to the box on page 254 before beginning.)

Open the **T**ools menu and choose Merge Codes. Then choose Field.

1. Use the Date Text feature to position the date at **Pos 4"** two inches from the top of the page. Follow the date with a quadruple space.

2. Strike **Shift-F9** and look at the list of Merge codes. Choose **1** Field and then key **1** to request Field 1. Strike **Enter**. {FIELD}1 ~ will be entered. Be careful not to delete the tilde accidentally. It MUST be in place for your merge to work. Strike **Enter** again twice so the code is followed with a double space.

3. Key *Dear* and space once. Strike **Shift-F9**, choose **1** Field, and then strike **3** to request Field 3. Strike **Enter** once. Key a colon. Strike **Enter** twice. Your document should look like the top of the letter in Figure 22-2.

4. Key the remaining copy in Figure 22-2 as the body of the letter. Use the macro named with your initials for the closing, and then key *Enclosure* a double space below the author's name.

5. Exit from the letter, saving it as **dentist.pri**.

```
                        (Current Date)



{FIELD}1~

Dear {FIELD}3~:

Thank you, {FIELD}3~, for agreeing to sell 50 tickets to the
Annual Dentist's Ball scheduled for the second Saturday
night of next month.

Your pack of 50 tickets is enclosed.  Remember that the
price per ticket is $5.  You might remind folks who are
hesitant to buy that the price at the door will be $6.
```

We really appreciate your willingness to help with this
worthwhile project. As you know, the proceeds from the ball
will be used to provide scholarships for students from next
year's graduating class who are interested in studying
dentistry.

You may turn in the cash from your sales and any unsold
tickets at the door the evening of the ball. We are hoping
that you won't have any unsold tickets to return.

Again, thank you. See you at the Ball!

                              (Use the macro created with your
                              initials for the closing.)

Enclosure

Figure 22-2

TEMPLATE DISK USERS:

1. Follow Steps 1-3 of the exercise.
2. Instead of keying the body of the letter, retrieve **dent1.pri** from
    the template files.
3. Proofread and save the document as directed.

CREATING A SECONDARY FILE

Now we'll create the secondary file (sometimes known as the list).
Follow along carefully so that the merge will be successful. The example
will be a letter sent to several dentists regarding their participation in an
annual fund-raiser. You will see how easy it is to send a group of letters
without keying each one individually.

Lesson 22 Exercise 2

Open the **T**ools menu
and choose Merge
Codes. Then choose
Field.

Open the **T**ools menu
and choose Merge
Codes. Then choose
End Record.

(Template disk users: Refer to the box on page 255 before beginning.)

1. Key the record in Figure 22-3. Strike **F9** to insert the End Field codes
    as shown. (Do not strike Enter when inserting an End Field code. The
    hard returns are inserted automatically after End Field codes.)

2. At the end of the record, strike **Shift-F9** and **E** for End Record. The
    hard page break will be inserted automatically.

3. Prepare the records in Figure 22-4 the same way. Begin each new
    record on the line directly below the hard page break.

```
Dr. Thomas Tartar
1234 Dentist Court
Appleton, WI 54911-4556{END FIELD}
555-4444{END FIELD}
Tom{END FIELD}
{END RECORD}
===================================
```

Figure 22-3

4. Check your work carefully. There must be the same number of fields in each record. Each field must contain the same information as the corresponding fields in other records.

5. Exit from the document, saving this list of dentists (your secondary file) as **dentist.sec**. Do NOT print the secondary file.

```
Dr. Benjamin R. Bitewing
456 Dentist Court
Appleton, WI 54911-4566{END FIELD}
555-3456{END FIELD}
Ben{END FIELD}
{END RECORD}
===================================
Dr. Cap Cruz
678 Physician's Way
Appleton, WI 54911-4567{END FIELD}
555-8978{END FIELD}
Cap{END FIELD}
{END RECORD}
===================================
Dr. Rhonda Sawtooth
679 Physician's Way
Appleton, WI 54911-4567{END FIELD}
555-1234{END FIELD}
Rhonda{END FIELD}
{END RECORD}
===================================
```

Figure 22-4

TEMPLATE DISK USERS:

1. Follow Steps 1 and 2 in Exercise 2 to create the first record.
2. With the cursor in position for the second record, retrieve **dent1.sec** from the template. You will need to affirm that you want to retrieve the file into the work already on the screen.
3. Follow Steps 4 and 5 to check the list and save it.

MERGING THE FILES

Once you have created your secondary and primary documents, it is a simple matter to merge them together. To do so, you must always begin with a clear screen. Let's do it!

Lesson 22 Exercise 3

Clear the screen, if it is not already clear, using your **Alt-x** macro. Follow the steps below to merge your documents.

Choose **M**erge from the **T**ools menu.

1. Strike **Ctrl-F9** and choose **1 Merge**. A prompt will ask for the name of the primary document. Key *dentist.pri* and strike **Enter**.

2. At the prompt for the secondary file, key *dentist.sec* and strike **Enter**.

3. *** Merging *** will appear in the lower left corner of the screen. Then your merged documents will appear on the screen. When the merge is complete, your cursor will appear at the bottom of the last letter.

4. Use **Home**, ↑ to move backwards through your document a screenful at a time, and look at the merged letters. Check your letters with Print Preview. Do they look good? Do you see any major errors? Is the spacing correct around the recipient's first name in the first paragraph? Are you impressed with your fantastic knowledge? (You should be!)

5. Print the letters and exit from them, saving them as **dentist.mrg**.

Now that you have completed all of the steps for a successful merge, you're on your own as you practice it again. In Exercises 4 and 5, you will key another primary document as well as the names and addresses to create another secondary document. Finally, you will merge them.

Lesson 22 Exercise 4

1. Key the copy in Figure 22-5 to create a primary file using normal letter spacing. Be careful to get the spacing exactly correct around the Merge codes in the first paragraph.

2. Exit from the document, saving it as **billing.pri**.

```
                            (Current Date)


{FIELD}1~
{FIELD}2~
{FIELD}3~

Dear {FIELD}4~:
```

Your bill in the amount of {FIELD}5~ is now {FIELD}6~ months
overdue. What has happened?

If there is a problem with your most recent dental work,
come in and let me check it. If you are having financial
problems, please let me know. Perhaps we could work out
some kind of payment schedule.

I'm hoping to hear from you within a few days.

(Use the macro created with your
initials for the closing.)

Figure 22-5   The Primary File (billing.pri)

Lesson 22 Exercise 5

1. Key the copy in Figure 22-6 to create a secondary file. Because each line of the address was a field in the primary file, you will need three Field codes for each line of the address in the secondary file.

2. Exit from the document, saving it as **billing.sec**.

3. With both the secondary and primary files created and saved, use Merge to merge **billing.pri** with **billing.sec**.

4. Check over your work carefully. Then print the completed letters and save them as **billing.mrg**.

```
Mrs. Susan Student{END FIELD}
1234 Smith Street{END FIELD}
Xenberg, WI 55555-0111{END FIELD}
Susan{END FIELD}
$374.50{END FIELD}
3{END FIELD}
{END RECORD}
==================================
Mrs. Sara Shaw{END FIELD}
611 Dalton Road{END FIELD}
Buchanan, MI 45369-0099{END FIELD}
Sara{END FIELD}
$417.57{END FIELD}
6{END FIELD}
{END RECORD}
==================================
```

Figure 22-6 The Secondary File (billing.sec)

MORE ABOUT SECONDARY FILES

Sometimes called an "address file" or a "list," a secondary file can contain all types of information. The same secondary file can be merged with primary documents such as mailing labels, contracts, form letters, lists, wills, and reports.

A secondary file contains individual records. Files must be made up of records that are exactly the same size; that is, each record must have the same number of fields. You have a great deal of freedom, however, in choosing how much information to put into one field.

The rule for preparing secondary files is: If Field 3 of one record contains information such as a phone number, then Field 3 of every record in that file must contain a phone number—or nothing at all. If you don't have the information to put in the field, the End Field code must still be there.

As you know, the number of lines in addresses vary. You don't have to have the same number of lines or words within each field. For example, you might have two address lines in Field 2 of one record and five address lines in Field 2 of another record.

File and record size are limited only by the disk space available.

KEYBOARD MERGE

Merging secondary and primary documents is a good way to produce customized documents when you have a number of them to prepare at one time. Another kind of merge is available for situations where you need to prepare only one or two letters or forms at a time and it's not efficient to create a secondary file for the merge.

This procedure is usually called a *keyboard merge*. (In some programs, it is called a "screen" merge.) With a keyboard merge, you prepare a primary file only. During the merge, you key the variable information. The code used in the primary document in a keyboard merge is sometimes known as a "stop" code. In WordPerfect, it is an {INPUT} ~ code that is inserted by striking **Shift-F9** and then **3 Input**.

A message may be included to the left of the tilde (~) each time you insert an Input code. Then when you perform the merge, the message appears as a prompt at the bottom of the screen telling you what information is needed at each merge location. As with the merges using primary and secondary documents, you must be careful not to delete the tilde character or your merge won't work! Let's try a keyboard merge. Read through all of the instructions for this exercise before beginning.

Lesson 22 Exercise 6

Open the **T**ools menu and choose Merge Codes. Then choose Input.

1. Key the paragraph in Figure 22-7. Use double spacing. At the location for each {INPUT} ~ code, strike **Shift-F9** and key **3** or **I** for Input.

2. At the **Enter Message** prompt, key the information that is shaded in the paragraph. It is shaded here so that you can more easily distinguish what goes with each Input code. On your screen, it will look quite normal.

3. Exit from the paragraph, saving it as **refer226.pri**.

This is a referral of {INPUT}patient name~ to your care. {INPUT}He/She~ lives at {INPUT}address~. {INPUT}patient name~ is a {INPUT}male/female~ who is {INPUT}age~ years old. {INPUT}He/She~ has a blood pressure of {INPUT}blood pressure~ and is suffering from {INPUT}symptoms~. A complete medical chart is available upon request.

Figure 22-7

Lesson 22 Exercise 7

1. Look at the variable information for the two patients shown in Figure 22-8. To merge the primary document with that variable information, begin with a clear screen. Then strike **Ctrl-F9** and choose **1 Merge**.

2. At the prompt for the primary document, key **refer226.pri** and strike **Enter**. At the prompt for the secondary document, strike **Enter**.

3. The document will appear with the cursor waiting for you to key the first piece of information. Notice the prompt at the bottom of the screen telling you that you need to key the "patient name." Key *Isabella Legg* and strike **F9** to move the cursor to the next "blank."

4. Continue moving through the document. Follow the prompt to fill in the information about Ms. Legg and strike **F9** after each piece of information you enter.

Patient 1

Isabella Legg
333 Erie Street
Epsonville, IA 49876
Female
Age: 33
Blood Pressure: 98/58
Symptoms: dizziness

Patient 2

Harley Hartmann
77 Yoman Court
Yaleston, IA 49879
Male
Age: 77
Blood Pressure: 180/95
Symptoms: chest pains and
          shortness of breath

Figure 22-8

---

5. After entering Ms. Legg's "symptoms," strike **F9** to add the final sentence and end the merge.

6. Strike **Ctrl-Enter** for a hard page break. Then strike **Ctrl-F9** and choose **1 Merge** to start the process over. This time, fill in the information for Harley Hartmann. When you finish, again strike **Shift-F9** and choose **1 Quit** to end the merge.

7. Print the referrals and exit from them, saving them as one document named **refer.227**.

Keyboard merges can be very useful. The preceding exercises provide a simple example of how a keyboard merge might be used in the medical environment. You can use this feature for recurring letters and reports.

Another simple yet effective application of a keyboard merge is with a memo. We'll take the **memo.frm** you created in an earlier lesson and change it into a primary file to be used in keyboard merges.

Lesson 22 Exercise 8

Choose Merge **C**odes from the **T**ools menu and then choose **I**nput.

Choose Merge **C**odes from the **T**ools menu and then choose **M**ore.

1. Retrieve **memo.frm**. Position the cursor somewhere in the **To:** line and strike **End** to move the cursor to the tab stop set at 2".

2. Strike **Shift-F9** and choose **3 Input**. Strike **Enter** at the **Enter Message** prompt. (The requested information is pretty obvious!)

3. Use the same procedure to insert an {INPUT} ~ code on the **From:** line.

4. Position the cursor on the **Date:** line and strike **End**. Reveal your codes and find the Date Code [Date:3 1,4] and delete it. Strike **Shift-F9** and choose **6 More**. A small window resembling Figure 22-9 will open in the upper right corner of the screen showing a list of merge codes.

5. Strike **d** to move to that alphabetic segment of the list. The highlight will land on the {DATE} code, and that's the one you want. Strike **Enter** to position it in your document.

6. Add an {INPUT} ~ code to the **Subject:** line the same way you added them to the first two lines of the memo.

7. Strike **Page Down**. Your cursor should be a double space below the **Subject:** line. If it isn't, make any adjustments necessary.

```
{CHAR}var ~ message ~
{COMMENT}comment ~
{CTON}character ~
{DATE}            (^D)
{DOCUMENT}filename ~
{ELSE}
{END FIELD}     (^R)
{END FOR}
{END IF}
{END RECORD} (^E)
```

Figure 22-9

8. Add a final {INPUT} ~ code, this time with a message that says *Key Memo*.

9. Exit from your memo, saving it this time as **memo.pri** to remind you that it is a primary document.

Now that you have your primary document prepared and saved, we'll use it for a keyboard merge.

Lesson 22 Exercise 9

(Template disk users: Refer to the box below before beginning.)

1. Using the **memo.pri** primary document and Merge, prepare the memo illustrated in Figure 22-10.

2. Send the memo to the *Department Staff*. It will be from you. The subject will be *Ergonomics and Orthopedics*.

3. When you finish keying the body of the memo, remember to use **Shift-F9** and **1** Quit to end the merge.

4. Print the document and exit from it, saving it as **ergo.229**.

Lewis Wickerscheim, from the local medical center, will be visiting our office on Thursday of next week. He will work with each employee individually, reviewing ergonomic factors in the way our employees do their work.

We have hired Mr. Wickerscheim for this consultation because of an increased incidence of tendinitis and carpal tunnel cases in the work places throughout the country. We feel that a little prevention early in our use of computers and automated equipment will save many of you pain and our insurance company many dollars in the years to come.

Please be prepared to cooperate with Mr. Wickerscheim and follow through on the suggestions he makes. His goal is to make you more comfortable at your workstations and eliminate any residual effects you might otherwise suffer from your work at your desks and at your computers.

Also, please clean up your workstations prior to Thursday so that Mr. Wickerscheim sees you in your best light.

Figure 22-10

TEMPLATE DISK USERS:

1. Begin the merge and complete it up to the keying of the message.
2. Retrieve **ortho** from the template disk.
3. End the merge, print, and save the document as directed.

SUMMARY

This lesson has introduced you to one of the most powerful applications in word processing—Merge. You learned how to create a secondary file or list and how to insert the codes that make a merge work. You learned how to create a primary file or shell document and how to design the document so it matches the secondary file with which it will be merged. Then you learned how to join the two using the merge process.

You learned that not all secondary documents are the same. Some consist of only a few fields in each record. Others have many fields in each record. You'll learn even more about secondary files in Lesson 23.

As you can see from the exercises in this lesson, using Merge can make you a more efficient worker. You'll find no end of ways to use Merge to speed up your work! You're nearly ready to begin Lesson 23, where you'll acquire some additional tools for the merge process. Enjoy!

LESSON 22 NOTES:

TRUE/FALSE

Each of the following statements is either true or false. Indicate your choice in the Answers column by circling T for a true statement or F for a false statement.

Answers

1. A macro is a way of streamlining your work by saving a series of keystrokes to be reused. (Les. 21, Obj. 1) . . . .   1.   T   F

2. The first thing you must do to set up a macro is give it a name. (Les. 21, Obj. 2) . . . .   2.   T   F

3. A macro may only be used once in each document. (Les. 21, Obj. 3) . .   3.   T   F

4. Commands can be added to a macro, but you can never delete anything. (Les. 21, Obj. 3) . . . .   4.   T   F

5. More than one macro can be linked together. (Les. 21, Obj. 4) . . . . . .   5.   T   F

6. In a merge, the list is known as the secondary file. (Les. 22, Obj. 1) . . .   6.   T   F

7. The exact same kind of information must be included in the same field of each record. (Les. 22, Obj. 2) . . . .   7.   T   F

8. A primary file is a document containing codes where information from a secondary file will be merged. (Les. 22, Obj. 3) . . . .   8.   T   F

9. A secondary file must be showing on the screen when you initiate a merge. (Les. 22, Obj. 4) . . . .   9.   T   F

10. In order to complete a merge, you must have both a secondary document and a primary document. (Les. 22, Obj. 5) . . . .   10. T   F

COMPLETION

Indicate the correct answer in the space provided.

Answers

1. Is there any limit to the kinds of applications for which macros might be used? (Les. 21, Obj. 1) . . . .   1. _____

2. What extension does WordPerfect give to a macro? (Les. 21, Obj. 2) . . . .   2. _____

3. What is the maximum number of characters you can use for a macro name? (Les. 21, Obj. 2) . . . .   3. _____

4. After giving the Start command when using a named macro, what must you key? (Les. 21, Obj. 2) . . . . .   4. _____

5. What is the key combination you must use to add certain keystrokes to a macro when you are in the macro editor? (Les. 21, Obj. 3) . . . .   5. _____

6. What is the word for one piece of information in a record? (Les. 22, Obj. 1) . . . .   6. _____

7. Every record in a list must have the same number of _____. (Les. 22, Obj. 2) . . . .   7. _____

8. What code separates records when you are preparing a secondary file? (Les. 22, Obj. 2) . . . .   8. _____

9. Must all the fields of a secondary file be used when you prepare a primary file? (Les. 22, Obj. 3) . . . .   9. _____

10. What code is used to insert the date automatically in a merge document? (Les. 22, Obj. 5) . . . .   10. _____

11. List one or two things that you've done in the past that could have been done more efficiently using Merge.

_____

12. List one or two things that you've done that could have been done more efficiently had you known how to use macros?

_____

REFERENCE

Turn to the alphabetized section of the *WordPerfect Reference*. How many sections have to do with macros? Page through those sections. You've learned material from four of those sections. List the four about which you have some knowledge.

_____

In the Merge section of the *Reference*, the user is continually referred to an appendix for more information. What is the name of that appendix and how many pages long is it?

_____

LESSON 23
Putting Merge to Work

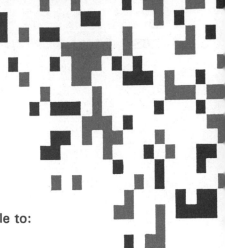

OBJECTIVES

Upon completion of this lesson, you will be able to:

1. Use named fields in your merges.
2. Use Merge for tabulation work.

Estimated Time: 1 ½ hours

In Lesson 22 you learned the terminology associated with Merge and the basics of creating primary files and secondary files. You learned to combine those primary and secondary files into finished documents. Best of all, you learned that a great deal of your time can be saved by using Merge to streamline your work.

In Lesson 23 you will learn that there are a number of things you can do to expand the power of Merge in your work. None of the applications here are difficult providing you will take the time to think about what you are doing and how you are being asked to do it. What's more, these applications might give you some ideas about how you can use Merge in your work. Have fun!

SECONDARY FILES WITH NAMED FIELDS

As mentioned in Lesson 22, you may name your merge fields to make your secondary and primary files easier to prepare. This is especially useful in cases where there are many fields in each record. One advantage of naming the fields is that when keying the secondary file, WordPerfect prompts the information to be included in each field. In keying the names and addresses of the dentists in Lesson 22, for example, the prompt might have been **name and address** or **phone**.

The advantage of using named fields in the creation of the primary document is that there is no guessing regarding which field you are requesting. You ask for it by name rather than having to try to figure out the field in which the first name or phone number is recorded.

You get to determine the names of the fields. They are keyed as part of a special Merge code called *field names* inserted at the beginning of the secondary file. Let's create a secondary file as part of a simple exercise so you can see how naming merge fields works.

Lesson 23 Exercise 1

(Template disk users: Refer to the box below before beginning.)

Choose Merge Codes from the Tools menu and then choose More.

1. Beginning on a clear screen, strike **Shift-F9** and choose **6 More**. Strike **f** for Field and strike ↓ once to highlight the Field Names code as illustrated in Figure 23-1. Strike **Enter** to choose the code.

2. A prompt will appear at the bottom of your screen asking for the field name for Field 1. Key *name and address* and strike **Enter**.

```
{END WHILE}
{FIELD}field ~           (^F)
{FIELD NAMES}name1 ~ ...nameN ~ ~
{FOR}var ~ start ~ stop ~ step ~
{GO}label ~
{IF}expr ~
{IF BLANK}field ~
{IF EXISTS}var ~
{IF NOT BLANK}field ~
{INPUT}message ~
```

Figure 23-1

3. A prompt will appear asking for the name for the second field. Key *phone* and strike **Enter**. A prompt will appear asking for the name for the third field. Key *first name* and strike **Enter**.

4. Finally, strike **F7** to tell WordPerfect you have named all of the fields and are ready to create the secondary file. The field names will appear across the top of the screen, separated by tildes. A hard page break separates the Field Names code from the first record. The top of your screen should look much like Figure 23-2. In the lower left corner of the screen, you are being prompted to key the **name and address** for the first record.

```
{FIELD NAMES}name and address~phone~first name~~{END RECORD}
================================================================
```

Figure 23-2

---

5. Key the name and address for Dr. Robert Root, as illustrated in Figure 23-3. Strike **F9** to enter the {END FIELD} code after the ZIP code. Follow the prompts at the bottom of the screen, and continue keying the information for Dr. Root. Insert an {END RECORD} code. Then key the information for the remainder of the dentists in the list.

TEMPLATE DISK USERS:

1.   Follow Steps 1-4 of Exercise 1.
2.   Retrieve **dent2.sec** from the template disk.
3.   Follow Steps 6-8 of the exercise to check and save the file.

6. Check your work to be sure that all of the information for each of the dentists is included. Notice that Ms. Cusp is without a phone number. The {END FIELD} code must still mark the place for the phone number.

7. Finally, we'll add the records you keyed in Exercise 1 of Lesson 22. With the cursor positioned below the final Hard Page code, retrieve **dentist.sec**.

8. Check spacing and Merge codes. Then exit from the document, saving it as **dent-23.sec**

```
Dr. Robert R. Root                      Ms. Carol C. Cusp
655 Longview Drive                      121 Carnation Drive
Appleton, WI 54911-9662{END FIELD}      Appleton, WI 54911-0066{END FIELD}
555-4321{END FIELD}                     {END FIELD}
Robert{END FIELD}                       Carol{END FIELD}
{END RECORD}                            {END RECORD}
==================================      ==================================
Dr. Betty Bridges                       Dr. Gingi Vitis
679 Physician's Way                     543 Meadow Lane
Larsen, WI 54947-1212{END FIELD}        Neenah, WI 54956-1001{END FIELD}
555-4444{END FIELD}                     555-9999{END FIELD}
Betty{END FIELD}                        Gingi{END FIELD}
{END RECORD}                            {END RECORD}
==================================      ==================================
Dr. Bernie Brush                        Dr. Dinah Driller
1234 Dentist Court                      445 Dobson Drive
Larsen, WI 54947-1213{END FIELD}        Denmark, WI 54208-4332{END FIELD}
555-5555{END FIELD}                     555-9876{END FIELD}
Bernie{END FIELD}                       Dinah{END FIELD}
{END RECORD}                            {END RECORD}
==================================      ==================================
```

Figure 23-3

You can't print a secondary file because the Hard Page codes between the records cause each record to be printed on a separate page. You can, however, make a usable list of dentists by merging your secondary file with a primary file that lists the dentists' names, addresses, and their phone numbers in columns.

In this exercise you must use a new code—the {PAGE OFF} code. The Page Off code disables the hard returns between the records in your secondary file. If you recall, when you merged the secondary file with the primary file for letters, each letter printed on a separate page. In this case, you want all of the doctors listed on one page. Think about what is happening as you follow along!

Lesson 23 Exercise 2

Choose Merge Codes from the Tools menu and then choose Field.

1. On a clear screen, strike **Shift-F9** and choose **1** Field. At the **Field** prompt, key *name and address* and strike **Enter**.

2. Strike **Alt-F6** for Flush Right and follow the instructions in Step 1 to request the *phone* field. Then strike **Enter**.

3. Strike **Enter** two more times so the cursor is a double space below the Field codes. Strike **Shift-F9** and choose **4 Page Off**. Your screen will look much like Figure 23-4.

```
{FIELD}name and address~                                     {FIELD}phone~

{PAGE OFF}
```

Figure 23-4

---

4. Exit from the document, saving it as **dentists.pri**.

5. Merge **dentists.pri** with **dent-23.sec**.

6. Center the title *CALLING LIST* in all caps, 2 inches from the top of the paper. Follow it by a quadruple space. Your list of dentists should look much like the thumbnail illustration here.

7. Print your list of dentists and exit from it, saving it as **dentists.232**.

PLANNING SECONDARY FILES

In the merge exercises you've completed so far, your options regarding how you could use the information in your dentist secondary file were limited. A separate field was needed for the dentist's first name so that the name could be used in the greeting of the letter. Had the name been separated into a number of fields in the secondary file, it could have been used both in the inside address as well as in the greeting. In addition, you would have had the option of greeting some of the doctors more formally (e.g., Dr. Vitis instead of Gingi).

Usually you know ahead of time how the information in a secondary file will be used. You can configure the fields in the records so that they will best fit your needs. In designing the layout of a secondary file, it is important to remember that all the records in the entire file must be keyed in the same way. You MUST be consistent about what is in each field.

Let's look at some other ways the records in the secondary files might have been divided into fields. Figure 23-5 illustrates four possible schemes that might be used in setting up the secondary file. And the list of schemes goes on, depending on the information needed and how that information will be used.

	Scheme 1	Scheme 2	Scheme 3	Scheme 4
Field 1	title	title	title	inside address
Field 2	first name	name	first name	telephone
Field 3	middle initial	street address ..	last name	
Field 4	last name	city	street address	
Field 5	street address ..	state	city, state ZIP	
Field 6	city	ZIP	telephone	
Field 7	state	telephone		
Field 8	ZIP			
Field 9	telephone			

Figure 23-5

Notice that in Scheme 1 above, a separate field is used for the middle initial. If you don't know the initial, an End Field code must still be inserted for that field, just as you did for the missing telephone number earlier in the lesson.

Had you used Scheme 1, the opening lines of the letters you created in Lesson 22 would have looked like those illustrated in Figure 23-6. Notice the spaces between "words" so the names don't run together when the merge is completed.

```
{FIELD}1~ {FIELD}2~ {IF NOT BLANK}3~{FIELD}3~ {END IF}{FIELD}4~
{FIELD}5~
{FIELD}6~, {FIELD}7~ {FIELD}8~

Dear {FIELD}1~ {FIELD}4~:
```

Figure 23-6

Notice also the peculiar {IF NOT BLANK} and {END IF} codes in the first line. These two codes go together and must be used to accommodate the middle initial that appeared in some of the dentists' names. Without the codes, extra space would be left for the initial.

These codes can also be used if your secondary file contains names of people in business where a company name appears in some records and not in others. When the questionable material is on a line by itself, a question mark can be used instead of the {IF NOT BLANK} and {END IF} codes (e.g., {FIELD}3?~).

We won't work with the {IF NOT BLANK} and {END IF} codes in this lesson, but we will work with a secondary file where each field contains a smaller piece of information. We'll begin by creating the file. That file is illustrated in two columns in Figure 23-7. It is a large file, and yours will be in one long column at the left. Once created, it will be useful in all kinds of applications.

Lesson 23 Exercise 3

(Template disk users: Refer to the box on page 272 before beginning.)

1. Key the file illustrated in Figure 23-7. Use named fields as illustrated. Key the records in the left column and then continue to the column on the right. Some records are broken from one column to the next. Work carefully.

```
{FIELD NAMES}Account Number~Title~First Name and Middle Initial~Last Name~
Street Address~City~State~ZIP~Phone~Amount Due~Months Overdue~~{END
RECORD}
===========================================================================
4439{END FIELD}                        $342.59{END FIELD}
Mr.{END FIELD}                         3{END FIELD}
Bill B.{END FIELD}                     {END RECORD}
Bloom{END FIELD}                       ===============================
543 Bixby Street{END FIELD}            8821{END FIELD}
Bloomington{END FIELD}                 Ms.{END FIELD}
OK{END FIELD}                          Mari{END FIELD}
74562{END FIELD}                       Gold{END FIELD}
405-555-9975{END FIELD}                231-A Garden Street{END FIELD}
$789.56{END FIELD}                     Gardena{END FIELD}
1{END FIELD}                           ME{END FIELD}
{END RECORD}                           04940{END FIELD}
===============================        207-555-7782{END FIELD}
2399{END FIELD}                        $34.79{END FIELD}
Mrs.{END FIELD}                        1{END FIELD}
Daisy D.{END FIELD}                    {END RECORD}
Ditson{END FIELD}                      ===============================
7632 Ann Street{END FIELD}             2310{END FIELD}
Dixonville{END FIELD}                  Mr.{END FIELD}
DE{END FIELD}                          Gary G.{END FIELD}
19811{END FIELD}                       Gardenia{END FIELD}
302-555-1490{END FIELD}                143 Gingham Grove{END FIELD}
$45.39{END FIELD}                      Gillingham{END FIELD}
4{END FIELD}                           TX{END FIELD}
{END RECORD}                           75921{END FIELD}
===============================        806-555-5561{END FIELD}
5488{END FIELD}                        $1,056.23{END FIELD}
Ms.{END FIELD}                         1{END FIELD}
Pearl{END FIELD}                       {END RECORD}
Poppy{END FIELD}                       ===============================
6732 Polk Street{END FIELD}            3296{END FIELD}
Pittsburgh{END FIELD}                  Miss{END FIELD}
WI{END FIELD}                          Betty{END FIELD}
54461{END FIELD}                       Blum{END FIELD}
715-555-4453{END FIELD}                657 Johnson Drive{END FIELD}
$125.90{END FIELD}                     Jackson{END FIELD}
2{END FIELD}                           MN{END FIELD}
{END RECORD}                           56143{END FIELD}
===============================        218-555-8223{END FIELD}
7811{END FIELD}                        $126.98{END FIELD}
Mrs.{END FIELD}                        2{END FIELD}
Heather{END FIELD}                     {END RECORD}
Hillman{END FIELD}                     ===============================
145 Highland Street{END FIELD}         6223{END FIELD}
Heightstown{END FIELD}                 Mrs.{END FIELD}
ND{END FIELD}                          Lily L.{END FIELD}
58344{END FIELD}                       Larsen{END FIELD}
701-555-3378{END FIELD}                2324 Landskron Lane{END FIELD}
```

Lexington{END FIELD}
IL{END FIELD}
61764{END FIELD}
217-555-7723{END FIELD}
$763.64{END FIELD}
3{END FIELD}
{END RECORD}
================================
4534{END FIELD}
Miss{END FIELD}
Flora{END FIELD}
Frank{END FIELD}
123 Fantasia Court{END FIELD}
Farmington{END FIELD}
MI{END FIELD}
48066{END FIELD}
906-555-2753{END FIELD}
$56.90{END FIELD}
3{END FIELD}
{END RECORD}
================================
4821{END FIELD}
Ms.{END FIELD}
Petunia{END FIELD}
Peters{END FIELD}
543 Park Place, S.W.{END FIELD}
Perryville{END FIELD}
TX{END FIELD}
76682{END FIELD}
903-555-1956{END FIELD}
$992.57{END FIELD}
4{END FIELD}
{END RECORD}
================================
1492{END FIELD}
Mrs.{END FIELD}
Rose R.{END FIELD}
Ramirez{END FIELD}
6789 Robin Lane{END FIELD}
Rockton{END FIELD}
RI{END FIELD}
02954{END FIELD}
401-555-8931{END FIELD}
$41.50{END FIELD}
1{END FIELD}
{END RECORD}
================================
5692{END FIELD}
Miss{END FIELD}
Veronica{END FIELD}
Vorpahl{END FIELD}
453 Valley Drive{END FIELD}
Vail{END FIELD}
VT{END FIELD}
05432{END FIELD}
802-555-7624{END FIELD}
$291.67{END FIELD}
2{END FIELD}
{END RECORD}
================================
8611{END FIELD}
Ms.{END FIELD}

Iris{END FIELD}
Inge{END FIELD}
987 Ibsen St., N.E.{END FIELD}
Indianapolis{END FIELD}
ID{END FIELD}
83634{END FIELD}
208-555-9075{END FIELD}
$117.98{END FIELD}
2{END FIELD}
{END RECORD}
================================
7392{END FIELD}
Ms.{END FIELD}
Marguerite{END FIELD}
Montalvo{END FIELD}
199 Morninglory Lane{END FIELD}
Memphis{END FIELD}
MD{END FIELD}
20660{END FIELD}
301-555-6673{END FIELD}
$553.98{END FIELD}
4{END FIELD}
{END RECORD}
================================
1357{END FIELD}
Mr.{END FIELD}
Sam S.{END FIELD}
Solomon{END FIELD}
5454 Sunshine Drive{END FIELD}
Stockholm{END FIELD}
SC{END FIELD}
29315{END FIELD}
803-555-2789{END FIELD}
$697.54{END FIELD}
2{END FIELD}
{END RECORD}
================================
7913{END FIELD}
Mr.{END FIELD}
Adelbert{END FIELD}
Aster{END FIELD}
67 Anklam Avenue{END FIELD}
Anchorage{END FIELD}
FL{END FIELD}
33412{END FIELD}
305-555-8642{END FIELD}
$78.76{END FIELD}
1{END FIELD}
{END RECORD}
================================
1246{END FIELD}
Mr.{END FIELD}
Julius{END FIELD}
Jacobs{END FIELD}
872 Jenkins Street{END FIELD}
Johnson{END FIELD}
NJ{END FIELD}
08466{END FIELD}
908-555-0864{END FIELD}
$2,459.21{END FIELD}
1{END FIELD}
{END RECORD}

```
7654{END FIELD}
Mr.{END FIELD}
Peter{END FIELD}
Periwinkle{END FIELD}
871 Parkside Avenue{END FIELD}
Pottsville{END FIELD}
NY{END FIELD}
13571{END FIELD}
315-555-5664{END FIELD}
$15.23{END FIELD}
6{END FIELD}
{END RECORD}
==============================
1209{END FIELD}
Mr.{END FIELD}
Charles{END FIELD}
Cosmos{END FIELD}
90-C Carlton Place{END FIELD}
Canton{END FIELD}
CA{END FIELD}
93518{END FIELD}
619-555-8765{END FIELD}
$643.43{END FIELD}
3{END FIELD}
{END RECORD}
==============================
8656{END FIELD}
Mr.{END FIELD}
George{END FIELD}
Gaillardia{END FIELD}
654 Godins Street{END FIELD}
Georgetown{END FIELD}
GA{END FIELD}
31754{END FIELD}
912-555-9112{END FIELD}
$135.79{END FIELD}
1{END FIELD}
{END RECORD}
==============================
6673{END FIELD}
Miss{END FIELD}
Gina{END FIELD}
Goldenrod{END FIELD}
876 Galley Drive{END FIELD}
Galveston{END FIELD}
OH{END FIELD}
43866{END FIELD}
216-555-7732{END FIELD}
$79.67{END FIELD}
4{END FIELD}
{END RECORD}
==============================
7531{END FIELD}
Mrs.{END FIELD}
Fern F.{END FIELD}
Fennimore{END FIELD}
543 Franklin Way{END FIELD}
Framingham{END FIELD}
FL{END FIELD}
```

```
32523{END FIELD}
904-555-9786{END FIELD}
$735.88{END FIELD}
2{END FIELD}
{END RECORD}
==============================
8675{END FIELD}
Miss{END FIELD}
Dandi{END FIELD}
Lyons{END FIELD}
131 Liverpool Avenue{END FIELD}
Lexington{END FIELD}
WI{END FIELD}
54861{END FIELD}
608-555-5656{END FIELD}
$45.92{END FIELD}
1{END FIELD}
{END RECORD}
==============================
9002{END FIELD}
Mr.{END FIELD}
Chris{END FIELD}
Carrington{END FIELD}
345 Columbine Circle{END FIELD}
Concord{END FIELD}
CA{END FIELD}
94512{END FIELD}
916-555-1032{END FIELD}
$932.55{END FIELD}
4{END FIELD}
{END RECORD}
==============================
0116{END FIELD}
Ms.{END FIELD}
Zola{END FIELD}
Zinnia{END FIELD}
111 Zeininger Lane{END FIELD}
Zacksville{END FIELD}
AZ{END FIELD}
85436{END FIELD}
602-555-7021{END FIELD}
$123.11{END FIELD}
5{END FIELD}
{END RECORD}
==============================
```

TEMPLATE DISK USERS:

Retrieve **flowers** from the template disk. Check over the file and save it as **flowers.sec**. You will be using it for a number of exercises.

Figure 23-7

2. Check your work over carefully. Make certain there are 11 {END FIELD} codes in each record! There should be 25 records.

3. Save this secondary file as **flowers.sec**, since each person in the list has a flower in his or her name. Exit from the document without printing.

Lesson 23 Exercise 4

(Template disk users: Refer to the box below before beginning.)

1. Create a primary document to be sent to the customers in the **flowers.sec** list. Format it in the usual way.

2. The letter is illustrated in Figure 23-8. Save this primary document as **flowers.pri**. Note that some of the fields of the secondary file are not used in this letter.

3. Merge **flowers.pri** with **flowers.sec**. Depending on your equipment, it could take a while! Print ONLY the first four letters. Save the merged letters as **flowers.234**.

TEMPLATE DISK USERS:

Create the opening lines of the letter as directed. Position the cursor a double space below the greeting and retrieve **flo.pri** from the template disk. Follow the instructions in the exercise to save, merge, and print.

```
(current date)


{FIELD}Title~ {FIELD}First Name and Middle Initial~ {FIELD}Last Name~
{FIELD}Street Address~
{FIELD}City~, {FIELD}State~ {FIELD}ZIP~

Dear {FIELD}Title~ {FIELD}Last Name~:

A recent check of our Accounts Receivables revealed that you have an
outstanding balance of {FIELD}Amount Due~.

Perhaps your payment and this letter have crossed in the mail.  If so,
please disregard this notice with our thanks.  If not, please make
arrangements to pay your bill in full by the end of the month.

As you know, our company policy is that all invoices are to be paid
within 30 days of delivery of the merchandise.  If your account
continues to be overdue, we will have to refuse future orders from you
unless they are accompanied by full payment.
```

Our next quarterly catalog of merchandise should arrive in your mailbox
shortly. You will find that we have an entirely new line of merchandise
which is certain to please you and your family as well as your
customers.

Please send your payment so that your account is cleared, and you can
order some of the fine merchandise featured in the new catalog.

Sincerely,

Andreas Anthony
Manager of Accounting

Figure 23-8

MERGE IN TABLES

You can also merge into a table. The nice thing about table merges
is that you can set up columnar material without having to calculate the
placement of the tab stops. Instead, simply adjust the column sizes and
center the table horizontally. Voila! You have a table that looks like you
spent all day figuring the placement of the columns!

Let's assume that Andreas Anthony is your boss, and he would like
a list of the customers whose accounts are overdue. He would like the
following information: customer's last name, state where the customer
does business, amount overdue, phone number. We will set up a table
merge to list this information. This merge requires the use of two new
codes: {LABEL} and {GO}. You will see how they are used in the table
to create a merge that works.

Lesson 23 Exercise 5

1. Create a table that has four rows and four columns. Enter the
   information shown in the table in Figure 23-9. Remember to move
   from cell to cell with the Tab key.
     When you are entering the codes into the table, the codes for each
   cell will probably be on a single line in the cell instead of split on extra
   lines as illustrated in the figure.
     The table will become VERY wide and the cells will adjust auto-
   matically. You needn't worry about the size of the table, because the
   information that will go in cells during the merge doesn't take nearly
   as much room as the codes that request that information.

2. The {LABEL} code comes from the **6 More** list of codes. Key *top* at the
   prompt for the label. The {NEXT RECORD} code can be selected from
   the regular Merge codes. The {GO} code also comes from the **6 More**
   list, and again you will key *top* at the prompt. This cycles the merge
   back to the top of the Merge codes.

OVERDUE ACCOUNTS			
Customer	State	Amount Due	Telephone
{LABEL}top~{FIELD}Last Name~	{FIELD}State~	{FIELD}Amount Due~	{FIELD}Phone~ {NEXT RECORD}
{GO}top~			

Figure 23-9

3. After keying the information into the cells, save your VERY wide table as **flo235.pri** and exit from it.

4. Merge **flo235.pri** with **flowers.sec**. After the merge is completed, strike **Ctrl-F3** and choose **3** Rewrite to bring the table back to size.

5. You will end up with a very neat table that looks a lot like the thumbnail illustration here.

6. The table will have double lines between most of the rows. You will need to fix those lines so that all lines inside the table are single lines.

7. Make this table attractive. You may refer back to Lesson 16 to review how to format tables. Here are some suggested improvements.

   • Decimally align the figures in the Amounts Due column.

   • Decrease the width of the column that contains the state abbreviations.

   • Add some space above and below the title and enlarge the font used in the title. You might also like to remove the lines around the title and the column headings.

   • If you change the sizes of the columns, be certain to go to Options and center the table horizontally.

8. You can probably think of other things to do to improve the appearance of this table. Finally, print your table of overdue accounts. Then exit from it, saving it as **overdue.235**

SUMMARY

This lesson only addressed two WordPerfect features. Much of the work you did with those two features reviewed material you have covered in previous lessons. Along with this good review, you acquired some very useful skills as you progressed through the lesson.

- You learned to work with named fields in your merge.
- You learned to merge a secondary file into a table to prepare lists without the pain of figuring tab stop locations.

Perhaps you know more about Merge than you think you want to, but if you use WordPerfect 5.1 much at all, you will find a use for most of these features. It's such great fun!

LESSON 23 NOTES:

LESSON 24
Document Assembly

OBJECTIVES

Upon completion of this lesson, you will be able to:

1. Use Merge to assemble documents from standard text.
2. Fill in variable information while merging.

Estimated Time: 1 ½ hours

In Lessons 22 and 23 you used Merge to combine lists of names and addresses with letters and table formats. By now you are probably pretty good at merging secondary files with primary files.

Secondary files can also be used as what's known as *standard text* for repetitive documents. This is sometimes called *boilerplate*. When used in this way, standard text is stored on the disk, with each sentence or paragraph considered a merge field. The sentences or paragraphs can then be retrieved as needed with a simple primary document.

Examples of this concept may be found in law or medical offices where portions of documents tend to be similar in nature. Actually it can be used in any kind of establishment where documents need to be personalized yet have a degree of standardization.

USING DOCUMENT ASSEMBLY

To set up a document assembly application, you must first create the secondary file. In the exercises in this lesson, the secondary file will contain frequently used sentences and paragraphs. Study Figure 24-1. Note that the paragraphs are numbered. Each numbered segment of text is a field in one large secondary file. Steps for preparing this secondary file are in Exercise 1.

From the secondary file, a reference copy must be prepared. The reference copy is a printout of the material in the secondary file. It is used by the person (author or boss) who will select the sentences or paragraphs to be used in the letter. The administrative assistant should also keep a copy of the reference document. The reference document will be prepared in Exercise 2.

After the secondary file is created, your document assembly materials are ready for assembly of the office documents. In this application, letters will be prepared by merging the secondary file with primary documents or *shell* documents. You will do this in Exercise 3.

PREPARING THE MATERIALS

The first step in preparing a document assembly application will be to save the paragraphs and create the reference copy for the author's use.

Lesson 24 Exercise 1

(Template Disk Users: Refer to the box below before beginning.)

Create the secondary document.

1. Start with a clear screen. Key the first sentence in Figure 24-1. Pay attention to this instruction! **Follow the sentence with a period and two spaces, but do NOT strike Enter.** Do not key the item number that is shown in parentheses.
   (These items are shown with extra space between them to make it easier for you to follow the text when keying. Do not double space anywhere when keying this standard text.)

2. Strike **F9** to insert an {END FIELD} code. The hard return will automatically be inserted.

3. Key the second item, followed with a period, two spaces, and another {END FIELD} code.

4. Continue until you come to Item 22. Key that exactly as it appears, with a double space between the closing and the company name. Strike **Enter** four times to leave room for the signature. End the text with the {END FIELD} code.

5. Proofread the entire document carefully. (When using a computer, an undetected error has a nasty habit of coming back to haunt you over and over again.) Save the document as **clancy24.sec** and close it.

TEMPLATE DISK USERS:

1. The paragraphs in Figure 24-1 have been saved with the name **assembly**. Open the document and check to see that the {END FIELD} codes are all in place.
2. Exit from the document, saving it as **clancy24.sec**.
3. Prepare the reference document and letters.

---

(1) Thank you for your phone call regarding our line of automated office equipment.

(2) Thank you for your letter inquiring about our automated office equipment.

(3) Thank you for stopping at our booth at the recent PC trade show in your area.

(4) As you know, we specialize in computers for the mobile professional.

(5) Our line of laptop, notebook, and hand-held computers is unequalled by any other company in the industry.

(6) Our laptop computers are small and lightweight, but boast all of the conveniences of a fully equipped desktop computer.

(7) Our notebook computers come with their own light-weight carrying case, or they will fit comfortably in one side of most briefcases, leaving room for your important business papers.

(8) Our hand-held computers have multi-function programs, offering you full-time management and database features as well as the capability of preparing to-do lists and notes to yourself.

(9) Our hand-held computers come complete with ports and software that enable you to plug into desktop equipment for data transfer, printing, and monitor usage.

(10) All of our portable products come with extended life batteries to give you hours of uninterrupted computing, away from electrical outlets.

(11) The VGA video displays on all of our laptop and notebook computers provide the user with sharp, easy to read, high-resolution images.

(12) A catalog about our full line of portable computing products is enclosed.

(13) A brochure describing the product about which you inquired is enclosed with this letter. Please take a few minutes to look it over to learn more about our products and services.

(14) Our salesperson for your area will call you in the next few days.

(15) The business card for our salesperson in your area is enclosed with this letter. Please call to arrange for a demonstration of any of our products.

(16) We are looking forward to working with you in an effort to equip you with the best portable computer equipment available on the market today.

(17) Our current, up-to-date stock of equipment means that you never have to wait for an order to be filled.

(18) You may place your order by mail on the enclosed form, or you may call our toll-free order department at 1-800-555-4567 and place your order through one of our knowledgeable telephone sales representatives.

(19) If you would like a list of satisfied customers in your region, please call our toll-free information line at 1-800-555-4566.

(20) We are confident that you will find our products worth the price and will return to CLANCY'S COMPUTERS again and again for your computer needs.

(21) Our staff of highly trained service technicians can solve most of your problems over the telephone. If your computer purchased from CLANCY'S COMPUTERS needs repair, send it directly to the nearest service center. You are guaranteed a 4-day turnaround time on repairs. The service center locations are listed on the enclosed brochure.

```
(22) Sincerely yours,

CLANCY'S COMPUTERS


Clem Clancy, President
```

Figure 24-1

The reference document is prepared once the secondary file has been keyed and saved. The reference document is used only by you and the boss to select the paragraphs to be used in the letters. The sentences are numbered ONLY on the reference copy.

Lesson 24 Exercise 2

Create the reference document.

Choose Merge Codes from the Tools menu. Then choose Field.

1. Center *CLANCY'S COMPUTERS* at the top of a clear screen. Center *Standard Sentences* a double space below the title. Quadruple space.

2. Key the numeral *1* at the left margin, followed by Indent (F4). Strike **Shift-F9** for the Merge menu and request Field 1. Double space.

3. Follow the same procedure to request Field 2, and continue until all 22 fields have been requested. Your document will look like the portion of the document illustrated in Figure 24-2.

```
              CLANCY'S  COMPUTERS

              Standard  Sentences


1    {FIELD}1~

2    {FIELD}2~

3    {FIELD}3~

etc.
```

Figure 24-2

---

4. Proofread carefully, check the format, and exit from the document, saving it with the name **clancy24.pri**. Do not print the document.

Choose **Merge** from the Tools menu.

5. Strike **Ctrl-F9** and choose **1 Merge**. At the prompt for the primary document, key **clancy24.pri** and strike **Enter**. At the prompt for the secondary document, key **clancy24.sec** and strike **Enter**.

   (Whenever you can't remember the exact name of your primary or secondary files, you can strike **F5** to list your files. Before striking **Enter**, amend the prompt at the bottom of the screen to read **a:*.pri** or **a:*.sec** to get a list of primary or secondary documents.)

6. When the merged reference document appears in the window, check it over for format. If you find an item broken from one page to the next, block the entire item and strike **Shift-F8**. You will be asked if you wish to protect the block. Respond with **Y** for Yes and the entire block will move to the next page. (This is called "block protect.")

7. If the document looks good, print it. If it doesn't, adjust the formatting and spacing. Then exit from it, saving it with the name **clancy24.par** (short for paragraphs).

CREATING THE LETTERS

The standard material has been created and saved. A copy of the standard text has been prepared that will be used as a reference. Now let's see how easy it is to assemble a letter using these stored materials.

Lesson 24 Exercise 3

Figure 24-3 shows letter skeletons for your document assembly exercise. Each skeleton includes the date, the inside address, and the salutation. Following the salutation is a series of numbers in parentheses. These numbers list the paragraphs needed from the stored paragraphs for the letters.

Each letter has several paragraphs. In the cases where more than one number is on a line, the paragraphs with those numbers will be joined together into a single paragraph. Follow these instructions to create the letters.

1. On a clear screen, strike **Enter** six times to position the date 2 inches from the top of the paper. Use the Date Text code to insert the date. Quadruple space.

2. Key the inside address and salutation for the first letter as shown in Figure 24-3. Strike **Enter** twice after the salutation.

3. Request Field 1. DO NOT SPACE. Request Field 4. Double space between paragraphs.

4. Request Fields 6, 7, and 10 for Paragraph 2. Double space.

5. Request Fields 12, 18, and 20 for Paragraph 3. Double space.

6. Request Field 22, double space, and key your reference initials. Double space and key *Enclosure*. Your letter will resemble Figure 24-4.

7. Use **Ctrl-Enter** to add a hard page break. Then prepare Letter 2 in the same way.

8. Prepare all four letter skeletons, separating them with hard page breaks. Exit from the document, saving your four letter skeletons as **clancy-3.pri**.

9. Merge **clancy-3.pri** with **clancy24.sec**. Page through your four letters and check them with Print Preview to be sure they look good. Then print the letters and exit from them, saving them as **clancy.let**.

Mr. Samuel Sampson
14 Singletary Circle
South Bend, SD 77402

Dear Mr. Sampson :

(1)(4)

(6)(7)(10)
(12)(18)(20)
(22)
(reference initials)
Enclosure

Miss Sing Ho Lee
992 Lighthouse Lane
Los Altos, AR 72776

Dear Miss Lee :

(2)(5)
(9)(11)(13)
(14)(16)
(22)
(reference initials)
Enclosure

Ms. Stella Severson
177 Sensenbrenner Lane
Sarasota, NC 32413

Dear Ms. Severson :

(3)(5)
(8)
(17)(19)(21)
(16)
(22)
(reference initials)
Enclosure

Mr. James Jillian
731 Jackman Way
Jonesboro, WI 54811

Dear Mr. Jillian :

(1)(9)
(11)(21)(10)
(15)
(22)
(reference initials)
Enclosure

Figure 24-3

```
(current date)


Mr. Samuel Sampson
14 Singletary Circle
South Bend, SD 77402

Dear Mr. Sampson:

{FIELD}1~{FIELD}4~

{FIELD}6~{FIELD}7~{FIELD}10~

{FIELD}12~{FIELD}18~{FIELD}20~

{FIELD}22~

(ref)

Enclosure
```

Figure 24-4

Now that you know how easy it is to prepare a letter using document assembly, you get to make up a letter using the standard paragraphs prepared in Exercise 1.

Lesson 24 Exercise 4

1. Supply the name and address of someone you know who would dearly love to have a notebook computer.

2. Prepare a letter skeleton for that person, using your own selection of paragraphs from the **clancy24.sec** prestored paragraphs. Save the letter skeleton as a primary document. You may name it, but don't forget what name you use.

3. Merge the primary document you just prepared with **clancy24.sec**. Look over the letter to be sure it makes sense. Then print and exit from it.

DOCUMENT ASSEMBLY WITH INPUT CODES

There will be times when you will want to include variables in your document assembly paragraphs to provide additional information. You may include an {INPUT} ~ code in the fields of the secondary file. As the document is merged, WordPerfect will stop at each Input code and prompt you to enter the correct variable. This is especially useful in legal applications such as wills where you can use prerecorded paragraphs and fill in the pertinent information for the particular client as the paragraphs are merging into the shell. Let's practice by amending some of the paragraphs you used in the preceding exercise.

Lesson 24   Exercise 5

1. Retrieve **clancy24.sec**. Revise Paragraphs 14 and 15 as shown in Figure 24-5. The prompt to be included at the {INPUT} code is highlighted as in earlier lessons.

Our salesperson for your area, {INPUT}district salesperson~, will call you within the next few days.

The business card for our salesperson in your area, {INPUT}district salesperson~, is enclosed with this letter. Please call {INPUT}him/her~ at {INPUT}salesperson's telephone number~ to arrange for a demonstration of any of our products.

Figure 24-5

---

2. Save the secondary document again, this time as **clancy-v.sec** (with variables).

3. Merge **clancy-4.pri** with **clancy-v.sec**. The cursor will first stop at the {INPUT} codes for you to input the appropriate information. Remember to strike **F9** after you key the information at an {INPUT} code to move to the next code.

   For Paragraph 14 of the letter to Miss Lee, the area representative for Arkansas is Cathy Krueger. For Paragraph 15 of the letter to Mr. Jillian, the Wisconsin salesperson is Juan Romero. His phone number is 414-555-1299.

4. Since Paragraphs 14 and/or 15 are used only in the letters to Miss Lee and Mr. Jillian, print only those two letters. (Position the cursor on the page to be printed and choose **2 P**age from the Print menu.)

5. Wasn't that fun? Exit from your letters, saving them as **clancy-5.let**.

PARAGRAPHS AS DOCUMENTS

Another method of document assembly preferred by some word processing users involves the combining of whole documents into a final, usable document. You learned early in your training that you can open two documents at once—one on the Doc 1 screen and the other on the Doc 2 screen. Then you can block chunks of text to move from one document to another. Like the document assembly in this lesson, this method saves rekeying of text that is being reused.

Another alternative is to create the sentences and/or paragraphs that will be reused and save each as a separate document. The assembly of the final document is performed by simply retrieving the individual sentences and paragraphs in order. It is not a merge operation unless your paragraphs contain variables like the example in Exercise 5. In that case, you would assemble the paragraphs by retrieving them. Then you would save the document and fill in the variable information using a keyboard merge. Let's try a short sample exercise so you can see how it works.

Lesson 24 Exercise 6

1. List your files. From the menu at the bottom of the List Files screen, choose **7** Other directory and key *para*. Affirm that you would like to create a directory named **para**.

2. On your List Files screen, move the highlight to the **para** directory and choose **7** Other directory again. Follow the prompts to make a permanent move to the **para** directory.

3. Key the short paragraphs in Figure 24-6. Strike **Enter** twice at the end of each paragraph and save it with the name in parentheses at the end of the paragraph.

4. Then create two VERY short letters using the letter skeletons in Figure 24-7. The procedure is to key the opening material for the letter, including the current date, inside address, and salutation followed by a double space. Use **Shift-F10** to retrieve the paragraphs in order.

5. End each letter with your closing macro.

6. Separate the letters with a hard page break. Print both letters and save the document as **para.let**. Save the document in your **para** directory.

7. Finally, list your files to see the files in the **para** directory. Move the highlight to **Parent <Dir>** and choose **7** Other directory. Follow the prompts to make a permanent return to your root directory.

This is a short exercise using an alternative method of document assembly. It is very easy. (**p1**)

This exercise in document assembly uses paragraphs saved as whole documents. It is great fun.(**p2**)

I can retrieve each sentence or paragraph individually to make up my document. (**p3**)

The final document is made up of sentences or paragraphs that have been individually saved and retrieved. (**p4**)

Whatever method is used for document assembly, the time saved in preparing the final documents easily offsets the up-front time in preparing the materials. (**p5**)

```
Document assembly saves much time in the preparation of
documents, once the preliminary work of creating, proof-
reading, and saving the paragraphs is complete. (p6)
```
Figure 24-6

```
Letter 1 to Miss Mary Sunshine, 549 Sunnyview Road,
Sarasota, FL 34343.  Paragraphs 1, 3, and 5.

Letter 2 to Mr. Ronny Ronson, 776 Running Road, Ringwald, UT
84066. Paragraphs 2, 4, and 6.
```
Figure 24-7

SUMMARY

If you had to key the lengthy document containing the paragraphs in this lesson, you are probably not convinced that document assembly is such a great tool. Actually, it is. Once the paragraphs are keyed and proofread, you don't ever have to key them again. And all that proof-reading time can be saved, too.

Some authors are reluctant to use document assembly because they feel they can improve on the way something has been said before. You may have to do a hard sell to convince your boss that he or she can make your office run more efficiently by "automating" the documents or document parts that are used repeatedly. Good luck!

LESSON 24 NOTES:

TRUE/FALSE

Each of the following statements is either true or false. Indicate your choice in the Answers column by circling T for a true statement or F for a false statement.

Answers

1. A special Merge code enables you to name your fields when you prepare a secondary document. (Les. 23, Obj. 1) . . . .   1. T F

2. You may not use more than eight characters in the name of a field when naming the fields in a secondary document. (Les. 23, Obj. 1) . . . .   2. T F

3. When you are preparing to merge into a table, you must count the number of records so you can create a table that has enough rows to accommodate all of the records in the merge. (Les. 23, Obj. 2) . . . .   3. T F

4. After you've merged a secondary file into a table format, you may not edit the lines and the column widths of that table. (Les. 23, Obj. 2) . . . . . .   4. T F

5. When you use a secondary document for document assembly, each paragraph is followed by an {END RECORD} code. (Les. 24, Obj. 1) . .   5. T F

6. A reference copy is simply a numbered list of the paragraphs included in the secondary file. (Les. 24, Obj. 1) . . . .   6. T F

7. The letter skeleton primary file prepared for a document assembly application includes codes requesting certain fields. (Les. 24, Obj. 1) . .   7. T F

8. If you include {INPUT} codes in the secondary file, WordPerfect stops during the merge for you to enter information. (Les. 24, Obj. 2) . . . . .   8. T F

9. The information that is keyed at the locations of the {INPUT} codes during a merge is always the same. (Les. 24, Obj. 2) . . . .   9. T F

COMPLETION

Indicate the correct answer in the space provided.

Answers

1. Why shouldn't you print a secondary file? (Les. 23, Obj. 1) . . . .   1. _____

2. What item must you choose when the Merge Codes menu is showing to open the window with the LONG list of Merge codes? (Les. 23, Obj. 1) . . . .   2. _____

3. What code do you put in a primary document to tell WordPerfect not to insert a hard page break before the next record? (Les. 23, Obj. 2) . . . .   3. _____

4. What two codes go together in a table merge to cycle the merge back to get the next record? (Les. 23, Obj. 2) .   4. _____

5. If you use Merge for document assembly, are the stored paragraphs considered a primary or secondary file? (Les. 24, Obj. 1) . . . .   5. _____

6. What is the name of the list of paragraphs used by the boss in a document assembly application? (Les. 24, Obj. 1) . . . .   6. _____

7. Where does the message prompt appear when a merge stops at an {INPUT} code for you to enter variable information from the keyboard? (Les. 24, Obj. 2) . .   7. _____

8. Which do you think you would like the best about document assembly—the fact that you only have to key the paragraphs once or the fact that you only have to proofread them once?

_____

9. Which application in Lessons 23 and 24 did you like the best? Were there any you didn't understand?

_____

REFERENCE

What does the *WordPerfect Reference* tell you in the Merge section about primary and secondary documents created in Previous Versions of WordPerfect?

_____

Do the illustrations in the Merge section of the *Reference* use numbered fields or named fields?

_____

LESSON 25
Sort

OBJECTIVES

Upon completion of this lesson, you will be able to:

1. Discuss the reasons for using Sort.
2. Use Line Sort.
3. Use Paragraph Sort.
4. Use Merge Sort.
5. Use Table Sort.
6. Select records.

Estimated Time: 2 hours

In the last three lessons you've been working with Merge. While there are a variety of documents that might be created using Merge, combining a standard or shell document (the primary document) with a list of names and addresses is probably one of the most frequently used applications.

If the list of names and addresses to be merged is relatively small, sorting the documents for distribution after printing isn't a big problem. When the list is large, however, and post office demands for ZIP code order are taken into account, hand sorting can be a big job.

With WordPerfect, hand sorting is unnecessary because WordPerfect has a tool called Sort that enables you to sort the records in a secondary file before it is ever merged with a primary file. What's more, you get to direct the sort. The list can be sorted in any number of ways:

- in alphabetic order by name
- in ZIP code order
- by ZIP code and alphabetized within each ZIP code grouping
- by company name
- by amount owed
- by months overdue for payments

Depending on your needs and the content of the secondary file, the list can be sorted by just about any other criteria. In addition, WordPerfect can be directed to select certain records from your lists.

TYPES OF SORT

There are four types of records that WordPerfect can sort:

- Line   lines of any kind of text separated from each other by a hard return or soft return
- Paragraph   groupings of text separated from each other by two or more hard returns
- Merge Record   records in secondary files separated from each other with End Record codes
- Table Row   horizontal rows in WordPerfect tables

Unless your cursor is in a WordPerfect table when you open the Sort dialog box, the default will always be a line sort. Let's learn about Sort as you practice some examples of each of the types.

LINE SORT

We'll begin with Line Sort. Follow the steps in Exercise 1.

Lesson 25 Exercise 1

Choose **S**ort from the Tools menu.

1. Key the list of names in Figure 25-1. Add your own name to the list.

2. With the list showing, strike **Ctrl-F9** and choose **2 S**ort. Strike **Enter** for each of the two prompts telling WordPerfect that the Input file and Output file are both on the screen. That means that the document to be sorted is showing on the screen, and you'd like it on the screen when it is finished.

3. This opens the Sort menu, which takes half of the screen. It looks frightening, but it's not so bad. We'll analyze it shortly. For now, we'll use the defaults. Strike **1** Perform Action to sort your list.

4. Voila! Your list of names should now be sorted alphabetically.

5. Save the list as **sort1** in case you need to retrieve it again for the next exercise.

```
Alberta
Dale
Judy Anne
Elizabeth
Pedro
Walter
Betty
Earl
```

Figure 25-1

Pretty easy, wasn't it? That's about as basic as a line sort can be. The people in our list, however, probably would not normally be sorted by first name. Let's give them last names and learn more about Line Sort.

Lesson 25 Exercise 2

1. Amend your list by adding a surname for each of the people in the list as follows: *Alberta Weigel, Betty Boneske, Dale Nelson, Earl Wiesmann, Elizabeth Reichert, Judy Anne Boneske, Pedro DePino, Walter Anderson.* Use your own last name.

Choose **S**ort from the Tools menu.

2. Strike **Ctrl-F9** and choose **2 Sort**. Strike Enter twice. Let's look at the Sort menu.

```
----------------------- Sort by Line -----------------------

Key Typ Field Word          Key Typ Field Word          Key Typ Field Word
  1   a    1    1             2                           3
  4                           5                           6
  7                           8                           9
Select

Action                            Order                           Type
Sort                              Ascending                       Line sort

1 Perform Action; 2 View; 3 Keys; 4 Select; 5 Action; 6 Order;
7 Type: 0
```

Figure 25-2

This menu is pretty simple when you get a handle on what it's all about. When you open it, the cursor is at the bottom, waiting for you to choose from the seven menu items. We'll discuss the first three of those items in order. Later we'll look at the rest of the choices in the menu.

1 Perform Action. This is the item you will use last, after you've made all the choices that need to be made in the menu. You've already "performed" using the default settings.

2 View. This choice allows you to return temporarily to your document to look for information that might be needed in setting up the sort.

3 Keys. When you choose Keys, your cursor will be moved into the top part of the menu where nine keys may be set. Look at the Keys section. The keys are numbered across, from 1 to 9. Each key is an instruction to WordPerfect to direct your sort. You will NEVER use all nine keys. In fact, it is unlikely that you will ever use more than three keys. The rest will remain empty.

As a default, only the first key is set. Let's talk about the three settings—**a 1 1**. **Typ** is the kind of sort. There are two kinds:

- Alphanumeric (**a**), which may include words, a combination of letters and numerals, or numbers of equal length, like social security or telephone numbers.
- Numeric (**n**), which includes numbers of unequal length or numbers containing periods or commas, like 3,451 or $5.30.

Also set is the **Field**, which is the same kind of field with which you worked in Merge. In Line Sort, each column in a line is considered a field.

Finally, the last thing set is **Word**. In the list on your screen, Alberta is Word 1, and Weigel is Word 2. But Judy is Word 1, and Anne is Word 2. To be consistent in identifying the last name, count from the right. In your list, the last name is always considered Word -1. You'll have a chance to set Keys shortly.

That's all for now. We'll finish Exercise 2 and then come back to the menu to do some other things later.

3. Key **3 Keys** to move the cursor to the Key1 position. Strike → twice to move the cursor to the Word section of Key1.

4. Key **-1** to change the setting. You don't even have to delete the number that's already there.

5. Strike → to move the cusor to the Key2 setting. You need to set Key2 to get the Boneskes in alphabetic order by first name. Set Key2 at **a 1 1**. When you perform this sort, Key1 will sort first, putting all the last names in alphabetic order. Wherever there are duplicates, it will sort the first names because of your Key2 setting.

6. Strike **F7** to exit from the Keys section of the menu.

7. Strike **1 Perform Action** to sort your list. Now the names in the list should be rearranged with Walter Anderson on top and Earl Weismann on the bottom. Your name should be properly included. Betty Boneske should come before Judy Anne Boneske.

8. Isn't that amazing? Save this list as **sort2** but keep it open for the next exercise.

Now that you know how to deal with first and last names, let's learn how WordPerfect sorts fields. You worked with fields in Lessons 22 through 24. You'll find that this isn't much different.

The names that are in the list on your screen are considered Field 1 of the information to be sorted. We will add some Field 2 information to the list. Then we'll sort it—first by ZIP code, then by city.

Lesson 25 Exercise 3

1. Strike **Page Up** to move your cursor to the top of the list. Go to your tab ruler and use **Ctrl-End** to delete all tab stops. Then set a left tab at + 2.5″. Exit the tab ruler.

2. Tab once following each name and key the city, state, and ZIP code information as illustrated in Figure 25-3. Key **Home, space** between the words in *Butte des Morts* to make WordPerfect think it's all one word. Include your address information opposite your own name. Each city, state, and ZIP code in Column 2 represents Field 2 of the list.

```
Walter Anderson          Phoenix, AZ 88471
Betty Boneske            Oshkosh, WI 54901
Judy Anne Boneske        Menasha, WI 54952
Pedro DePino             Butternut, WI 54914
Dale Nelson              Butte des Morts, WI 54927
Elizabeth Reichert       Milwaukee, WI 53211
Alberta Weigel           Hendersonville, NC 28739
Earl Weismann            Ladysmith, WI 54848
```

Figure 25-3

---

3. Now we'll sort by ZIP code. Open the Sort menu and choose **3 Keys**. The ZIP code is the last word in Field 2. It is alphanumeric because each ZIP code has the same number of characters. Therefore you must change the settings for Key1 to **a 2 -1**. (Do you understand that setting?)

4. With the cursor at the end of Key1, strike **Ctrl-End** to delete the Key2 settings. Strike **F7** to exit from Keys.

5. Perform the sort. Check the numbers carefully. Is the order correct? Save the document as **sort3**, but keep it open for the next exercise.

The trick of putting a hard space between two words you'd like considered as one word works very well when you are working with names such as River Falls, Little Chute, North Dakota, Butte des Morts, Vanden Boom, Van Hoof, La Barre, etc. When the adjoining words are keyed with a hard space, WordPerfect treats them as a single word.

Lesson 25 Exercise 4

Can you sort this list by the name of the city? You're on your own. (Hint: The city is the first item in Field 2.) When you finish, keep the document open for Exercise 5. Don't save it.

Let's take this practice one step further and do a numeric sort. Follow the instructions in Exercise 5 carefully.

Lesson 25 Exercise 5

1. Strike **Page Up** to move your cursor to the top of the list. Reveal your codes. Position the cursor just to the right of the Tab Set code.

2. Set a DECIMAL tab at +5.75" and exit from the tab ruler. Find the old Tab Set code and delete it, leaving only the one you just set. (Keep your document clean!)

3. Tab once following each ZIP code number and key these dollar amounts in a single column opposite the names and addresses. Make up a number for yourself. (It doesn't matter who gets which number.)

455	998	1334	110
24	2390	1199	786

4. Go to the Sort menu. Set Key1 at **n 3 1**. (This is a numeric sort on Word 1 of Field 3. Do you understand that setting? You should. If you don't, ask your instructor to help you understand. It's important!)

5. Exit from the Keys portion of the menu and perform the sort. Did the list rearrange so the person with the smallest debt is at the top?

6. Return to the Sort menu. Key **7** Order and change the sort from the default of Ascending (getting bigger) to Descending (getting smaller).

7. Perform the sort again. Were the results what you expected? Print the document. Then exit from it, saving it as **sort5**.

Congratulations! You are now an expert at Line Sort. All the principles you learned here will be applied in the other kinds of Sort, so be sure you're comfortable with Line Sort before moving on.

PARAGRAPH SORT

Anything separated by two hard returns can be sorted in Paragraph Sort. It can be one line or several, and the lines in the paragraph may each end with a soft return or a hard return. Paragraph sort may be used to arrange bibliographies in alphabetic order. You could also use Paragraph Sort for the names and addresses you keyed in Lessons 22 and 23 if they weren't in Merge format.

Let's use Merge to put those addresses into a usable list. Then we'll sort them using Paragraph Sort.

Lesson 25 Exercise 6

1. Create a primary document to look like Figure 25-4. It will list only the names and addresses of your **dent-23.sec** document. If you remember, the name and address field was called just that—name and address. The blank line between the {FIELD} code and the {PAGE OFF} code will cause the dentists to be separated by a double space.

2. Save the primary document as **dent-256.pri**.

3. Merge **dent-256.pri** with **dent-23.sec**. The result should look much like the portion of the list illustrated next to Figure 25-4.

```
{FIELD}name and address~

{PAGE OFF}
```

Figure 25-4

4. Go to the Sort menu and choose **7 Type** from the menu at the bottom. Then choose **3 Paragraph**. Notice that an additional component has now been added to each of the Keys columns. You now have the opportunity to identify which line of a field you'd like to consider in the sort.

5. If necessary, change the sort order to Ascending. Sort this list by last name of each dentist. The information for each dentist is considered a field. Each dentist's name is the last word in the first line of the field. Therefore, your setting for Key1 should be **a 1 1 -1**. Do you understand? Set Key1 appropriately and perform the action.

6. Now change the setting for Key1 so that it will sort by ZIP code number and perform the sort. Can you do it without help? If so, hearty congratulations!

7. Print your sorted list and exit from it, saving it as **sort.256**.

That was a simple exercise in Paragraph Sort. Obviously, it can be used for other kinds of paragraphs as well as the names and addresses of our illustrious dentists. Of the four kinds of sort, this may be the least useful to you.

MERGE SORT

In the previous exercise using Paragraph Sort, you merged to get rid of the Merge codes in the original list. In Merge Sort, you work with the secondary documents, complete with their Merge codes. The End Field codes serve to separate one field from another.

Lesson 25 Exercise 7

1. Open **dent-23.sec**. Delete the line with the Field Names code and the Hard Page code so that the first dentist's title is the first thing in the document.

2. Use **F10** to save the repaired list as **dent-257.sec**. This document is identical to the **dent-23.sec** list except that the fields are no longer named.

3. With the list showing on the screen, open the Sort menu. Change the Type to **1 Merge**. We'll sort this list of dentists in a number of ways.

4. Sort alphabetically by name. We'll first arrange the dentists alphabetically. Since the dentist's name is the last item in the first line of the first field, you must set Key1 at **a 1 1 -1**. Perform the sort. Are your dentists arranged alphabetically?

5. Sort alphabetically by city. Since the city is the first word in the last line of Field 1, your setting will be **a 1 -1 1**. Key the appropriate setting and sort the list.

   In this example, the city, state, and ZIP code were on Line 3 in all records. But that's not always true. In some addresses there are a total of four or five lines, making it necessary to count from the bottom to find the line with the city.

6. Finally, sort by ZIP code. Can you figure out how to set up the sort on your own?

   If you were using 5-digit ZIP codes and had several dentists with the same ZIP code, you could set Key2 to alphabetize the dentists by last name within the ZIP area. With 9-digit ZIP codes, this is not necessary since each dentist has a different ZIP code.

Now we'll prepare the list so you can print it. Since the list currently appears in the window, you ought to be able to print a copy to keep for your records. However, the problem is that each record is separated by a hard page break, which causes the information for each dentist to print on a separate page.

We'll make this list more appropriate for printing by replacing the End Record and Hard Page codes with two hard returns. In this way, not only will your names print in a list, but each record will be separated from the one above it by a blank line.

Lesson 25 Exercise 8

1. Strike **Home, Home, ↑** to return to the top of the list. Strike **Alt-F2** for Replace. Choose **N** at the Confirm? question.

2. At the →Srch: prompt, strike **Shift-F9** and E for an {END RECORD} code. Then strike **Ctrl-Enter** to insert a Hard Page code. Strike **F2**.

3. At the **Replace with** prompt, strike **Enter** twice. Strike **F2** one final time to start the replacement. Your {END RECORD} and {HPg} codes will automatically be replaced with two hard returns.

4. Look through your list. View it with Print Preview. The {END FIELD} codes will remain, but they won't print. Print the list of dentists that are in ZIP code order. Then exit from the document, saving it as dentlist.258.

If you would like more practice with Merge Sort, you may retrieve **dent-257.sec** and sort it in different ways. Do not save it again with the same name because you'll need it in its present form for later exercises.

TABLE SORT

You can also sort the rows of text in a table. Let's practice on the large table you created at the end of Lesson 23.

Lesson 25 Exercise 9

1. Open **overdue.235**. Move the cursor to the *B* of *Bloom* in the first row of the customers of the table.

2. Turn on Block. Move the cursor down through the table, blocking the entire table except the rows containing the title and column headings.

3. Strike **Ctrl-F9**. You will be taken directly into the Sort menu. At the top, the menu will tell you that you are sorting a table. We'll practice sorting this table two ways.

4. Sort alphabetically. Key1 should be set at **a 1 1 1**. Perform the sort. Check your work. Are your customers in alphabetic order?

5. Sort by amount due. Block the list as in Step 2. Go to Sort and change the Cell setting to 3 (which represents the third column in the table). Change from an alphanumeric sort to a numeric sort. Perform the sort.

6. Look through the list. You'll find that the double line below the customer named Zinnia moved with the name and is now in the middle of the table. (This didn't affect the alphabetic sort because Zola Zinnia was the last name in the list before and after that sort.)

7. Block the customers again. Return to the Sort menu and change from Ascending to Descending so the customers owing the greatest amount are at the top of the list. Then sort the customers again.

8. Fix the line under Zinnia, making it a single line. Then go to the bottom of the table and end it with a double line. Print your sorted list and exit from it, saving it as **overdue.259**.

Now that you are so good at Sort, that exercise seemed like a piece of cake, didn't it? Let's look at the final feature of the Sort menu—Select.

SELECT

WordPerfect enables you to separate certain records from a list. For example, you might want to send a mailing to everyone in a particular city or town. Perhaps you'd like to send a reminder letter to all customers whose bills are more than 60 days overdue.

By identifying the field where the Select criteria is found and giving WordPerfect the command to select, a large list can be cut down to exactly the records with which you wish to work. Select uses the Sort menu. Let's try a couple of exercises.

Lesson 25 Exercise 10

1. Retrieve **dent-257.sec**. This is the combined list of your secondary files. Open the Sort menu.

2. Set Key1 at Alphabetic and ask for the FIRST word of the LAST line of Field 1. (That's the name of the city.)

   With some lists, you could use the ZIP code number for Select. That won't work with this list, however, because the last four digits of the ZIP codes are different. So for this exercise, we'll sort by city.

3. Set Key2 to alphabetize the list by last name. (The setting would be **a 1 1 -1**.) Strike **F7** to get the cursor out of the Keys section.

4. Choose **4 Select** from the menu at the bottom. Your cursor will be moved to the Select portion of the Sort menu.

5. Key the command *key1 = Appleton* and strike **Enter**. This command tells WordPerfect to look at the word identified in Key1 and eliminate any records that do not have Appleton in that position.

6. Set the order for Ascending.

7. Perform the action. Your resulting list should include only those dentists who have Appleton addresses, and they should be alphabetized. Print the list and exit from it, saving it as **dent-250.sec**.

Lesson 25 Exercise 11

1. Retrieve **overdue.259**. This is the table listing the customers who have large overdue accounts. The last time you worked with this list, you sorted it so that the largest accounts are at the top of the list.

2. Block everything in the table except the rows containing the title and the column headings.

3. Open the Sort menu and go to the Keys section. Set Key1 and **n 3 1 1** because we are going to select only the largest accounts. Go to Key2 and strike **Ctrl-End** to remove the settings there. Then strike **F7** to exit the Keys portion of the menu.

4. Choose **4 Select**. Key the following command: *key1 > = $500.00* and strike **Enter**. This tells WordPerfect to look for amounts greater than or equal to $500.

5. Set Order at Descending.

6. Finally, perform the action. Look at the list that results. The column headings and title should still be in place. The customers with accounts in excess of $500 should be listed with the greatest number at the top and the smallest at the bottom.

7. Note that the lines at the bottom of the table need to be repaired again. Fix the lines and print the table. Then exit from it, saving it as **overdue.251**.

SUMMARY

Now you know how to use WordPerfect Sort and Select. These WordPerfect features are much like what's known as a database. Like most other WordPerfect tools, there's more to learn. The *WordPerfect Reference* or the *Workbook* contain additional information, and practice can help you to be better at Sort and Select. For now, you know how to
- sort lines, paragraphs, merge records, and table rows, and
- select certain records from a list.

LESSON 25 NOTES:

Review Exercise

(Template disk users: Refer to the box on page 300 before beginning.)

1. Clear all tab stops. Then set left tabs at +3.0" and +5.0".

2. Key the list of seniors and their college choices in Figure 25-5. Key the names at the left margin and tab to the other columns. Use **F10** to save the list as **seniors.25r** so you can retrieve it again, if necessary.

3. Go to the Sort menu and be sure it is set for Line sort. Check the order. You want Ascending.

4. If anything appears in the Select portion of the menu, go to Select and use **Ctrl-End** to delete it. Exit from the Sort menu.

TEMPLATE DISK USERS:

1.   Retrieve **seniors** from the template disk.
2.   Set the tabs as directed in Step 1. Then skip to Step 3 to complete the remaining steps in the exercise.

We will sort this list in a number of ways. How much of it can you do on your own?

5.   Sort alphabetically by last name. You should be able to do this by yourself. When you finish, print the list and save it as **sen-alp.25r**, keeping it on the screen for the next part of the exercise.

6.   Sort alphabetically by college and then alphabetically by name within the college groups. (Set the college sort in Key1 and the last name sort in Key2. You'll need Key3 to alphabetize the first names of the Peterson boys.) When you finish, print the list and save it as **sen-col.25r**. Keep it on the screen.

7.   Sort females only in alphabetic order by last name. You'll need to use Select for this. Can you do it? (Hint: key1 = female) Print the list and exit from it, saving it as **sen-gal.25r**.

8.   Retrieve **seniors.25r** and repeat Step 7, this time for the males. Print the list and exit from it, saving it as **sen-guy.25r**.

9.   Retrieve **seniors.25r** one more time and make an alphabetized list of those students who have chosen Oshkosh as the college where they wish to further their education. Check the list, print it, and exit from it, saving it as **sen-osh.25r**.

Kelly Lewis	Female	Eau Claire
Jenny Leksander	Female	Oshkosh
Dick Peterson	Male	Oshkosh
Mark Chang	Male	Milwaukee
Anne Gonzales	Female	Marion
Stephanie Roderick	Female	Silver Lake
Juan Perez	Male	Oshkosh
Steve Kolb	Male	Milwaukee
Mark Anderson	Male	Whitewater
Randy Peterson	Male	Oshkosh
Sharon Fisher	Female	Green Bay
Diane Krebs	Female	LaCrosse
Bee Yang	Female	Oshkosh
Lisa O'Connell	Female	Menasha
Brad Bradley	Male	Madison

Figure 25-5

LESSON 26
Envelopes and Labels

OBJECTIVES

Upon completion of this lesson, you will be able to:

1. Set up an envelope form and create an envelope.
2. Set up a labels form for dot matrix printers.
3. Set up a labels form for laser printers.
4. Create an envelope macro.

Estimated Time: 1 hour

In Lessons 22, 23, and 25 you worked with mailing lists. You created lists and sorted them. You created the primary letters or shell documents, and you combined those standard documents with mailing lists to create letters. With those tools, you discovered how easy it is to prepare documents to be sent to a number of addresses, whether it is several or several thousands.

All of those letters or documents, however, don't do you or your company much good stacked on your desk or that of your boss. You must come up with a way of getting them in the mail. You have a number of alternatives for distributing your documents: facsimile, electronic mail, special courier services, and the postal service. If you choose to use the postal service, there are really only three choices for preparing your mailing: envelopes, labels, or window envelopes. To use window envelopes, you simply need to position the inside address in a specific location on the letter. Labels and envelopes require the insertion of a code telling WordPerfect the appropriate paper size and type.

To use a paper size different than the standard 8½-inch by 11-inch that you have been using throughout the course, you must strike **Shift-F8** and **2 P**age for the Page Format menu. Do that now. Note that item **7** Paper Size looks somewhat like this little illustration.

Choose Paper Size from the Page Layout menu.

7 - Paper Size	**8.5" x 11"**
Type	**Standard**
Labels	

This setting always tells you what kind of paper you have chosen. If you wish to change the paper size, strike **7** or **S** to open a menu that looks much like Figure 26-1. Your Paper Size/Type menu will vary according to two things:

Format: Paper Size/Type

Paper type/Orien.	Paper Size	Pr.	Loc	Font Type	Double Sided	Labels
2 5/8" x 1" - 5160	8.5" x 11"	No	Contin	Port	No	3 x 10
Envelope - Wide	9.5" x 4"	Yes	Manual	Land	No	
Labels - Wide	4" x 1"	No	Contin	Port	No	1 x 1
Legal	8.5" x 14"	No	Contin	Port	No	
Legal - Wide	14" x 8.5"	No	Contin	Land	No	
Standard	8.25" x 10.75"	No	Contin	Port	No	
Standard	8.5" x 11"	No	Contin	Port	No	
Standard	8.5" x 11"	No	Contin	Port	No	
Standard - Wide	11" x 8.5"	No	Contin	Land	No	
Standard - Wide	17" x 11"	No	Contin	Land	No	
[ALL OTHERS]	Width _ 8.5"	Yes	Manual		No	

1 Select; 2 Add (Create); 3 Copy; 4 Delete; 5 Edit; N Name Search: 1

Figure 26-1

- What kind of printer description is chosen when you look at this menu, and
- Whether additional labels or paper sizes have been added.

No matter which printer is selected, a standard 8.5" by 11" paper size will be available. The list illustrated here is especially large and has capabilities available only on some laser printers. If you are working with a dot matrix printer, your list of available paper sizes will undoubtedly be quite different. Let's look at your list.

Choose Paper Size from the Page Layout menu.

Lesson 26 Exercise 1

1. Strike **Shift-F8** and choose **2 Page**. In the Page Format menu, choose **7 Paper Size**.

2. Look at the paper size choices available to you. Do you see an envelope size? Do you see label sizes listed? If any labels are listed, they are probably there because your instructor or another student added them. WordPerfect doesn't automatically include labels because there is such a wide variety of label sizes from which to choose.

3. Strike **F7** to exit back to your working screen. If you have another printer available, change to that printer. Then return to the Paper Size/ Type menu to see what paper sizes are available for the new printer.

4. Return to the working screen and your original printer description.

Now that you have seen a list of those paper sizes available on your printer(s), let's learn about preparing envelopes.

ENVELOPES

With a laser printer, envelopes are usually fed in the Landscape orientation. The envelopes go through the printer small end first, and the print will be sideways on the envelope when it's finished. Some brands of printers work best if the envelopes are hand fed individually. Other printers have special envelope feeders.

With many styles of dot matrix printers, envelopes are harder to feed. In some cases, the envelopes may be affixed to a backing sheet that has tractor feed holes at the sides like continuous paper. The printer needs to be quite wide to accommodate the standard No. 10 envelopes. They are an inch wider than a normal sheet of paper, and the backing paper with the tractor holes needs to be an inch wider than the envelopes.

Fortunately, WordPerfect knows enough about your printers so it is unlikely that you will be allowed to set up a paper size/type that your printer can't handle. It is important to choose your printer before working with odd-sized paper. When you have created a new setting, that setting is then saved with your printer description.

Lesson 26 Exercise 2

1. Check your printer setting. Then go to the Paper Size/Type menu.

2. Look for the envelope setting. It will be either 9.5″ x 4″ or 4″ x 9.5″. If it is there, move the highlight to that choice and strike **1 Select** to choose it. Return to your working screen. Skip to Step 5.

3. If no envelope setting appears, choose **2 Add** to open the Format Paper Type menu. Choose **5 Envelope**. That opens the menu illustrated in Figure 26-2.

Format: Edit Paper Definition

	Filename	HPLASIII.PRS
1	Paper Size	8.5″ x 11″
2	Paper Type	Envelope
3	Font Type	Portrait
4	Prompt to Load	No
5	Location	Continuous
6	Double Sided Print	No
7	Binding Edge	Left
8	Labels	No
9	Text Adjust - Top	0″
	Side	0″

Figure 26-2

Format: Paper Size	Width Height
1 Standard	(8.5″ x 11″)
2 Standard Landscape	(11″ x 8.5″)
3 Legal	(8.5″ x 14″)
4 Legal Landscape	(14″ x 8.5″)
5 Envelope	(9.5″ x 4″)
6 Half Sheet	(5.5″ x 8.5″)
7 US Government	(8″ x 11″)
8 A4	(210mm x 297mm)
9 A4 Landscape	(297mm x 210mm)
o Other	

Figure 26-3

4. Choose **1** Paper Size. Another menu will open that looks much like Figure 26-3. Here you will choose the envelope setting and return to the Paper Size/Type menu.

5. With the highlight on the envelope form, strike **1** Select. Look at the Paper Size/Type code in Reveal Codes. Then use Print Preview to see how your blank envelope will look.

Now that you have the proper setting for your envelope, you need to place the address on the envelope in the proper location. The following exercise assumes the return address is preprinted.

Lesson 26 Exercise 3

1. Go to the Line Format menu and change your left margin to 4.5". Change the right margin to 0.5".

2. Go to the Page Format menu and change your top margin to 2.0" and the bottom to 0.5".

    Please note that most laser printers have an area around the edges of the paper where no text may be printed. This is called the no-print zone. The size of that zone varies according to the printer. If the setting you key for the margins conflicts with your printer's capabilities, your setting will be changed to an acceptable setting. The half-inch settings you've entered for the right and bottom margins will be more than adequate.

3. Close the menu and key your name and address for the envelope.

4. Look at the envelope with Print Preview. If it looks good, print it. You may use a regular envelope to print this exercise, or you may cut a piece of paper so it measures 9.5 inches by 4 inches. Get help from your instructor if you don't know how to feed the envelope through the printer. Exit from the document, saving it as **myadress.263**.

    Note that even if you were unable to create the envelope form and print the envelope, you can make the margin settings and print your address in the proper location on a full sheet of paper.

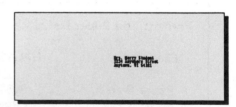

LABELS

WordPerfect 5.1 for DOS makes label preparation quite easy for you. The program comes equipped with a macro that lists a wide variety of standard label sizes from which you may choose for your label needs. The newer your WordPerfect program is (upgrade dates will vary), the more label choices you will have.

Your local stationery supply store also helps make label preparation easy by carrying a wide variety of labels from which you may choose. Again, you must consider your printer when choosing the labels type.

Dot Matrix Printers

If you are working with a dot matrix printer, in all likelihood you will use labels that are about 4 inches wide and 1 inch tall. Your labels will feed through the printer in a single row. Other sizes are available. For example, you can get labels that feed through the printer in a double row; two labels beside each other are about the width of a piece of paper.

The labels we will set up in the next exercise will be dot matrix labels that come in a single row. If you have labels of this type to print, you can adjust the distance between the tractors on the printer to accommodate the narrow "paper" as it feeds through the printer. Whether you have a laser printer or a dot matrix printer, follow the steps in this exercise to set up single feed labels. For this exercise, we will pretend we have labels of that type. Then we'll print them on your normal paper.

Lesson 26 Exercise 4

Choose Macro from the Tools menu.

1. Look in the Paper Size/Type menu for a 4" x 15/16" label. If that label size is there, read the steps below to set up the label. If that label size is not there, follow these steps to set it up.

2. With a clear screen, strike **Alt-F10** and key *labels* to start the labels macro.

3. A small window will appear resembling Figure 26-4. It contains a list of labels for either laser printers or dot matrix printers. The appearance of that window will vary depending on the release date of your WordPerfect software. Figure 26-4 is from the 3-9-92 software release.

   Note that under the window you are told that Shift-F3 will change to the opposite kind (laser or dot matrix). (WordPerfect opens the correct window for the printer driver you have chosen when you run the macro.)

4. Use the arrow keys to look down through the list. Notice that the list includes shipping labels, name tags, rotary index

Tractor Fed (dot matrix) Label Definitions

Number	Name	Width x Height	Columns x Rows
4013	Avery	3 1/2" x 15/16"	1 x 1
4014	Avery	4" x 1 7/16"	1 x 1
4020	Avery	3" x 15/16"	1 x 1
4022	Avery	4" x 1 15/16"	1 x 1
4031	Avery	3 1/2" x 15/16"	3 x 1
4060	Avery	3 1/2" x 1 7/16"	1 x 1
4065	Avery	4" x 15/16"	1 x 1

(PgUp-Dn, or ↑ or ↓ arrows)
Switch (Shift-F3) for Page (laser) printer labels
Enter to create label

Figure 26-4

labels (for rolodex address files), and a wide variety of other label sizes. Again, this list will vary depending on the software release date.

5. Move the highlight to the label that measures 4" x 15/16". In this list, it is an Avery label, #4065. If that label size isn't available, choose a similar size. Strike **Enter** to choose that label size.

6. At the prompt, key **1** to tell WordPerfect that this will be a **Continuous** kind of label.

7. Return to the Paper Size/Type menu. Position the highlight on the selected label and key **1** Select to put the code in your document.

8. Look at the code with Reveal Codes. Then use Print Preview to see just what that blank label will look like.

Now that the label size is set up, let's use the labels for something useful. In Lesson 23 you worked with a list of dentists, **dent-23.sec**. Now we'll prepare labels so you can "mail" those letters.

Lesson 26 Exercise 5

1. Set your left margin at 0.25". Set the right margin at 0".

2. Insert a Center Page (top to bottom) code (from the Page Format menu) to center the text on the labels.

3. On your working screen, request Field 1. (The {FIELD}1~ code will be the only thing showing on your screen.)

4. Save the label format as **labsing.pri** (that's single labels, with the letters *lab* first so all your labels will appear together in your file list).

5. Merge **labsing.pri** with **dent-23.sec**. Note that the labels are separated from one another with a double rule (that's a page break, of course).

6. Use Print Preview to see a label. Strike **Page Down** to look at the next label.

7. Return to your working screen and print your labels. WordPerfect will print them in a row on one sheet of paper because it thinks you have label paper in the printer.

8. Print your page of labels and exit from them, saving them as **lab5.mrg**.

Let's take a moment to analyze what you did to prepare these labels. You first made sure the proper label size was in the Paper Size/Type list. If it wasn't there, you added it. Then you created a primary file for the single row of labels. Finally, you merged that primary file with an existing secondary file and printed the labels.

The printed labels, if you used plain paper, looked much like the lists of dentists you prepared in earlier lessons. The difference was evident when you used Print Preview. WordPerfect showed your label on a piece of paper the size of a label. When you printed lists of dentists in earlier lessons, Print Preview showed those dentists all on one page.

Now let's apply what you've learned to the preparation of labels using a laser printer.

Laser Printer

If you have a laser printer, the labels you will probably use come on a standard sheet of paper. If the labels are one inch high, the labels are considered 3 x 10 labels (30 per page). A half-inch of space is unusable at the top and bottom of the page because of the no-print zone. If you wish to use larger labels, you can choose the 2 x 7 size (2 labels across and 7 labels from top to bottom—a total of 14 per page).

When printing labels on a laser printer, you must buy labels that are specifically manufactured for laser printers. If you don't, the heat applied to the paper in the laser printing process can either ruin the labels, or cause them to become jammed in your printer. This is NOT a fun thing to have happen. Also, some laser printers have a "door" that opens at the back of the printer for the labels to eject. This eliminates the need for the labels to go around the last tight roller in the printer. (This is useful for envelopes, too!)

When preparing labels for a laser printer, there is one extra step that you must NOT ignore. The Paper Size/Type code must go in a special place called Initial Codes. The instructions for your exercise will help you do this correctly. If the Paper Size/Type code is placed in your document like you did in the single-feed labels for the dot matrix printer, your labels will print one to a full sheet of paper, no matter how you try to manipulate the primary document.

Labels are costly. In all likelihood, you will practice printing your labels on your regular classroom paper. The Labels format can be prepared, anyhow. Follow along.

Lesson 26 Exercise 6

1. Go to the Paper Size/Type menu and look at the choices available. If 3 x 10 labels measuring 2⅝" x 1" appear in the list, do NOT select them again. Skip to Step 5. Otherwise they will continue to accumulate, and the list will get long.

2. Run the *labels* macro and look at the list of labels available for laser printers. (If the dot matrix list appears, use **Shift-F3** to switch to the other list.) The list that appears for the laser printer will look much like the one for dot matrix printers in Figure 26-4.

Choose **Document** from the **Layout** menu.

3. Find the 3 x 10 labels that measure 2⅝" x 1". Choose that label size and add it to your Paper Size/Type list. Return to your working screen.

4. On a clear screen (reveal your codes, if you must, to make sure there are no lingering codes), strike **Shift-F8** and choose **3 Document**.

5. Choose **2** Initial Codes. You will be taken to a special Initial Codes screen with the ruler across the center. ON THIS SCREEN, go to the Paper Size/Type menu and choose your 3 x 10 labels. Look at the code as it appears on your special screen. Strike **F7** a number of times to return to your document. On your way back to your working screen, you will come to the Format menu twice—once when you exit the Paper Size/Type menu and then when you exit from Initial Codes.

6. Look in Reveal Codes. The Paper Size/Type code will NOT show here.

7. Enter a Center Page (top to bottom) code to center the label information on the label. Then enter a {FIELD}1 ~ code.

8. Save the label format as **lab3col.pri** and exit from it.

Lesson 26 Exercise 7

1. Merge **lab3col.pri** and **dent-23.sec**.

2. Check your labels with Print Preview. They should look like the thumbnail illustration here.

3. Print the entire set of labels. Note that Benjamin Bitewing has a problem. You may remove the middle initial to make his name fit on one line, if you'd like.

4. Save the exercise as **lab7.mrg** and exit from it.

Let's try one more exercise with labels to help you feel comfortable with them. This will include the 2 x 7 labels we discussed earlier. They are larger and would better accommodate longer names such as that of Dr. Bitewing. The instructions will be less specific, so you can test your knowledge as you go.

Lesson 26 Exercise 8

1. Check your list of paper sizes to see if a 2 x 7 label is there (Avery #5162, perhaps?). If it's not, run the *labels* macro to add it to the list.

2. Back on your working screen, go to the Document Format menu and choose Initial Codes.

3. Once in Initial Codes, go to the Page Format menu and choose the 2 x 7 label form. Return out of the Page Format menu and the Document Format menu to your working screen.

4. Enter the Center Page code and the {FIELD}1 ~ code. Save your label format as **lab2col.pri** and exit from it.

5. Merge **lab2col.pri** with **dent-23.sec**. Look at your labels in Print Preview before printing.

6. Save the merged document as **lab8.mrg** and exit from it.

ENVELOPE MACRO

You have primary documents prepared for each time you wish to merge a secondary document with a label format. But setting up an envelope for each letter you prepare is unnecessary. In the final exercise for this lesson, you will prepare a macro that lifts the address from a letter and automatically places it in the correct position on an envelope. Follow along carefully.

Lesson 26 Exercise 9

Choose **M**acro from the **T**ools menu.

1. Open the letter named **berry.197**. Position the cursor at the beginning of the *M* for *Mrs. Susan Sanderfoot*.

2. Strike **Ctrl-F10** to define a macro. Name your macro **envelope**. You do not need to give it a description.

3. When **Macro Def** begins blinking in the lower left corner of the screen, turn on Block (**F12**).

4. Strike **F2** for Search and strike **Enter** twice. Strike **F2** again to tell WordPerfect to search for two hard returns. (The cursor will move to the bottom of the inside address.) Strike **Ctrl-F4** and choose first **1 Block** and then **2 Copy**.

5. Strike **Shift-F3** to move the cursor to the Doc 2 screen. WordPerfect is still waiting for you to strike **Enter** to complete the move. Don't do it yet!

6. Go to the Page Format menu and then to the Paper Size/Type menu and choose your envelope form. Back at the Page Format menu, set your top margin at 2″ and the bottom at 0.5″.

7. Go to the Line Format menu and set the left margin at 4.5″ and the right margin at 0.5″. Return to your working screen and strike **Enter**. The address you copied from the letter should be on the Doc 2 screen.

8. Strike **Ctrl-F10** to end your macro. Print the envelope and close the document without saving.

With the envelope macro, you should be able to position the cursor at the beginning of the inside address of any letter and run the macro. The envelope will be prepared on the Doc 2 screen, and you can print it before or after you print your letter. Isn't that clever?

SUMMARY

In this lesson you learned to set up a document of a size other than the standard 8½ x 11-inch document. You learned that you can print envelopes on some laser printers and on some dot matrix printers and that the envelope format may be selected from the Paper Size/Type menu.

You also learned that you can create a variety of label types, depending on the kind of printer you have. With the labels, you learned that the Paper Size/Type code must go in a new location—the Document Initial Codes, which is accessed by choosing Document from the Format menu. You might feel this lesson took you through envelopes and labels very quickly. It did. You will have a chance to review creating your primary document in some of the exercises yet to come, but once the label and envelope forms for your printer are listed in the Paper Size/Type menu, it's easy to choose the form and create the primary document!

COMMAND SUMMARY

Feature	Function	Menu	Lesson
Block Protect	Block Text, Shift-F8		24
Create Directory	F5	File	20
Define Macro	Ctrl-F10	Tools, Macro	21
End Record Code	Shift-F9, E	Tools, Merge Codes	22
End Field Code	F9	Tools, Merge Codes	22
Envelope	Shift-F8, P	Layout, Page	26
Field Names	Shift-F9, M	Tools, Merge Codes	23
{INPUT} ~ Code	Shift-F9, I	Tools, Merge Codes	22
Keyboard Merge	Shift-F9, I	Tools, Merge Codes	22
Labels	Shift-F8, P	Layout, Page	26
Macro Edit	Ctrl-F10	Tools, Macro	21
Merge	Ctrl-F9, M	Tools, Merge	22
Password	Ctrl-F5, P	File	20
Play Macro	Alt-F10	Tools, Macro	21
Request Field	Shift-F9, F	Tools, Merge Codes	22
Select Files	Ctrl-F9, S	Tools, Sort	25
Sort	Ctrl-F9, S	Tools, Sort	25
Text In	Ctrl-F5	File	20
Text Out	Ctrl-F5	File	20

LESSON 26 NOTES:

Name _____ **Date** _____

TRUE/FALSE

Each of the following statements is either true or false. Indicate your choice in the Answers column by circling T for a true statement or F for a false statement.

Answers

1. WordPerfect automatically knows whether you have Line Sort, Merge Sort, or Paragraph Sort text on the screen. (Les. 25, Obj. 1) . . . .   1.   T   F

2. Text that is separated by two hard returns will be sorted as a Line Sort. (Les. 25, Obj. 2) . . . .   2.   T   F

3. Numbers can be sorted in ascending or descending order. (Les. 25, Obj. 2) . . . .   3.   T   F

4. Merge Sort is used for secondary files (Les. 25, Obj. 4) . . . .   4.   T   F

5. In order to sort the lines of a table, your cursor must be in the table when you open the Sort dialog box. (Les. 25, Obj. 5) . . . .   5.   T   F

6. WordPerfect allows you to set the criteria for Select. (Les. 25, Obj. 6)   .   6.   T   F

7. Once the envelope form is on the list in the Paper Size/Type menu, it doesn't need to be added again. (Les. 26, Obj. 1) . . . .   7.   T   F

8. You are very limited in the kinds of labels that you can prepare using WordPerfect. (Les. 26, Obj. 2 & 3) . . . .   8.   T   F

9. The Center Page (from top to bottom) code places the address in the middle of the label. (Les. 26, Obj. 2 & 3) . . . .   9.   T   F

10. Your envelope macro sets up the envelope form so you can key the address onto it. (Les. 26, Obj. 4) . . . .   10.   T   F

COMPLETION

Indicate the correct answer in the space provided.

Answers

1. Which type of sort is used for items in tabular columns? (Les. 25, Obj. 1-5) . . . .   1. _____

2. Which type of sort is used for numbers of unequal lengths? (Les. 25, Obj. 1-5) . . . .   2. _____

3. When sorting or selecting a ZIP code that's on the same line as the city and state, what number do you key in Word to select the ZIP code? (Les. 25, Obj. 1-5) . . .

3. _____

4. If you wish to print standard size envelopes attached to a backing sheet on a dot matrix printer, what is a prerequisite of that printer? (Les. 26, Obj. 1) . . . . .

4. _____

5. What are the measurements of a standard No. 10 envelope? (Les. 26, Obj. 2) . . . .

5. _____

6. What kind of a printer prints a single row of 1" x 4" labels (laser or dot matrix)? (Les. 26, Obj. 2) . . . . .

6. _____

7. What is the size of the paper holding the labels that are printed on a laser printer? (Les. 26, Obj. 3) . . . . . .

7. _____

8. Where must you put the Paper Size/Type code when you are preparing a label format for use on a laser printer? (Les. 26, Obj. 3) . . . .

8. _____

9. Why do you suppose you had to block a section of your table in Lesson 25 before you could sort it?

_____

10. Can you think of something you do regularly that can be done more easily now that you know how to prepare envelopes and labels?

_____

REFERENCE

Turn to the Sort: Select Records section of the *WordPerfect Reference*. Look at the symbols that can be used in Select statements. List 3 of the symbols and what they mean.

_____

Turn to the Paper Size/Type section of the *Reference*. What does the Codes section tell you about the location of the Paper Size/Type code and how many of those codes you may have per page?

_____

LESSON 27
Styles

OBJECTIVES

Upon completion of this lesson, you will be able to:

1. Discuss the need for styles.
2. Create a WordPerfect style.
3. Save a style library.
4. Revise a WordPerfect style.
5. Use Styles to format your documents.

Estimated Time: 2½ hours

WHAT ARE STYLES?

In Unit 4 you will learn to create documents like newsletters and brochures, and you'll learn about some of the tools WordPerfect has available for the layout of pages of magazines and newspapers. An important concept in page layout is consistency. If the layout of page 3 is similar to the layout of page 2, and the page layout for May is similar to the layout for March and April, the reader will be comfortable with the document. Most people find it difficult to read a document that looks entirely different on each page.

WordPerfect provides you with a feature called Styles. A style is a combination of formatting codes (and sometimes text) that can be called upon when needed. Styles are given a name, are listed in what's known as a Styles menu, are saved as a style library, and can be used to format documents more easily.

There are a number of other WordPerfect features that resemble Styles. Let's review them and look at differences and similarities.

- Macros. As you learned in Lesson 21, a macro is a collection of keystrokes that may include codes or commands as well as text. You can usually start a macro by striking **Alt-F10** followed by the name of the macro or by striking **Alt** along with a predetermined alphabetic character. You have created some macros and have been encouraged to look for ways to use macros to enhance your productivity.

    Macros can be any length and can be used as many times as needed. WordPerfect makes it possible for you to edit macros, and macros are saved with the **.wpm** extension. Macros are usually saved in the macros directory, although for this course, you have been saving them on your data disk.

- **Format Documents.** The term "format document" is used in some word processing programs. This concept is not included in this course, but the theory is that you can enter all of the codes needed for a regularly used format and save those codes as a document. Then, to prepare that kind of document, you begin by opening the document containing all of those formatting codes.

  For all practical purposes, the results of a format document and a macro are identical. The major difference is that a format document is normally opened when you are beginning a document. A macro can easily be played anywhere.

- **Styles.** A style, then, is much the same except that it is accessed in yet another way. There are some other major differences that set Styles apart from the features listed above.

  ▶ A style can be the format for something you use regularly—like a parallel columns or newspaper columns format. Each time you need that format, rather than go to the column definition menu to define your column, you can access the style with the column margins already set.

  ▶ Several styles can be saved together to make up a library or collection of related styles. Each style in that library has a name as well as a description that identifies the style.

  ▶ Style libraries are created and then saved on disk using the **.sty** extension.

  ▶ You can use the Enter key in a variety of ways in a style.

  ▶ There are two varieties of styles.

    a. **Open** styles are similar to open codes. When you turn on an open style, it affects the remainder of the document or stays in effect until you turn on another style.

    b. **Paired** styles are like paired codes because you turn on the style to use it and turn it off when you no longer need it.

Styles can be saved with your other documents on either your data disk or the hard drive of your computer. Since you want your styles available wherever you are working on WordPerfect, for this course it is desirable that your styles be saved on your data disk.

Your instructor may have already set up your computer so your styles are automatically saved on your data disk, but let's look to see if the setting is correct.

Open the File menu and choose Setup. Then choose Location of Files.

Lesson 27 Exercise 1

1. Strike **Shift-F1** and choose **6** Location of Files.

2. Look at **5** Style Files. The setting should be **a:** if you are working on a hard disk system and saving your documents on a data disk or **b:** if

you are on a dual floppy system. If you are saving your documents on the hard drive, the setting should reflect the correct directory.

3. Beneath that line is a place to list the library filename that you wish to use as the default.

    For this course, the setting for that line should be empty. When you are working with WordPerfect on the job, you may have a style library that you use regularly. If so, you can name that style library in the Library Filename location, and that style library will automatically be loaded for you and ready to be used each time you start WordPerfect.

4. Make any adjustments necessary for Styles in this menu and strike Enter until you are returned to your working screen.

CREATING A STYLE

The **Alt-F8** menu is used to create styles, edit them, save them, and use them. Your first style will be a letter format that you can use whenever you wish to create a letter. It is an open style that includes letterhead information and sets the font for the body of the letter.

Follow along carefully. When working with Styles, it sometimes seems that you insert a large number of codes for a very small result. The payoff comes later when your style is put to work for you.

Lesson 27 Exercise 2

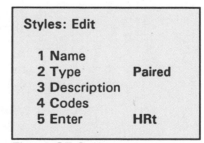

Choose **Styles** from the **Layout** menu.

1. Strike **Alt-F8** to access the Styles menu. It should be empty, and it will look much like Figure 27-1.

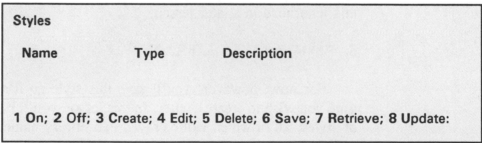

Styles

Name	Type	Description

1 On; 2 Off; 3 Create; 4 Edit; 5 Delete; 6 Save; 7 Retrieve; 8 Update:

Figure 27-1

2. Choose Option **3** to tell WordPerfect you would like to **Create** a style. This brings up a new menu as illustrated in Figure 27-2.

3. First we will name the style. Choose **1 Name** and key *Letterhead*. Then strike Enter.

4. Choose **2 Type** and change the style type to **2 Open**. The last item in the

Styles: Edit

1 Name
2 Type   **Paired**
3 Description
4 Codes
5 Enter   **HRt**

Figure 27-2

menu will disappear. Choose **3** Description and key *Letterhead and setup for letters*. Strike **Enter**.

5. Choose **4** Codes. The screen will split so you can see the codes as you enter them, much like when you use Reveal Codes. It is on this screen that you will enter the codes to format your letter.

Choose **Very Large** from the **Font** menu.

6. Give the Center and Bold commands. Then strike **Ctrl-F8** and choose **1** Size. Choose **6** Vry Large and key your entire name. Return to the Font Size menu and choose Normal. Turn off Bold.

7. On the next line, also centered, key *WordPerfect Expert* in italics. Follow it by centering your address, using as many lines as your address takes. Strike **Enter** once when you're finished with your address. (Are you watching the codes accumulate on the screen?)

Choose **Normal** from the **Font** menu.

8. Strike **Ctrl-F8** and choose **3** Normal to return to the default font. Strike **Enter** three more times. Change the side margins to 1.25″. Tab six times. Insert the Date code followed by another quadruple space.

9. Strike **F7** twice to return to the Style menu and see the line that says you have an open style named *Letterhead*.

Your letterhead is now set up and ready to be used for creating letters. There are quite a variety of things you could have done differently in setting up this letterhead. You could have changed the top margin to a half inch to save space on the page. You could have used a proportional font, providing your printer can handle proportional fonts. (You'll learn about using fonts in Lesson 33.) You could have left the side margins at the defaults or changed them to yet a different setting. It is also possible to add graphics to your letterheads. In fact, we'll add some graphics to this letterhead in a later lesson.

SAVING A STYLE LIBRARY

For now, however, you'll save this style so it's available the next time you wish to create a letter. In this lesson you'll be creating a number of styles, all of which will be saved in a library named with your name.

Lesson 27 Exercise 3

1. You should still be in the Styles menu with your *Letterhead* style showing. Choose **6** Save.

2. At the prompt for the name of the style, key your first name followed by the **.sty** extension (i.e., **sandra.sty**). Strike **Enter**. The style library will be saved on the disk you specified.

3. With the highlight on the Letterhead style, turn on the style with **1** On. Your cursor should be in place for the inside address of a letter.

4. Key a brief letter to your instructor telling him or her about a school activity in which you participate and really enjoy.

5. Print the letter and exit from it, saving it as **activity.273**.

When you exited from your letter in the exercise above, the style library was cleared from memory. Once you open a style library, the only way you can clear it from the memory of your screen is to use **F7** to exit from the document. (Don't exit from WordPerfect, however.)

USING A STYLE

Lesson 27 Exercise 4

(Template disk users: Refer to the box on page 318 before beginning.)

1. On a clear screen, go to the Styles menu and choose **7 Retrieve**. At the prompt, key the name you gave your style library (i.e., **sandra.sty**). When it appears, your Letterhead style should be there.

2. Retrieve your Letterhead style, and key the letter illustrated in Figure 27-3. Send the letter to Ms. Maralyn Howard, 34 Henry Street, Howards Grove, MN 55334. End the letter with your Closing macro.

3. Proofread, print, and exit from your letter, saving it as **gui.274**.

Thank you for your inquiry about working with GUI software. GUI stands for Graphical User Interface (pronounced "gooey") where little pictures called "icons" are used to represent computer functions. The theory is much like the use of stick figures on restroom doors instead of signs like "Men" and "Women." The rationale behind the theory is that pictures communicate more effectively than words, especially for those who don't read well.

Typical GUI interfaces include the use of menu bars, buttons, and icons. A mouse is required for pointing and clicking to choose various icons or menu choices. The text usually appears on the screen the same as it will appear on your paper. This is called WYSIWYG (pronounced "wizzy wig"), and it stands for "what you see is what you get."

A number of operating environments give you a GUI interface. Apple's Macintosh was the leader. Windows and OS/2 are newer GUI operating systems. Even some DOS-based programs are being developed with GUI characteristics, such as WordPerfect 6.0 for DOS.

Test results show that GUI users work faster and more accurately; they express lower frustration and fatigue

```
levels and are better able to explore and learn the software
on their own.  Won't you give GUI a try?
```

Figure 27-3

TEMPLATE DISK USERS:

Follow the steps in Exercise 4 with the exception of keying the body of
the letter. Retrieve **gui** from the template disk for the body of the letter.

Now it's time to work with a paired style. We'll add this paired style
to your style library. This is a style to be used for formatting the side
headings in your reports.

Lesson 27 Exercise 5

Choose **St**yles from
the **L**ayout menu.

1. Strike **Alt-F8** to open the Styles menu and retrieve your style library.

2. Choose **3 C**reate to begin a new style. Name the new style *Side
   Heading* and for the description, key *formats side headings in a larger
   font*. This is a paired style so you don't need to change Option 2.

3. Choose **4 C**odes. Because this is a paired style, a [Comment] code will
   appear. The [Comment] code separates the beginning codes from the
   ending codes. The Comment is actually a place marker that represents
   the text being formatted, as you'll see when you work with your style.

4. Go to the Font menu and choose **1 S**ize. Choose Large.

5. Turn on Bold.

6. Strike **F7** to return to the Styles menu. You'll now see a line that says
   you have a paired style named Side Heading as well as your Letterhead
   style.

7. Save your style library, using the same name as you did in Exercise 3,
   and use **F7** to exit to your working screen. Affirm the replacement of
   your old style library.

Now that you've created another style and saved it, let's try out this new
style. We'll also look at the style codes and learn about how they work in your
documents.

Lesson 27 Exercise 6

Choose **St**yles from
the **L**ayout menu.

1. Strike **Alt-F8** to return to the Styles menu.

2. Move the cursor to the Side Heading style and choose **1 O**n.

3. Key your entire name. Strike **Enter** twice and key your name again.
   Both occurrences of your name should appear in an odd color.

4. Reveal your codes. Observe the Style Off code just to the right of the cursor. If you had continued keying, that code would have continued to push to the right to accommodate the text you were keying, and it would continue to be formatted in the Side Heading style.

5. Strike **Page Up** to return the cursor to the beginning of your document. The highlight will be directly on the Style On code. When the code is highlighted, you can see the individual codes in it. Strike → once so your cursor is on the first letter of your name. Now look at the code.

6. Strike **Page Down** and look at the codes that turn off Bold and Large. With your cursor highlighting the Style Off code, key the words *is VERY smart!* (Of course you are!)

7. Strike **Alt-F8** to open the Styles menu again and choose **2** Off to turn off Styles. (You could have accomplished the same thing by striking the **End** key to move the cursor past the Style Off code.)

8. Strike **Enter** twice and key your name again. It should be in the normal color. Use Print Preview to look at the names formatted in large, bold type and the name in normal type.

9. Finally, exit the document without saving. (Remember that this clears your style library from memory, but you already saved it in the previous exercise. If you had saved the document, the styles would have been saved with the document, also.)

Now that you have created a style and saved it in a library on your disk, let's use it in a more practical way by applying the style to a document you have already created. The document you will use for this exercise is **pc-care.154**. You worked with this document in Lesson 15 when you were experimenting with footnotes and endnotes, and you should have moved it to the **Unit-2** directory in Lesson 20. If you do not have the document, you may rekey **pc-care.14r** for this exercise.

Lesson 27 Exercise 7

Choose **S**tyles from the **L**ayout menu.

c

Choose **S**tyles from the **L**ayout menu.

1. Go to the **Unit-2** directory and retrieve **pc-care.154**. Go through the document and remove the Bold codes surrounding the side headings.

2. Strike **Alt-F8** for the Styles menu. If you exited properly at the end of the previous exercise, the menu will be empty.

3. Strike **7** Retrieve and retrieve your style library from your disk. Exit from the Styles menu.

4. Move the cursor to the beginning of the first side heading. Turn on Block and strike **End** to block the entire side heading. Strike **Alt-F8** and turn on Side Heading from your style library.

   The side heading you blocked should turn to the same odd color as your name in the last exercise because you have applied the style to it. Use Print Preview to see if the side heading is large and bold.

5. Go through the rest of the document and format each side heading in the same manner. Remember to block the text to be formatted before choosing the style from the Styles menu. When you finish, page back through the document to be certain that all six of the side headings are properly formatted.

6. Keep the document on the screen as you read on.

At this point it is important that you understand the distinction of a style. When you opened this document, the side headings were already bolded. You COULD have gone through the document and added the Large setting to each of the side headings, and the document would look the same as it does now.

The difference with using Styles is that each side heading has also been assigned a "side heading" designation. So any changes you make to the Side Heading style will automatically affect all of the side headings in your document. Let's try it.

Lesson 27 Exercise 8

Choose **Styles** from the **L**ayout menu.

Choose **A**ppearance from the **F**ont menu.

1. Strike **Alt-F8** to open the Styles menu. With the highlight on the Side Heading style, choose **4** Edit and **4** Codes to open the Codes screen.

2. Strike **Ctrl-F8** and choose **2** Appearance and then **4** Italic. This will add italics to the bold and large formatting for your side headings. Exit from the Codes screen and the Styles menu. Page through your document. Did the side headings show in color or in italics? Use Print Preview. Are all of your side headings italicized now? They should be! (If your printer can't print italics, the side headings will be underlined.)

3. Do an interim save of your document. Save it in the root directory of your disk, and call it **pc-care.278**. Keep the document open.

This, then, is the beauty of the style. No matter the length of your document, any part of that document identified with a particular style will take on the attributes of that style if the style is edited. In addition, when a portion of the document needs multiple formatting attributes (i.e., bold, large, and italic), you can format that text with only one step!

Let's add another style to this document. In order to do so, you need to add some text to be formatted. The text you will add is a list. When working with double-spaced manuscript format, listings are normally single spaced. The style you will create will change the list to single spacing and tighten the space between the tab stops a little.

Lesson 27 Exercise 9

1. Amend the end of the first paragraph of the section about Equalizing the Power so the last sentence reads as illustrated in Figure 27-4.

Choose **D**efine from the **T**ools menu.

2. Strike **Shift-F5** to go to the Outline menu. Change the definition to Paragraph and turn on Outline. Key the list following the paragraph. The list will be double spaced because the text is set for double spacing. At the end of the fourth item in the list, turn off Outline.

```
. . . outlet will equalize the power coming to your PC and
give it some protection from several types of fluctuations.¹
1.    Power high, which is also known as a spike or a surge.
2.    Power low, which is also known as a brownout.
3.    Blackout, which is an extended brownout.
4.    Dirty power, or electrical pollution.
```

Figure 27-4

---

3. Open the Styles menu and create another style called *Listing*. For the description, key *Single-spaced list format*.

4. On the Codes screen, insert a code changing to single line spacing.

5. Clear all tabs. Set a left tab at 0.4″. Then exit from the Codes screen and return to the Styles menu.

6. Your library now has three styles. Save your style library with the same name and close the menu.

Choose **S**tyles from the **L**ayout menu.

7. Use Block to block the entire enumeration in your document. Strike **Alt-F8** to open the Styles menu. Choose Listing. Your list will change to single spacing, and the indent after the numeral will be a little less than a half inch.

8. If necessary to make it look right, adjust the placement of the hard returns on either side of the Style Off code so the list is followed by only one blank line. (This may be necessary depending on the size of the chunk of text you blocked before applying the style.)

9. Do another interim save of the document. Call it **pc-care.279**.

Lesson 27 Exercise 10

1. Delete the second paragraph of the Defuse Static Electricity part of the document, and rekey the paragraph so it looks like Figure 27-5. Then apply the style before keying the list as follows:

   a. After the word *include*: turn on Outline. (WordPerfect remembers from the earlier definition the kind of outline you need.)
   b. Then select Listing from your list of styles. Strike **Enter** twice for the first numeral (you need the extra Enter to get the blank line because your style has you set up for single spacing.)
   c. Key the list as shown. Because you are between the two formatting codes, the list should be formatted with single spacing and the decreased tab spacing following the numerals.
   d. At the end of Item 6, turn off Outline.

Actually, in this case you don't need to turn off the style because the text following the list was already in place. Had this been a new document that you were keying for the first time, you would have needed to move the cursor past the Style Off code before continuing with the document so the original spacing would be restored.

```
There are a number of ways to help eliminate PC problems

caused by static electricity.  They include:

1.  Antistatic carpeting and furniture
2.  Proper grounding
3.  Carefully monitored air humidity
4.  An antistatic pad or first-touch strip under your
    computer
5.  Antistatic sprays
6.  Good common sense
```

Figure 27-5

---

e. Adjust the line spacing, if necessary, so one blank line separates the listing from the text before and after it. THINK about where a hard return causes a single space and where it causes a double space!

2. Print the revised document and exit, saving it as **pc-care-270**.

In the previous exercises, we used two different ways of adding a listing to an existing document. In the first instance, you defined your outline, turned on Outline, keyed the listing, blocked it, and applied the Listing style to format it. In the second instance, you turned on Outline, turned on the Listing style, and keyed the items in the listing. Then you had to turn off Outline.

Your Listing style is fine for working with documents that have already been keyed. More practical, however, is to change that style so that you don't have to mess with defining the outline and turning Outline on and off each time you prepare a list. You can do that by adding the outline definition to the Listing style. Let's do that and practice a short sample exercise to see how well it works!

Lesson 27 Exercise 11

1. Retrieve your style library. Go to the codes section of the Listing style.

2. Position your cursor on the Comment code (anything you add will be added before the code).

3. Go to the Outline menu and define Paragraph numbering. Turn on Outline.

4. While still in the Styles menu, save your style library yet again with the same name. Return to your working screen (don't turn on any style).

5. Set double spacing and key the sentences at the beginning of Figure 27-5. Immediately following the word *include*: go to the Styles menu and turn Listing on.

6. Strike **Enter** twice (for the blank line) and continue to key the listing.

7. When you finish the last item, strike the → key to move the cursor past the Style Off code. Check to see if Outline is turned off and the spacing changed back to double by striking **Enter** a couple of times.

8. Reveal your codes and position the cursor on the Style Off code. You will see that it includes an Off code for everything you turned on in the On portion of your Listing style.

9. Exit from your practice document without saving it.

As you can see, styles can be configured to meet just about any need you might have in document creation. Sometimes they require a little fine tuning. You know enough about simple style creation at this point so you can probably do that with ease. But there's more!

"ENTER" OPTIONS

As mentioned earlier in the lesson, you have three choices regarding how the Enter key can be used in working with paired styles. The default setting is for the Enter key to perform the usual Enter function.

You can set the Enter key so that it will turn off your style or, in some rare instances, turn the style off and on again. When you are working with a style that usually ends with the striking of the Enter key, it is convenient to have the Enter key turn off the style. An example of that might be the side headings we worked with earlier in the lesson.

You won't need to retrieve the **pc-care** document again, but we'll amend the Side Heading style so it is turned off when you strike Enter. Then we'll practice with it.

Lesson 27 Exercise 12

1. On a completely cleared screen, open the Styles menu and retrieve your style library from your disk.

2. Move the cursor to the Side Heading style and choose Edit to open the Codes window.

3. Choose **5 Enter**, and you'll see the following little menu across the bottom of the screen:

`Enter 1 HRt; 2 Off; 3 Off/On:`

4. Choose **2** so the style is turned off when you strike Enter. Return to the Styles menu and turn on the Side Heading style.

5. Key your name. It should be in that usual odd color.

6. Strike **Enter** twice and key your name again. (The first time you struck Enter, nothing appeared to happen. Actually, you were turning off the style. The second time you struck Enter, the cursor returned to the beginning of the next line in the normal manner.)

7. Use Print Preview to look at your names. The first should be in large, bold, and italic type. The second should be in normal type.

8. Return to the Styles menu and save your styles again with the same name. Then exit from the practice document without saving it.

Let's create one more style to accompany your Letterhead style. In Lesson 21 you created a macro to copy the address from a letter onto an envelope format. This is fine when you have a letter with which to work. There will be times when you'll need to prepare envelopes and there will be no letters from which to copy the addresses. If you can print envelopes on your printer, you can use an envelope style to save some setup time for those envelopes. If you can't print envelopes, check with your instructor about skipping this exercise.

Lesson 27 Exercise 13

1. On a clear screen, retrieve your style library. Then choose **3 Create** to begin a new style.

2. Name the style *Envelope* and skip the description. Change the setting to reflect that this is an **O**pen style.

3. Go to the Codes screen and enter the following codes:
   a. Envelope size paper (Format, Page, Paper Size/Type)
   b. Margins: Top: .3"; Bottom: .5" (Format, Page, Margins)
             Left: .3"; Right: .5" (Format, Line, Margins)

4. Key your name and return address for that portion of the envelope.

5. Strike **Enter** until the line count is somewhere around 2". Then set a left margin at 4". That's it!

6. Return to the Styles menu. Save your style library again.

7. Turn on the Envelope style and prepare an envelope for the letter you sent to Maralyn Howard in Exercise 4. Use Print Preview to see if your envelope looks good. If not, see if you can figure out what went awry and fix it.

8. Strike **Ctrl-Enter** for a hard page break, start the style again, and prepare an envelope to send to your best friend.

9. Print and exit from the document, saving it as **env2.713**.

THE WORDPERFECT STYLE LIBRARY

WordPerfect is shipped with a style library called **library.sty**. It includes a number of prestored styles that are primarily intended for a legal office, although you might find some of them useful in your work. If you wish to look at the styles in the prestored library at your convenience, you can find it by following these steps.

1. Strike **Alt-F8** and choose **7 Retrieve**.
2. At the Filename prompt, strike **F5**.
3. When the directory prompt appears at the bottom of the screen, key **c:\wp51*.sty**. This tells WordPerfect to list all of the styles saved in the **wp51** directory.
4. Move the highlight to **library.sty** and choose **1 Retrieve**.

The individual styles in the library will then be listed on your screen, and you can edit them, turn them on, or use them in the normal manner.

SUMMARY

This lesson introduced you to one of the greatest time savers available in word processing. Not only can the use of styles save you many hours in formatting your documents, but it helps you to work with consistency. You don't need to remember a lot of settings to be used over and over—you set them once and then let the styles do the formatting.

Whenever you use a style to format your documents, that style is saved with the document. If the style is part of a library, the entire library is saved with the document.

You can have as many libraries as you want. In this lesson, you combined all of your styles into one library. In real life, you would probably have a library to hold the styles related to the creation of letters, for example, and another library to hold the styles for the creation of reports. It is important to remember to save your style library each time you add a style to it, otherwise the style will be lost for use with other documents.

In this lesson you learned how easy it is to edit a style. You also experienced how changing a style can affect an entire document that has styles attached to the document parts. You learned that if you wish to apply a paired style to text that has already been keyed, you must first block the text to be formatted and then apply the style. Blocking is not necessary if you wish to insert an open style.

This lesson probably didn't provide you with enough practice so that you feel entirely comfortable with the use of styles. Like so many of the other features of WordPerfect that you've learned, you need to spend some time with styles in your own work—set up styles that will best serve you, try them out, edit them, and use them. Like macros, this feature is useful to you only if you remember to take advantage of it!

LESSON 27 NOTES:

LESSON 28
Table of Contents and Index

OBJECTIVES

Upon completion of this lesson, you will be able to:

1. Mark text for a table of contents.
2. Define and generate a table of contents.
3. Mark text for an index.
4. Define and generate an index.
5. Prepare and use a concordance file.

Estimated Time: 2 hours

In a number of your WordPerfect lessons you have worked with lists of one kind or another. You've learned that WordPerfect provides you with helpful tools to number paragraphs, outlines, and bulleted lists.

There are other kinds of lists that WordPerfect can help you prepare. Two of them are covered in this lesson—a table of contents and an index. Both of these features are quite useless for short documents. When you are preparing a longer document, however, they can be wonderfully helpful. This lesson contains a multiple-page document that you may need to key. If the template disk is available, you may retrieve it rather than keying it. Either way, you will have an opportunity to "mark" it for both a table of contents and an index. You can learn as you go!

TABLE OF CONTENTS

In using the Table of Contents feature, the person preparing the text uses the WordPerfect Mark Text feature to mark text to be included in the table of contents. In addition, that person may designate just how that table of contents is to be displayed. When the document is completely keyed and marked, a simple command tells WordPerfect to look at all of the marked text and the page number of the marked text. It then will generate a table of contents, complete with page numbers and dot leaders, and will then position that table of contents in the desired location.

Look at Figure 28-1. This is a portion of the table of contents you will be preparing in this lesson. Your learning steps will refer you to that figure as you proceed.

Figure 28-1

Preparing the Text

When working with a document in which you'd like an automatically generated table of contents, you may key the text and then go back to mark it for the table of contents. An alternative is to mark the text as you are keying the document.

In the exercises that follow, you may use either procedure unless, of course, you are retrieving the document from the template disk. In that case, you'll mark text that has already been keyed. Follow the instructions carefully so your text is appropriately marked when you finish.

Lesson 28 Exercise 1

(Template disk users: Refer to the box on page 329 before beginning.)

1. Look at Figure 28-2. The text contains circled words and phrases. Beside each word or phrase is a number from 1 to 3. These represent the levels in the table of contents. You'll note that all side headings are Level 1 items. All paragraph headings are Level 2 items, and Level 3 items are miscellaneous key words picked out of the text.

2. Now look at Figure 28-1 and see how the Level 1 items are displayed at the margin in the Table of Contents and how the Level 2 items are indented one indent level. Both are followed by dot leaders and a page number. The Level 3 items are displayed in wrapped format with the page numbers in parentheses following the words or terms.

3. Now key the long document in Figure 28-2. Begin with a header that includes the document name at the left and the page number at the right. Suppress the header on the first page and protect the document against widows and orphans. Leave a 2-inch top margin on the first page and double-space the document.

4. When you've keyed something that should be included in the table of contents, block that item by highlighting it on the screen.
   You may block it by positioning the cursor at the beginning of the word or phrase, striking **F12** to turn on Block, and then using the arrow keys to move the cursor until the entire word or phrase is

blocked. Do NOT include Underline codes in the blocked text. You may reveal your codes to help you avoid the codes in the underlined words.

Choose Table of Contents from the Mark menu.

5. With the text blocked, strike **Alt-F5** to open the Mark Text menu. A small menu will appear at the bottom of the screen:

Mark for: 1 ToC; 2 List; 3 Index; 4 ToA:

6. From the menu, choose **1 ToC** for Table of Contents. A prompt will appear asking for the table of contents level. Respond by keying the proper level number according to the numeral beside the word(s). Strike **Enter**.

7. Reveal your codes and look at the two Mark Text codes surrounding the word or phrase. Turn off Reveal Codes again.

8. Continue until the text is all keyed and the circled words have all been marked for the appropriate level. Proofread your document carefully and page through it looking for bad page breaks and obvious problems. Remember that you can use Block Protect to keep a side heading with the text in the paragraph below, if necessary. Use **F10** to save the document as **ergomark.281**. Do not exit the document.

TEMPLATE DISK USERS:

1. Open **ergo** from the template disk.
2. Follow the steps in Exercise 1 to format the document, mark the text, and save the document as **ergomark.281**.

OFFICE ERGONOMICS

Introduction

In recent years one of the hottest topics in the office has to do with office "ergonomics." Ergonomics has many definitions. Usually the term ergonomics refers to the relationship between workers, their equipment, and their surroundings. The primary goal of office ergonomics is for workers to be safe and comfortable at their work. The secondary goal of office ergonomics is increased productivity and morale. The overall understanding is that an office that is designed around the employee will be an office that will best serve the employer.

Ergonomics touches the office from many directions--from computerized equipment to the furniture housing that equipment to the decor of the office. This report will select some of the more important aspects of office ergonomics and explore them briefly.

Computer Terminals [1]

Computer terminals have been blamed for so many ailments and maladies. Research has steadfastly refused to prove that there is any substance to the complaints that computer terminals are to blame. But a common-sense approach to these terminals in the work place can prevent even the complaints.

Display Screens [2]. Many factors need to be considered in the installation of computer monitors (or VDTs or CRTs or display screens). One factor is the clarity of the character on the screen. What about character size [3]? Can the illumination [3] be adjusted? What color [3] is the screen, and what is the color of the character? What about flicker [3]? Much of this can be assessed by spending a little time at the screen before the decision to purchase is made. In some cases, the colors available are determined by the software to be used on the computer.

Another consideration when looking at display screens is glare [3]. Some vendors build their monitors with a silky surface on the screen--a surface that is much less likely to glare than the shiny surface of others. Products are available that will cut the glare, and lighting and placement in the work room will make a difference in the amount of glare the worker will be subjected to from the screen.

Keyboard [2]. The keyboard should be separate from the equipment, connected by cord, so that the worker can move it around to a convenient location. It should be quite flat and some provision could be made for the worker to rest his or her hand while waiting for the computer to respond. In addition, the keys on the keyboard are best, of course, if their arrangement is much like the arrangement of the keys on a typewriter. It makes the transition between equipment much easier for the worker when key locations are similar.

Breaks [2]. Obviously not part of the computer work station but an important consideration for people who use one is regular breaks. The experts recommend a 15-minute break each 2 hours for people who work intensely with computers or computer terminals as the major part of their job. During that 15-minute break, the worker should move around--rotate the shoulders and head, walk briskly to the water fountain or around the office, and look out the window or across a large expanse of area to make the eyes focus on something other than the recommended 20-inch distance to the display screen.

(Lighting and Decor)[1]

While not quite so obvious in how workers perform in an office setting, the lighting and decor of the office can have quite an impact on productivity.

(Ambient vs Direct Lighting)[2] It is widely felt that the lighting in an open office arrangement should be ambient (indirect) lighting at a relatively low level. The employees should certainly be able to see as they move around the office but the usual high level of overhead direct lighting is not so widely accepted as it was at one time. In fact, direct lighting has been blamed for glare on display screens, on papers, on desks, and has been found to be largely responsible for worker fatigue in general.

(Task Lighting)[2] The alternative is low-level ambient lighting with task lighting at the work station for work such as reading and other close work. Many companies have experimented with this arrangement and have found it to be highly successful.

(Color)[2] It has been long known that color influences moods, morale, and attitude. This is just as important in the office as it is in the mental institutions and prisons where color is widely used to affect the behavior of the residents. Color designers change the popular colors like fashions in clothing change. Bottle green was popular. Then purple became the rage. Whatever the color, the decorating should be tastefully done so as not to be too soothing while not being aggravating to those who must live with it all day.

The color of the furniture should also be considered. One expert recommends that furniture should be light colored but not white, and it should be finished with a non-glare surface.

(Furniture)[1]

There has been quite a revolution in office furniture with the advent of computerized equipment.

(Desk)[2] designers have a whole new set of considerations in their attempt to place the (display screen)[3] the (keyboard)[3] and (disk drives)[3] (on desktop computers) in locations that are correct for the worker. The keyboard needs to be adjustable at a height of about 26 inches from the floor for most workers, and the display screen should be arranged so the top of the screen is even with the worker's eye level, about 20 inches away.

A wide variety of apparatus are available to drop the keyboard below the front of an existing desk or place the display screen on a swivel arm that can be moved freely out of the way when not in use. And the central processing unit and disk drives may be placed on the floor beside the desk so that the entire desk top is free for the worker to use for other tasks.

(Chair)[2] It is estimated that the biggest single factor in worker productivity is the chair. The most important aspect of a chair is that it promotes good posture. It should be easily adjustable and should support the lower back. The height of the seat should be low enough so the worker's heels rest firmly on the floor when seated all the way back in the chair.

Again, the customer will find a wide variety of chairs available on the market. Some of the more futuristic ones have no back and the worker is supported partially by a leg rest. One expert recommends that the worker assume a standing position with one foot elevated--on a footrest. The assumption is that standing posture is better than the sitting posture allowed by most office chairs.

(Summary)[1]

There's a great deal more involved in office ergonomics than the few topics listed above. And everyone who works with this area of office ergonomics considers himself or herself an expert. A huge variety of products and services are available from the vendors and consulting agencies to help office managers design a work station that promotes comfort and productivity for the office worker.

Figure 28-2

Positioning the Table of Contents

Once the text has been prepared, the table of contents page must be formatted and a code must be placed in the document at the location for the table of contents. Then the command to generate is given. Voila! Your table of contents automatically appears.

Normally the table of contents goes before the first page of text and is preceded by the title page. You need to think about page numbering, because the first page of text should be considered page 1.

All of these considerations will be dealt with in the next exercise. Follow along carefully so your document ends up looking just right!

Lesson 28 Exercise 2

1. Strike **Home, Home, Home, ↑** to return to the top of your document above all codes. Strike **Ctrl-Enter** to insert a hard page break.

2. Make sure the cursor is just below the page break and go to the Page Format menu. Change the page number to 1 so that WordPerfect considers the first page containing text as page 1.

3. Reveal your codes. At the top of that first page of text you should have a Header code, a Page Numbering code, a Widow/Orphan code and a Suppress code (in any order).

4. Strike **Home, Home, ↑** to move the cursor above the page break. Go to the Page Format menu and tell WordPerfect that you would like this page numbered with small Roman numerals beginning with *i* (choose **1 New Page Number** and key i followed by **Enter**). You would like this page number in the bottom center of the page (choose **4** and then **6**).

You want that small *i* at the bottom of the Table of Contents page only. This page number is in addition to the one in the header at the top of the first page of text. Unless you discontinue the centered Roman numeral, the remaining pages will have two page numbers—one at the top of the page in the header and the centered Roman numeral at the bottom of the page!

You can discontinue the centered numeral by inserting a No Page Number code in a position where it will not affect the page on which it is inserted but will affect the rest of the pages in the document.

5. Return to your document screen and strike **Enter** once (one printing character or command is all that is needed to keep a command from working on the current page). Go to the Page Numbering section of the Page Format menu. Choose **4** and then **9** to turn off Page Numbering.

6. Strike **Enter** five more times to give the Table of Contents page a 2-inch top margin. Center *TABLE OF CONTENTS* followed by a quadruple space.

With the pages all prepared and numbered, you must insert a code in your document that tells WordPerfect what you'd like the table of contents to look like and where it will go. As with most other WordPerfect features, the program makes setup of the table of contents easy.

Lesson 28 Exercise 3

Choose **Define** from the **M**ark menu.

1. Strike **Alt-F5** for the Mark Text menu. Choose **5 Define**, which opens a menu that looks like Figure 28-3.

2. Choose Option **1** to Define Table of Contents. A new menu will appear that looks like Figure 28-4.

```
Mark Text: Define

 1 Define Table of Contents
 2 Define List
 3 Define Index
 4 Define Table of Authorities
 5 Edit Table of Authorities Full
   Form
```

Figure 28-3

```
Table of Contents Definition

 1 Number of Levels          1
 2 Display Last Level in      No
   Wrapped Format
 3 Page Numbering    Level 1  Flush right with leader
                     Level 2
                     Level 3
```

Figure 28-4

   a. Since you have three levels of information, you must change the first option to **3**.

   b. Study Figure 28-1. You will see that the characteristics of the display screens are listed horizontally and separated by semicolons. This is the wrapped format about which WordPerfect was asking you to make a decision in Option 2 of the Table of Contents definition menu. Set it at **Yes**.

   c. The third section of this menu has changed as you made your choices for parts 1 and 2. It is prompting you that the third level will have page numbers in parentheses following the entry. You may use the defaults here, although there are a number of other options for page number placement.

3. Strike **Enter** until the menu disappears. Reveal your codes to see what the Table of Contents Define code looks like. It says you've defined the markings for a table of contents with three levels. The code is also positioned at the location for the table of contents. Be careful about that or you may get some strange results! The table of contents will be inserted exactly where the cursor is positioned when you define the table of contents.

Choose **Generate** from the **M**ark menu.

4. Move your cursor to the right of the code. Strike **Alt-F5** to open the Mark Text menu again and choose **6 Generate**.

5. From the impressive Generate menu, choose **5 Generate Tables, etc.** Note that the same selection is used to generate all tables and lists. Answer **Yes** to the question about replacing existing tables, lists, etc.

   The computer will work for a short time. It is actually looking through and finding the marked text and adding that information to the table of contents. Presently, your table of contents will appear, looking just as you expected it to look after you studied Figure 28-1.

6. Preview your table of contents with Print Preview. Is your page number centered at the bottom? Is the table on a page by itself? Does it look good?

7. Finally, strike **Home, Home, Home, ↑** again to go to the top of your document. Add another hard page command. Above that hard page break, create a title page as you did in Lesson 14.

8. Proofread your document carefully, checking the accuracy of the page numbers. Then print it and exit from it, saving it as **ergo.283**.

INDEX

An index could be described as an alphabetical listing of topics or terms and where they can be found in a document. It is usually the very last item in a document. Turn to the index at the back of this book and study it. Note that not only are the topics listed alphabetically as individual items, in some instances they are also listed in indented format under main heading sections.

In the next exercises you will be creating an index to accompany your ergonomics document. Your index will look much like the portion of an index illustrated in Figure 28-5.

You will discover that, as with the Table of Contents feature, you must mark the text to be included in the index. Marking text for an index is usually a little more complex than marking the text for a table of contents. In an index, reference is made to each occurrence of the word or phrase. In the table of contents, the topics are listed as they are introduced.

You may mark the text for an index manually—that is, go through the document and block each word or phrase to be included in the index. For each word or phrase, you must then mark the text in a manner that is similar to that for the table of contents. There is a better way . . . .

```
ambient lighting  3
breaks  2
chair  5
character size  2
color  2, 4
computer terminal  1, 3
decor  1, 3
desk  4
```

Figure 28-5

The Concordance File

It is usually much more efficient to prepare what is known as a *concordance* file. The concordance file is a separate document containing a list of all the terms you want in the index. With the list prepared, Word-Perfect will search the text for each occurrence of each word and will insert the page numbers for each entry into the index.

When using the concordance file, the first step is to choose the words to be included in the index and key them as a list. The words or phrases can be keyed in any order, but the generation of the index is quicker if the words are listed alphabetically before the command to generate the index is given. An efficient way to manage that is to key the words or terms and use WordPerfect Sort to alphabetize them.

The words or terms illustrated in Figure 28-6 might be included in an index for the document about office ergonomics with which you were just working. We'll practice using this list.

Lesson 28 Exercise 4

1. Key the words or terms in Figure 28-6 in a single column at the left margin.

2. Use Sort to alphabetize the list. The default settings in the Sort menu are probably the correct settings for this kind of sort. When the list has been alphabetized, exit from the document, saving it as **concord**.

computer terminals	decor	color
display screen	direct lighting	glare
illumination	desk	breaks
flicker	disk drives	ambient lighting
keyboard	furniture	task lighting
	character size	chair

Figure 28-6

Positioning and Defining the Index

You must tell WordPerfect where in your document you'd like the index to be generated. While you can position the index anywhere in a document, the usual place that people will look for an index is at the end of the document.

As with the table of contents, you must define the index—that is, tell WordPerfect how you would like it to look. When you define the index, WordPerfect inserts a code at the position of the cursor. The index will be generated at the location of that code. WordPerfect offers you several index styles, as you'll see in the next exercise.

Lesson 28 Exercise 5

1. Open **ergo.283** and strike **Home, Home, ↓** to move the cursor to the very end of the document, at the bottom of the last page. Change from double spacing to single spacing.

2. Strike **Ctrl-Enter** for a hard page break. Then center the word *INDEX* two inches from the top of the page, followed by a quadruple space.

Choose **Define** from the **Mark** menu.

3. Strike **Alt-F5** to go to the Mark Text menu. Choose **5 Define** and then **3 Index**. A prompt will appear asking for the name of your concordance file. You called it **concord**. Key that name and strike **Enter**.

> **Index Definition**
>
> **1 No Page Numbers**
> **2 Page Numbers Follow Entries**
> **3 (Page Numbers) Follow Entries**
> **4 Flush Right Page Numbers**
> **5 Flush Right Page Numbers**
>   **with Leaders**

4. A new menu will appear that looks much like Figure 28-7. It asks where you'd like the page numbers. In the sample shown in Figure 28-5, the page numbers follow the entries. Choose Option 2.

Figure 28-7

Generating the Index

Finally, when the code is in place, you can generate your index. The concordance file must be named and the code must be positioned at the desired location for your index. When you give the command to generate, you will again be asked about existing tables, lists, etc. Again you will answer **Yes** to the question.

Lesson 28 Exercise 6

Choose **Generate** from the **Mark** menu.

1. Strike **Alt-F5** for the Mark Text menu. Choose **6 Generate**.

2. Choose **5 Generate tables, indexes, etc.** You will see a prompt reminding you that all previous lists and tables will be eliminated. Respond with **Yes** to tell WordPerfect that you wish to continue.

3. A counter will appear to be counting the pages as they are scanned for words to be added to the index. Your table of contents will be regenerated at the same time, and a new one will take the place of the old one.

4. Check the appearance of your index. Then print only the index page of your document. Resave the document as **ergo.286** and exit from it.

This was a simple index with all items aligned at the left margin. One of the WordPerfect features enables you to create an index with an indented format so that you can have main items in the list and others as subheadings under the main ones, as shown in the index in this book.

You will not practice creating an index with two levels here, but it is a fairly simple process to work with the concordance file to identify which items are to appear at the left margin and which will be indented as subheadings.

SUMMARY

This lesson has provided you with a brief introduction to the use of lists in WordPerfect. In addition to a table of contents, you could generate a list of figures, a list of tables, and a list of equations. If you worked in a legal environment, lists of tables of authority could also be generated automatically using WordPerfect.

Your most painstaking part of this lesson was preparing the document so that the table of contents could be generated. In one way or another, any text to be included in a list must be marked just as you marked the material for the table of contents. While it seems like a lot of work to mark the text, it is a real time saver in the long run because once the text is marked, you can revise the document to your heart's content and then regenerate your lists. They will always reflect the correct page number for the marked text.

The concordance file you prepared in this lesson was a simple listing without subheadings. If you would like to work with subheadings, the Index: Concordance and Mark Text portion of the *Reference* gives specific instructions for subheadings in an index.

You may be a little unsure about the creation of lists in WordPerfect after this introduction. If your job includes the preparation of long documents, you will want to review this lesson and work with documents of your own so that you can become skilled in the preparation of lists.

COMMAND SUMMARY

Feature	Function	Menu	Lesson
Define Index	Alt-F5, D	Mark	28
Define T of C	Alt-F5, D	Mark	28
Generate	Alt-F5, G	Mark	28
Index	Alt-F5, I	Mark	28
Mark Text	Block Text, Alt-F5	Mark	28
Setup	Shift-F1	File	27
Styles	Alt-F8	Layout	27

LESSON 28 NOTES:

TRUE/FALSE

Each of the following statements is either true or false. Indicate your choice in the Answers column by circling T for a true statement or F for a false statement.

Answers

1. People are more comfortable with a document where the pages have common layout elements. (Les. 27, Obj. 1) . . . .   1. T   F

2. Styles are listed in a style library as they are created. (Les. 27, Obj. 2) .   2. T   F

3. Once a style is created, the only way you can revise it is to redo it completely. (Les. 27, Obj. 4) . . . .   3. T   F

4. Once the elements of a document have been marked, you can change its style by retrieving the document and applying the new style. (Les. 27, Obj. 5) . . . .   4. T   F

5. In order to include items in the table of contents, the text to be included must be marked. (Les. 28, Obj. 1) . . . .   5. T   F

6. You get to choose the level of the item to be included in the table of contents. (Les. 28, Obj. 1) . . . .   6. T   F

7. You get to choose the arrangements of page numbers and indents in the table of contents. (Les. 28, Obj. 2) . . . .   7. T   F

8. The same command that you use to generate a table of contents is used to generate an index or list. (Les. 28, Obj. 3) . . . .   8. T   F

9. Items in an index generated by WordPerfect are always listed at the left margin. (Les. 28, Obj. 4) . . . .   9. T   F

10. If you prepare a list of the words you'd like included in the index, WordPerfect can alphabetize the list and find all occurrences of each word. (Les. 28, Obj. 5) . . . .   10. T   F

COMPLETION

Indicate the correct answer in the space provided.

Answers

1. For what reason would you use a style for a regularly produced multiple-page document? (Les. 27, Obj. 1) .   1. _____

2. How many ways can the Enter key be used in a style? (Les. 27, Obj. 2) . . . .   2. _____

3. What is the code that separates the beginning codes from the ending codes in a paired style? (Les. 27, Obj. 2) .   3. _____

4. What is the extension used in the document name when you save a style library? (Les. 27, Obj. 3) . . . .   4. _____

5. Can you add style features to a document that has already been keyed? (Les. 27, Obj. 5) . . . .   5. _____

6. How many Mark codes appear for each "chunk" of text you mark for the table of contents? (Les. 28, Obj. 1)   6. _____

7. What is the word that describes what you do when you tell WordPerfect how you would like your table of contents to look and where you would like it placed in the document? (Les. 28, Obj. 2) . . . .   7. _____

8. The table of contents you prepared in this lesson had how many levels? (Les. 28, Obj. 3) . . . .   8. _____

9. Where is an index usually located in a document? (Les. 28, Obj. 4) . . . .   9. _____

10. What is the name of the kind of file you can create to make it easier to select the words or phrases included in an index? (Les. 28, Obj. 5) . . . .   10. _____

11. Which of the features covered in Lessons 27 and 28 did you like the best? Why?

_____

REFERENCE

Turn to the Style section of the *WordPerfect Reference*. When you wish to delete a style from your style library, WordPerfect gives you three choices. What are those choices?

_____

In the Index, Concordance and Mark Text section of the *Reference*, an explanation is made using "Birds" as an example. What is the *Reference* trying to tell you with this example?

_____

LESSON 29
Feature Bonanza

OBJECTIVES

Upon completion of this lesson, you will be able to:

1. Work with Redline and Strikeout.
2. Number the lines in your documents automatically.
3. Create a master document.
4. Use Advance to position text on the page.
5. Create document comments.
6. Create a document summary.
7. Work with Line Draw.

Estimated Time: 2¼ hours

REDLINE AND STRIKEOUT

Redline and Strikeout are features that may be chosen from the Appearance portion of the Font menu. Redline is used to indicate text to be added to a document. Strikeout is used to indicate text that is suggested for deletion from a document.

Redline and Strikeout have many uses. One that is particularly helpful is in making suggested changes to a document that other people have to approve. If the changes are approved, a single step will delete the text marked with strikeout and remove the markings from the redlined text.

To mark text with either redline or strikeout, the text to be marked should be blocked. Then the appropriate marking may be chosen from the Font menu. The marked text is surrounded with paired codes.

On your screen, the text marked with strikeout will usually have a horizontal line through it, although the appearance of text marked with strikeout varies, depending on your video display terminal (VDT). When printed, a horizontal line will print through text marked with strikeout.

Text marked with redline will be displayed in red on color VDTs. On monochrome VDTs you may need to go to the Redline Method portion of the Document Format menu and choose an alternative method to see your text marked with redline.

Text marked with redline will print with a shaded background on some printers or will be highlighted in some other way on different kinds of printers. Let's create some text and try both Redline and Strikeout.

Lesson 29 Exercise 1

(Template disk users: Refer to the box below before beginning.)

1. Key all parts of the short paragraphs illustrated in Figure 29-1. Can you see the words through the strikeout and redline?

2. After you have keyed the text, block the first sentence to highlight it.

Choose **A**ppearance and then **R**edline from the **F**ont menu

3. With the text blocked, strike **Ctrl-F8** for the Font menu and choose **2 Appearance**. From the menu that appears, choose **8 Redln**. The sentence will appear in red if you have a color VDT or else it will be highlighted in a different way, depending on your equipment.

Choose **A**ppearance and then **S**trikeout from the **F**ont menu

4. Block the second sentence. With the text blocked, go to the Font Appearance menu and choose **9 Stkout**. The text may appear with a line through it as illustrated in the figure.

5. Mark the text in the rest of the paragraph in the same way, using Figure 29-1 as the guide for what should be marked with redline and what should be marked with strikeout.

6. Position the cursor anywhere in the document and reveal your codes. Look at the beginning and ending Redline codes. Look at the beginning and ending Strikeout codes.

7. Print a copy of this marked document. We will use it for a couple of exercises, so use F10 to save it as **redline.291** and keep it open.

This is text created for the purpose of testing the redline and strikeout features. ~~This is text created for the specific purpose of testing the redline and strikeout features.~~ These features are used in revising documents where a group of people must approve the revisions. An example of the use of redline and strikeout is in revising the constitution of a large or small organization. ~~An excellent example of the use of redline and strikeout is in revising the constitution of a large organization.~~

Copies of the document with the suggested revisions marked with redline and strikeout may be distributed to the membership. Then the revisions may be voted on as a whole or individually. ~~Each revision may then be approved or disapproved individually.~~

Figure 29-1

Now we'll assume the document has been discussed by all interested parties and the corrections have been approved. Follow the steps in Exercise 2 to remove the redline markings and the text marked with strikeout.

TEMPLATE DISK USERS:

Retrieve **redline** and follow Steps 2-7 of Exercise 1.

Lesson 29 Exercise 2

Choose **Generate**
from the **Mark** menu.

1. With the marked document showing in the window, strike **Alt-F5** and choose **6 Generate**. This menu (illustrated in Figure 29-2) should be familiar to you from Lesson 28.

Mark Text: Generate

1 Remove Redline Markings and Strikeout Text from Document
2 Compare Screen and Disk Documents and Add Redline and Strikeout
3 Expand Master Document
4 Condense Master Document
5 Generate Tables, Indexes, Cross-References, etc.

Figure 29-2

2. Choose **1** Remove . . . from this menu. Key **Y** to answer the prompt that appears at the bottom of the screen.

3. Print a copy of the revised document and save it as **redline.292**. Keep the document open in the window.

In the above exercise, you worked with whole sentences to be added to the text (redline) or deleted from it (strikeout). The same thing could be accomplished by working with the affected phrases of the text rather than the complete sentence. Care must be taken in those instances to make sure the sentence makes sense after the changes have been made.

It should also be noted that if the revisions are not all approved but some of them are, it is a relatively simple procedure to delete the strikeout markings around text that will remain in the document and delete the suggested redline text. You may wish to retrieve the document and practice this later on your own.

Document Compare

The Document Compare feature can be used to compare two similar documents. You currently have the revised document showing in your window. You can compare this document with the marked document saved on your disk. When you compare, the text that has been deleted will be added to the document and marked with strikeout so you can see the differences in the documents. Let's try it.

Lesson 29 Exercise 3

Choose **Generate**
from the **Mark** menu.

1. Strike **Alt-F5** and choose **6 Generate** again to return to the same menu you just used.

2. This time choose **2** Compare Screen & Disk Documents . . . Word-Perfect will ask for the name of the document to be compared. We called it **redline.291**. Key that document name and strike **Enter**. The results of the comparison will appear on the screen. Notice that the differences are marked with strikeout.

3. Close this document without saving. If you wish to work more with Redline, Strikeout, and Compare, you have the **redline.292** document on your disk or you may use any other document.

Document Compare can be used to compare just about any two similar documents that you have. It is an easy way to highlight differences between documents—especially in instances where you can't remember what changes were made to a document.

That's enough about redline and strikeout for now. Let's learn about another neat WordPerfect feature.

LINE NUMBERING

WordPerfect will number the lines of your document automatically. You can tell WordPerfect to number the lines of a multiple-page document continuously, or you can set it to number beginning anew on each page. You can also set whether or not blank lines will be numbered, although WordPerfect only numbers those lines left blank because of a hard return. In other words, if you have a document set for double spacing, the blanks between the lines won't be counted.

Let's try numbering the ergonomics document you marked for a table of contents and index in Lesson 28.

Lesson 29 Exercise 4

1. Retrieve the document named **ergomark.281**. (This should be your ergonomics document without title page, table of contents, or index.)

2. Position the cursor at the left margin opposite the title of the document.

3. Go to the Format menu and choose **1 Line**. Then choose **5 Line Numbering**.

Open the **Layout** menu and choose **Line** and then **Numbering**.

Change the prompt from No to **Yes**. A menu like Figure 29-3 should appear. It offers choices regarding line numbering.

Format: Line Numbering	
1 Count Blank Lines	**Yes**
2 Number Every n Lines, where n is	**1**
3 Position of Number from Left Edge	**0.6"**
4 Starting Number	**1**
5 Restart Numbering on Each Page	**Yes**

Figure 29-3

4. Study the settings. Note that the default is to count blank lines and restart numbering on each page. Look at where the numbers will be positioned. Leave all the default settings and strike **Enter** until you return to your document screen.

5. Reveal your codes and look at the Line Numbering code. Since line numbers don't show on your working screen, use Print Preview to see what the printed document will look like.

    Note that the blank lines between the title and the first paragraph are counted (because they contain hard returns) but the blank lines between lines in the paragraph are NOT counted, because double spacing caused them.

6. Print your document and exit from it, saving it as **ergonum.294**.

That was pretty easy, wasn't it? There are some additional things you should know about line numbering.

- Footnotes ARE numbered with line numbering but headers and footers are NEVER numbered.
- When you look at your numbered document in Print Preview, each page will appear to begin with the number 1, even when you have numbering set at Continuous. This peculiarity occurs because Print Preview takes too long to format the document with continuous numbering. Printed pages WILL be numbered continuously.
- As you saw in the menu, you can change the position of the numbers. Otherwise they are printed just to the left of the lines of the document, at 0.6 inches.
- When giving the Line Formatting command, position your cursor at the beginning of the page or the beginning of the text to be counted. You can do this anywhere in the document, and you can turn it off anywhere, too.
- You can remove numbering by deleting the [Ln Num:On] code.

While line numbering isn't used for the majority of documents you might create using WordPerfect, it's useful when working with documents that will be discussed. With lines numbered, people can refer to the lines by number so there is no confusion about the text being discussed.

MASTER DOCUMENT

WordPerfect has a Master Document feature that helps you manage extremely large documents. When you are using Master Document, parts of that large document can be saved as separate documents (called subdocuments). The subdocuments are then named in the Master Document but are never assembled all together ("expanded") as one document unless you wish to generate a table of contents or an index.

When using the Master Document feature for a table of contents, a list, or an index, you would mark each individual document and save it. Then you would create the master document, expand it, and generate the appropriate list. Because WordPerfect is considering all of the subdocuments to be part of the master document, the page numbers will be appropriately entered in the index or table of contents.

The exercises that follow don't include either the index or the table of contents. This is just a brief introduction to master documents.

Lesson 29 Exercise 5

1. Create a document that says: *This is Document 1*. Follow the sentence with two hard returns.

2. Save the document on your disk as **doc1**. Do not close it.

3. Change the *1* to a *2* and save the document again, this time as **doc2**.

4. Continue changing the number and saving the documents until you have ten different documents saved in ten different document files. Clear the screen.

Now that you have your "dummy" documents prepared, you will include them as you prepare your master document.

Lesson 29 Exercise 6

Choose **S**ubdocument from the **M**ark menu

1. On a new document screen, create your master document. Strike **Alt-F5** and choose **2 S**ubdocument. At the prompt for the subdocument, key **doc1** and strike **Enter**. A box will appear on the screen, listing the name of your first subdocument.

```
Subdoc:   DOC1
```

2. Follow the same procedure to add **doc2**. Then continue until boxes appear on the screen containing all ten of your subdocument names.

3. Use Print Preview to view your document. What you'll see is an empty page because no text is included at this point. The boxes are merely "comment" boxes.

4. Reveal your codes and look at the subdocument codes in your document. Save your document on your disk as **master.296**.

Now that you have created your master document, you need to prepare it for printing. You must expand the document to print it. When you expand it, all ten documents will be retrieved into your master document. In order for Expand to work, WordPerfect must be able to find the documents. If you have them saved on a disk, be certain that the disk is in Drive A when you expand the master document.

Choose **Generate** from the **Mark** menu

5. Strike **Alt-F5** and choose **6 Generate**. (The menu illustrated in Figure 29-2 will appear. This is most likely becoming a familiar menu for you!)

6. Choose **3 Expand Master Document**. Now each subdocument has a "start" and an "end" comment line.

7. Look at your document with Print Preview. You'll see the text of the ten documents. Print your simple expanded master document.

8. Return to the Mark Text: Generate menu and choose **4 Condense Master Document**. You will be asked if you would like to save the individual documents. Since you didn't change any of them, you may respond with **No**. Close your master document without saving it again.

These little exercises didn't exhibit the power of the master document. You need to have much longer documents to really see this feature at work. As mentioned above, this is a way of including a number of subdocuments into one document to generate the index, a list, or a table of contents for a document made up of many pages. You did discover, however, how easy it is to work with the master document.

ADVANCE

Choose **Other** and then **Advance** from the **Layout** menu.

Advance can be used to position text at an exact location on the page. You can advance up, down, right, left, or to a particular position or line. The Advance feature is chosen from the **Other** menu that is the fourth choice in the **Format** menu.

Advance: 1 Up; 2 Down; 3 Line; 4 Left; 5 Right; 6 Position

If you choose to advance up, down, left, or right, the measurement begins at the position of the cursor when the command is given. If you choose to advance to a "Line," the measurement begins at the top edge of the paper. For "Position," the measurement begins at the left edge.

Advance can be used to replace extra hard returns for the purpose of moving a portion of text to a certain location. For example, if you always wish to begin the date of your letters 2 inches from the top of the page, you can insert an "advance to Line 2 inches" code in your document rather than striking **Enter** six times before inserting the date.

While this doesn't seem especially significant, it becomes very important for applications like filling in forms or positioning text within graphics. You'll work with forms in Lesson 35, and you'll find that you must measure very carefully and have your paper aligned perfectly before printing a document with Advance codes.

Before practicing with Advance, let's check your paper placement in your printer.

Lesson 29   Exercise 7

1. Beginning on a clear screen, with your cursor at Line 1" and Pos 1" (in the upper left corner), key your entire name.

2. Print the document that contains your name. Then find a ruler and measure the distance from the top of the paper to your name. Is it exactly one inch?

3. Measure the distance from the left edge of the paper to your name. Is it exactly one inch?

If the measurements aren't exactly correct, you must either adjust the paper in the printer or make allowances for the discrepancy. With a laser printer, you'll likely have to make allowances, since the paper can't be adjusted in most laser printers. If you have a dot-matrix printer, you can usually adjust the paper both vertically and horizontally. Have your instructor help you make these adjustments.

Lesson 29   Exercise 8

Choose **Other** and then **Advance** from the **Layout** menu.

1. Strike **Page Down** to move the cursor to the end of your name. Strike **Shift-F8** and choose **4 Other** and then **1 Advance**.

2. Choose **3** Line. At the prompt, key **5.5** and strike **Enter**.

3. Choose Advance again and choose **6 Position**. Key **4.25** and strike **Enter** until you return to your working screen. (You can see that your cursor hasn't moved, but look at the **Line** prompt in the status line. It always identifies your position.) The position you've chosen should be the exact center of the page.

4. Key a capital **X**. Do NOT strike **Enter**.

5. Return to the Advance menu and choose **1 Up** and key **2.25**. Then return to Advance and choose **4 Left**. Key **1.65**. Return to the working screen and key your name again.

6. Print your document. Fold the paper both ways. Is your *X* in the exact center? Does the final printing of your name fall on a diagonal between the beginning of the first printing of your name and the *X*? Your document should look much like Figure 29-4.

7. Look at the screen. Does the *X* come between your names or is it at the bottom, the way it appears on the paper? Exit from your document and save it as **advance.298**.

Figure 29-4

That's a brief overview of Advance. You are probably getting an idea of how it could be used in some of the documents you must create. You'll be using the feature more in the lessons in Unit 4.

DOCUMENT COMMENT

If you have a problem remembering to make required changes or perform certain tasks when working with some of your documents, you can use the WordPerfect Document Comment feature to plant comments in your documents. These comments will show on the screen when you have a document open, but they are not printed. They are simply reminders to you or anyone else using the document.

Choose Comment from the Edit menu.

You must use **Ctrl-F5** for the Text In/Out menu if you wish to place a comment in your document. You used this menu in Lesson 20 when you worked with text conversion and passwords. A document comment appears in a box that looks much like the subdocument box in the Master Document feature. If you look at the comment in Reveal Codes, you will see a simple [Comment] code. If you wish to remove the comment from a document, simply delete the code. Let's experiment!

Lesson 29 Exercise 9

Choose Comment from the Edit menu.

1. Open clancy24.par. With the cursor positioned at the top of the document, strike **Ctrl-F5** and choose **4 Comment**. The following menu will appear:

   Comment: 1 Create; 2 Edit; 3 Convert to Text

2. Choose **1 Create**. A box will appear on the screen. In the box, key the text in Figure 29-5. You will need to key the characters of the word *{FIELD}*, including the brackets, as part of the text.

```
These are the prestored paragraphs to be used in creating
Clancy's Computers' standard letters.  Each sentence or
paragraph is saved as a field in the clancy24.sec document.
Create a shell document as a primary document, using {FIELD}
codes to request each field as needed.
```

Figure 29-5

3. When you finish, strike **F7** to exit from the document. Reveal your codes to see the code. Then use Print Preview to see what the comment looks like in your document. (It doesn't show, does it?)

Comments can be edited by choosing **Edit** in the menu. You can also change a comment to normal text in your document, or normal text can be changed to a comment. Let's play.

4. Position the cursor near the comment in your document. Return to the Text In/Out menu and choose **4 Comment**. Then choose Option **3** to convert the comment to text. (Use Print Preview to affirm that it really is part of the document.)

5. Now return to the document and block the entire paragraph that originally was the comment. Strike **Ctrl-F5**. You will be asked if you wish to create a comment. Key **Y** for Yes. The text is boxed and again becomes a comment. Finally, close the document without saving it.

Comments are easy to work with and quite useful in documents where you must remember what should be done or how to do something. For some reason, WordPerfect users tend to try to remember everything and forget that document comments are great reminders.

DOCUMENT SUMMARY

A document summary is a brief on-screen synopsis of a document. It is the document summary you will see if you "Look" at the contents of a file when you have your files listed.

Look at Figure 29-6 to see the items included in the Document Summary. Note that the first item, Revision Date, has no menu item. It changes automatically each time you revise a document. The majority of the items are quite self-explanatory. Let's add a document summary to your **master.296** document.

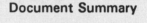

Document Summary

  Revision Date
1 Creation Date
2 Document **Name**
  Document Type
3 Author
  Typist
4 Subject
5 Account
6 Keywords
7 Abstract

Figure 29-6

Lesson 29 Exercise 10

1. Open **master.296**.

2. Strike **Shift-F8** and choose **3** Document and **5** Summary.

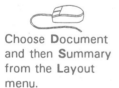

Choose **D**ocument and then **S**ummary from the **L**ayout menu.

3. Fill in the Document Name and skip the Type. Key names for the Author and the Typist (probably your name for both in this case).

4. For Subject, key *master document*. An Abstract is a description of the document. Choose Abstract and key *This is a practice master document that contains ten practice subdocuments.* Use **F7** to exit the Abstract portion of the menu.

5. Leave the other items in the menu blank. Strike **Enter** to return to your document. Save your document again, using the same name.

6. List your files and move the highlight to the **master.296** document. Strike **6** Look to see the summary of the document.

7. Return to your working screen.

That was pretty easy, wasn't it? We'll leave the summary on the **master.296** document. If you wish to add a summary to any of your other documents, do it now for practice.

LINE DRAW

WordPerfect's Line Draw feature enables you to draw horizontal and vertical lines. Your lines can be created with a variety of typographic characters as well as normal single or double lines.

When you strike **Ctrl-F3** and choose **2 Line Draw**, the following menu appears:

    1 |; 2 ‖; 3 *; 4 Change; 5 Erase; 6 Move:

If you choose **1**, moving the cursor with the arrow keys will draw a single line. If you choose **2**, you will draw a double line. If you wish to move the cursor to a different location without drawing a line, choose **6 Move**. If you make a mistake, you can erase the line with **5 Erase**. Let's try an exercise and then learn additional facts about Line Draw.

Lesson 29 Exercise 11

Choose Line Draw
from the Tools menu.

1. On a clear screen, strike **Enter** 5 times. Use Center to center your name. Move the cursor back to the first letter of your name and make a note of the **Pos** setting in the status line.

2. Backspace once to delete the Center code. Then space with the space bar until your name is returned to the same **Pos** number.

3. Strike ← three times to move the cursor away from your name.

4. Strike **Ctrl-F3** and choose **2 Line Draw**. Then choose **3** and use the arrow keys to draw a box of asterisks around your name. Use Erase and Move as needed to make the box frame your name attractively.

5. Print your little drawing and exit from it, saving it as **draw29.11**.

Now let's analyze what you just did.

• First, you can't draw a line in the margin. That's why you added the hard returns above your name—to give you some room above your name for the line. This is also true with the side margins.

• You shouldn't try to draw a line around something that has been positioned with Tab or Center. You can use those features to determine the desired position of the text, but then you should delete the Tab or Center commands and space the text into place as you did in Exercise 11.

- If your text is double spaced, the vertical lines will only appear on every other space. To get solid vertical lines, you'll have to key double-spaced text with two hard returns between each line. UGH!
- Some printers will print alphabetic or numeric characters instead of the desired vertical or horizontal lines.
- You used asterisks for your name because if you wanted a single line or a double line around your name, it would have been much easier to do it using the Tables feature. The **4 Change** option gives you additional choices for the kinds of lines you can draw.
- Line Draw works much more efficiently with a fixed pitch font— that is, a font where each character takes exactly the same amount of space as all other characters. You'll learn more about fonts in Lesson 33. The default font in WordPerfect is a fixed-pitch font. Line Draw does NOT work well with proportional fonts.

Lesson 29 Exercise 12

1. Return to Line Draw and experiment a little with the **4 Change** option. Clear your screen and prepare the little organization chart illustrated in Figure 29-7. Don't waste a lot of time trying to make it perfect!

2. When you finish, print the chart and save it as **org29.12**.

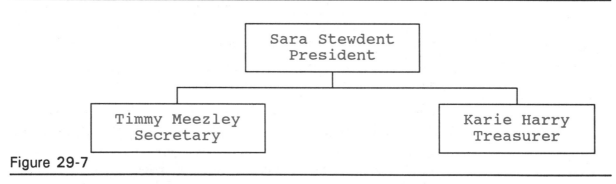

Figure 29-7

MATH

In Lesson 16 you used some WordPerfect math in the tables you created. You don't need to use a WordPerfect table to perform math calculations. A number of math functions can be used:

+ The + in a math problem causes WordPerfect to add the numbers above it, resulting in a subtotal.
= This character adds the subtotals above it, resulting in a total.
* The asterisk gives a grand total of all totals above it.

T and **t** allow you to put extra subtotals into a column.

N, **-**, and **( )** force numbers to be negatives.

Setting Tabs

To use Math, you must set tabs to position the columns. You will set tabs for all columns except the one at the extreme left. WordPerfect doesn't consider the column at the extreme left to be a column because that position normally contains text. For ease of use, we'll refer to that area as the *left-text area*. If you don't want the left-text area to begin at the default left margin, don't set a tab for it. Instead, reset the margin at the desired location for that material.

Let's try a simple math problem.

Lesson 29 Exercise 13

1. Clear all tabs and set one at +2.5" and another at +4.5". Return to your working screen.

2. Strike **Alt-F7** and choose **3** Math followed by **1** On to turn on Math. The word **Math** should appear in the lower left corner of the screen. (If it is not there, your math won't work!)

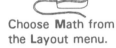

Choose **Math** from the **Layout** menu.

3. Key *Joan*. Tab once and key *250.00*. Tab again and key *400.00*. Strike **Enter**.

4. Key the rest of the exercise exactly as it appears in Figure 29-8. Note the use of + for subtotals, both - and ( ) for negatives, = for a total, **T** for inserting extra subtotals, and finally, * for a grand total.

5. When you finish, strike **Alt-F7** and choose **3** Math and **4** Calculate. When calculated, your problem should look like Figure 29-9. If it doesn't, follow the steps for the exercise and try again. Use a calculator to see if the math totals are correct. (Can you do it in your head?)

Choose **Math** from the **Layout** menu.

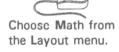

Choose **Math** from the **Layout** menu.

6. When everything is correct, strike **Alt-F7**, choose **3** Math, and turn off Math. Print the document and exit from it, saving it as **math29.13**. (Note that the functions aren't printed with the columns.)

```
Joan          250.00        400.00
Sam           350.00       -105.00
John         -100.00        110.00
                +             +
Trudy         279.58        425.00
Hue           432.78       (100.00)
Jesse        (200.00)       400.00
                +             +

                =             =

           T4,920.00     T3,500.00

                *             *
```

Figure 29-8

```
Joan                          250.00                    400.00
Sam                           350.00                   -105.00
John                         -100.00                    110.00
                              500.00+                   405.00+

Trudy                         279.58                    425.00
Hue                           432.78                   (100.00)
Jesse                        (200.00)                   400.00
                              512.36+                   725.00+


                            1,012.36=                 1,130.00=


                           T4,920.00                 T3,500.00

                            5,932.36*                 4,630.00*
```

Figure 29-9

Defining Columns

In the simple exercise above, you simply added and subtracted *down* a column. Sometimes you wish to calculate *across* columns. To do so, you must define the columns. Let's look at the Math Define menu illustrated in Figure 29-10. We'll begin at the bottom of the menu.

Note that you can use parentheses or minus signs for negative numbers. You already knew that. Then the menu tells you that you have four choices of column types. Just read about them for now.

- **Calculation** columns are for calculations and are set with **0**.
- **Text** columns will hold descriptions or text of some kind (not counting the left-text area). Text columns are set with **1**.

```
Math Definition      Use arrow keys to position cursor

Columns              A B C D E F G H I J K L M N O P

Type                 2 2 2 2 2 2 2 2 2 2 2 2 2 2 2 2

Negative Numbers     ( ( ( ( ( ( ( ( ( ( ( ( ( ( ( (

Number of Digits to  2 2 2 2 2 2 2 2 2 2 2 2 2 2 2 2
  the Right (0-4)

Calculation     1
  Formulas      2
                3
                4

Type of Column:
     0 = Calculation   1 = Text    2 = Numeric   3 = Total

Negative Numbers
     ( = Parentheses (50.00)       - = Minus Sign -50.00
```

Figure 29-10

- **Numeric** columns hold figures and totals. Numeric columns are set with **2** and are the default setting.
- **Total** columns are used to display totals from the column to the immediate left, just as in accounting. Use **3** for a Total column.

Above the listing of column types is a place to put calculation formulas. If you choose **0** to make a column a calculation column, your cursor will be positioned for you to enter the formula. The formula may be complicated, or it may be a simple formula such as the calculation of sales tax on an item.

You may use + for Add, - for Subtract, * for Multiply, and / for Divide in your formulas. You may also use +/ to average the numbers in a numeric column and =/ to average the numbers in a totals column.

At the top, you may define as many as 24 columns. They are not all shown in Figure 29-10. The columns are labeled A, B, C, and so forth. Column A is the location of the first tab stop. It is NOT the left-text area.

Note that parentheses are the default for negative numbers for all columns, and two places past the decimal is the default in the number of digits section. Let's try the short multiplication exercise in Figure 29-11. Study it. Note that the left-text area is empty.

Lesson 29 Exercise 14

Choose **Math** from the Layout menu.

1. Set tabs at +2.0", +3.5", and +5.0".

2. Strike **Alt-F7** followed by **3** Math and **3** Define. Your cursor is under the **2** that tells you Column A will be numeric. That's correct. Strike →. Column B is also numeric. Strike → again.

3. Column C will be a calculations column. Key **0** and watch the cursor move to Formula 1. Key *a*b* to tell WordPerfect to multiply Column A times Column B. Strike **Enter**.

4. Since you're working with whole numbers, cursor to the Number of Digits area and change Columns A, B, and C to zero (0) digits.

5. Exit the Column Definition menu and turn on Math. (Look for **Math** in the prompt position at the bottom of the screen.)

6. Key the exercise in Figure 29-11. Tab to the first column and key *5*. Tab to the second column and key *7*. Tab to the third column and watch the exclamation mark (!) appear. Strike **Enter**. Repeat the procedure for the second and third rows.

7. Leave a blank line before the total. Then tab to the third column, backspace to delete the exclamation mark, and key + to total the numbers in the column. Strike **Enter** and turn off Math.

8. Return to the Math menu and calculate. Check the multiplication and addition. Did the exercise work the way it should have?

9. Print your exercise and exit from it, saving it as **math29.14**.

5	7	!
12	6	!
3	12	!
		+

Figure 29-11

One other thing you should know about Math is that if you have text to follow the math problem, you should return to the Math menu after you calculate your problem and turn off Math. You probably noticed that the money columns aligned just fine, even though you set left tabs for all of them. That's because Math automatically assumes all numeric columns will be aligned at the decimal. If you don't turn off Math and you try to indent a paragraph, some really weird things will happen!

SUMMARY

Well, you've reached the end. As implied in the title of the lesson, quite a number of useful (?) and easily learned features are included here. You learned to use Redline, Strikeout, and Document Numbering for discussions about documents that affect a number of people.

Document Comments and the Document Summary are features that should be helpful to you in your work. Perhaps you will have cause to use the Master Document and Line Draw. Another feature covered in this lesson was Advance. As mentioned earlier, Advance will be used in some of your future lessons. Math, too will be practiced again. In fact, you'll have an opportunity to do a math problem in Lesson 30. Lesson 30 is another of those Review and Practice lessons where you have an opportunity to brush up on all kinds of skills. You'll want to work carefully to prepare for the production tests that follow that lesson.

Obviously, you are not yet an expert at any of these features, but you have enough background so you can become good at them when you need them. Good luck!

LESSON 29 NOTES:

TRUE/FALSE

Each of the following statements is either true or false. Indicate your choice in the Answers column by circling T for a true statement or F for a false statement.

Answers

1. Redline is used to indicate text that might be deleted. (Obj. 1) . . . .   1.   T   F

2. Text to be marked with strikeout must first be blocked. (Obj. 1) . . . . . .   2.   T   F

3. WordPerfect line numbering always begins with *1* at the top of each page. (Obj. 2) . . . .   3.   T   F

4. When using line numbering, footnote lines are always numbered. (Obj. 2)   4.   T   F

5. A master document is a shell-type document that provides links to a number of documents saved on your disk. (Obj. 3) . . . .   5.   T   F

6. You can use Advance to move from the current page to a page in a different document. (Obj. 4) . . . .   6.   T   F

7. If you advance to a certain line, that distance is measured from the left edge of the paper. (Obj. 4) . . . .   7.   T   F

8. A document summary is text that shows in a box in your document reminding you to do something with that document. (Obj. 5 & 6) . . . . .   8.   T   F

9. When you position the highlight on a document with a summary in List Files and choose the Look option, you'll see that summary. (Obj. 6) . . . . . .   9.   T   F

10. Line Draw can be used to create display documents like organization charts. (Obj. 7) . . . .   10. T   F

11. WordPerfect Math provides you with a tool that enables you to add, subtract, multiply, and divide. (Obj. 7) . . . .   11. T   F

COMPLETION

Indicate the correct answer in the space provided.

Answers

1. What is the feature to use when you wish to indicate text to be added to a document? (Obj. 1) . . . .   1. _____

2. Which is displayed on the screen with a horizontal line through it, redline or strikeout? (Obj. 1) . . . .   2. _____

3. How redline and strikeout appear on your screen is dependent on what piece of hardware? (Obj. 1) . . . . . .   3. _____

4. When you tell WordPerfect to pull all subdocuments into a master document, what is the term used? (Obj. 3) .   4. _____

5. You can advance six ways. What are the other two besides up, down, left, and right? (Obj. 4) . . . .   5. _____

6. What piece of hardware might need to be adjusted for your advance to be exactly correct? (Obj. 4) . . . . . .   6. _____

7. What is the name of the feature that enables you to add nonprinting information to a document? (Obj. 5) . . .   7. _____

8. What is the name of the feature that can be used to keep track of the author, typist, and date of creation of a document? (Obj. 6) . . . .   8. _____

9. Considering all of the features you learned about in this lesson, which one do think will be most useful to you?

_____

10. Considering all of the features you learned about in this lesson, which one do you think will be least useful to you?

_____

REFERENCE

What does the *WordPerfect Reference* tell you must be showing on the screen if you wish to delete a Document Summary from your document?

_____

What does the *Reference* recommend be adjusted when using Advance to fill in preprinted forms?

_____

What does the Line Draw section of the *Reference* tell you about the use of Repeat in drawing lines?

_____

LESSON 30
Review and Practice

OBJECTIVES

Upon completion of this lesson, you will have reviewed:

1. Merge with Sort and Labels.
2. The use of Styles.
3. Line Numbering, Redline, and Strikeout.
4. Document Assembly.
5. WordPerfect Math.

Estimated Time: 2¼ hours

SORT, MERGE, AND LABELS

The first set of exercises requires you to create and revise a primary document, a secondary document, and a set of merged documents, complete with labels and envelopes. Before merging, however, you will use Sort to arrange the names in the secondary file in alphabetic order. Read through this entire application before beginning so you know what's ahead. You will be using many of the skills acquired in the lessons in this unit.

Lesson 30 Exercise 1

1. Key the names and addresses in Figure 30-1 using the following secondary file format:

Field 1	title{END FIELD}
Field 2	fname{END FIELD}
Field 3	lname{END FIELD}
Field 4	streetaddress{END FIELD}
Field 5	city{END FIELD}
Field 6	s/p{END FIELD}
Field 7	ZIP{END FIELD}
Field 8	country{END FIELD}
	{END RECORD}

You may use numbered fields or named fields, although the primary file will be illustrated with field names to help you know what information is required in each instance.

If you use named fields, be careful to spell the field names correctly in both the primary and secondary files. If you use numbered fields, of course the numbers in the primary file must match those in the secondary file. As you remember from Lesson 23, naming the fields makes the creation of the secondary file easier because as you are entering the information, WordPerfect prompts you (in the prompt location at the lower left of the screen) with the field information requested for that location.

In the list of fields in Step 1 of this exercise, "fname" represents first name, "lname" represents last name, "s/p" represents state or province, and "number" represents the ZIP code or postal number. (Note that these addresses are not all equal. Some things, like postal numbers, are missing from some of them. Remember that each record must have an equal number of {END FIELD} codes. Think!!)

2. Proofread carefully. Then use **F10** for an interim save of the secondary file as **obea301.sec**. Keep it open in the window.

3. Sort the secondary file in alphabetic order by last name of the speaker. Check to be certain your sort was done correctly.

4. Save the sorted file again with the same name and exit from it.

```
Mr. Graham Magnan
498 Elm Street
Winnipeg, MB B7Y 8X7
CANADA

Mrs. Luisella Notman
1395 S. Columbia Road
Toronto, ON P8R 5J2
CANADA

Ms. Avanell Scott
755 Winnipeg Street
Mississauga, ON A2R 9D1
CANADA

Mr. Miles Cougler
776 Chestnut Street
Fort Erie, ON L3A 9X9
CANADA

Mrs. Suzan Seitz
4 Pelikano Street
Nikosia
CYPRUS

Miss Mary Ricci
45 Portage  Place
Appleton, WI 54913
USA
```

```
Ms. Dauna Childs
1322 Ventura Blvd.
Los Angeles, CA 99754
USA

Mrs. Nancy MacCallum
21 Madison Road
Cincinnati, OH 45027
USA

Miss Alain Cousineau
135 River Drive
Weston, ON M7L 1G7
CANADA

Mr. Peter Szymski
201 St. Clair Avenue
Georgetown, ON Y6B 4T8
CANADA

Miss Lori McBride
120 W. Adelaid
North York, ON R6B 7E3
CANADA

Mr. Berndt Scholz
Schonbornstr 25
Zeusleben 8727
GERMANY
```

Figure 30-1

Lesson 30 Exercise 2

Figure 30-2 contains the letter for use as a primary file to be merged with the secondary file created in Exercise 1. Use the current date. Enter the correct field name or field number codes to place the recipient's first name in Paragraph 1 and city in Paragraph 3.

Position the letter attractively on the page. When you finish, save the letter as **obea302.pri** and exit from it.

(current date)

{FIELD}title~ {FIELD}fname~ {FIELD}lname~
{FIELD}streetaddress~
{FIELD}city~, {FIELD}s/p~ {FIELD}number~
{FIELD}country~

Dear {FIELD}title~ {FIELD}lname~:

Thank you, {FIELD}fname~, for your participation as a presenter at our recent province teachers' conference in Toronto. The conference was a huge success, thanks to the members of the committee, the people who attended, and especially those who shared their expertise as speakers.

In this world of changing technologies, it is important that we share our methods, our knowledge, our successes, and our failures with one another. In this way we can build a better educational environment for our students of today and tomorrow--hopefully at a cost that encourages rather than hinders the educational process.

The committee joins me in expressing our appreciation, and we hope your return trip to your home in {FIELD}city~ was pleasant. Please visit us in Toronto again soon.

Sincerely,

Muriel Anderson
Chairperson

Figure 30-2

Lesson 30 Exercise 3

1. Merge the letter with the sorted list of speakers. Page through the letters to make certain everything is correct. If it isn't, close the

document. Then open and check your primary and secondary documents to find out where the problem is before merging again.

2. Print only the first four letters by choosing **5 Multiple Pages** in the Print menu and keying *1-4* at the prompt. Do not print all 12 of the letters.

3. Save the 12 letters as **obea303.mrg**. Then exit from the document.

In the next exercise you will prepare labels for mailing the letters prepared in Exercise 4. You will modify the **labsing.pri** document you prepared in Lesson 26. This primary document is for 4- by 15/16-inch labels in a single row.

When you created the labels primary document, you were working with a secondary file where the entire name and address were considered one field. In this application, the name and address take up eight fields.

Lesson 30 Exercise 4

1. Open **labsing.pri** and adjust the field codes so they resemble one of the examples in Figure 30-3 (depending on whether you used field names or numbers).

```
{FIELD}1~ {FIELD}2~ {FIELD}3~
{FIELD}4~
{FIELD}5~, {FIELD}6~ {FIELD}7~
{FIELD}8~


        or


{FIELD}title~ {FIELD}fname~ {FIELD}lname~
{FIELD}streetaddress~
{FIELD}city~, {FIELD}s/p~ {FIELD}number~
{FIELD}country~
```

Figure 30-3

---

2. Save the primary document as **lab-mf.pri** and close it. (The *mf* in the document name stands for "many fields." Perhaps you can think of a better document name that you would be more likely to remember when you need it again!)

3. Merge your secondary file with the modified labels primary file. Print the "labels" on plain paper. Save the labels file as **obea304.lab**.

REDLINE, LINE NUMBERING, STYLES, AND ENVELOPES

Well, you thought you had Muriel's letters ready to be sent. What you didn't count on was that her committee decided at the last minute that the letters needed a more businesslike tone and that the addresses should be printed directly onto the envelopes, rather than on labels. So you have some more work to do on this project. The next exercise will prepare the letter with revisions for the committee to discuss. Then you will need to use your envelope style to prepare the envelopes for the mailing. Follow along carefully.

Lesson 30 Exercise 5

1. Look at Figure 30-4. It is the body of the same letter you prepared in Exercise 2, but it contains suggested material to be added (shown with redline) and suggested material to be deleted (shown with strikeout).

2. Retrieve obea302.pri and add the redline material and format the material to be deleted with strikeout. Remember that you may turn on Redline and key the material to be added. On the other hand, you must block the text to be marked with strikeout before choosing the Strike-out attribute. Be careful to mark your text in such a way that the punctuation will be correctly positioned when (and if) you remove the redline markings and the strikeout text. THINK!

3. When you finish with those repairs, return to the top of the document and turn on Line Numbering so the letter can more easily be discussed at the committee meeting.

4. Print the revised letter, complete with markings, and exit from it, saving it as obea305.pri.

Thank you, {FIELD}title~ {FIELD}lname~ {FIELD}fname~, for your participation as a presenter at our recent province teachers' conference in Toronto. The conference was a huge success, thanks to the people who attended, the members of the committee, the people who attended, and especially those who shared their expertise as speakers.

In this world of changing technologies, it is important that we share our methods, our knowledge, our successes, and our failures with one another. In this way we can build a better educational environment for the our students of today and tomorrow--hopefully at a cost that encourages rather than hinders the educational process.

The committee joins me in expressing our appreciation, and we hope your return trip to your home in {FIELD}city~ was pleasant. Please visit us in Toronto again soon. We hope you will have an opportunity to return to Toronto in the near future.

Figure 30-4

The committee has met and approved most of the corrections to the letter. The change in the second paragraph, however, was not approved. You must now finalize the primary document and once again prepare the mailing.

Lesson 30 Exercise 6

1. Retrieve obea305.pri and delete the redlined word *the* in the second paragraph. Remove the strikeout markings from around the word *our*.

2. Go to the Generate menu and choose to delete strikeout text and redline markings.

3. Check the letter over carefully to see that it reads well and that the punctuation is correct, especially around the added or deleted text.

4. Find the Line Numbering code at the top of the document. Delete it.

5. Resave the letter, this time as obea306.pri, and exit from it.

6. Merge the letter you just revised with obea301.sec.

7. Print the first four letters and save the merged letters as obea306.mrg. Keep the letters on the screen for the next exercise.

Lesson 30 Exercise 7

1. Go to your Doc 2 screen and retrieve your style library. Turn on the Envelope style.

2. Return to the Doc 1 screen and block the inside address (the name and address of the recipient) on the first letter. Copy that block to the envelope form on the Doc 2 screen.

3. Strike **Ctrl-Enter** for a hard page break and turn on the Envelope style again.

4. Copy the inside address of the second letter to the second envelope.

5. Continue with this procedure until you have prepared an envelope for each of the 12 recipients of the letter.

6. Print (if you can) the first four envelopes. Save the envelopes as obea307.env and close the document.

You should be getting pretty good at thinking your way through problems like the ones faced in these exercises. Exercise 7 had a flaw, in case you didn't notice it. The problem here was that the envelope style contained your own return address. You probably would use Muriel's return address on envelopes to accompany a letter of this type—or at least the return address of the organization for which you're working. Actually, you could have an envelope style of this type that could be used with envelopes preprinted with the company's return address.

DOCUMENT ASSEMBLY

Remember Clancy's Computers? A prospective customer has contacted your boss wanting more information about hand-held computers.

Lesson 30 Exercise 8

1. Using the format you used in Exercise 3 of Lesson 24, set up a primary document for a letter to be sent to Mr. Jeffrey Anglin, 4457 Angel Road, Ann Arbor, MI 43778. Include paragraphs 3 and 4 in the first paragraph, 8 and 10 in the second paragraph, 13 and 21 in the third paragraph, 18 in the fourth paragraph, and 22 as the closing. Be sure to include the reference initials and Enclosure notation.

2. Exit from the primary document, saving it as **clanc308.pri**.

3. Merge the primary document with **clancy24.sec**.

4. Use your envelope style to prepare an envelope to accompany the letter.

5. Print both the letter and the envelope. Save the letter as **clanc308.let**. DO NOT save the envelope.

WORDPERFECT MATH PLUS MERGE

Math can be mixed with various types of applications. In this next exercise Math will be combined with a keyboard merge where you used {INPUT} ~ codes for the insertion of variable information. The form you will create is illustrated in Figure 30-5. Study the form. Then follow the steps below to set up the form, complete with math.

Lesson 30 Exercise 9

1. Begin with a clear screen. Center the first five lines at the top as shown. (You may use your own company name, address, and telephone number, if you wish.)

2. Key *Bill to* in bold at the left margin. Turn off Bold and use Flush Right to insert the Date Merge code.

3. On the next line, insert the {INPUT} code. You don't need a message with the {INPUT} code.

4. Key *Ship to:* as shown. Flush right the *Invoice No.:* line on the same line. Put the {INPUT} code for *Ship to* on the next line and key the *Terms:* and *Order No.:* lines as shown.

5. The column headings will be shown in bold, also. Use the space bar to position them. Space to **Pos 5.5"**, turn on Bold, and key *Unit* on a line by itself. Turn off Bold and strike **Enter**.

XYZ CORPORATION

1234 Anywhere Street
Somewhere, WI 55555
Phone 414-555-5678

INVOICE

Bill to: {DATE}
{INPUT}~

Ship to: **Invoice No.:** {INPUT}~
{INPUT}~

Terms: {INPUT}~

Order No.:   {INPUT}~

			Unit	
Stock #	Description	Quan.	Price	Amount

Figure 30-5

---

6. Put the remaining column headings on the next line at the following positions. Begin by turning on Bold and Underline and keying *Stock #*. Turn off Bold and Underline after the word *Amount*.

Stock #	1.2"
Description	2.5"
Quan.	4.4"
Price	5.4"
Amount	6.6"

7. Space twice after *Amount*. Then turn off Bold and Underline and strike **Enter** twice.

8. Voila! Your form is now set up. Do an interim save, calling the document **inv-309.pri**. Then we'll deal with the math.

Lesson 30 Exercise 10

1. Clear all tabs. Set new tabs at +0.3", +1.6", +3.6", +4.6", and +5.9".

2. Go to the Math Define menu and insert the following settings.

• Column A is a text column—the numbers are all the same length and they are purely informational. No calculations will occur. Note that you've left your margin alone, and you will need to tab to get to the stock number column.

• Column B is a text column.

- Column C is a numeric column, but it should be set for whole numbers. Change the number of digits to zero.

- Column D is OK. It is numeric and has two decimal places.

- Column E is a calculation column. The formula should be **c*d** because you are multiplying quantity times unit price.

3. Check all of your settings. Then exit from the Math Definition menu and turn on Math.

4. Add one final {INPUT} ~ code to your document so the cursor will move to this location when you are filling in the form.

5. Reveal your codes and study the codes at the end of the document. After the line of underlined column headings, you should have two [HRt] codes to put your cursor a double space below the column headings. Then you should have a Tab Set code, a Math Define code, the Math On code, and the {INPUT} ~ code. If your document is missing something or if the codes are out of place, follow the steps above and redo the document. Obviously, it must be correct to work.

6. Exit from the document, saving it as **Invoice.pri.**

Now you can use your invoice form to fill in the pertinent information each time a sale is made. Study Figure 30-6. It contains information for three customers. Exercise 11 will walk you through the first customer. You'll be on your own for the other two. If your form is set up correctly, this exercise will be a piece of cake for you!

Bill to: CUSTOMER #1
Mr. Jason Jackson
Jackson's Dry Goods
5432 Jackson Drive
St. Joseph, NJ 01010

Ship to:
Jackson's Dry Goods
6565 Main Street
St. Joseph, NJ 01010

Invoice No.: 6787   **Terms:** 30 days   **Order No.:** 930
- -
0132   Sweatshirts   36   14.95
9420   Sweatpants   24   24.95
5492   T-shirts   48   7.95
2304   Caps   15   2.95
= =

Bill to: **CUSTOMER #2**
Mrs. Harley Hershome
Hendricks Hat Shop
4531 Holcomb Way
Hersheyville, OH 34972

Ship to:
Hendricks Hat Shop
431 Ohio Street
Hersheyville, OH 34972

Invoice No.: 6788   **Terms:** 10 days   **Order No.:** 231
- -

1145   Cowboy Hats   15   79.50
4302   Straw Hats   10   19.75
3290   Riding Derbys   8   43.50
4493   Homburgs   12   97.95
= =

Bill to: **CUSTOMER #3**
Mr. Hiram Henderson
Hiram's Haberdashery
46 High Avenue
Hendersonville, NH 11023

Ship to:
Same

Invoice No.: 6789   **Terms:** net 30 days   **Order No.:** 1349
- -

2314   Silk Shirts   18   88.40
5488   Silk Ties   36   27.50
2236   Novelty Briefs   6   12.50

Figure 30-6

Lesson 30 Exercise 11

1. Give the command to merge. Key in the name of the primary document, **invoice.pri**. Strike **Enter** at the prompt for the secondary document since you are merging from the keyboard.

2. Part of the document should appear on the screen with the current date in place and the cursor at the spot for the "Bill to" information. Key in Mr. Jackson's name and address.

3. Strike **F9** to continue the merge. The cursor will stop at the location for the invoice number. Key in the appropriate invoice number.

4. Continue keying the appropriate material and using **F9** to move from {INPUT} ~ code to {INPUT} ~ code. After keying the order number, strike

F9 one last time. The cursor will stop at the beginning of the line for the first item to be ordered. **Math** will be showing at the lower left.

5. Tab once and key the stock number. Tab again and key the first description. Tab to key the quantity and again for the unit price. Tab one final time for the ! to show in the Amount column. Strike **Enter**.

6. Follow the instructions above until all items for Jason Jackson's order have been keyed. Then strike **Enter** an extra time and tab to the Amount column. Delete the ! and replace it with +.

7. Strike **Enter** and give the command to calculate.

8. Turn off Math. (It is important that you not skip this step!)

9. Strike **Shift-F9** and choose **1** Quit to end the merge.

Your first invoice is completed. Are you excited? It wasn't too hard. The reason you had to turn off Math is that if you had left it turned on as you proceeded to the next invoice, the total at the bottom of the next invoice would include the total from the first invoice. By turning off Math, you are assuring that Hendricks Hat Shop doesn't get billed for the order sent to Jackson's Dry Goods.

Now you can prepare the other two invoices. They will be pages 2 and 3 of the same document.

Lesson 30 Exercise 12

1. Strike **Ctrl-Enter** for a hard page break.

2. Begin again with the command to merge, this time filling in the invoice for Customer #2. When you've calculated the invoice, turned off Math and Merge, and inserted another hard page break, you can follow through with the third customer.

3. Print your invoices.

4. Use your envelope style on the Document 2 screen and prepare envelopes for each of the invoices. (Block and copy the "Bill to" portion of the invoice to use for the address on the envelope.)

5. Exit from the invoice document, saving it as **inv3012.mrg**. Do not save the envelopes.

FILE MANAGEMENT

Create a directory to hold your work for Unit 3. Then use **Alt-F5** to mark all of the documents in your file list and copy those documents into the Unit 3 directory. That will clear your root directory to make room for the work you'll be doing in Unit 4.

SUMMARY

Congratulations on the good work you did in this lesson, which reviewed quite a lot of information you had learned earlier. Hopefully you're more comfortable with some of the WordPerfect features than you were when you finished the lessons covering those features.

You should now be ready for the production tests that follow this lesson. Ask your instructor for more specific information about what will be covered on the tests and arrange for about a half hour each on them.

LESSON 30 NOTES:

Unit 4

WordPerfect Graphic Tools

LESSON 31
Graphic Boxes

OBJECTIVES

Upon completion of this lesson, you will be able to:

1. Learn the characteristics of the different types of graphic boxes.
2. Insert graphic boxes into your documents.
3. Change the characteristics of graphic boxes.

Estimated Time: 1 ½ hours

Quite often when we think about word processing and graphics, we are thinking about working with page layouts—that is, designing attractive pages for multiple production. The documents might be newsletters, brochures, business reports, resumes, or magazine articles.

Regardless of the final product, the design elements are the same. Page layout is simply the arrangement of type, white space, and graphics. If it is attractive and easy to follow, people will read it. If it is neither attractive nor easy to follow, no matter how interesting, people probably won't read it.

WordPerfect provides you with a number of design elements that enable you to make attractive documents. These design elements include columns (which you already know how to use), graphic boxes, graphic lines, and, if your printer has the capability of printing them, fonts of every imaginable size!

This lesson will help you work with graphic boxes. You will learn about graphic lines in Lesson 32 and fonts in Lesson 33. This is not a primer in page layout. Indeed, whole courses are necessary for that training. A certain amount of artistic talent is also helpful for designing attractive documents. The person aspiring to excellence in page layout will study layouts of everything he or she reads and then will adopt the layouts that look good, discarding those that are unattractive.

Let's learn about WordPerfect graphic boxes.

KINDS OF GRAPHIC BOXES

WordPerfect provides you with four kinds of graphic boxes from which to choose—Figure, Text, Table, and User boxes. These boxes all have different characteristics but are much the same. A fifth kind—Equation boxes—will be saved until Lesson 34. In the next section you will find an example of each of the others with a discussion of how these boxes might be used.

Figure Box

Figure boxes are most often used for charts, graphic images, and diagrams, but they may also contain text. The caption is beneath the figure as Figure 1, Figure 2, etc. The default setting for Figure boxes includes a single line enclosing the figure into a box. Approximately a sixth of an inch of white space surrounds the box on the outside.

Figure 1 — Figure Box

Graphics can be retrieved from the 30 prerecorded graphics that come with WordPerfect 5.1, from WordPerfect 5.0, clip art, *DrawPerfect*, or WordPerfect *Presentations*. They can be scanned or created in one of the numerous graphic formats acceptable to WordPerfect. They can then be included in your document. The WP graphic illustrated here is one of the graphics that came with your WordPerfect 5.1 program.

Text Box

Text boxes may be used for sidebars, quotes, or any kind of text to be set off from the remainder of the document. Graphics or charts may also be placed in Text boxes. They may be captioned with Arabic numerals.

> Text boxes can be sized to attractively frame the text or graphic material included in them.

1 — Text Box

The default setting for Text boxes includes a heavy black line at the top and at the bottom with shading in the background. Approximately a sixth of an inch of white space surrounds the box on the outside as well as the text on the inside of the box.

Table Box

Table boxes may be used for maps, statistical data, and WordPerfect tables, as well as any kind of chart or graphic. Table boxes look much like Text boxes. The main difference is that Table boxes have a white background instead of the

Table 1 — Table Box

Sam	$34.99
Bea	4.67
Jo	78.92

shading in Text boxes. If a caption is used, the Table box caption (Table I, Table II, etc.) is located above the box.

User Box

User boxes can be used for anything to be offset in a document—text, graphics, tables, diagrams, charts, etc. User boxes have no lines of any kind, nor do they have shading. Captions aren't necessary. If a caption is used, it comes with a simple numeral.

1 — User Box

This good idea light bulb is another WordPerfect graphic. Without the caption, you could place it anywhere in your text when suggesting something you think is especially "bright."

CREATE A BOX

You are probably itching to use some of the graphics, so let's try an exercise or two to give you the basics of working with graphic boxes. Then we'll take a look at the options.

Lesson 31 Exercise 1

Open the Graphics menu.

1. Strike **Alt-F9** for the Graphic menu. A line menu will appear across the bottom of your screen that looks much like this:

```
1 Figure; 2 Table Box; 3 Text Box; 4 User Box; 5 Line; 6 Equation:
```

We'll begin with a Figure box, so choose **1 Figure** and then **1 Create**. A menu will appear that looks much like Figure 31-3.

Choose Figure and then Create.

2. Choose **1 Filename**. We'll ignore the rest of the menu for now. At the Filename prompt, key **c:\wp51\balloons.wpg** and strike **Enter**. This tells the computer to look in the WP51 directory on Drive C.

   If you have a computer without a hard drive, you may need to access a special disk for the graphics. Even if you have a hard drive, your computer may be set up differently. If the directions above don't work, check your spelling carefully and try again. If it still doesn't work, ask your instructor for help in locating the graphic images.

3. When **balloons.wpg** appears on the line opposite **1 Filename**, strike **F7** to return to your document.

4. All you will see is a line in the upper right corner with **Fig 1** in the middle of it. This is your graphic, but it doesn't show on the screen. Go to Print Preview to see how the graphic will look in your document. If you are working on a color monitor, your balloons should appear in color looking much like Figure 31-2. (Too bad you can't print color without a special color printer!)

Figure 31-2

5. Return to your working screen and reveal your codes to see what the code for a Figure box looks like. Print your document and keep it open.

THE GRAPHIC BOX MENU

Now that you have a graphic box in your document, let's return to the menu where you may make adjustments to fit your graphic into your document. You've already seen the menu. Let's look at it in depth.

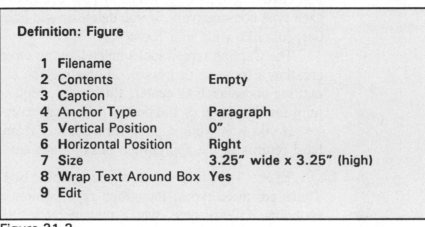

Definition: Figure

1 Filename
2 Contents   Empty
3 Caption
4 Anchor Type   Paragraph
5 Vertical Position   0"
6 Horizontal Position   Right
7 Size   3.25" wide x 3.25" (high)
8 Wrap Text Around Box   Yes
9 Edit

Figure 31-3

Lesson 31 Exercise 2

1. Strike **Alt-F9** and **1** Figure. At the next menu, choose **2** Edit rather than **1** Create because we are going to work with the existing graphic.

2. A **Figure Number?** prompt will appear. If your cursor is above your graphic code, WordPerfect will prompt you with **1**. If the cursor is below the graphic code, it will prompt you with **2**. You want Figure **1**.

3. The Figure 31-3 menu will appear with **balloons.wpg** as the filename. Keep it open as we discuss the parts of the menu. Then we'll work with changes in the settings.

    This next section contains a lot of reading. Stick with it and learn what's presented. It will make your work with graphic boxes much more meaningful!

Choose Figure and then Edit from the Graphics menu.

Filename.   As you know, this is where you specify what you'd like in the box. You may retrieve text, a table, or a graphic image. If you don't want anything in the box, you can leave the filename slot empty. For example, you could make it the exact size to paste a photograph into the finished page.

You don't have to know the exact name of the text or figure you'd like in the box. While WordPerfect is waiting for you to name your graphic, you can strike **F5** for List Files to find the desired material.

Contents. This setting will report what is in the figure, for example a graphic or text. If you retrieve something into a graphic box, it replaces the current contents of a box. If you wish to delete whatever is in a box, you can choose Contents and strike **Ctrl-End**.

Caption. This menu choice is where you key the information to be included in the caption. The words **Figure 1** will appear when you choose Caption, but you may delete that and key your own text, if you wish. If you have a number of graphics in your document, WordPerfect numbers each type consecutively. If you delete or add one, the rest will all renumber, just like with your footnotes.

The Caption screen looks much like the screen you see when you are creating a footnote or header. In creating the caption, you may use formatting codes such as center, flush right, bold, etc. If the caption is too long for the width of the box, it will wrap to the next line.

If you want your caption further away from the box, you can insert hard returns in the appropriate place to add that space.

Type. Type refers to how your graphic box is attached to your text. There are three types: Paragraph type, which moves with the text surrounding it; Page type, which remains at a fixed position on the page; and Character type, which is attached to a certain keystroke. The default for Type is Paragraph.

The code for a Paragraph type box is placed at the beginning of the paragraph. If the paragraph is too near the bottom of the page or if the box won't fit in the place where the paragraph is to begin, WordPerfect "bumps" the box to the top of the next column or page.

The Page type box is fixed on the page. The code should be inserted at the very top of the page or WordPerfect will bump it to the next page.

Character type boxes are treated like a single character no matter how large or small they are. Character type boxes are the only type allowed in footnotes and endnotes.

Vertical Position. This works together with Type. With a Paragraph type graphic, for example, choosing a vertical position of 0" tells WordPerfect to begin the box even with the first line of the paragraph. If you are in the process of keying a paragraph when you create the box, the box code will be placed at the beginning of the paragraph, but the vertical position prompt will reflect the distance you are from the top of the paragraph when you create the box.

With a Page type of box, the box can be aligned with the top or bottom of the page, or it can be centered on the page. If you choose Full Page as the type, the graphics box will fill the entire page within the margins and will be on a page by itself. With a Character type box, you have the choice of whether the remaining text on the line will be printed in line with the top, middle, or bottom of the box.

Horizontal Position. Like vertical, the horizontal position is dependent on the box type. A Paragraph type enables you to select a horizontal position that places the box at the left of the paragraph, the right of the paragraph, centered between the margins, or filling the entire area from left to right margin. A Page type box may be aligned with the left or right margin or centered between margins.

Size. WordPerfect gives you three options in the Size menu: Set Width, Set Height, and Set Both Width and Height. When you set the width, WordPerfect calculates the height of the box so the original shape of the image is maintained. If you set height, the width is automatically calculated so the graphic keeps its proportion. If you set both width and height, you are allowed to enter the measurements. If, however, the width and height don't match the shape of the graphic in the box, the box size may change but the graphic will stay the same size.

If you are working with a box containing text, you may set the width or the width and height. If you set only the width, WordPerfect calculates the height of the box containing text to allow adequate room for the text.

Wrap Text Around Box. This default is set at **Yes** because normally you will want the text to wrap around the graphic. However, you may change that setting to **No**, and the text will print right over the top of the graphic box. When using **No**, the box outline won't be shown on the screen. To see the box on screen, you must use Print Preview.

Edit. The Edit menu gives you an interesting array of things you can do with a figure. Let's try an exercise in which you'll work with Edit.

WORKING WITH BOXES

Lesson 31 Exercise 3

1. Strike **F7** to exit from the current graphic menu back to your working screen. Then use **F7** again to exit from the document without saving so you are returned to a clear screen.

2. Create a new figure by striking **Alt-F9** and choosing **1** Figure and **1** Create. At the filename prompt, retrieve the graphic called **pencil.wpg**. You may key the filepath (i.e., **c:\wp51\pencil.wpg**), or you may strike **F5**, move to the WP51 directory, and select the **pencil** graphic from the alphabetized list.

3. With the Definition: Figure menu still showing, choose **9** Edit. A large graphic of a pencil will appear with menu choices at the bottom.

Choose **Figure** and then **Create** from the Graphics menu.

Notice that on the right side of the menu you are prompted to use the **Goto** function (**Ctrl-Home**) to return the graphic to its original status. Use it whenever you need as you "play" with this pencil.

4. Use the **Arrow** keys to move the pencil up, down, right, and left in the box. Use **Page Up** and **Page Down** to make the pencil larger or smaller while keeping the same proportion.

5. Use the Number Keypad + and - keys to rotate the pencil in the box. Note that striking **Ins** causes a percentage figure to appear in the lower right corner of the screen where you can set a percentage that affects the cursor keys, Page Up, Page Down, scaling, moving, and rotating as well as the + and - keys.

6. Experiment with **Move**. You'll be prompted for a horizontal and vertical distance to move the pencil in the box.

7. **Scale** gives you an opportunity to enter an **X** and **Y** axis. If you set one at 50 percent and the other at 100 percent, you will see a distortion of the original pencil. Experiment with it.

8. **Rotate** enables you to turn the pencil every which way. You can set any number of degrees for the rotation. A prompt will ask whether you would like a mirror image. **Invert** changes a white-on-black to a black-on-white image.

9. Fix the pencil so it looks the way you want it to look. Then strike **F7** to return to the Definition: Figure menu.

You certainly have managed quite a few changes to that lowly pencil. This exercise has given you a taste of just what can be done to edit your graphics. Now let's experiment with changing the size of the graphic and its position on the page.

Lesson 31 Exercise 4

1. Choose 7 **Size** and look at the line menu that appears:

`1 Set Width/Auto Height; 2 Set Height/Auto Width; 3 Set Both; 4 Auto Both`

2. Choose **1** and set the width at 6 inches. Let the height set automatically. Return to your working screen and use Print Preview to see your BIG pencil.

3. Return to the Definition: Figure menu for Figure 1 (remember to choose Edit). Choose Size again. This time set both height and width. Set the width at 6 inches and the height at 3 inches. Your graphic should look much like Figure 31-4.

Figure 31-4

4. Return to the Definition: Figure menu one more time. Give the pencil a caption of your choice. Rotate or scale it however you wish.

5. For Anchor Type, choose **2 Page**. You will be asked how many pages to skip. Just strike **Enter**.

6. For Vertical Position, choose **3 Center**. For Horizontal Position, choose **1 Margins** and **3 Center**.

7. Return to your working screen and use Print Preview to evaluate your pencil. If it meets your discriminating approval, print it and save it on your disk as **pencil.314**. Close the document.

You must be tired of the pencil by now. You have had plenty of opportunity to see what you can do with that pencil—or with any graphic, for that matter. But wait . . . there's more!

Lesson 31 Exercise 5

1. Strike **Alt-F9** and **1 Figure**. You've already created and edited a figure. The third choice, **3 New Number**, simply allows you to assign a different number to your figure if you'd like.

2. Choose **4 Options**. Look at the menu that appears. It should look much like Figure 31-5.

3. Look at the smorgasbord of choices available in this options menu! Choose **1 Border Style**. Note that in the menu that appears at the bottom, you have seven choices with regard to the border around your Figure box. Strike **Enter** as many times as necessary to accept the Single setting for all four sides.

4. Choice **2**, Outside Border Space, can be set at any portion of an inch. This refers to the amount of space between the graphic and the text surrounding it.

5. Choice **3**, Inside Border Space, deals with the amount of space between the graphic and the box surrounding it.

6. The rest of the choices deal with numbering, the caption, and gray shading. Note that the setting for shading for a Figure box is 0%. If you remember from earlier in the lesson, the only kind of graphic box with shading set as a default is the Text box, but you can use shading in any of the four kinds of graphic boxes.

7. Spend a moment or two exploring the options in this menu. Then return to your working screen. Reveal your codes and delete the Figure Options code.

Cropping

One of the limitations on WordPerfect graphic images is that you can't change them in any way. In other words, you couldn't get rid of that line the pencil was drawing. It had to be there, no matter which way you turned your pencil.

Choose **Figure** from the Graphics menu. Then choose **4 Options**.

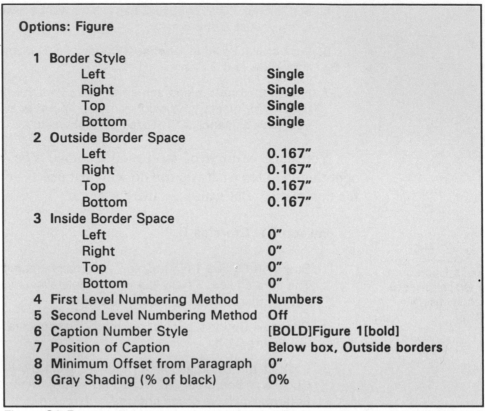

Options: Figure

1	Border Style	
	Left	**Single**
	Right	**Single**
	Top	**Single**
	Bottom	**Single**
2	Outside Border Space	
	Left	**0.167"**
	Right	**0.167"**
	Top	**0.167"**
	Bottom	**0.167"**
3	Inside Border Space	
	Left	**0"**
	Right	**0"**
	Top	**0"**
	Bottom	**0"**
4	First Level Numbering Method	**Numbers**
5	Second Level Numbering Method	**Off**
6	Caption Number Style	**[BOLD]Figure 1[bold]**
7	Position of Caption	**Below box, Outside borders**
8	Minimum Offset from Paragraph	**0"**
9	Gray Shading (% of black)	**0%**

Figure 31-5

Another of the graphics is a clock that ALWAYS gives the same time. You can turn the clock backwards, upside down, and cornerwise, but the time will never change. This is also true of graphics retrieved into WordPerfect from another program. Your graphic image must be just as you want it in that other program before you import it into WordPerfect.

Now that you know everything there is to know about graphic boxes (HA!), here are some exercises so you can see how they look and how they work in your documents.

Lesson 31 Exercise 6

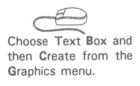

Choose **Text Box** and then **Create** from the Graphics menu.

1. Strike **Alt-F9**. Choose **3** Text Box and **1** Create to create a text box.

2. On the Definition: Text Box screen, you can do all the things you learned when working with Figure boxes. If you wished, you could choose **1** Filename and retrieve a text file saved on your disk.

3. Instead, choose **9** Edit. This will take you to a special screen. Key the information included in the Text box example on page 373.

4. When you finish, exit from the box and return to your working screen. Note that now the line indicating the graphic box says **TXT 1.**

5. Use Print Preview to look at your document with Text box.

6. Return to the same text box by following the appropriate steps to Edit Text Box 1. Change the word *included* to *contained*.

7. Change the horizontal position to Center. Return to the document and print it. Exit from it, saving it as **txt.316**.

Lesson 31 Exercise 7

Choose **User** Box and then **Create** from the Graphics menu.

1. Open **pc-care.279** (in your Unit-2 directory). Position the cursor to the left of the Tab for the first line of the first paragraph.

2. Strike **Alt-F9**. Choose **4 User** Box and **1 Create**. Choose **pc-1.wpg** from the list of graphic images.

3. Change the width (auto height) to 2 inches.

4. Return to your document and use Print Preview to see how the computer looks on the page.

5. Print only the first page of the document and use **F10** to save it as **pc-care.317**.

Lesson 31 Exercise 8

1. Put your cursor at the beginning of the part about making backups.

2. Create a Text box. In that Text box, key the last sentence of the first paragraph: *Protect yourself by making backups of critical data*.

3. Set the width of the box at 1.7 inches. Then print the page. This is known as a "pull-quote."

4. Strike **Page Up** to move your cursor well above the Text box and go to Text Box Options.

5. Change the Border Style to Left-Thick, Right-Thick, Top-None, Bottom-None. Use Print Preview. Do you like this arrangement better?

6. Try some of the other options with regard to border and print a page showing the style you like best.

7. Close your document, saving it as **pc-care.318**.

Lesson 31 Exercise 9

1. On a clear screen, clear all tabs. Then set a left tab at 0.3" and a decimal tab at 1.5". Key the little table illustrated in the Table box example on page 343. Save it on your disk as **table** and clear the screen.

2. Create a Figure box. For the filename, retrieve your **table** document.

3. Return to your working screen and use Print Preview to look at your table in a Figure box. It doesn't look very good, does it?

4. Return to your Figure box and edit it. Change the width to about 2.2".

5. Choose **9** Edit and add a hard return above the table and below it to give some room inside the box. (The default for a Text box or a Table box has inside border space. If you had used either of those, it would not be necessary for you to add space.)

6. Now look at your little table in Print Preview. Is it better? Print your table and exit from it, saving it as **table.319**.

SUMMARY

This has been a quick overview of graphic boxes and how they can be used. You learned the difference between the four kinds of boxes—Figure, Text, Table, and User. You learned how to put graphics and text into those boxes. You also learned the difference between the Page, Paragraph, and Character types and how to adjust the placement and size of the boxes. You didn't get any practice with Character boxes in this lesson, but a later lesson will include some of that. In fact, you'll be working with graphic boxes in a number of exercises in the remaining lessons. The only way you'll get good at working with graphics is to use them, and you'll have plenty of opportunity for that!

All four kinds of boxes can be used for any text or graphic. The default settings are what make them different. You learned that you can change those settings so that one kind of box can look exactly like a different kind, if you wish.

The advantage of having the four kinds of boxes is that when generating lists using the Mark Text feature, you can generate a list of each of the different kinds of boxes. For example, if you set up a page at the beginning of your document for tables and positioned the Define List code in the appropriate place, WordPerfect would make a list of your tables at the same time it's generating the Index or the Table of Contents.

You are sure to find graphic boxes useful in the creation of your lovely documents!

LESSON 31 NOTES:

LESSON 32
Graphic Lines

OBJECTIVES

Upon completion of this lesson, you will be able to:

1. Add horizontal and vertical lines to your documents.
2. Change the default settings for horizontal and vertical lines.

Estimated Time: 1 hour

Graphic lines are a powerful way of adding interest and clarity to any document. WordPerfect graphic lines are easy to insert and easy to edit. You can use horizontal and vertical lines of any length, width, or darkness to make your documents more attractive.

Compare the two letterheads illustrated in Figure 32-1. They contain the same information and are arranged in a similar manner. The major difference is the addition of the graphic lines in the sample at the right.

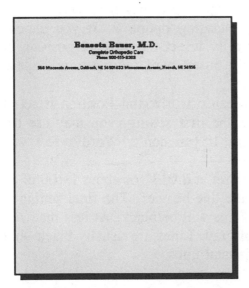 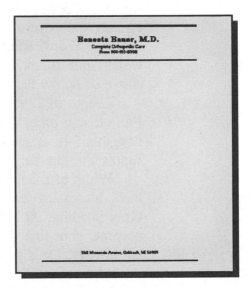

Figure 32-1

WordPerfect is incredibly intuitive when you are working with graphic lines. If you position your cursor correctly before inserting the line and ask for "help," WordPerfect will supply most of the critical measurements for your line placement and length. The toughest part of working with graphic lines is that they don't show in your document unless you use Print Preview.

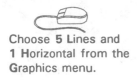

Choose **5** Lines and
1 Horizontal from the
Graphics menu.

The Graphics menu is used to insert a horizontal or vertical graphic line into your document, just like the graphic boxes you worked with in Lesson 31. Strike **Alt-F9**, choose **5** Line and then **1** (Create Line) Horizontal. Let's look at the menu for a horizontal line.

HORIZONTAL LINES

The menu that appears when you order up a horizontal line in Word-Perfect looks like Figure 32-2.

The default setting for Horizontal Position is Full, so the line will extend from the left to the right margin. Other choices include placing a shorter line against the left or right margin. You may also center the line or key the number of inches from the left margin where you wish the line to begin.

Graphics: Horizontal Line	
1 Horizontal Position	**Full**
2 Vertical Position	**Baseline**
3 Length of Line	
4 Width of Line	**0.013"**
5 Gray Shading	
(% of black)	**100%**

Figure 32-2

Vertical Position is set for Baseline. This means the line is aligned at the bottom of the line of text where the code is placed. If you wish the line to begin elsewhere, you can set the position of the line by choosing option 2. If you choose Specify, WordPerfect will automatically insert the vertical position at which your cursor is located. You can insert hard returns to add space above or below the line.

Length of Line has no setting because Horizontal Position is set at Full. If any other choice is made in the first setting, you may use the Length of Line setting for your line. If you don't, WordPerfect will supply the line length for you.

Width of Line, as you can see, is set at 0.013" or about 1/100 of an inch. Increasing that setting makes the line heavier. The final setting is Gray Shading. At 100 percent, your line will be black. At less than 100 percent, your line will be a shade of gray. Lines are usually black—but not always! Let's practice with horizontal lines.

Lesson 32 Exercise 1

Choose **5** Lines and
then **1** (Create)
Horizontal from the
Graphics menu.

1. On a clear screen, strike **Alt-F9** and choose **5** Line and then **1** (Create Line) Horizontal. Strike **Enter** to accept the defaults and position a horizontal line in your document. You will be returned to your document screen.

2. Reveal your codes and look at the code for the horizontal line. Notice all the information it provides about the line.

3. Then use Print Preview to view the line. It was easy, wasn't it? Delete your horizontal line by deleting the code or by clearing the screen. Remember Alt-x?

Now let's use the Horizontal Line feature to do something useful. We'll create the form illustrated in Figure 32-3. Follow along carefully.

Lesson 32 Exercise 2

Choose **5 Lines** and then **1** (Create) Horizontal from the Graphics menu.

1. Key *Name* and space once. Strike **Alt-F9**. Choose **5 Line** and **1 Create**.

2. Choose **1 Horizontal Position** and then **5 Set Position**. A prompt will appear at the bottom of the screen telling the location of your cursor.

3. Strike **Enter**. That cursor position will be reflected opposite the first choice in the menu, and the distance from the cursor to the right margin will be reflected at **3 Length of Line**.

4. Strike **Enter** to accept the settings and to return you to your document screen. You may check the appearance of the first line of your form using Print Preview, if you'd like. Strike **Enter** twice to leave a double space before the next item in the form.

5. Follow the exact same procedure for the address, telephone number, and children's lines of the form.

Name _____

Street Address _____

City, State, ZIP Code _____

Telephone Number _____

Children's Names and Ages _____

Dues (check one): Individual ($3.00) _____

                   Family ($5.00) _____

Date _____

Figure 32-3

You're doing great! If you remembered to space once before inserting each line, your lines should begin a consistent distance from the end of the keyed line. And all of your lines should end squarely at the right margin.

Now let's try some different horizontal line features. In the remainder of the lines, we will also set the length of the line.

Lesson 32 Exercise 3

1. On the *Dues* line, key up to the colon, tab once (to **Pos 3"**), key *Individual ($3.00)*, and space once.

2. Insert the line and set the position. Before leaving the menu, choose **3 Length of Line** and key *.75* for a ¾-inch line. Strike **Enter** until you are returned to your document. Strike **Enter** twice to double space.

3. Tab to **Pos 3"** again and format the *Family* line the same way.

4. Use the normal procedure for the *Date* line but make that line *2.5* inches long.

5. Use Print Preview to see if your form needs any adjustments. If not print it and use **F10** to save it as **form.323**. Keep it on the screen.

Let's spruce up your form a bit! We'll change some of the other defaults for horizontal lines.

Lesson 32 Exercise 4

1. Strike **Page Up** to move the cursor to the top of the form, above all codes. Strike **Enter** twice. Move the cursor to the top again.

2. Go to the Create Horizontal Line menu and choose **4 Width of Line**. Key *0.05* to make the line about five times heavier than those in the form.

3. Choose **5 Gray Shading** and set it at 50 percent for a gray line.

4. Return to your document and strike **Page Down**. Strike **Enter** twice, if necessary, to add a double space below the *Date* line of the form.

5. Insert an identical line here. You have three choices regarding how to do this. Pay attention now. The review of theory in the first two methods is important to your efficient use of WordPerfect.

   a. Reveal your codes. Position the cursor ON the Horizontal Line code at the top of the document.
      • Turn on Block and strike → once. You have blocked the code.
      • Strike **Ctrl-F4** and choose to Copy the block.
      • Strike **Page Down** and then **Enter** to finish copying the code from the top of the document to the bottom.

   b. Reveal your codes. Position the cursor ON the Horizontal Line code at the top of the document.
      • Strike **Delete** to delete the code and place it in the temporary memory.

Choose **Block** and then **Copy** from the **Edit** menu.

- Without moving the cursor, key **F1** (Cancel) and **1** to Restore the code.
  - Strike **Page Down** and key **F1** and **1** again.
  c. Go through the steps of creating the line and setting all of the criteria for the line at the bottom, just like for the line at the top.

6. With both lines in place, preview your document and print it. Then exit from it, saving it as **form.324**. (The appearance of the gray line will vary by type and brand of printer.)

The advantage of copying the line in the exercise above rather than creating a new one is that you don't have to remember all the settings to get two identical lines. If you didn't try all three methods, take a few moments now and practice all three. Probably the most efficient was the second method, because the text to be copied was only one code. It was not necessary to block it. If the material you were repeating consisted of more than one code, you would need to use the first method and block the text to be copied.

Let's say you've decided you want to make the line a little darker. Fifty percent shading is a little too light. We'll adjust the shading.

Lesson 32 Exercise 5

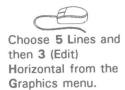

Choose **5 Lines** and then **3** (Edit) Horizontal from the Graphics menu.

1. Retrieve **form.324** and position the cursor just to the right of the horizontal line at the top of the form.

2. Strike **Alt-F9**. Choose **5 Line** and **3** (Edit Line) Horizontal. The menu with which you worked in the last exercise will appear, complete with your settings.

3. Change the Gray Shading to 75 percent.

4. Strike **Enter** to close the menu and repeat the process with the line at the bottom.

5. Print your revised form. Then exit from it, saving it as **form.325**.

As you can see, editing a line isn't difficult. The important thing to remember when you have a number of lines in a document is to position the cursor immediately following the Line code in your document before going to the Line menu and choosing to edit it.

VERTICAL LINES

Creating a vertical line is much the same as creating a horizontal line. In fact, the menu items are the same. The responses are different, however, because of the positioning. The default horizontal position setting for a vertical line is at the left margin, and the default vertical position is a full page. Let's start slowly and then create a game.

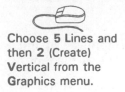

Choose **5 Lines** and then **2** (Create) **Vertical** from the Graphics menu.

Lesson 32 Exercise 6

1. Strike **Alt-F9**. Choose **5 Line** and **2** (Create Line) **Vertical**. Look at the Graphics: Vertical Line menu.

2. Strike **Enter** to accept all settings and enter a vertical line.

3. Look at the code in Reveal Codes and use Print Preview to see how it looks in the document with the default settings.

4. Clear your screen.

Lesson 32 Exercise 7

In this exercise you will create two horizontal and two vertical lines according to the instructions listed below. See if you can guess what game you will play with the results of this exercise.

1. Horizontal Line	Horizontal Position:	2.2"
	Vertical Position:	4.5"
	Length:	4.0"
2. Horizontal Line	Horizontal Position:	2.2"
	Vertical Position:	6.5"
	Length:	4.0"
3. Vertical Line	Horizontal Position:	3.2"
	Vertical Position:	3.5"
	Length:	4.0"
4. Vertical Line	Horizontal Position:	5.2"
	Vertical Position:	3.5"
	Length:	4.0"

When you finish, print your document. Perhaps you can get your teacher or a classmate to play with you. Save the document as **tic-tac.327** and exit from it.

Lesson 32 Exercise 8

1. Retrieve **columns.172** (Unit 2).

2. Position the cursor at the first character of the second column. (Remember that you can use **Ctrl-Home** followed by → to move the cursor to the column at the right.)

3. Go to the Vertical Line menu. Choose **1 H**orizontal Position and choose **3 B**etween Columns. Affirm at the prompt.

4. Choose **2 V**ertical Position and then choose **5 S**et position. Because your cursor is one inch from the top of the page, that information will be provided. The line length will automatically be set at 9 inches.

5. Return to your document screen and use Print Preview to look at the short document with the long line.

6. Position your cursor even with the last line of the document. Look at the **Ln** measurement in the status line. It should be at about 3.5". Mentally subtract the 1-inch top margin, which leaves 2.5".

7. Position the cursor to the right of the vertical line code in your document and use Edit to return to the menu to adjust the length of your line. Choose **3 Length of Line** and change the setting to 2.5".

8. Return to your document and view it with Print Preview. For some reason the line will probably be a little short. Return to the menu once again. Change the length to about 2.9" and preview again to see if it looks good.

9. Finally, print your columns with a vertical line between them and exit the document, saving it as **columns.328**.

That about covers graphic line basics. With what you learned in this lesson and a little experimenting, you should be able to use vertical and horizontal lines to give your documents a professional look!

One final exercise is included here. No specific steps are listed, so you'll need to think a little about how you'd like this document to look.

Lesson 32 Exercise 9

Create a letterhead that you can use for the letters you send—either yours or those of your boss. You may pattern it after the letterhead on the right in Figure 32-1, if you'd like, or you can do a number of different things with horizontal and vertical lines in preparing the format.

Include your name or your company name, address, phone number, and, perhaps, a FAX number. If you are doing a company letterhead, you may wish to include the names of the higher-level officials somewhere on the letterhead.

Plan your format before you begin. You may even wish to sketch it out first with pencil and paper. You might wish, also, to look at some samples of company letterheads for ideas. If your printer will cooperate, you may choose to use the Large or Extra Large setting for your name or the company name.

If you wish to have the lines go closer to the edges of the paper, change your margins before inserting the horizontal and/or vertical lines. You may make the margins as narrow as a half-inch without running into trouble with your printer.

When you finish, print your letterhead and exit from it, saving it as **letrhed.329**. We'll work with this letterhead again by applying different fonts in Lesson 33.

SUMMARY

This lesson provided you with a primer on horizontal and vertical lines. Once you understand the position and length settings, all you need is practice to be good at including lines in your documents. You will find that lines dress up all kinds of documents—business reports, newsletters, brochures, etc.

As with other graphic features, you should be careful not to overdo the use of graphic lines in your documents. Become a "critical consumer" of the documents you prepare. Evaluate whether they really look good or if you have used too many graphics. A junky document is hard to read, and the message is often lost.

COMMAND SUMMARY

Feature	Function	Menu	Lesson
Advance	Shift-F8, O	Layout	29
Comment	Ctrl-F5	Edit	29
Document Compare	Alt-F5, G	Mark	29
Document Summary	Shift-F8, D	Layout, Document	29
Figure Box	Alt-F9, F	Graphics	31
Generate	Alt-F5, G	Mark	28
Horizontal Line	Alt-F9, L	Graphics	32
Index	Ctrl-F5, I	Mark	28
Line Numbering	Shift-F8, L	Layout, Line	29
Mark Text	Block Text, Alt-F5	Mark	28
Master Document	Alt-F5, S	Mark, Subdocument	29
Redline	Ctrl-F8, A	Font, Appearance	29
Strikeout	Ctrl-F8, A	Font, Appearance	29
Table Box	Alt-F9, T	Graphics	31
Table of Contents	Alt-F5, C	Mark, Table	28
Text Box	Alt-F9, B	Graphics	31
User Box	Alt-F9, U	Graphics	31
Vertical Line	Alt-F9, L	Graphics	32

LESSON 32 NOTES:

Name _____ Date _____

TRUE/FALSE

Each of the following statements is either true or false. Indicate your choice in the Answers column by circling T for a true statement or F for a false statement.

Answers

1. The caption is always listed under a WordPerfect graphic box. (Les. 31, Obj. 1) . . . .   1. T F

2. Figure boxes may contain text. (Les. 31, Obj. 1) . . . .   2. T F

3. A Paragraph type graphic box moves with the paragraph to which it is attached. (Les. 31, Obj. 1) . . . .   3. T F

4. When you place a graphic in a document, you can see what that graphic will look like with Print Preview. (Les. 31, Obj. 2) . . . .   4. T F

5. You may choose between wrapping the text around the graphic box or having the text appear over the top of the graphic box. (Les. 31, Obj. 3)   5. T F

6. WordPerfect allows you to change the kind of lines surrounding a Text box. (Les. 31, Obj. 3) . . . .   6. T F

7. WordPerfect enables you to insert horizontal, vertical, and diagonal lines into your documents. (Les. 32, Obj. 1) . . . .   7. T F

8. Graphic lines may be used to prepare forms. (Les. 32, Obj. 1) . . . . . .   8. T F

9. The length, width, and blackness of graphic lines may be changed. (Les. 32, Obj. 2) . . . .   9. T F

10. A line may be placed between newspaper-style columns. (Les. 32, Obj. 2)   10. T F

COMPLETION

Indicate the correct answer in the space provided.

Answers

1. What kind of lines surround a Figure box? (Les. 31, Obj. 1) . . . .   1. _____

2. How is a Text box different from a Table box? (Les. 31, Obj. 1) . . . .   2. _____

3. How many WordPerfect 5.1 prestored graphic images are there? (Les. 31, Obj. 2) . . . .   3. _____

4. When you size a graphic and choose to set the width of the graphic only, what happens to the height? (Les. 31, Obj. 3) . . . .   4. _____

5. What can you do if you want to use a Table box but don't like the heavy black lines at the top and bottom? (Les. 31, Obj. 3) . . . .   5. _____

6. What color are the default graphic lines? (Les. 32, Obj. 1) . . . .   6. _____

7. When adding a horizontal line to your document, what menu must you access? (Les. 32, Obj. 1) . . . .   7. _____

8. What is the maximum length of a vertical line if you use the default margins? (Think!) (Les. 32, Obj. 2) . . . .   8. _____

9. What can you do to tell WordPerfect where to begin a line before you access the Graphic Line menu? (Les. 32, Obj. 2) . . . .   9. _____

10. Who won the tic-tac-toe game? . . . .   10. _____

11. Think of kinds of documents that you create that could be "dressed up" with horizontal or vertical lines. Name two of them.

REFERENCE

Turn to the Graphics, Formats and Programs portion of the *WordPerfect Reference*. As you know, the extension on WordPerfect graphics is **.wpg**. A list is provided of formats that WordPerfect supports. List two of them and the program from which they come.

Turn to the Graphic Lines portion of the *Reference*. A document is illustrated twice in that section. Study the layout of the document. What kind of document do you think it is? What graphic was used? How often is the document published? How many columns does it have? How many articles are included?

LESSON 33
Using Fonts

OBJECTIVES

Upon completion of this lesson, you will be able to:

1. Discuss type terminology.
2. Determine the fonts available to you.
3. Make font changes in your work.

Estimated time: 1 hour

Much earlier in your training you learned about the Font menu and the choices available there. One of the joys of working with WordPerfect 5.1 is the capability of using a variety of type to give your documents a professional appearance. Before you can work knowledgeably with type, however, some terminology needs to be defined.

TYPE TERMINOLOGY

- **Typeface**. One design of type. A typeface has a name, like Helvetica, Times, Swiss, and Univers.
- **Style**. A variation within a typeface. Some of the commonly used variations are italic and bold.
- **Typeface Family**. A group of all related sizes and styles derived from a master typeface.
- **Point Size**. The smallest unit of measure in typography is the point. One point equals approximately 1/72 of a vertical inch. Another way of saying it is that 72-point type is approximately one inch tall. Type is measured in points ranging from 6 points on the small end to several hundred points on the large end.

    The chapter opener at the top of this page is a 30-point font. The type you are reading is printed using a 12-point font. It is approximately the equivalent of a pica character on the typewriter, but more characters will fit on a line because it is proportionally spaced. A 10-point font is approximately the equivalent of an elite character on the typewriter. These two sizes are among the most popular point sizes used to prepare printed materials.
- **Font**. A set of all characters (letters, numbers, and symbols) in a particular typeface in a particular size. When you select a font (e.g., Times 12-point), you are specifying typeface and size.
- **Leading** (pronounced "ledding"). The vertical spacing between lines of type. The term comes from the days when strips of lead

separated the lines of type. In WordPerfect, leading is taken care of automatically, although if you wish to force a manual change, the setting for leading is made in the **6 P**rinter Functions portion of the **O**ther Format menu.

- **Kerning**. Adjusting the space between individual pairs of letters. Kerning, too, can be adjusted in the Printer Functions menu. You would be most likely to work with kerning and leading if you were working with very large fonts.

- **Serif**. The strokes or feet at the ends of the main strokes of letters. Examples of typefaces with serifs include Bitstream Charter, Dutch, and Times Roman. Serifs contribute to the readability of a typeface by helping the eye quickly differentiate between similar letters. You are reading serif type.

- **Sans Serif**. Type without serifs. The letters have no feet or curves at the ends of the main strokes. Examples of sans serif typefaces include Swiss, Helvetica, and Univers. Sans serif typefaces are most often used for headings, headers, and any portion of the well-designed page except long passages of text. Can you find an example of sans serif type on this page? Find one on page 395.

- **Display**. Decorative and novelty typefaces. These typefaces are used for special purposes like short announcements but are avoided for body text. They are quite hard to read. Examples of display typefaces include script and Bitstream Zapf Chancery.

- **Monospaced**. Often called fixed-pitch type. Monospaced type requires the same amount of space on the line for each character, regardless of the size of the character. Most of the work you have done in this course has been completed using Courier 10cpi, which is the default font in WordPerfect. It is monospaced. If you measure a horizontal inch in any document you've prepared, you will find that there are exactly 10 characters in that inch.

- **Proportional**. Type where characters take as much space as they need. Proportional type is characterized by the fact that wide characters like "m" and "w" take more space on the line than skinny characters like "i" and "t." Depending on the text, you can fit one-half to one-third more information on a line with proportional type than with monospaced type, and it's usually easier to read.

As you can readily see, there are lots of words referring to what you can do with text using WordPerfect 5.1. You may select a typeface as well as the point size for the document or portion of a document you are creating. Therefore, you can say you are selecting a font. All of the above definitions may be somewhat overwhelming to you. Let's see what this is all about. Here are some samples of fonts printed on a Hewlett Packard LaserJet III to illustrate the definitions.

This is 24-point Times. This is 16-point Times. This is 12-point Times. Times is a *serif* typeface. Notice the feet on the letters. Notice, too, the extra space between lines to make room for the "descenders," like the bottom of the *p*. In WordPerfect, that spacing is automatic. All of the characters in this paragraph are the same proportional typeface, but the letters obviously vary in size. Each size is a different font.

This is 24-point Univers. This is 16-point Univers. This is 12-point Univers. Note the lack of feet. Univers is a *sans serif* typeface. Again in this paragraph, the typeface is the same but the font varies because of the differences in size. Univers is also a proportional typeface.

```
This is Courier 10cpi and is the typewriter spacing
known to most typists as Pica. This is Courier 12cpi
and is known to most typists as Elite. Both 10-pitch and 12-
pitch Courier are monospaced fonts. When working with Courier
type and full justification, unsightly spaces are likely to
appear between words.
```

SOURCES OF TYPE

Hundreds of different typefaces are available today. Those mentioned above make up only a small portion from which you might be able to choose. What's available to you depends on your equipment configuration. Here are some of the possible options:

- **Resident Fonts.** Some of today's laser printers, such as postscript printers and the HP LaserJet III and IV, come equipped with what are known as scalable fonts. Scalable fonts are built into the printer circuitry. With scalable fonts, when you select a typeface, you can select any point size to accompany that typeface, and the printer will build the fonts as the document is printing. (This is referred to as "on the fly" formatting.)
- **Downloadable.** Companies such as Bitstream have designed fonts that can be printed on laser printers. These fonts must be purchased and assembled on the hard drive of your computer. They are then downloaded to the printer when your document calls for them. Because each font may take quite a large amount of space on the hard drive, you may choose to limit the available fonts to the typestyles and sizes you use most often.

- **Cartridges.** If you have a laser printer, you can probably plug one or more font cartridges into it. A font cartridge is a specially packaged circuit board that fits into the printer and offers a limited selection of font choices. Font cartridges are a relatively inexpensive way of building a font library.

USING FONTS

When you make a font change, a code is placed into your document. The code formats text from the place of insertion forward. You can make as many font changes in a document as you wish—that is, you can change back and forth between two or several fonts. In making font changes, however, format your document tastefully. Too many fonts spoil the appearance of a document.

Let's take a look at the fonts available to you. If you find that you have nothing more than a variety of Courier fonts, check with your instructor to find out what your procedure will be. Most of the exercises in this lesson will give you better results with fonts other than Courier 10cpi. If you find you are limited to Courier 10cpi and 12cpi, use Large, Very Large, Extra Large, etc., from the Size part of the Font menu to enhance your documents in the exercises that follow.

Lesson 33 Exercise 1

1. If you have a choice of printers to use, check with your instructor to see which printer to use for this exercise. Then go to the Print menu to choose the correct printer.

Choose Base Font
from the **Font** menu.

2. Strike **Ctrl-F8** and **4** Base Font to open the Base Font menu. If you have a printer with scalable fonts, you might see a menu that looks like Figure 33-1. Notice that with the exception of the Courier fonts, all the fonts illustrated in Figure 33-1 are scalable fonts. Theoretically, you can set any size you wish.

    If your printer is a dot-matrix printer, your menu might look more like Figure 33-2. Notice that these are all fixed-pitch fonts and they range from 5 characters per inch to 17 characters per inch.

    In all likelihood, your Base Font menu will be different from both of those illustrated.

3. Look at the sizes available to you. If your fonts are not scalable, how large can you go? What is the tiniest size listed? Do you understand the difference between characters per inch and points?

4. Move the highlight to a sample typeface and size (font) and choose it. (If you have scalable fonts, you'll choose the typeface and then key the size at the prompt.) Back at your working screen, key a sentence that identifies that font. For example, key *This is 12-point Times.* Strike **Enter** twice.

```
Base Font

  CG Times (Scalable)
  CG Times Bold (Scalable)
  CG Times Bold Italic (Scalable)
  CG Times Italic (Scalable)
  Courier 10cpi
  Courier 10cpi (Bold)
  Courier 10cpi (Italic)
  Courier 12cpi
  Courier 12cpi (Bold)
  Courier 12cpi (Italic)
  Line Printer 16.67cpi
  Univers (Scalable)
  Univers Bold (Scalable)
  Univers Bold Italic (Scalable)
```

Figure 33-1

```
Base Font

  NLQ  5cpi
  NLQ  5cpi Emphasized
  NLQ  6cpi
  NLQ  6cpi Emphasized
  NLQ 10cpi
  NLQ 10cpi Emphasized
  NLQ 10cpi Half-height
  NLQ 10cpi Half-height Emphasized
  NLQ 12cpi
  NLQ 12cpi Emphasized
  NLQ 12cpi Half-height
  NLQ 12cpi Half-height Emphasized
  NLQ 17cpi
  NLQ 17cpi Half-height
```

Figure 33-2

5. Return to the Base Font menu and choose a different font. At your working screen, key a sentence identifying that font.

6. Repeat the procedure for two more fonts (maximum of four fonts altogether). Your finished document might look like Figure 33-3.

7. Print your document. You may find that the printer will take a great deal of time printing your sample with four different fonts. Be careful not to try too many fonts. Some printers have limited memory. If you try to print lots of different fonts on one page, the printer will not correctly size some of the fonts.

This is 18-point Times.

This is 12-point Times Bold Italic.

This is 10-point Univers.

This is 14-point Univers Bold.

Figure 33-3

8. Save your practice as **fonts.331** and exit from it.

Lesson 33 Exercise 2

1. Retrieve **form.325**. Change to a proportional font for the entire form.

2. View the form with Print Preview. Did the change of fonts mess up your lines? Is there too much space between the words and beginnings of the lines?

3. This is good practice for you. You get to delete each of the graphic lines (reveal your codes to find the codes and delete them) and replace them, using the same procedure you used when you created the form in the first place. (It's easier to delete and redo the lines than to try to edit them to get the correct placement and length.)

4. When you finish, check to see how it looks. Then print the form and save it again, this time as form.332.

Lesson 33 Exercise 3

1. Open pc-care.318. Change to a 12-point proportional font, if you can. If that choice is not available, choose a different font that would look good in a manuscript.

2. Make any changes to the graphics in your document. Use Print Preview to check the appearance of the entire document.

3. Print your newly revised document and exit from it, saving it this time as pc-care.333.

Lesson 33 Exercise 4

1. Open columns.328. Go to the bottom of the first column and delete the Vertical Line code and the Hard Page code that divides the single column into two columns.

2. Return to the top and change to a 12-point proportional font.

3. Add returns so the document has a two-inch top margin. Center the title *WORDPERFECT COLUMNS* followed by a quadruple space.

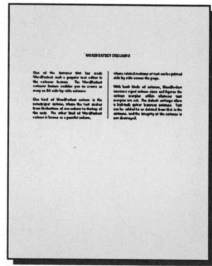

4. Count the lines and divide the single column into two columns again. Add the vertical line between columns and adjust it so it is exactly the right length to bisect the columns.

5. When you finish, check the document for appearance. It should look much like Figure 33-4.

6. Print a copy of the document. Then exit from it, naming it columns.334.

Figure 33-4

Lesson 33 Exercise 5

Retrieve the letterhead you created in Lesson 32. Try out your available fonts in this letterhead. If you have proportional fonts, use one of them. They are much more professional in appearance. Use a variety of sizes, if you can.

Add a graphic image to your document. This may mean that you must move the centered information at the top either to the right or left to make room for the graphic. You may use any of the kinds of graphic boxes about which you learned in Lesson 31. Spend a few minutes with this letterhead developing an attractive form. When you finish, print your revised letterhead and save it as **letrhed.335**.

SUMMARY

What you can do with fonts in your documents using WordPerfect varies according to your printer and the fonts available. If you have a laser printer, you don't necessarily have many fonts from which to choose. In fact, some dot matrix and ink jet printers give you a wider selection of fonts than some laser printers.

This lesson does little more than introduce you to the world of fonts and how they can be used to improve the appearance of your documents. With some practice and by learning from looking at the layouts of documents, you can become skilled in the use of fonts to prepare documents that are attractive and easy to read.

If you should discover on the job that you don't wish to be bothered with the Courier 10cpi setting (the default), you can go to Initial Codes in the Setup menu (Shift-F1) and insert a code setting the font you would like as a default. Then, until you change it, that font will automatically be set each time you begin a new document.

LESSON 33 NOTES:

Review Exercise

Illustrated below is a resume created with Graphics Lines. Adapt the resume to your situation. Use a proportional font, if one is available. Vary the locations, shading, and thickness of the lines and the spacing between sections of text as necessary to prepare an attractive resume for yourself. Print the resume, save it as **resume.33r**, and close it.

SARA STEWDENT
2726 North Bluemound
Menasha, WI 54952
555-7890

EMPLOYMENT OBJECTIVE

To be employed as an administrative assistant in a company that uses WordPerfect.

EXPERIENCE

Hug-a-Leg Hosiery Co., Menasha, WI
Internship position, Administrative Assistant
(1991 to present)

Clara's Computers, Appleton, WI
Part-time, Administrative Assistant
(1990 to 1991)

Schimmelpfennig Schimmelpfennig Krizenesky Hall & Vanderlinden SC, Kaukauna, WI
High School Co-op Position, Secretarial
(1989-1990)

Singing Pines Girl Scout Camp, Winchester, WI
Scout Leader and Counselor
(1985-1990)

Leo's Custard Stand, Menasha, WI
Carhop
(1987-1989)

EDUCATION

Butte des Morts Business College, Winchester, WI
Administrative Assistant--Information Processing
Associate Degree, May, 1992

Kaukauna High School, Kaukauna, WI
Graduated in 1990

HOBBIES & INTERESTS

Scouting, church youth group, sewing, knitting, bicycling, hiking, reading, and gardening

REFERENCES

Available upon request.

LESSON 34
Graphic Mania

OBJECTIVES

Upon completion of this lesson, you will be able to:

1. Prepare statistical materials with the equation editor.
2. Work with ASCII characters.
3. Use the WordPerfect character sets for special characters.
4. Add dropped caps to your documents.
5. Print text over graphic images.

Estimated Time: 2 hours

THE EQUATION EDITOR

WordPerfect comes equipped with a marvelous equation editor for use in creating mathematical expressions for engineering and scientific purposes. The equation editor creates a graphic box for each equation, which sizes, positions, and aligns the elements of the equation. The equation box is much like the graphic boxes you created in Lesson 31. Equations can be printed on most printers. If the characters in the equation are not in the printer's font, they can be printed by WordPerfect as graphic characters on all printers with graphics capabilities.

Choose Equation and then Create from the Graphics menu.

The equation editor is accessed from the Graphics menu, which opens when you strike **Alt-F9**. You've already learned about all of the choices in this menu except the final choice, **6 Equation**.

Definition: Equation
1 Filename
2 Contents   Equation
3 Caption
4 Anchor Type   Paragraph
5 Vertical Position   0″
6 Horizontal Position   Full
7 Size   6.5″ wide x 0.333″ (high)
8 Wrap Text Around Box   Yes
9 Edit

Figure 34-1

Strike **Alt-F9** now. Choose **6 Equation** and **1 Create** for the Equation menu. It will look much like Figure 34-1. This menu should look familiar to you because it is similar to the menus for other kinds of graphic boxes. Ignore all of the choices now except **9 Edit**.

Strike **9 Edit** to start the equation editor. It will look like Figure 34-2. Keep the equation editor open so it is showing on your screen while you read about it.

The equation editor is divided into three windows. The large section at the top on the left is the display window. It is here that you may view your equations as you create them by striking **Ctrl-F3** (screen). Below the display window is the editing window. This window is your workspace while you are creating equations.

	Commands
	OVER
	SUP or ^
	SUB or _
	SQRT
	NROOT
	FROM
	TO
	LEFT
	RIGHT
	STACK
	STACKALIGN
	MATRIX
	FUNC
	UNDERLINE
	OVERLINE
	{
	}
	HORZ
	VERT

Screen Redisplay; List Commands; Switch Window; Setup Options   500%

Figure 34-2

The window at the right is the equation palette. It is from the palette that you can choose the items to make up the equations. There are eight menus in the palette, including commands, large and small symbols, Greek characters, arrows, and others. You can move your cursor to the palette by striking **F5** (list). You may then use the **Page Down** key to page through the palette until it cycles back to the beginning menu. We'll work with the equation palette shortly.

Items can be chosen from the palette for inclusion in the equation. Many of them can be directly keyed into the editing window. Let's try a simple equation so you can get the feel of the editor.

Lesson 34 Exercise 1

1. With the cursor in the editing window of the equation editor, key the following simple line: $a + b = c$

2. Use **Ctrl-F3** to view the equation in the display window. Note that even though you keyed spaces between the elements of the equation, none appear. The spaces inserted in equations with the space bar only make it

$a+b=c$

easier to see the equation as you edit it. If you would like the spaces to appear around the elements, they must be inserted with the tilde (~) character. It should look like this when keyed: a~ + ~b~ = ~c. Locate the tilde on your keyboard.

3. Remove the spaces from your equation and replace them with ~ characters. The ~ does not show when the equation is printed. Use **Ctrl-F3** to view the equation again.

$$a + b = c$$

4. Edit your equation so it looks like this in the editing screen:
   a~ + ~b over d~ = ~c
   Space with the space bar before and after the word **over**. View the equation again. Is this the way the equation was supposed to look or should the entire $a + b$ section be above the line? You can fix that by adding curly braces to the elements above the line. Curly braces are the shift of the square bracket keys.

$$a + \frac{b}{d} = c$$

5. Edit the equation: {a~ + ~b} over d~ = ~c

$$\frac{a + b}{d} = c$$

6. View the equation.

7. Use **F7** as many times as necessary to leave the equation editor. Notice the line with EQU 1 near the top to show where the equation will appear. Then use Print Preview to look at the equation the way it will be printed. Note that it won't be nearly as large on the paper as in the equation editor. You may remember seeing at the bottom of the equation editor that the equation is enlarged to 500%.

8. Reveal your codes and look at the equation code. Note that the contents of the equation box don't show anywhere in your document unless you use Print Preview.

Lesson 34 Exercise 2

1. Strike **Enter** a couple of times to leave some room below your first equation box and return to the equation editor to try another simple exercise.

2. Strike **F5** to move your cursor to the equation palette and cursor down to **SQRT** (square root). Strike **Enter** to enter that function into your equation.

3. Space once and key the rest of the equation: *144 ~ = ~ 12*

4. View your equation. Now remove the space between the square root function and 144 and view the equation again. See how important the spaces are in creating an equation. Put the space back into the equation. Then close the equation editor and strike **Enter** twice. There should now be an EQU 2 box on your working screen.

$$\sqrt{144} = 12$$

Now you have the basics for working with equations. Any of the commands, symbols, or functions in the equation palette may be accessed in the same way you accessed the square root symbol. For example, you can choose **sup or** $\hat{}$ from the equation palette and key the numeral to get superscripted (raised) numerals. An alternate method is to shift and strike **6** for a caret character ($\hat{}$) to cause the character to be superscripted.

Lesson 34 Exercise 3

With your knowledge of equations, create the following equation. Use normal brackets found on the keyboard. When you finish, print the document with all three of your equations and exit from it, saving it as **equation.343**.

$$\frac{d}{dx} [7y^4] + \frac{d}{dx} x^3y + \frac{d}{dx} [x] = 0$$

Lesson 34 Exercise 4 (Challenge Exercise)

Here is one last exercise using the equation editor. This is a challenge exercise. You may skip it with your instructor's permission if you've had enough equations. If you get stuck, the code for this equation is shown at the end of the lesson near the lesson summary.

Hint 1: You can put braces within braces providing they're used in pairs.

Hint 2: Choose the superscript and subscript codes from the equation palette.

$$Q = \frac{B^{n+y^2} + C_i D_j}{\sin^2(A^2 + B^2) - \cos^2(C_i + DC_j)^2}$$

Print your document and exit from it, saving it as **equation.344**.

Once an equation has been created, it can be sized and moved around in a document just like you sized and moved your other graphic images. This may be more than you ever wanted to know about equations. However, if you have a need for them in your work, this feature will be extremely valuable to you.

ASCII CHARACTERS

The Appendix of the *WordPerfect Reference* contains much useful information for creating characters not included on the keyboard. In Appendix A, for example, 255 ASCII characters are illustrated along with instructions for inserting those characters into your documents. You may look at Appendix A at your leisure. Let's practice with some of the characters.

Lesson 34 Exercise 5

1. Turn on Num Lock (if it isn't already on). Hold **Alt** and **use the Number Keypad** to key the number *14*. When you release **Alt**, a couple of music notes should appear. (Why would you want music notes in your document?????)

2. Key *ni* and hold **Alt** while you key *164* on the Number Keypad. End with the letter *a*. You should have a Spanish word meaning child on the screen: niña

3. Strike **Enter** twice and keep the document on the screen for the next exercise.

WORDPERFECT CHARACTER SETS

Another method of getting different kinds of characters is using the character sets that are illustrated in Appendix P of the documentation. There are a total of 11 predefined character sets. Some of the characters are the same as those in the ASCII list in Appendix A. Others are repeated in several of the character sets listed in Appendix P.

Choose Characters from the Font menu.

To access special characters from the character sets, you must use the **Compose** command, which is either **Ctrl-V** or **Ctrl-2**. When you strike either of these, you'll see **key =** in the lower left corner of the screen. Key the number of the set followed by a comma and the number of the desired character.

A section of Character Set 4 (the one you'll probably use most frequently) is illustrated in Figure 34-3. In Appendix P, each row contains 30 characters. In each set, the fourth character in the first row is Character 4. The fourth character in the second row (beginning with **30**) is Character 34. The **1** and **2** above the zeros tell you that you must add 10 or 20 to the number in the row directly below. For example, the ‰ character in Figure 34-3 is 10 plus 3 in row **60**. It is Character 4,73.

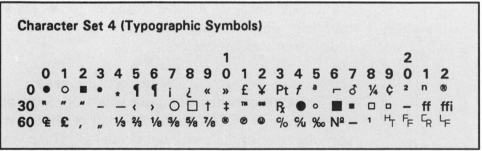

Figure 34-3

The bold numerals are your key to reading the character set tables. For example, since this is Character Set 4, the ℞ symbol is 4,43. The fraction ¼ is 4,18. Study Figure 34-3 until you understand the numbering. What would be the numbers for ™? How about ⌐?

Lesson 34 Exercise 6

Choose **Characters**
from the **Font** menu.

1. Strike **Ctrl-V** and enter the fraction ⅞ by keying *4,69*. You may see a small white square on the screen instead of the fraction, depending on your VDT. (This happens with quite a number of the characters, but most printers will print the characters anyhow.)

2. Use Print Preview to see the actual character on the screen.

3. Reveal your codes and position the cursor ON the fraction. The character set and number should show. Strike **End** to move the cursor past the fraction.

4. Strike **Enter** twice to prepare for the next exercise.

Bullets. Many of the characters in the 11 character sets are not characters you will use with regularity. But there are a few that might be useful to you. Bullets are an example of something you might use often enough to make a macro useful.

A bullet is used to introduce a listing of items that don't necessarily follow a specific order. Bullets introduce items in a list like this listing of all the sources of bullets.

°   Character Set 2, Number 2
●   Character Set 4, Number 0
○   Character Set 4, Number 1
•   Character Set 4, Number 3
●   Character Set 4, Number 44
○   Character Set 4, Number 45
☺   Character Set 5, Number 8 (Whoops! Not a bullet!)
○   Character Set 6, Number 33
•   Character Set 6, Number 34

Please note that you should NEVER mix bullet styles like this. You should choose one and use it for all of the listings in a document!

Check Boxes.   Another character for which you might have use, especially when working with forms, is a check box. Check boxes are little boxes used for choices.

☐ Yes or ☐ No
☐ Male or ☐ Female

These check boxes were made with 4,38. Some additional choices are ☐ (4,48), or ☐ (5,24). If you think all of these are too small, you can vary the sizes of the check boxes (and all of the other characters in the character sets) by changing the font or print size. An easy choice is to go to the Font Size menu (**Ctrl-F8, 1** Size) and choose **7** Extra Large before entering your character set and number.

Lesson 34 Exercise 7

1. Practice making some bullets and check boxes. Use Print Preview to see how your bullets and check boxes will look when printed.

2. Vary the sizes of your check boxes with Large, Very Large, and Extra Large. If you have a variety of font sizes available, try using a 30- or 40-point font for one of your check boxes to make it larger. What size do you like best?

3. When you have had enough practice, print the document containing all of your practice with special characters. Save the practice as **char.347** and exit from it.

While it seems like quite a job to change print size and choose a character from the character set, a macro would do the job very nicely if you need to use a particular character a number of times.

Lesson 34 Exercise 8

Key the sentences in Figure 34-4. Use WordPerfect character sets for the required characters. The number of each special character is shown in parentheses following each sentence. Print a copy of the exercise and exit from it, saving it as **char.348**.

It might cost $1.70 or more to buy £1 of British money. (4,11)

The cake was baked in a 350° oven. (6,36)

"¿Dónde está su niña?" asked Carmelita. (4,32) (4,8) (1,59) (1,27) (1,57) (4,31)

"Let's go to the beach." (4,32) (4,28) (4,31)

I can create check boxes with 4,38 □ and 4,48 ▫. If I want larger ones, I can use a quarter-inch empty Figure box.

Figure 34-4

DROPPED CAPS

One of the attention-getting devices used in magazine articles is known as a *dropped cap*. This is actually a very large capital letter at the beginning of the article. The text for the first paragraph wraps snugly around this large letter. There are a number of ways of creating dropped caps. We will choose an easy

O ne of the fea
made WordPerfe
ular text edit
umns feature. T
columns feature
create as many ε
side columns.

method of adding a dropped cap to one of your documents. We'll use a User box (because it doesn't have any lines).

Lesson 34 Exercise 9

1. Go to your Unit 2 directory and retrieve **columns.172**. Delete the letter *O* at the beginning of the document.

2. Go to the Graphics menu and tell WordPerfect you'd like to set the options for a User box.

3. In the Options menu, set **2 O**utside border to 0" on all four sides. Exit from the Options menu.

4. Create your User box. Skip down the menu to **6 H**orizontal position. Change it to Left.

5. Go to **7 S**ize and set both the height and width. Set the width at 0.3" and the height at 0.4".

6. Choose **9 E**dit. On the edit screen, go to the Base Font menu and choose a font WITH serifs that is large—a good size is 30 points, if you have that size available. (If you don't have 30-point fonts, choose a font that is smaller and then choose Extra Large from the Size menu.) Key a capital *O* and exit from the Edit screen.

7. Exit all the way back to your document. Turn on Hyphenation to even the line endings a little better.

8. Use Print Preview and see how your dropped cap looks at the beginning of that first paragraph. Note that the text could wrap better under the dropped cap. Boxes often appear to have too many blank lines beneath them.

9. Print your document. Then exit from it, saving it as **drop-cap.349**.

If you use a lot of dropped caps in your work, it can be tedious to set up the format each time. You could block the Options code together with the User box code and save them on your disk. Then each time you need a dropped cap, all you'd have to do is go to the User box edit screen and change to the desired letter. (Obviously your dropped caps won't all be *O's*!) An alternate method might be to make a macro that contains the Option codes and the creation of the User box. Then whenever you run the macro, you can go to the User box edit screen and change the letter.

TEXT IN GRAPHICS

Earlier in your work with graphics, you learned that text doesn't have to wrap around the graphic. Sometimes you will want your text to print over the top of the graphic. In fact, a number of the WordPerfect graphic images are designed with that in mind. Look at the 30 graphics illustrated in Appendix B of the *WordPerfect Reference*.

Placing the text appropriately in the graphic is a different kind of challenge. You ought to be able to print the graphic, measure, and then use Advance to position the text. However, when you use Advance, the graphic covers the text. The next alternative is to print the graphic, measure, and then watch the status line as you use Enter and the space bar to position your text. Let's practice.

Lesson 34 Exercise 10

1. Create a Figure box. In the location for the filename, key **burst-1.wpg**. Set the width to 5 inches. (Let the height set automatically.)

2. Set **6** Horizontal position at Center and **8** Wrap to **No**.

3. Print the Burst graphic. On the printed copy, put a pencil dot in the middle of the white part of the Burst. (You should be able to do this pretty well by eye.)

4. Use a ruler and measure the distance from the left edge of the paper to the dot in the center of the Burst. Did you get approximately 4 inches?

   Then measure from the top of the paper to the dot. Did you get approximately 2.5 inches? Record both measurements.

5. Reveal your codes to be certain your cursor is to the RIGHT of the Figure code. Strike **Enter** until the **Line** indicator is at about 2.5 inches.

6. Watch the **POS** indicator as you use the space bar to move the cursor to the correct position at 4.6 inches. Choose the Center command.

7. Key the following message in bold: *IT'S A BOY!!*

8. Use Print Preview to look at the graphic before printing. You may need to make a slight adjustment in the location of the text.

9. Print your announcement. Then exit from it, saving it as **boy-34.10**.

Using a ruler and the WordPerfect graphics capabilities, you can do some other interesting things. For example, you can produce your own greeting cards. The birth announcement you will produce in Exercises 11 and 12 is a good example of what you can do.

All of the text in this card is printed on one side of a sheet of paper. You may have to print the parts of the announcement separately because some printers don't print rotated text (upside down or sideways printing).

Look at Figure 34-5. It represents a sheet of paper folded in quarters. Quarter 1 is the front of the card. Quarter 3 is the inside message portion of the card. Quarter 1 must be printed upside down on the page so that when the card is folded, the printing will be right-side up. Figure 34-6 illustrates what page 1 will look like when you finish. Figure 34-7 illustrates page 3. Let's work with this format.

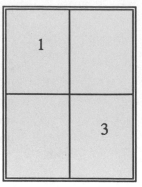

Figure 34-5

Lesson 34 Exercise 11

1. Take a sheet of scratch paper and fold it into quarters. Counting the front of the card as page 1, number the pages of the card. Open up the paper. Does it look like Figure 34-5? Is the numeral for page 1 upside down?

2. We'll begin with page 1. Set the following margins:
    Left 4.75"; Right 0.5"; Top 6.7"; Bottom 0.5"

Those margins position the banner vertically and give you half-inch side margins on the quarter of the page with the banner.

3. Create a User box containing the **banner-3.wpg** graphic. Change Anchor Type to **Page** (strike **Enter** at the pages to skip the prompt) and Horizontal Position to **Center**.

4. Set the width (auto height) at 3 inches. (It will automatically adjust to a number that's a little smaller.) Change Option 8 to **No** (don't wrap text around the graphic).

5. Print the page containing the graphic. Fold it to make certain the banner is completely within the appropriate quarter. Open the paper. Using a pencil or pen, place a small dot in the exact center of the banner. Measure from the top of the page to the dot, approximately 7⅝ inches.

6. On your working screen, set Center Justification (Line format menu).

7. Strike **Enter** and watch the status line until your cursor is approximately on Line 7.6" or 7.7".

8. Key in bold: *IT'S A BOY!!* Check your work with Print Preview. Does the position of the text need to be adjusted? If so, make any necessary adjustments. Then print the page to be sure it is OK.

9. Strike **Ctrl-Enter** for a hard page break. We'll use some of the same settings for the inside of your announcement.

Figure 34-6

Lesson 34 Exercise 12

1. Change the top margin to 7.25". Center Justification should still be turned on.

2. Key the lines for the message in the announcement as illustrated in Figure 34-8. (You may make up your own text, if you wish.) Use character set symbol 4,17 for the ½ in Peter's birth length. Add extra hard returns to space your information attractively.

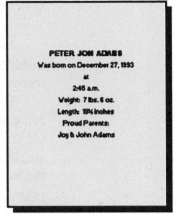

Figure 34-7

3. Use Print Preview to check your work. Make any adjustments necessary.

4. Print the inside of the announcement (page 2) only. If you can feed the page already printed with the banner through the printer again, turn it the other way and do so. If you can't print again on the same paper, print it on a new sheet and cut and paste your two pages together to make the announcement.

5. Save the entire document as **baby-34.12** and exit from it.

```
        PETER JON ADAMS
      was born on May 27, 1993
                at
              2:45 a.m.
        Weight: 7 lbs. 6 oz.
        Length: 19½ inches
          Proud Parents:
          Joy & Jon Adams
```

Figure 34-8

In preparing this announcement, most of the measurements were provided for you. In real life, you would probably spend some time working with an application like this, experimenting and measuring to get appropriate spacing and margins.

Figuring and using margins for applications of this type are important. For example, had you not set the margins for the text in this exercise, you wouldn't have been able to use Center Justification to position your text horizontally. You would have had to have determined the center of each "page," set a tab, tabbed to that position, and given the center command for each line.

If you found that you needed to do quite a bit of this kind of application, you would probably develop a format to be saved as a style or a macro to make the job easier. Avoid starting a new formatting job whenever you can!

BORDERS

Another relatively simple graphic application is the use of borders. Borders are used on one-page brochures, letterheads, and certificates of recognition.

There are a number of ways to put a border around your work. You can create a large, single-cell table using the cell margins as the border. Or you could use a Graphic box. The Figure box, as you remember, has single lines all around. Another alternative is a prepared border. One of the WordPerfect 5.1 graphics is a border. The WordPerfect drawing program (DrawPerfect or Presentations) includes a variety of borders from which you may choose. Other borders are available as clip art from a variety of sources.

Because your margins are set at one inch, you will need to change those margins whenever you want your border to be closer to the edges of the page. Let's try a simple border exercise using the border available as a WordPerfect graphic. We will use the default margins.

Lesson 34 Exercise 13

1. Tell WordPerfect you would like to create a Figure box. At the filename location, key **border-8.wpg**.

2. Make the following settings:

   4 Anchor Type at **Page**
   5 Vertical Position at **Full Page**
   6 Horizontal Position at **1** Margins and then **4** Full
   7 Size will automatically prompt at **6.5"** wide and **9"** high
   8 Wrap text around figure at **No**

3. Choose **9** Edit. You can see that the border is fine from side to side, but it isn't tall enough. Choose **2** Scale and strike **Enter** for the X axis at 100. Set the Y axis at 195% and strike **Enter**. That should fill the page. You can work by trial and error when you don't know the correct percentage to set. For example, 200% was too big here.

4. Exit all the way back to your document screen. Nothing will show. Use Print Preview to look at your border.

This border is fine if you can put something into it. In this case, we will make it a display document, although you could use a border of this type for a letterhead, if you wanted.

You set Option 8 to make the text print over the graphic. That's important in this exercise because we'll put some text inside the border. This will be a certificate of recognition.

You may use BIG or small fonts as you wish and bold wherever you'd like. If you use a variety of fonts, you should probably adjust the space between certificate parts to make it attractive. When you finish, your certificate will be even fancier than the thumbnail illustration in Figure 34-9.

Lesson 34 Exercise 14

1. Reveal your codes so you can see your cursor as you move it to the RIGHT of the Figure box code. Strike Enter six times.

2. Turn on Center Justification and key the text in this certificate as illustrated in Figure 34-10. Use Enter to space the lines attractively.

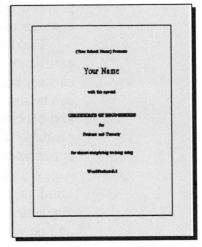

Figure 34-9

(Your school name) Presents

(YOUR NAME)

with this special
CERTIFICATE OF RECOGNITION
for
Patience and Tenacity
for almost completing training using
WordPerfect 5.1

Figure 34-10

---

3. Use Print Preview to check the spacing and the fonts you used for your certificate. Make any adjustments necessary. If you wish, you can turn off Center Justification and add a line on each side near the bottom—one line for your instructor's signature and one for the date.

4. Print a copy of your certificate to show your instructor. Then you can take it home and put it on the refrigerator! Exit from the document, saving it as certif34.14.

SUMMARY

Whew! You finally finished. Reflect for a moment on what you learned in this lesson about dressing up a document. You created equations using the WordPerfect equation editor. You learned to include a variety of odd characters in your documents by using ASCII characters or the WordPerfect character sets.

You discovered that dropped caps—while they look difficult—are really pretty easy to add to your documents. When you do work using proportional fonts, they really dress up the appearance of various display-type documents.

Finally you used graphics for the creation of a greeting card and a certificate. The certificate was created using a border. As mentioned earlier, borders can be created in a number of ways. What's more, they can be used for everything from memo forms to letterheads to newsletters and brochures as well as certificates. If you put your mind to it, you can probably think of a few other places where borders would enhance the appearance of your work.

With the skills you've acquired in this and the previous lessons, your mind is probably abuzz with ideas for document creation. Study the available graphic images. Think a little about greeting cards, brochures, and newsletters. You'll have an opportunity to create one of your own in Lesson 36, and it will probably be easier for you if you've given it some thought beforehand.

Solution to Exercise 4:

Q~ = ~{B^{n+y^2}~ + ~C_iD_j} over {sin^2(A^2~ + ~B^2)~-~cos^2(C_i~ + ~DC_u)^2}

LESSON 34 NOTES:

TRUE/FALSE

Each of the following statements is either true or false. Indicate your choice in the Answers column by circling T for a true statement or F for a false statement.

Answers

1. When discussing type, the word "point" is used to refer to how many strokes it takes to make up a character. (Les. 33, Obj. 1) . . . .   1. T F

2. Leading is the vertical space between lines of type. (Les. 33, Obj. 1) . . .   2. T F

3. When you specify Univers 12-point, you are specifying typeface and size. (Les. 33, Obj. 1) . . . .   3. T F

4. A sans serif typeface has little feet at the ends of the main strokes of the letters. (Les. 33, Obj. 1) . . . .   4. T F

5. Monospaced or fixed-pitch type takes the same amount of space for each letter. (Les. 33, Obj. 1) . . . .   5. T F

6. The WordPerfect equation editor is actually another kind of graphic box. (Les. 34, Obj. 1) . . . .   6. T F

7. The code for ASCII characters is entered using Alt and the Number Keypad. (Les. 34, Obj. 2) . . . .   7. T F

8. The WordPerfect character set codes are entered using Alt and the Number Keypad. (Les. 34, Obj. 3) . . . .   8. T F

9. A dropped cap is simply a large letter in a User box. (Les. 34, Obj. 4) .   9. T F

10. The default is set so that text is automatically printed over the top of graphic images. (Les. 34, Obj. 5) . . . .   10. T F

COMPLETION

Indicate the correct answer in the space provided.

Answers

1. What is the word used to describe type where each letter takes as much space as it needs? (Les. 33, Obj. 1) . .   1. _____

2. What is the name describing the little feet at the ends of the main strokes of a letter? (Les. 33, Obj. 1) . . . . .   2. _____

3. When you work with downloadable fonts, which piece of hardware houses those fonts? (Les. 33, Obj. 1) . . . .   3. _____

4. Given a proportional and a monospaced font that are the same size, which will fit more characters on a line? (Les. 33, Obj. 1) . . . .   4. _____

5. Approximately how many points would a font be that is about one-half inch tall? (Les. 33, Obj. 1) . . . .   5. _____

6. What character forces a space in an equation? (Les. 34, Obj. 1) . . . .   6. _____

7. If you wish to use ASCII characters, must Num Lock be on or off? (Les. 34, Obj. 2) . . . .   7. _____

8. From which two sets of keystrokes may you choose to tell WordPerfect you'd like to use a character from one of the character sets? (Les. 34, Obj. 3) . . . .   8. _____

9. With how many character sets does WordPerfect provide you? (Les. 34, Obj. 3) . . . .   9. _____

10. Why is it best not to try to use too many fonts when you are creating a single document?

_____

11. With your knowledge and/or experiences with office work, which of the features covered in this lesson is most likely to be useful to you? How will you use this feature?

_____

REFERENCE

Turn to the Font section of the *WordPerfect Reference* where you are told about three different places you can go to set the font(s) for a document. What are those three places?

_____

What does the Font section of the *Reference* tell you about the PRINTER.TST document?

_____

Turn in the *Reference* to Appendix P. Which of the character sets would be most useful to you if you did business with European countries? Which set would be must useful in a scientific environment?

_____

LESSON 35
Forms

OBJECTIVES

Upon completion of this lesson, you will be able to:

1. Use WordPerfect to fill information into preprinted forms.
2. Work with forms prepared using WordPerfect.
3. Create forms using the WordPerfect Tables feature.

Estimated Time: 3 hours

The business world is swamped with forms! It seems everywhere you turn you are requested to fill out a form for this and a form for that. If you go to the doctor or dentist, you must fill out insurance forms. If you want to get married, you must fill out a form for the marriage license. Forms are used to register your car or apply for auto insurance. You can't even buy computer hardware or software without having to fill out a registration form! And if you think forms are bad in everyday life, they are the nemesis of life in the office!

Some forms must be filled out by hand. Others may be filled out at the typewriter, where you have the dubious pleasure of aligning the print point with the printed line before keying the information. In today's business office, many forms are filled out using the computer. With the computer, you can't see where the printing will be on the form until the document comes out of the printer, so you often have the feeling you're working in the dark. And not only are computers being used to supply the information requested on a form, in many cases they are being used to design new forms.

In this WordPerfect training, you have worked with all of the tools that make it possible for you to complete or create forms. You've worked with Advance. You've worked with horizontal and vertical lines. You've worked with tables. What's more, you've measured with a ruler, which is a critical tool in preparing information for a preprinted form.

In fact, the preparation of preprinted forms is a very good place to start this lesson. From there, we'll progress to the creation of forms. This lesson includes quite a bit of reading. Don't be discouraged by the amount of it!

PREPRINTED FORMS

Some printers, such as laser and ink jet printers, allow you to feed single sheets. You'll be preparing your forms and then printing on them

NOTE: The exercises in this section of the lesson assume you have a printer that allows you to print on a sheet of paper a second time.

as though they were forms received in the mail. If your printer feeds only continuous paper, you may still complete the exercises, but your information will be printed on plain paper rather than on the form. Then you can hold the two sheets of paper up to the light to see whether the print aligns with the form.

Whenever you need to fill information into a preprinted form, you'll need to use your ruler. You need to measure the distance from the top of the form and the side of the form so you can properly position the information that is to be keyed into the form. If you have a ruler that measures in tenths, that will be helpful to you. If it doesn't you'll have to figure a little to adjust the numbers to correlate with the computer's tenths of an inch.

Let's learn as we practice. We'll fill in your form so it looks much like Figure 35-1.

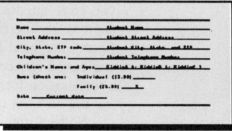

Lesson 35 Exercise 1

1. List your files. Find and print form.325.

Figure 35-1

2. On the printed copy, measure from the top of the paper to a spot just shy of the Name line. Make any necessary adjustments for your printer and jot down that distance.

   Do you remember from Lesson 29 whether your printer aligns text exactly or if it is off a little bit? If not, you'll be experimenting this first time through, and you'll probably need to print your form again for a good finished copy.

3. Measure the distance from the left edge of the paper to a location where you could begin the information for all of the lines up to Dues. Jot down that number. (There isn't any reason why you can't begin them all at the same horizontal location, providing the information fits on the line.)

4. On a clear screen, strike **Shift-F8** and choose **4 Other** to go to the Other Format menu. Set Advance to Line to bring your text to the correct distance from the top of the page.

   You can key a fraction, if you wish, and WordPerfect converts it to tenths. For example, 1 1/8 in WordPerfect is converted to 1.125.

5. You may use Advance to Position to achieve the horizontal placement or, since it doesn't need to be very exact, you may strike **Tab** until you reach the position for the text. Key your name.

Choose **O**ther and then **A**dvance from the **L**ayout menu.

6. Lucky you! The form was created with double spacing, so you need merely to strike **Enter** twice and strike **Tab** to the correct position for your street address. Continue this way until you've filled in everything up to Dues.

7. Figure the location for an **X** for either family or individual dues. Position the X and key it.

8. Decide on the location for the date and key it.

At this point, the text showing on your screen doesn't look like much. You need to print it on the form to find out whether or not it will be appropriately aligned. An important point about forms was briefly addressed in Step 6 of the exercise. Because the form was created with double spacing, once you properly located the information for the first line, the rest didn't need to be figured.

Forms are often NOT created with straight double spacing. Sometimes the lines to be filled in are too far apart or too close together to use regular double spacing. When that happens, you'll probably need to use Advance to position the text for each line of the form. Obviously, that's more time consuming. Let's print the information onto the form and see how well you did with your measuring and adjusting.

Lesson 35 Exercise 2

1. Put your printed copy of the form into the printer so you can print on it again.
   - If you have a laser printer, you will feed the form the same way you feed envelopes. You may need to have your instructor help you feed the sheet of paper a second time.
   - If you have a dot matrix printer, you will need to print the information on a fresh sheet of paper and hold up the two copies to the light to see how well they are aligned.

2. Print the form.

3. Check the alignment of the information to the line. A very small slice of white should show between the bottoms of the characters and the lines on which they rest. This makes the information easier to read.

4. If your alignment is good, save the information for your form as **form.352** and exit from the document.

5. If your alignment is not good, return to the Advance code at the top of your document and make the amount of the advance greater or smaller to lower or raise the text and try again. You'll probably need to print an extra copy of your form for the second (and additional if necessary) try.

Obviously, once you've discovered the amount of the discrepancy between your measurements and what the printer actually produces, your time of trial and error is pretty much ended. You can jot down the amount of the discrepancy and make the adjustment BEFORE you print the next form.

WORDPERFECT FORMS

The exercises above treated the form from Lesson 32 as though it were a preprinted form that came from a source other than WordPerfect. If a form is a WordPerfect form, you can simply retrieve it and fill in the appropriate information right on the lines. Let's try it.

Lesson 35 Exercise 3

1. Again, retrieve **form.325**.

2. Move your cursor to the Name line and strike the **End** key. The cursor will stop at the beginning of the graphic line. If you reveal your codes, you'll see that the cursor is just to the right of the Graphic line code. (Actually, this works equally well whether you position your cursor BEFORE the graphic line code or AFTER it, but it must be on the same line as the Graphic line code.)

3. Tab to **Pos 4"** and key your name. As you can see, the graphic line is not affected.

4. Following the same procedure, fill out the remainder of the form.

5. Print your form and exit from it, saving it as **form.353**. Label the hard copy so you can distinguish it from the one in Exercise 2.

6. Examine your form closely. You'll find that the words are a little too close to the line for easy reading. The fact that it was so easy to prepare is an attractive tradeoff.

7. If you wish, you may use Advance to raise the text a little above each of the lines and reprint your revised document.

When you created the form you used in Exercises 1 and 2, you used graphic lines that began at the cursor and extended all the way to the right margin. Graphic lines can be any length you set them to be, and they can begin and end anywhere you specify.

Another method of adding lines in a form is to set WordPerfect so it underlines the spaces when you tab. The advantage to doing it this way is that you can end the lines wherever you want without having to measure. You'll see as you work with it. When you finish, your form should resemble Figure 35-2.

Name _____ Social Security # _____

Address _____

City _____ State ___ ZIP _____

Figure 35-2

Lesson 35 Exercise 4

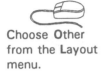

Choose **Other** from the **Layout** menu.

1. Begin with a clear screen. Strike **Shift-F8** and choose **4** Other and **7** Underline.

2. Leave Spaces set to **Yes**. Set Tabs to **Yes**. (Now when you tab, the underline will be added.)

3. Key *Name* and space once. Strike **F8** to turn on Underline.

4. Strike **Tab** until your cursor is at **Pos 4.0"**. Turn off Underline and space once.

5. Key *Social Security #* and space once. Turn on Underline and tab to **Pos 7.5"**. Turn off Underline and strike **Enter** twice.

6. Key *Address* on the next line. Space once and turn on Underline. Strike **Tab** until the cursor is at **Pos 7.5"**. Turn off Underline.

7. Insert the last line the same way, tabbing five times after City, twice after State, and three times after ZIP.

8. Print your form and exit from it, saving it as **form.354**.

This form is primarily made for writing. If you wanted to key information onto the lines, you'd have to use typeover, and it would take some fiddling. As you can see, there are advantages to either way of creating the lines when preparing forms.

USING TABLES FOR FORMS

The forms with which you worked in the exercises above were all pretty simple forms. You can use some of the same methods to work with more complex forms at your leisure (or when the need arises). What you'll probably discover is that the majority of the forms you create will be done using the WordPerfect Tables feature. Using Tables, you can create some pretty fancy forms that even look good. Let's experiment.

Figure 35-3 is a shortened version of a daily time sheet for a worker where detailed records must be kept of the work completed. This sheet is designed for a production office environment but could be customized for a manufacturing job.

The form illustrated in the figure was actually created with two tables, one directly over the other. You could leave space between the tables, if you wished. In this case, the form looks fine with no space between the parts.

Lesson 35 Exercise 5

Choose **Tables** from the Layout menu.

1. Create a table that consists of two columns and four rows to make up the heading section. Did you remember that you begin to create a table with **Alt-F7**?

2. Use a large font for the heading of the form and a small or fine font for the rest of the text in the form.

3. Join cells, change the lines, and fill in the information as shown in the figure. (Refer to Lesson 16 for help, if you need it.)

DAILY TIME SHEET

Employee:	
Department:	Date:
Company:	Total Hours:

Job. No	Kind of Work	Began		Finished		Hours

Instructions: Enter the type of work on each job, listing the exact time you started and finished that job. List "Miscellaneous" for time not billable.

Figure 35-3

4. Move your cursor out of the table and create another table, this one with 7 columns and 12 rows.

5. Shade the heading section, adjust the appropriate lines from single to double, and add the headings. Remove all lines from the last row and key the instructions as shown.

6. Make any adjustments necessary to make the form attractive.

7. Print your form and exit from it, saving it as **form.355**.

That wasn't so bad, was it? You did the work with little direction, and your form is probably lovely. Let's try something a little more complicated. Figure 35-4 shows an invoice form for a company called Helium Happiness. It includes math to figure the extensions, tax, and total. Read ALL of the instructions before beginning.

Lesson 35 Exercise 6

1. Study Figure 35-4 and read through all of the steps for this exercise. Then create a table that looks just like it. Here is a list of some miscellaneous information that may be of use to you.
   - The graphic is named **balloons.wpg**.
   - Remember to block groups of cells for formatting.
   - The Ship To and Bill To sections each are made up of four rows. The top row is shaded with a thick line at the top and no line at the bottom. The other three rows in that section are joined.
   - You will need to do a lot of joining of rows or columns. Start at either the top or bottom and "carve" out the areas for each piece of information.
   - Remember when you work with table lines that not all lines are equal. The line at the top of a cell may still be there, for example, when you delete the line at the bottom of the cell above it.
   - Note the shading of certain sections of the table. Block a vertical or horizontal area to be shaded and then choose Shading from the Lines portion of the table editor.
   - Format the cells containing the column headings with Center justification.
   - Format Columns A and C with Center justification.
   - Format Columns D and E with Decimal justification.
   - The cells containing the words *Subtotal, Tax, and Total* are right justified.
   - In the first cell under Amount, put the formula **a*d**. Copy the formula down as many times as necessary so it formats all of the rows above the Subtotal row. (When you add formulas to these cells, 0.00 will appear in the cells. That's OK. Just delete the zeros so the cells are empty again.)
   - In the cell for the Subtotal, put the formula **+** to add the figures above it.
   - In the cell for the Tax, put the formula that multiplies the Subtotal times 5% tax. For example, if the cell containing the subtotal is Cell E19, the formula for the tax would be **e19*.05**.
   - In the cell for the Total, put a formula that adds the contents of the two cells above it, for example, **e19+e20**.
   - Format all of the cells ABOVE the Amount column (the cell containing the Invoice Number and Order Date, the Ship To area, and the Bill To area) as follows. In the table editor, block the cell and choose **2 Format, 1 Cell, 1 Type,** and **2 Text**. If you don't do this, any numerals in the addresses or invoice number will be added into the Subtotal.

Invoice No:
Order Date:

Helium Happiness
778 Hearthstone Hill
Hoopstown, NH 12998

Ship To:

Terms:

Ship Date:

Bill To:

Ship Via:

Handling:

Salesperson:

Quan.	Description	Color	Unit Price	Amount

NOTE: Included are an up-to-date catalog and a brochure for the winter sale. Thank you for your order!

Subtotal	
Tax	
Total	

Figure 35-4

2. You will no doubt run into some snags in this exercise. It is a real challenge. If you are persistent, you can do it! Remember to save frequently (each time with a new name) when you are working on a table of this magnitude. Then, if you really mess it up, you can retrieve the appropriate earlier version and take it from there.

3. If you wish, you can create two separate tables as in the previous exercise. By doing so, your Ship To and Bill To parts of the invoice may be wider than the combined Color, Unit Price, and Amount columns. That gives you more room for the Description column.

4. When you finish, print your invoice and exit from it, saving it as invoice.356.

ORGANIZATIONAL CHART

There are a wide variety of other things you can do with WordPerfect Tables to create the forms necessary in your job. For example, you can use a table made up of many cells and carve out an organizational chart. By joining some cells and turning off all the lines of others, you can create an organizational chart that looks perfect. No one will ever guess you used the Tables feature to create it. Usually you will want to map out the chart before you begin, perhaps using graph paper.

The beginning of such an organization chart is illustrated in Figure 35-5. Note that all of the lines for the tables are still there, but those to be used for the organizational chart have been illustrated with heavy lines so you can see how the chart will evolve. Eventually, in a chart of this kind, you would tell WordPerfect not to display the lines of the cells not used. Also, note that a space separates the two tables. That's just so you can see where one begins and the other ends. You would delete that hard return to make your chart look like one big chart.

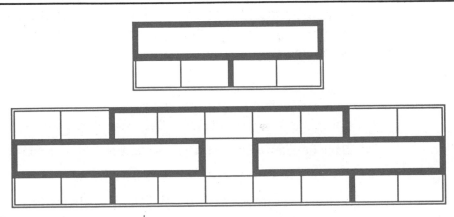

Figure 35-5

Lesson 35　Exercise 7

1. Create a three-tier organizational chart for a fictitious business. You may be the big chief, if you'd like. You may include anyone you'd like as your supportive staff.

2. Start by preparing the two tables illustrated in Figure 35-5. Add a third tier to the chart. Center your name on one line and strike **Enter** after your name to center your official title on the next.

3. When your organizational chart is beautiful, give it a title, print it, and exit from it, saving it on your disk as **org.357**.

SIDE-BY-SIDE TABLES

WordPerfect allows you to use a maximum of 32 columns in a table. Occasionally you may want to create a form that has more than 32 columns. While this usually isn't practical with the paper turned in the portrait orientation, there is plenty of room for more than 32 columns when the paper is used in the landscape orientation.

If you wish to prepare a wider table, you can do so by placing two tables side by side. An Advance code is used to bring up the second table to the same line as the first table. Let's prepare a small sample to see how it works. If your printer can't print using the landscape orientation, ask your instructor if you should skip the exercise.

In this exercise, we'll create a table that consists of a total of 37 columns. The first column will be locked in width at 1 inch. The remainder of the columns will be locked in width at ¼ inch to guarantee even spacing. You will also change the space within each cell so that no space surrounds the text keyed into the cell.

The math for this problem has been figured so that the form will have ½-inch side margins, leaving 10 inches for the table—one inch of which is used by the first column and 9 inches for the 36 quarter-inch tables. As you work through the exercise below, try to understand what you're doing and why you're doing it.

Lesson 35　Exercise 8

1. Go to the Page Format menu. Set Paper Size/Type at standard—wide.

2. Back in your document, change the side margins to 0.5 inches.

3. Create a table that is 21 columns by 5 rows.

4. While in the table editor, do the following things to your table:

   a. Choose **6** Options. In the first section, change Left and Right Spacing between Text and Lines to 0. Leave the Top and Bottom settings.

b. Also, in the Options menu, note the third setting. The table will be placed to the Left on the page. Return to the table editor.

c. Position the cursor in Cell A1. Choose **2 Format**, **2 Column**, **1 W**idth. Key 1.0 and strike **Enter**.

d. Block all of Row 1 except Column A. Return to the Width setting and set the columns at 0.25 inches.

e. Block all of Row 1 except Column A again. Format all columns with Center justification.

f. Block all of Column U. Change the line at the right to **1 None**.

5. Exit from the table editor and strike **Page Down** to move your cursor out of the table.

6. Go to the Advance menu and tell WordPerfect to advance to Line 1″. This moves the beginning of the second table to the same place the first table began. If your first table begins at a location other than one inch from the top of the page, you'll note that measurement and use it for the second table.

7. Create another table, this time with 16 columns and 5 rows. Format the table as follows:

a. Go to Options and change the Left and Right Spacing to 0 as in Step 4 above. (WordPerfect may remember your settings from the previous table.)

b. While in the Options menu, set the table to be aligned at the Right.

c. Set the width of all columns at 0.25 inches.

d. Set the justification of all columns to Center justification.

e. Change the line at the left of Column A to a single line.

8. Your work should now look much like Figure 35-6. Use Print Preview and see if the tables are joined so that they look like one big table.

9. We won't bother to key anything in the table. Save your big table as form.358 and exit from it.

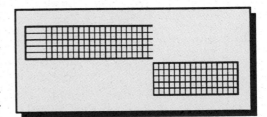

Figure 35-6

FORMS WITH LABELS

Another way you can create forms is by using a labels set-up. For example, if you want to have two 5½″ x 8½″ pages side by side on a landscape sheet, you COULD use newspaper-style columns, but you wouldn't be able to number the pages automatically. Using a label style that turns each half sheet into a label that's 5½ inches wide and 8½ inches tall, you can enter a page numbering code, and the "pages" will number automatically, even though they are on the same sheet of paper. The result could look much like Figure 35-7.

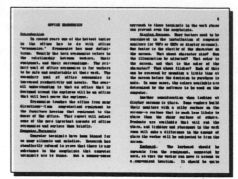

Figure 35-7

If you're confused, don't worry about it. In the next exercise you will use the Labels feature (actually the same theory) to create raffle tickets. What's more, you'll learn a new pair of merge codes that enable you to make multiple copies of the ticket quite painlessly, and the tickets will be numbered as well. One page of your tickets will look much like the thumbnail illustration in Figure 35-8. For this exercise, your label format will use the paper in the normal portrait orientation. We'll start by setting up the label format.

Lesson 35 Exercise 9

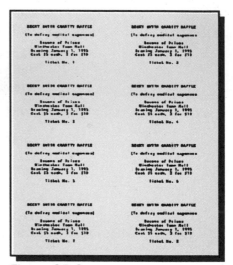

Figure 35-8

1. Go to your Page Format menu and choose Paper Size/Type. Study the list of available sizes. Can you find one for Labels-Wide, 8½ x 11, 2 columns by 4 rows? If so, you may choose it and skip to Exercise 10. If not, you'll have to create it using the following steps.

2. Choose Add and then Labels. Then choose 8 Labels and Y for Yes. This brings up the Format: Labels menu.

3. Choose Item 1 and set the label size at 4.25" wide and 2.75" high.

4. Choose Item 2 and set number of columns at 2 and rows at 4.

5. Change all choices in Items 3 and 4 to 0.

6. Strike F7 to exit from the menu. You will probably see a message in the prompt line saying that the margins are being changed to accommodate your printer. Then Item 5 will report the new margins. Look at the margins WordPerfect gives you. If the left and right margins aren't equal, change the smaller number of the two so the smaller and larger numbers match. If the top and bottom margins aren't equal, make them both the size of the larger number.

7. Strike **F7** again to return to the Paper Size/Type menu. Your new label size should be there. Choose that label form.

8. Go to the Format menu and set Justification at Center.

With the Labels paper size chosen, you can now prepare your tickets. Since you will be able to get 8 tickets on a sheet of paper, we'll prepare only three sheets of tickets—a total of 24 tickets. Actually, you could set the numbering for as many tickets as you wished to prepare. You could also start the numbering at any number. We'll begin with 1 and the numbering will be consecutive.

The form will be a primary document that includes the {FOR} merge code and the {END FOR} merge code. Between those codes will be the information to be included on the tickets and the instructions to WordPerfect regarding the numbering of the tickets. Follow along carefully!

Lesson 35   Exercise 10

*From the **T**ools menu, choose **M**erge Codes and then **M**ore.*

1. Strike **Shift-F9** for the Merge menu and choose **6** More for the long list of merge codes.

2. Strike **F** to move the cursor to the F section of codes and move down two codes to the {FOR}var~start~stop~step~ code. Choose it. You will be asked for a number of pieces of information. Fill them in as follows: variable = **x**   strike **Enter**
   start = **1**   strike **Enter**
   stop = **24**   strike **Enter**
   step = **1**   strike **Enter**
   In this code, **x** tells WordPerfect that another **x** will appear somewhere in the document to give the position for the number. The first **1** tells WordPerfect to start numbering at **1**, while **24** tells WordPerfect to stop numbering at **24**. The final **1** tells WordPerfect to count in increments of **1**. You could set it to number only even numbers, such as *2, 4*, and *6* or odd numbers such as *1, 3,* and *5.*

3. Back on your document screen, you will see the results of the code you just entered. Go to the Page Format menu and choose the Center Page (top to bottom) code. Key **Y** for Yes so the information will be centered vertically on each label.
   Placement of this code is very important! It MUST follow the final tilde of the {FOR} statement, and it MUST be before your first text on the "label" so that each "page" is centered on its own label.

4. Key the information illustrated in Figure 35-9 as the text for your labels. Following the words *Ticket No.*, add a code that refers WordPerfect to the {FOR} code. This positions the ticket number. Add this code as follows:
   Return to the **6** More merge codes and strike **V** to go to the V section of codes. The only one there is {VARIABLE}var~, and that's the one you want. Choose it and set the variable at *x* (again).

5. Strike **Ctrl-Enter** to add a hard page break. Then return one final time to the **6 More** merge codes and strike E. Move to the **{END FOR}** code and insert it into your document. This code ends the loop that tells WordPerfect to go back and repeat the text and add the next numeral.

6. Your label form will look much like Figure 35-10. Save it as **lab.frm** and exit from the document.

```
BECKY SMITH CHARITY RAFFLE

(To defray medical expenses)

      Dozens of Prizes
    Winchester Town Hall
   Drawing January 1, 1995
   Cost $5 each, 3 for $10


       Ticket No.
```

Figure 35-9

Your form is now complete and ready to be used. Remember that it is a primary file. There will be no secondary file to merge with it.

Lesson 35 Exercise 11

1. Give the command to merge. Key **lab.frm** as the name of the primary file. Strike **Enter** at the prompt for the secondary file.

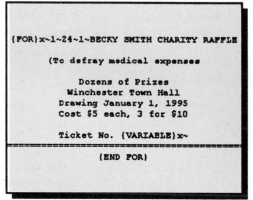

Figure 35-10

2. Your tickets will appear in a column at the left separated by Hard Page codes. Use Print Preview to see how they are spaced on the page. Your page should look like Figure 35-8. If it does not, you probably should check your Paper Size/Type code and prepare your primary document again.

3. If your tickets look good, print all three pages. Then exit from the document, saving it as **ticket35.11**.

   If you want to print only one paper full of labels, choose **5 Multiple** pages from the Print menu and list pages 1-8. Each label is considered a page. Therefore, one page would be only one label. You have eight labels on a piece of paper, so you need to print eight pages to fill a sheet of paper. Are you confused? Try it!

4. Fold the sheet of paper into eighths or cut one page of tickets apart. You should be able to make them exactly the same size, and the writing on each ticket should be attractively placed.

SUMMARY

Wow! This was another lesson filled with exciting and useful Word-Perfect features! You learned a number of ways of filling in forms and creating new forms. Few of the procedures were new to you, but combining them gives you some very interesting possibilities.

One concept you should have gathered from this lesson is that not only is every job different, so is every form. How you will attack those forms when you confront them on the job will depend on how difficult they are, how much time you have available to design them, and who you might contact for help if you should run into trouble. The final form, for example, uses a simple but very effective {FOR} and {END FOR} loop that tells the computer to continue doing whatever the commands are within the loop 24 times. (Of course, that number can be changed for more or fewer "tickets.") This technique would make perfect sense to someone who has had some training in computer programming but seems a little foreign to the non-programming professional.

At any rate, it is important that you remember that you have the skills to master forms, and you should look upon them as a challenge!

COMMAND SUMMARY

Feature	Function	Menu	Lesson
Characters	Ctrl-V or Ctrl-2	Font	34
Compose	Ctrl-V or Ctrl-2	Font	34
Equation	Alt-F9, E	Graphics	34
Fonts	Ctrl-F8, F	Font	33
Underline Tabs	Shift-F8, O	Layout, Other	35

LESSON 35 NOTES:

Name _____ Date _____

TRUE/FALSE

Each of the following statements is either true or false. Indicate your choice in the Answers column by circling T for a true statement or F for a false statement.

Answers

1. The Advance feature is very useful in aligning the information to be printed onto a preprinted form. (Obj. 1) . . . .   1.   T   F

2. Most preprinted forms have been prepared using straight double spacing. (Obj. 1) . . . .   2.   T   F

3. You can key information to appear on a graphic line that was inserted using the WordPerfect program. (Obj. 2) . . . .   3.   T   F

4. The setting that allows you to turn on Underline and use Tab to insert lines must be reset for each document in which you wish to use it. (Obj. 2) . .   4.   T   F

5. Two tables can be created and made to look like one big table. (Obj. 3) .   5.   T   F

6. You can format a number of cells in a table by first blocking the cells to be formatted and then applying the formatting. (Obj. 3) . . . .   6.   T   F

7. When working with a complicated table format, it is a good idea to save your work often. (Obj. 3) . . . .   7.   T   F

8. Advance is used to position the second table when you create one big table out of two smaller tables placed side by side. (Obj. 3) . . . .   8.   T   F

9. WordPerfect allows you to set the width of a cell so that a number of cells can be exactly the same size. (Obj. 3) . . . .   9.   T   F

COMPLETION

Indicate the correct answer in the space provided.

Answers

1. In positioning text to be printed on a preprinted form, may you use Advance for horizontal position or vertical position or both? (Obj. 1) . . . .   1. _____

2. When preparing text to be printed on a preprinted form, does the form show on the screen? (Obj. 1) . . . . . .   2. _____

3. When printing text on a preprinted form, should the text touch the lines of the form? (Obj. 1) . . . .

3. _____

4. You have learned three ways to include horizontal lines in a form created using WordPerfect. List all three. (Obj. 2 & 3)

4. _____

5. _____

6. _____

7. What format must you apply to cells in which there are numerals that shouldn't be included in a math total? (Obj. 3) . . . .

7. _____

8. What is the character that tells WordPerfect to multiply? (Obj. 3) . . . .

8. _____

9. You can tell WordPerfect to number parts of a document automatically—all on the same page—when you use what feature? (Obj. 3) . . . .

9. _____

10. What were the three new merge codes that you used in the tickets exercise? List all three and briefly describe your understanding of each. (Obj. 3)

_____

_____

_____

REFERENCE

The Forms Fill-In portion of the Tables section of the *WordPerfect Reference* refers to *Lesson 30: Forms Fill-In* of the *WordPerfect Workbook*. If a *Workbook* is available, look up Lesson 30. How many pages are in the lesson? What feature did you learn about in Lesson 29 that WordPerfect suggests you might use to help with forms fill-in?

_____

_____

LESSON 36
Review and Practice

OBJECTIVES

Upon completion of this lesson, you will have reviewed the use of:

1. WordPerfect styles.
2. Graphic lines and boxes.
3. Fonts and characters.
4. Footers and page numbering.

Estimated Time: 3 hours

SETTING UP A MASTHEAD STYLE

The style that you will use in this lesson is a masthead style. A masthead is the title area of a document that is produced on a regular basis. For example, the first page of each of the lessons in this book have a commonality about them. The front of your daily newspaper or favorite monthly magazine has lines and the name of the publication in a font that doesn't change from issue to issue. That masthead helps you to feel comfortable with your publication because it is familiar.

It follows, then, that if you are going to produce a publication regularly, each issue of that publication will have the same characteristics. The best way to ensure that sameness and to save yourself keystrokes is to create a style that includes all the codes and settings for that masthead. Let's create one.

Lesson 36 Exercise 1

1. Open the Style menu and retrieve your style library. The library is probably in the Unit-3 directory on your disk and is saved in a document called **student.sty**.

2. Give the command to create a new open style. Call it *Masthead* and describe it as *Masthead for Newsletter*. Go to the Codes screen.

3. Set margins at 0.5" on all four sides of the page.

4. Begin your masthead with a horizontal graphic line that goes from margin to margin. Use all of the defaults except Width of Line, which you should set at 0.06". On your working screen, strike **Enter** twice.

5. Change to a proportional font if you have one. Then choose Extra Large and Bold to center the name of the newsletter in all caps:

GOSSIP NEWS

6. Before striking Enter, return to the Font menu and choose **3 Normal** (to turn off the Extra Large font and Bold). Return again to the Font size menu and change to Fine. Strike **Enter** twice.

7. Create a one-row, one-column table with shading. In that table, key the information as shown in the one-cell table in the illustration of your masthead in Figure 36-1. Key the *Published In . . .* information at the left, and use Flush Right for the Date code. Change all of the lines around the table to a single line.

8. Back on your working screen, strike **Enter** twice and insert one more horizontal line, this one 0.03″ wide.

GOSSIP NEWS

| Published in Podunk Holler, WI | (current date) |

Figure 36-1

Now let's add some formatting that takes care of multiple-page newsletters. We need page numbering and a header to tie the document together. Also, since your newsletter will be in columns, you can save yourself time each time it is prepared by including the column setup as part of the masthead. You can also set the font for the newsletter. The next exercise will complete the setup of the masthead.

Lesson 36 Exercise 2

1. Use Reveal Codes so you can see to position your cursor just to the right of the two Margin Set codes. Create a footer to position a page number in the bottom center of all pages. Your footer will simply say *Page ^B*.

2. Insert a header to show on all pages except the first. The header should be another one-cell table, shaded, with the name of the newsletter at the left and the current date at the right. The header is illustrated in Figure 36-2.

| Gossip News | (current date) |

Figure 36-2

3. Strike **Page Down** to move the cursor below all lines and codes. Change to a 12-point proportional font. One with serifs is easier to read than a sans serif font.

4. Go to the Tab Set menu and delete the tab at 0.5". Set new tabs at 0.3", 0.6", and 0.9". Turn on Widow/Orphan control.

5. Go to the Columns menu and set up two newspaper columns. The one at the left should be 4 inches wide. Separate the columns with ½ inch. That leaves 3 inches for the column at the right.

6. Return to the Styles menu and save your style library—just in case!

Now let's set up a paired style for the article titles. Since titles are usually one-liners, the style will be set up to turn off when you strike **Enter**. This saves you from having to access the Style menu to turn on the style for the body of the following article. When you finish that, you will be ready to begin assembling or creating your newsletter.

Lesson 36 Exercise 3

1. Return to the Style menu and tell WordPerfect to create a style called *article.ttl*. For definition, key *Article Title Formatting.*

2. Go to the Font menu and choose Large. Turn on Bold. Give the Center command.

3. On the menu for the style, change the setting so striking Enter turns the style 2 Off. Font, Bold, and Centering will all be turned off when you strike Enter while using the style.

4. Return to the Style menu and save your style library again as **student.sty**.

5. Return to your document screen and exit from the document without saving it.

ASSEMBLING A NEWSLETTER

Now you can turn on your masthead style and use it for the preparation of a newsletter. Figures 36-4, 36-5, 36-6, 36-7, 36-8, and 36-9 provide the text for a number of articles to be assembled into the newsletter.

Follow the instructions after the articles carefully. When you finish, the first page of your newsletter will look much like the thumbnail illustration in Figure 36-3.

Figure 36-3

Our friend David D. was on the links last weekend and more than a little perturbed when the golf ball stopped about a foot short of its destination. In frustration at having to add one more stroke to an otherwise good game, David was just about to let his partner finish the hole when a wasp started buzzing around his head.

The wasp was persistent. David swatted and danced and tried to avoid the wasp. In doing so, he accidentally kicked his ball. Guess where it went! Does that count as a stroke?

Figure 36-4 (golf.36) Title: The Golfing Fiasco

The health services department is again looking for willing candidates to participate in the "Exercise the Pounds Off" competition. There are a variety of methods available for those who are particular about HOW they exercise. The duration of the exercise period depends on the method chosen. A listing is available in the health office, along with the rules of the contest.

If you're looking for the incentive to move your body, firm up some of the nether regions, and lose a few pounds in the process, stop in and sign up for your preferred form of torture. The contest begins the first Monday of next month. A prize will be awarded to the employee who completes the most successful program.

Figure 36-5 (health.36) Title: Health Habits

It seems love is blooming in the data processing department. A little bird has seen a diamond on the ring finger of Ashley and a special sparkle in her eye. Ashley has been seen on occasion lately with a fella named Charles who also has a special sparkle in his eye. Are there wedding bells in your future, Ashley?

Figure 36-6 (romance.36) Title: Spring Romance

In the continuing saga of Casey's cat, another escapade begs to be reported. This is the same cat that has on previous occasions nested in a pot of geraniums, eaten a whole pot of linguini, and fished the goldfish out of the goldfish tank.

The cat's name is Trouble, and that's what is usually afoot whenever the cat is near. Casey has been trying to teach the cat to climb. Since Trouble was raised in the house, it's good at jumping on furniture but not so good at climbing things like trees.

Last week Trouble was pestering the neighbor's dog. Apparently the dog had enough of Trouble's shenanigans and took after Trouble. There wasn't any place for Trouble to go except up the tree—and up, and up, and up.

You guessed it. Casey had to call for outside help to get Trouble out of the tree. Needless to say, Casey's cat is definitely in the doghouse these days.

Figure 36-7 (cat.36) Title: Casey's Cat

Many of his co-workers aren't aware of it, but our friend Ron in the accounting department has a real liking for old Mustang convertibles. In fact, he and his wife, Susi, have a matched pair of powder blue cruisers.

Ron takes great pride in the fact that he keeps his wife's car in perfect mechanical condition. He is less careful, however, with his own vehicle. His reasoning is that if something should break down, he can always fix it.

Earlier this week, Susi was preparing dinner for guests and sent Ron to the grocery store for a couple of forgotten items. While he was standing in line to get checked out, it began to rain. Of course, the top was down on his car. Ron paid for the groceries and hurried out to put the top up on the car.

The works in the top had been giving him some trouble, but it always worked eventually. This time he wasn't that lucky. It was pointing straight toward the sky when it got stuck, and even Ron, the mechanic, couldn't budge it in either direction. So Ron decided he'd keep himself and the interior of his car drier if he'd drive home and put the car in the garage.

Fortunately, even in its extended position, the car fit through the garage door. One of Ron and Susi's neighbors claims to have a snapshot of Ron driving his "disabled" car down the street while holding a bright red umbrella to protect himself and his groceries. Is that photo available for publication, Ron?

Figure 36-8 (mustang.36) Title: Photo Opportunity?

One of our more illustrious sports-minded employees umpires some of the local community baseball games. The way the story goes, he has a phobia about calling games. No matter how dark it gets, he feels that a ball game must be nine innings or more.

Recently when he refused to call a game, the pitcher, in desperation, huddled with his catcher and whispered,

"Listen. You keep the ball in your mitt. I'll wind up and pretend to throw it. You pop it into your mitt as though you caught it."

There were two strikes on the batter. The pitcher went through the motion and the catcher popped his mitt. "Strike three and you're out!" bellowed our friend, the umpire.

"Strike?" fumed the batter. "Are you nuts? That ball was two feet outside!"

Figure 36-9 (ball.36) Title: Baseball Fever

Lesson 36 Exercise 4

(Template disk users: Refer to the box below before beginning.)

1. Key the six articles illustrated in Figures 36-4 through 36-9. Single space between paragraphs and tab once to indent each paragraph.

2. Save each article using the name indicated in parentheses by the figure number (e.g. golf.36). (Following the filename is the title you'll use for each article when you assemble the newsletter.)

TEMPLATE DISK USERS:

The articles are saved on the template disk to eliminate keying. You may retrieve them as you assemble your newsletter.

Lesson 36 Exercise 5

1. Beginning on a clear screen, retrieve your style library and turn on the masthead style.

2. Turn on the article style and key *Casey's Cat* as the title of your first article. Strike **Enter** three times (one to turn off the style and twice more for the double space following the title).

3. Retrieve the article named cat.36. Strike **Page Down** to move the cursor below the article. Strike **Enter** twice.

4. Give the command for a horizontal line. Choose Horizontal Position and then Set Position. At the offset prompt, strike **Enter**. WordPerfect will determine the length of your line so that it fits within the column and position it in your document. Strike **Enter** again.

5. Follow Steps 2 & 3 again, this time retrieving **health.36**. For this one article only, don't include a line at the bottom because it will eventually be at the bottom of the column. Use Print Preview to see how your document is shaping up.

6. Continue in the same manner, retrieving **romance.36**, **mustang.36**, **golf.36**, and **ball.36** (in that order).

7. Do an interim save of your document, calling it **news.36**.

Now that the newsletter is assembled and the horizontal lines are in place, it's time to add some additional formatting to make the newsletter more appealing. You'll create dropped caps and add a graphic to the article about exercising. You will also add a vertical line and change the spacing. Follow along carefully.

Lesson 36 Exercise 6

1. At the beginning of the first article, delete the Tab and the first letter. Then set the user options and create a User box with a large letter to create a dropped cap. (Refer to Lesson 34 for help if you need it.)

2. Block the User options code and the User box codes and copy them to the beginning of each of the other articles. Then edit each of the User boxes to change the letter in the box to the appropriate one for that article. Repair the beginning of each of the articles.

3. Position the cursor somewhere in the first line of the Health article. Create a Figure box containing the graphic named **trophy.wpg**. Set the height (auto width) of the graphic at one inch.

4. Position the cursor at the beginning of the first line of the second column on the first page of your newsletter (beside the title of the article, if a new article begins in that column).

5. Create a vertical line. In the Vertical Line menu, choose Horizontal and tell WordPerfect to place the line between the columns. Strike **Enter** at the prompt that asks if the line should be to the right of Column 1.
   Choose Vertical and then Set Position. A prompt will show that your cursor is somewhere near 2 inches. Strike **Enter**. WordPerfect will fill in the length of the line. (You may need to return to the menu to make the line a little shorter if it extends closer to the bottom of your page than the articles on either side of it.)

6. Finally, do a search and replace to tighten the spaces between sentences. Search for a period followed by two spaces. Replace it with a period followed by one space. Do you remember how to do this? (Use these steps: Alt-F2, N for no confirmation, strike a period followed by two spaces, F2, strike a period followed by one space, and F2 again)
   This is the preferred method of spacing when working with a proportional font in published materials.

7. Preview your document to be sure it looks the way you think it should. You may need to adjust the spacing here and there to make it look good. Do an interim save of your newsletter, using the same name.

As you can see, your newsletter fills approximately a page and a half. You get to compose and add another article to the newsletter. You can tell a true story or make up something. You may key the article on a fresh screen, save it, and retrieve it into the newsletter, or you may key the article directly into the newsletter. You'll probably wish to add a vertical line on page 2 to match the line on page 1. If your article is quite short, you may wish to use Ctrl-Enter to divide the columns more equally on the page.

Lesson 36 Exercise 7

1. Following the guidelines in the paragraph above, add one more article to your newsletter.

2. Format the article with a dropped cap. You can insert a graphic into the article, if you wish.

3. Proofread and make sure everything is perfect. Then print your newsletter and exit from it, saving it as **news.367**.

Whew! There were a lot of parts to that newsletter. Much of it was preparation that won't need to be repeated—that is, the creation of the styles for the masthead and article titles—each time you prepare a new edition of the newsletter.

THE INVOICE FORM

The invoice form you created in Lesson 35 is probably lovely. It would be far more useful, however, if you would insert {INPUT} ~ codes so you could move through it more easily to prepare an invoice. Let's enhance that form and then use it to prepare some invoices.

Figure 36-10 shows the invoice you created in Lesson 35 but with a number of {INPUT} ~ codes added. Look at the locations for the codes.

Lesson 36 Exercise 8

1. Retrieve **invoice.356**. Insert {INPUT} ~ codes in each of the locations illustrated in Figure 36-10. Separate the {INPUT} ~ codes from the headings with two spaces. Don't insert any messages to accompany the {INPUT} ~ codes. The information requested is fairly obvious.
   Insert a {DATE} code on the Ship Date line.
   Note that in some cases, the input codes will not appear to fit comfortably in the space allotted. That's OK. The actual code has more characters than the information that will fill the space when the merge is completed.

2. Resave your invoice as **invoice.368** and exit from it.

Figure 36-11 provides the information to be filled into three invoices. Prepare the invoices and do the appropriate math as directed.

Invoice No: {INPUT}~
Order Date: {INPUT}~

Helium Happiness
778 Hearthstone Hill
Hoopstown, NH 12998

Terms: {INPUT}~

Ship Date: {DATE}

Ship Via: {INPUT}~

Handling: {INPUT}~

Salesperson: {INPUT}~

Ship To:

{INPUT}~

Bill To:

{INPUT}~

Quan.	Description	Color	Unit Price	Amount
{INPUT}~				

NOTE: Included are an up-to-date catalog and a brochure for the winter sale. Thank you for your order!

Subtotal	
Tax	
Total	{INPUT}~

Figure 36-10

Lesson 36 Exercise 9

1. Give the command to merge and list **invoice.368** as the primary file. Strike **Enter** at the prompt for the secondary file. The cursor will stop at the location for the invoice number.

2. Key the invoice number for the first customer and strike **F9** to move to the next {INPUT} ~ code. Look at a calendar to compute the correct order date.

3. Continue keying the information in the appropriate places, moving from one {INPUT} ~ code to another with F9.

4. When you get to the final {INPUT} ~ code in the cell to calculate, return to the table editor and choose Math and then Calculate. If the 0.00s bother you in the empty rows, you may delete them.

5. Do a mental check of the mathematics. Did everything work correctly?

6. Exit the table editor. Strike **F7** once and respond appropriately to exit the merge.

7. Enter a hard page break and begin again at Step 1. This time fill in the information for the second customer. Don't forget to terminate the merge between customers. If you don't, the totals will accumulate.

8. Continue until you have completed the invoices for all three customers.

9. Print the invoices. Then exit from the document containing the three invoices, saving it as **invoice.369**.

Customer 1

```
                    Invoice: #1237        Order date: Last week Tuesday
Martha Morningstar          (same name and address for billing and shipping)
443 Marietta Street         Terms: 2/10, n/30    Salesperson: Harry Henkel
Mortonville, MD 33433       Ship Via: UPS             Handling:  Rush!

12  #1415   5-inch          Red         @     2.50 each
10  #1662   12-inch         Blue        @     4.00 each
 5  #2110   14-inch         Silver      @     6.00 each
```

Customer 2

```
                    Invoice: #1238        Order date: Last week Wednesday
Charles Carlson             (same name and address for billing and shipping)
665 Cornelius Court         Terms:  Net 30       Salesperson: Hilda Harrison
Charleston, SC 22311        Ship Via:  Fed. Ex.  Handling:  Rush!

15  #2113   14-inch         Red         @     6.00 each
20  #1416   5-inch          Green       @     2.50
15  #1663   12-inch         Red         @     4.00
20  #1415   5-inch          Red         @     2.50
10  #2112   14-inch         Green       @     6.00
```

```
Customer 3

                      Invoice: #1239        Order date: Last week Monday
Georgia Gibson               Ship to: Georgia's Gift Shop (same address)
76 Gillingham Way            Terms:  Net 30        Salesperson: Hilda Harrison
Galveston, SC 22321          Ship Via: Fed. Ex.    Handling:  Rush!

45  #1414  5-inch       Silver    @      2.50 each
30  #1416  5-inch       Green     @      2.50 each
25  #1415  5-inch       Red       @      2.50 each
20  #1663  12-inch      Red       @      4.00 each
20  #1662  12-inch      Blue      @      4.00 each
```

Figure 36-11

While most of what you've been doing in your WordPerfect training has been pretty businesslike, saving all three of those invoices as a document really is NOT a good office procedure. The invoice for each customer should be saved in the customer's file. The businesslike approach probably would be to complete each invoice, print it, and save it.

If you like the idea of preparing them together and printing them all at once, you can still block each invoice and save it individually. If you do that, reveal your codes so you are certain to save all of the codes that belong to each invoice.

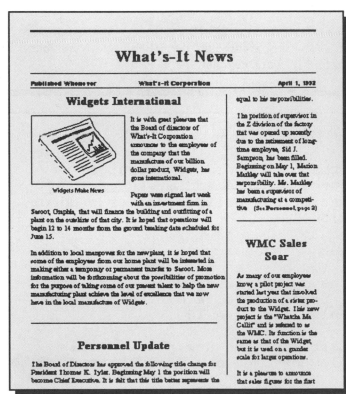

Figure 36-12

A NEWSLETTER

Now that you've had a break from the first newsletter created earlier in the lesson, let's create a different one. This newsletter is for a manufacturing company called "What's-It Corporation."

In Figure 36-12 you can study an edited version of part of the first page of the newsletter.

You may edit your Gossip News style for What's-It Corporation, or you may create a new style. If you edit the existing style and wish to keep the Gossip News style, you'll have to save it in a different library than the **student.sty** library.

The articles to be included in the newsletter are illustrated in Figures 36-13, 36-14, 36-15, and 36-16. You may write additional articles, if you'd like.

Lesson 36 Exercise 10

(Template disk users: Refer to the box below before beginning.)

You're pretty much in charge as you design and assemble another short newsletter.

If you study Figure 36-12, you'll see many differences between this first page and the first page of Gossip News. For example, paragraphs are NOT indented, but they are separated by a double space. The dropped caps at the beginnings of the paragraphs are missing. Justification is set at Left. The column at the left is nearly twice as wide as the column at the right.

Depending on the font you choose, the articles provided will extend nicely onto the second page. You may arrange the articles in any order you wish. Sometimes the arrangement of articles depends on how they fit on the page.

The graphic included in the newsletter in Figure 36-12 is named **news.wpg**. If you have time to "play" with this assignment, make the newsletter attractive and readable! Have fun. When you finish, save the newsletter as **news.360** and print a copy for your instructor.

TEMPLATE DISK USERS:

The articles in Figures 36-13 through 36-16 are saved on the template disk with the names shown in parentheses beside the figure numbers. You may retrieve the text for your newsletter.

```
                    Widgets International

It is with great pleasure that the Board of Directors of
What's-It Corporation announces to the employees of the
company that the manufacture of our billion dollar product,
Widgets, has gone international.

Papers were signed last week with an investment firm in
Sasoot, Graphia, that will finance the building and
outfitting of a plant on the outskirts of that city. It is
hoped that operations will begin 12 to 14 months from the
ground breaking date scheduled for June 15.

In addition to local workforce for the new plant, it is
hoped that some of the employees from our home plant will be
interested in making either a temporary or permanent
transfer to Sasoot. More information will be forthcoming
about the possibilities of promotion for the purpose of
taking some of our present talent to help the new
```

manufacturing plant achieve the level of excellence that we now have in the local manufacture of Widgets.

Sasoot is a tropical paradise. The weather is spring-like throughout the year, the natives are friendly, and the city has grown in the last ten years as people from the other seven continents have relocated and built office complexes and shopping areas.

Figure 36-13 (widgets)

Personnel Update

The Board of Directors has approved the following title change for President Thomas K. Tyler. Beginning on May 1, the position will become Chief Executive. It is felt that this title better represents the new direction of What's-It Corporation and affords Mr. Tyler status equal to his responsibilities.

The position of supervisor in the Z division of the factory that was opened up recently due to the retirement of long-time employee, Sid J. Sampson, has been filled. Beginning on May 1, Marion Markley will take over that responsibility. Ms. Markley has been a supervisor of manufacturing at a competitive firm and comes with a strong background in statistical process control.

Jan Hillshire has been hired as administrative assistant in the marketing department. This is a new position made necessary by increased paperwork due to government contracts. Jan is a graduate of the local technical college, and it is a pleasure to have her as a member of the staff.

Employees in the office in the evening might see a new face in the mail room. Andrea Arroyez has been hired for evening facsimile operations. Andrea is a high school student specializing in office occupations courses and is anxious to earn some money to help her with technical college next fall.

Figure 36-14 (per)

WMC Sales Soar

As many of our employees know, a pilot project was started last year that involved the production of a sister product to the Widget. This new project is the "Whatcha Ma Callit" and is referred to as the WMC. Its function is the same as

that of the Widget, but it is used on a grander scale for
larger operations.

It is a pleasure to announce that sales figures for the
first quarter of our fiscal year appear to support the need
for this type of product and that What's-It Corporation will
continue manufacture of WMCs. No expansion plans have been
made, however.

Figure 36-15 (wmc)

Plant #1 Conversion

The retooling and rebuilding of the production line at
What's-It Corporation's Plant #1 has begun. The management
has expressed gratitude that so many of the line workers
from Plant #1 were able to rearrange their vacations and
take them during this retooling process. Those Plant #1
employees who are still on the job will have different
responsibilities during this transition period.

When the work on the production line is completed, many of
the boring and the dangerous jobs will be completed by
automated manufacturing equipment. The use of robotics will
enable the company to save space in the manufacturing line
and therefore increase the capacity for production. In
addition, the production of Widgets will be more economical,
giving the company a greater profit margin on our products.

Some of our workers will be replaced by the automated
equipment. Those employees will be retrained for some of the
better jobs in the manufacturing process and will receive
raises commensurate with their positions.

Figure 36-16 (retool)

SUMMARY

With the exception of the revision and use of the invoice form, this
lesson has concentrated on newsletter preparation. The statistics tell us
that only about 22 percent of the office workers in today's office actively
use desktop publishing software to create page layouts. A much higher
number, however, use programs like WordPerfect for the occasional
informational brochure or office publications like those included in this
lesson. Obviously, these publications were intended to be less businesslike
and more fun, but the same skills can be applied to the more serious
documents.

You are nearly finished with this set of training materials. Immediately following this lesson is a short office simulation. The simulation is a set of jobs that are all related to a particular project that might be completed by the administrative assistant in any office around the world. It is intended to provide an overview of the skills learned in the lessons of this book. As you will find when you begin the simulation, fewer specific instructions are given with regard to HOW to complete the exercises. Instead, the instructions relate more to what is desired in the completed document. Find out from your instructor if you should begin the simulation.

Congratulations on your completion of these 36 lessons! Your understanding of the material in them should enable you to use Word-Perfect 5.1 to do just about anything required of you on the job. Obviously, you haven't learned everything that WordPerfect is capable of doing, but you have a good start. Most of the tips and tricks you would pick up at WordPerfect seminars have been included in your learning. What's more, if you have completed the Reference exercises at the ends of the lessons, you have a good understanding of the information available in the *WordPerfect Reference*. The *Reference* as well as this textbook should continue to provide you with most of the answers to your questions as you use the WordPerfect program. Again, congratulations and good luck.

LESSON 36 NOTES:

Office Simulation

The Eden PSI
Spring Seminar

Office Simulation

INTRODUCTION

At a recent meeting of the Eden Chapter of the Professional Secretaries International (PSI), your group decided to put together an educational seminar for the membership and other local administrative support staff. You have eagerly (?) volunteered to use your considerable Word-Perfect skills to help with this project.

In this simulation, you will be preparing the necessary paperwork for the seminar planning committee. Your work will usually be as a result of the planning meetings held by the seminar committee. The committee meets the first Tuesday of each month beginning in September of the current year. Nearer the seminar date, additional meetings may be held. The seminar is scheduled for the following April 1.

It will be your responsibility to prepare the advertising materials, assemble the list of those to be invited to the seminar, distribute those materials to the people on the list, follow up on the contacts with prospective speakers, make arrangements for seminar attendees to receive continuing education credits (CEU) for the seminar, handle the registrations as they are received, prepare an agenda for each meeting, and prepare the seminar program, among other things.

The committee has already made arrangements to hold the seminar at the Adams Hotel at 276 Wisconsin Avenue in downtown Eden, Wisconsin 53019. While most of the people who attend the seminar will be from the Eden area, Eve Warren, manager of the Adams, has agreed to set aside a block of rooms for seminar attendees who wish to spend a night or two. The hotel ballrooms have been reserved for the day of the seminar, along with a series of smaller meeting rooms to be used for the concurrent sessions.

This simulation begins with a training manual that includes the names of the committee members with whom you will be working and their responsibilities on the committee. Also included in the training manual is a copy of a sample letter on Eden PSI Chapter letterhead and a copy of an agenda prepared using Eden Chapter letterhead. The training manual provides general instructions about preparation of the documents in the simulation and the saving of those documents on your disk.

Your instructor may have a disk containing suggested solutions for the documents, but remember that these are suggestions, only. The prerecorded documents probably won't look good if printed on your computer, and you will probably wish to set up many of your documents using different formats.

TRAINING MANUAL

Your work will be coming to you from the members of the seminar committee. Here are their names, responsibilities, and phone numbers.

Georgia Gates, CPS . Chairperson 555-3778
Becky Brown . . . . . Speakers 555-7812
Joanne Dahleen . . . Food and Flowers 555-6234
Rhonda Evers, CPS . Registration 555-3791
Francis Fiera, CPS . . Facilities 555-0665
Tica Hayes . . . . . . Corporate Sponsors 555-2468
Jacob Jensen, CPS . . Publicity 555-2871
Erv Thorson, CPS . . Seminar Treasurer 555-2276
Whitney Woo, CPS . Exhibitors and Door Prizes . 555-1357
(your name) . . . . . . Word Processing Specialist . 555-____

Letters

The Eden PSI chapter letterhead is saved together with the envelope form as a style. The style library for the Eden PSI Chapter is in the [sim] directory on the template disk. (Please read the information in the box on page 454 before using the *Eden.sty* style library the first time.) Also included on the template disk is the PSI logo in a number of formats. These logos will be used in various jobs.[1]

Each time you wish to use the letterhead or the envelope format, retrieve the Eden style library and choose the desired form.

All letters should be prepared in block style. If possible, use a 12-point proportional font with serifs. The date should be a double space below the letterhead, and it should be followed

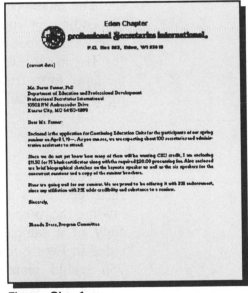

Figure Sim-1

with at least a quadruple space. In the case of very short letters, adjust

---

[1]The PSI logos used in this simulation are the registered trademarks of Professional Secretaries International®. They are to be used exclusively for the purposes of this simulation. Any other use of the logos requires written permission from Professional Secretaries International®, 10502 NW Ambassador Drive, P.O. Box 20404, Kansas City, MO 64195-0404.

the position of the letter on the page by leaving more space between the date and the inside address. The one-inch default margins are fine. Study Figure Sim-1 to see how your letters should look.

> Both the letterhead and envelope styles in the *Eden.sty* style library contain a Professional Secretaries International (PSI) graphic image. While the usual default setting in WordPerfect is for graphics to be saved with a document, this is not possible when the graphics are included as part of a style. Instead, WordPerfect looks in the default graphics library for the graphics.
>
> For this reason, the PSI graphics must be copied from the [sim] directory on the template disk to the WordPerfect default graphics library (usually WP51) before the styles containing the graphics can be used. The three PSI graphics used in this simulation are *ps-intnl.tif*, *circle-w.tif*, and *psi-glob.tif*. When the graphics are in the default graphics library, Word-Perfect can find the graphic each time it is needed for use in a style. Your instructor should copy those files for you. Check with your instructor before using the Eden letterhead or envelope styles to see if the graphics are available in the proper directory.

The envelope style is for a #10 envelope (9.5" x 4"). If possible (depending on your printing capabilities), prepare an envelope for each letter. Use paper cut to size for the envelopes.

If you can't do envelopes at all because of printer limitations, choose the label form from Lesson 26 that works best with your printer. Then, for all of the mailings, prepare labels for the envelopes.

Agendas

You will prepare an agenda for each meeting within the week following the preceding meeting. A copy of a sample agenda is provided in Figure Sim-2. In real life, you would make a copy of the agenda for each member of the committee and mail those agendas to the committee members. For this simulation, you need to prepare only one copy of the agenda. Place a small check mark to the left of the name of Seminar Chairperson Georgia Gates to identify that copy of the agenda as hers. Then prepare

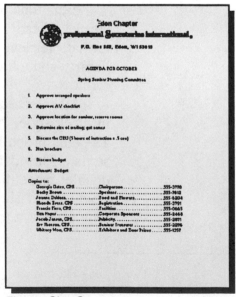

Figure Sim-2

an envelope to mail the agenda to Georgia at 399 Apple Valley Road, Eden, Wisconsin 53019.

Each agenda will have a copy of the budget attached. You will prepare the budget form as one of your first jobs. Each month it will be your responsibility to enter the figures provided to you by Seminar Treasurer Erv Thorson and update the budget.

Other Documents

Most of the remaining documents are one-of-a-kind documents. Many of them are forms. You may use any of the methods you learned about in Lesson 35 to create your forms. Keep in mind as you create the form that you will probably be expected to fill in the blanks on some of those forms. Create the form in such a way that you won't struggle later on when you are expected to complete the form.

You will also be working with Merge. Letters to the speakers, exhibitors, corporate sponsors, and prospective participants will be prepared using a primary file and a secondary file. In some cases, the same secondary file will be merged with more than one form letter.

Saving Your Documents

You will be creating quite a number of documents in planning this seminar. If you wish to save them on your data disk, you will want to create a Unit 4 directory and move all of the documents you created in Unit 4 into that directory. In that way, you can use the root directory for your simulation documents.

If your disk is getting full, you may delete most of the documents created in Units 3 and 4. Be careful not to delete any of your primary documents, however, because you will be using a number of them in your work for the simulation. Refer to Lesson 20 as a refresher in file management, if necessary.

An alternative would be to get a different disk for the simulation documents. If you put your simulation documents on a new disk, keep the data disk from your WordPerfect lessons handy so you can retrieve the primary documents when needed.

You will probably wish to name the documents by job. For example, in the first job you will be creating an audiovisual checklist. On the job you would probably name it something about "audiovisual." For the simulation, it would probably be easier to call it **job1**. Some jobs require the preparation of a number of documents. You can expand the document name to **job1a** or **job1b** for those jobs. This method leaves room in the extension for important information like **.pri** for primary documents and **.sec** for secondary documents (i.e., **job7a.pri** and **job7b.sec**).

General

Your work will be divided into months. The work for each month will come from source documents given to you by other members of the committee. The source documents begin on page 464. Most work will be as a result of the committee meeting held in that month. The jobs are all numbered consecutively, although some of them require the preparation of more than one document (such as the merge applications). Instructions are provided for most of the jobs, either in the preliminary materials for that month's work or on the source document for the job itself.

Much of the work will come to you in either rough draft or handwritten format. Be sure to study the information for each job in the monthly preliminary materials as well as on the source document itself before beginning the job.

Check your calendar to find out the date for the day after each of the committee meetings. It will usually be the second Wednesday of the month. Use that date for any work you prepare for that month.

You may prepare just one copy of each of the forms and documents. If you were taking the prepared documents to the committee meetings, you would make a copy for each of the committee members.

In real life you would have plenty of other office work to keep you busy without the complications of helping to prepare for the PSI seminar. In this simulation all you have to concentrate on is to efficiently prepare documents that you are proud to mail. Remember that you are member of a professional secretaries' group. Be professional in your work!

SEPTEMBER

The September organizational meeting of the Eden PSI seminar committee was a very productive meeting. The following topics were discussed and preliminary plans made.

- The date of the seminar—April 1, 19—
- The location for the seminar—the Adams Hotel in Eden
- Possible speakers and topics for the seminar
- The way the program for the day will be arranged
- Corporate sponsors who might help defray seminar expenses
- Audiovisual and room arrangement needs of the speakers
- The budget for the seminar

Job 1. Prepare a rough draft of the audiovisual (AV) checklist to be sent to the speakers. Use newspaper columns for the items and divide the columns somewhat evenly. Turn off Columns for the last section.

Use check boxes for the major items in the checklist. Short graphic lines or the underline can be used for the secondary items. Use graphic lines for the section at the bottom so the lines end evenly at the right of the page.

Job 2. Prepare a rough draft of the budget form. For the lines, set a tab stop at +4.5 and another at +5.5. Then you can tab to the stop and create a graphic line that begins at that position (set position) and is 0.7" long. After adding the line to the first item, block beginning with the first time you strike Tab to the end of the line. Use Ctrl-F4 and Copy. Then whenever you need that set of keystrokes, you can use Ctrl-F4, Retrieve, and Block. (You could also put that portion of the line into a macro to be retrieved at the end of each item.)

Job 3. This is a rough draft working program. Keep it simple.

Job 4. This job has several parts. Read through all of the instructions for this job before starting. Part **a:** Turn on your letterhead style. Then key the letter (the primary file).

Part **b:** Key the list of recipients of the letter (the secondary file). The secondary file should be arranged so that you can address the contact person as Ms. Aronstein, for example, in the salutation. The records will look like the sample in Figure Sim-3.

Part **c:** Sort the list by ZIP code and merge to prepare the letters.

Ms.{END FIELD}
Andrea{END FIELD}
Aronstein{END FIELD}
Andrea's Auto Body{END FIELD}
35 South Main{END FIELD}
Allentown, WI 53002{END FIELD}
{END RECORD}

Figure Sim-3

Part **d**: Use the envelope style (or label) format and enter the appropriate {FIELD} codes. Then save it as a primary file to be used throughout the simulation.

Part **e**: Prepare the envelopes (or labels). After merging with the primary file for the envelopes or labels, look through the list. You'll need to fix the one long company name in that list. Change it to two lines and tab the second line so it is slightly indented.

Part **f**: Finally, re-sort the list so the companies are in alphabetic order and print a list. Remember that when you want all of the names and addresses on one page, you must use the {PAGE OFF} code. Your primary file will look like Figure Sim-4.

At the beginning of the list, set up newspaper columns so you have two columns of names and addresses on the first page. Look through the list and insert hard page breaks as needed so none of the names and addresses are broken at the end of a column.

```
{FIELD}1~ {FIELD}2~ {FIELD}3~
{FIELD}4~
{FIELD}5~
{FIELD}6~

{PAGE OFF}
```

Figure Sim-4

Job 5. Print a copy of the budget sheet. Then use a pencil or pen to fill in the amounts on the dollar planner. Attach the budget to the October agenda.

OCTOBER

Job 6. Revise the AV checklist according to instructions.

Job 7. Use Merge to send confirmation letters to the speakers for the concurrent sessions. Prepare the merge. Print only the first letter for the group of speakers at 11:00 and the first letter for the group of speakers at 1:15. Attach the AV checklist, the envelope, and the format for handout layouts to each letter.

The letter to Ms. Cavness will be a two-page letter. Be sure to include the proper second-page heading (see Figure Sim-5) and the other appropriate attachments. Ms. Cavness will speak on two topics: "Thriving in a Changing World" and "Beyond the Office."

```
Ms. Cassie Cavness
Page 2
(date)
```

Figure Sim-5

Job 8. This is a confirmation letter for the hotel. Don't forget the envelope.

Job 9. The seminar committee has decided to send the local ZIP codes to PSI headquarters and pay PSI for labels to mail brochures to all of the PSI members in the immediate area. Rhonda has been in touch with PSI, and about 200 labels will be sent by PSI at a cost of $140. Members of your local group have been bringing in names and addresses of non-PSI members in the area that should be invited to the seminar. Those names and addresses are saved on the template disk as **job9a**. You need to add a few more names and addresses to the list and keep the list for the preparation of the labels next month.

Job 10. This job is to produce the brochure to be mailed to prospective seminar participants. A suggested solution is illustrated and includes all the information you'll need for the brochure. This solution assumes you can use an 8-point font. It is set up so that the brochure can be folded into thirds, and the registration portion is on the flip side of the address portion. This setup leaves the seminar participant with all of the pertinent information about the seminar after the registration portion has been torn off and returned.

If you can't squeeze the entire brochure onto two pages (to be printed back to back), you might wish to spread it out and put the registration portion on a separate half-sheet that will be inserted into the brochure for mailing. Use your imagination and your considerable design skills to create a brochure that's better looking than the suggested solution.

The **Professional Secretaries International** line is **ps-intnl.tif**. The PSI symbol is **circle-w.tif**. Both of the trademarks are in the **sim** directory of the template disk. Perhaps you can use the symbol somewhere on each side of your brochure.

Job 11. Make this agenda like the one for October. (Can you use the October agenda and just change the month and items in the list?)

NOVEMBER

Job 12. This is a letter to the corporate sponsors who have agreed to help with the seminar. You may use the same secondary file as the one you prepared in Job 4. You will need to delete the sponsors who are not participating and add a field listing the donation. After merging the letters, look at the paragraph where the donation is listed. You might need to edit the paragraph so it makes better sense. Prepare the envelopes (or labels) and submit one of each.

Job 13. Revise the brochure according to the instructions given. Then transmit it to the printer with Jacob's letter.

Job 14. Create a Figure box that is two inches wide and three inches tall. Space the information for the advertisement attractively in that box. You will need to choose a small font.

Job 15. Return to Lesson 26 and find the primary document named **lab3col.pri**. Retrieve it and customize it so that you can use it to merge with the list you created in Job 9 for mailing the brochures. Be sure to save the primary file with a different name than the original in Lesson 26 so that one will remain in case you need it again.

Sort the list of prospective seminar participants by ZIP code order before merging the secondary file with the primary file. Print all of the labels.

Job 16. Prepare the agenda for the December meeting. Take a few minutes to key the numbers for the Budget into the first column. They are not likely to change. It's the Actual amounts that will change. You may write in the few that Erv has supplied.

DECEMBER

Job 17. Create an invitation to join PSI. Rhonda has done all the work for you!

Job 18. A blank of the application for CEUs is saved on the template disk. The name of it is **applicat.ceu**. Fill in the information. Key the letter to PSI and include the biographies of the speakers. Don't forget an envelope.

Job 19. This is a simple Merge application to send letters to possible exhibitors. Use the same format for your primary and secondary files that you've been using to this point. Consistency will save you time.

Job 20. This is the seminar program. A suggested solution is provided for you, although you will probably be able to improve on the design. You may use the **circle-w.tif** graphic that is on the template disk for the PSI logo.

If you can print in the landscape orientation, use newspaper columns with a line length of about 4.3 inches. If your printer only prints in portrait orientation, set your margins so you have the same page size as the illustration but print each page on a separate sheet of paper. Then you can tape the pages together for printing purposes.

If your smallest font is too large to include all the information in the suggested solution, edit some of the text in the program to make it fit.

Job 21. This is the agenda for the January meeting.

JANUARY

Job 22. A suggested evaluation form is illustrated as a source document. The graphic at the top is a combination of the PSI logos you've used on past jobs. It is saved as one graphic on the template disk with the name **psi-glob.tif**.

Job 23. Proofread and correct the seminar program before printing the final copy to be sent to the printer.

Job 24. Jobs 24 and 25 require you to prepare tickets for the concurrent sessions and for the luncheon. They also involve preparing name tags for the seminar participants.

One of the better ways to do these jobs is to use the format with which you created raffle tickets in Lesson 35. That format was saved as **lab.frm**. If you remember, it enabled you to create a set number of tickets with numbering on the tickets. Since a limited number of people may attend some of the sessions, it will be nice to have the tickets numbered.

Your job will be to retrieve **lab.frm** or return to Lesson 35 and prepare it again. This time, however, you will prepare a copy of it for the luncheon and each of the eight concurrent sessions. When you merge each one of them, you will end up with enough tickets for each session. We'll begin with the luncheon tickets.

Retrieve **lab.frm** and change the number in the {FOR} line at the top from 24 to 120. Delete the portion of the line about the charity raffle. Key the information to be included on the luncheon ticket. At the bottom, remove the "Ticket No." portion but leave the {VARIABLE}x code. The tickets will be numbered, but no words will accompany the numbers. Save the revised form as **job24.pri**.

Use Merge to create the tickets. Remember that there is no secondary file. Print only one page of the tickets. To print only one page of the tickets, you must tell WordPerfect to print pages 1-8 because there are eight "pages" on one sheet of paper.

Job 25. Use the **lab.frm** for the tickets to the concurrent sessions. Prepare 20 tickets each for Sessions 1 and 5. Prepare 35 tickets each for the other six sessions. Remember to set the number in the {FOR} line at the top of each ticket and key the correct information for the session. Print the first "page" of tickets for each of the sessions.

Job 26. Now remove everything from **lab.frm** except the Paper Size/Type code and the Center justification code. Create a name tag with a very large (bold, if you'd like) first name in a sans serif font and a smaller last name. Use a normal size font for the city, state, and ZIP code. For this exercise, merge the name tag primary document with the list of prospective registrants you created in Job 9. You'll have about 55 name tags. Print only the first eight of them.

Job 27. Complete the agenda for the February meeting.

FEBRUARY

Jobs 28 through **31.** Since you did such nice work with these, all that's left is to check them over carefully for accuracy and print the final copies. If the copies you've already printed are perfect, you need not reprint them.

Job 32. This is the agenda for the March meeting.

MARCH

Jobs 33 and **34.** Work again with the shortened list of registrants you created in Job 9. Some of those people are registered for the hands-on sessions, and some didn't get their registrations in before the sessions were filled. Letters must be sent to all four groups of registrants. In Lesson 34, you can add a sixth field to the records in the secondary file to fill in the name of the replacement session.

Job 35. Send the letter to Ms. Cavness. You may need to fiddle with the margins or spacing in order to get the entire letter on one page. (It isn't long enough to justify a second page.)

Job 36. Send the letter to the speakers. You can use the same secondary file you used in Job 7.

Job 37. In creating the posters, use a sans serif font. This will be easier to read than a serif font. If you can't make big letters like requested, do the best you can. DO NOT clip the letters from the newspaper in anonymous note fashion!! Print all eight posters.

Job 38. The function sheet needed for this job is saved on the template disk with the name **function.** You may retrieve it, print it, and fill it out by hand for the hands-on sessions as directed. Francis has already completed the function sheets for the rest of the sessions.

Job 39. You can probably use the original list of vendors for this job. Delete those not exhibiting and add an extra field for the table number(s).

Job 40. This is the agenda for the April meeting.

APRIL

Job 41. Retrieve a copy of the evaluation and key the numbers in circles near the appropriate numerals on the evaluation. Fill in only this one form. Actually, there would be a form for each of the seven sessions.

Job 42. The participant list needs to be completed, listing all 98 of the seminar participants. The participant list is saved on the template disk as **partic**. Retrieve it and fill out only one page of the list with the information provided by Rhonda.

You may find when you fill in some of these forms that even with typeover turned on, some of the lines push to the next line. When that happens, finish keying the word or numeral. Then strike Delete until the lines are evened up again.

Job 43. Complete the Attendance Report. It is saved on the template disk with the name **attend**. You can get most of the information for the Attendance Report from the CEU application completed in Job 18. The number assigned by headquarters is WI4419.

Job 1

AUDIOVISUAL EQUIPMENT CHECKLIST

☐ 35 mm slide projector
__ no. carousels needed
__ remote control
__ extension cord
__ extra bulb

☐ screen
__ wall mount
__ portable
__ stage screen

☐ tape recorder

☐ videocassette player and monitor
__ 3/4 inch
__ 1/2 inch

☐ flip chart
__ no. of pads needed
__ markers

☐ easel

☐ board
__ whiteboard
__ markers
__ chalkboard
__ chalk
__ eraser

☐ pointer
☐ lectern with microphone
☐ podium with microphone
☐ lavalier microphone
__ 20-foot cord
__ 50-foot cord

☐ standing microphone
__ number needed

☐ table microphones
__ number needed

☐ overhead projector
__ acetate roll needed
__ blank transparencies
__ water soluble markers
__ extension cord
__ extra bulb

☐ display panel
__ extension cord

Please make a rough draft on Eden letterhead. Glad to have you on the committee! Thanks — Francis

Other: (please describe fully) _____
_____
_____

Job 2

DOLLAR PLANNER

	Budget	Actual
Revenue		
Target Number of Attendees @ $40 each	———	———
Contributions from Corporate Sponsors	———	———
Target Profit	———	———
Expenses		
Speakers		
Keynote—fee and transportation	———	———
Session Speakers—honorariums and transportation	———	———
Lodging and meals	———	———
Reproduction of speaker materials (consider who might donate this service)	———	———
Communication expenses (calls, mailings, etc.)	———	———
Complimentary registrations (actual costs)	———	———
Publicity		
Advertising	———	———
Brochure layout, printing, and mailing	———	———
Door prizes (consider donations)	———	———
Facilities		
Meeting room charges (check for hidden costs)	———	———
AV equipment (rental or setup costs)	———	———
Breaks	———	———
Seminar luncheon	———	———
Executive committee dinner	———	———
Participant Materials		
Printing of handouts	———	———
Program	———	———
Folders	———	———
Name tags	———	———
Pencil & paper (may be provided by hotel)	———	———
CEU Costs		
Certificates	———	———
$20 processing fee	———	———
Recording costs ($1.50 per person)	———	———

Please make this pretty! Thanks! Ew

Job 3

Proposed Program

8:00 a.m. – 9:00 a.m.

~~8 a.m. to 9 a.m.~~
      Registration; Continental Breakfast; Office Products
      Exhibits

9:00
~~9~~ a.m. ~~to~~ 10:30 a.m.
      Keynote Speaker

10:30 a.m. ~~to~~ 11:00 a.m.
      Break; Office Products Exhibits

11:00 a.m. ~~to~~ 12:15 a.m.
      Four concurrent sessions (one hands-on)

                    1:00
12:15 ~~to 1~~ p.m.
      Luncheon (included in cost of registration); Office
      Products Exhibits

1:15 p.m. ~~to~~ 2:30 p.m.
      Four concurrent sessions (one hands-on)

2:30 p.m. ~~to~~ 2:45 p.m.
      Break

2:45 p.m. ~~to~~ 4:00 p.m.
      Closing Session - Keynote speaker; wrap-up and
      evaluation; CEU certificates; door prizes.

[handwritten note: Please space this so there's room to add info at the next meeting. Use a 12-point proportional font. Thanks! Georgia]

Job 4   *(See next page)*

The Eden, Wisconsin, chapter of Professional Secretaries International is holding an educational seminar at the Adams Hotel in Eden on Saturday, April 1. It is anticipated that as many as 100 secretaries and administrative assistants from Eden and the surrounding area will attend the seminar.

As a representative of the program committee, I have been asked to contact you to see if (company) would be willing to help with our seminar. You can help by donating some of your products to be used as door prizes. Or your company could underwrite the expense of bringing in some of our speakers. Our keynote speaker is from the DePere area and a graduate of St. Norbert College. Another way you could help us would be by making a cash donation with which we may purchase door prizes or pay some of the costs of the seminar, such as the printing of handouts and program brochures.

Please let me know by November 1 whether (company) would be able to contribute in some way to our seminar. You may call me at 555-2468 between 8 a.m. and 4 p.m. on weekdays.

Job 4 (continued)

Mr. Stephen Paulus
Paulus & Paulus, Inc.
3380 Apple Valley Road
Eden, WI 53019

Mrs. Phyllis Jegen
Cross Construction
76 Green Bay Avenue
Eden, WI 53019

Miss Lucia Stumpf
Lucia's Lighting
3211 Apple Valley Road
Eden, WI 53019

Mr. David Warren
Sumner Publishing Company
327 Winding Way
Oostburg, WI 53070

Mr. George Dehart
Geohart Electronic Assembly
945 N. Main Street
Waupun, WI 53963

Mr. Wendell Lokensgard
Wendell's Marina
P.O. Box 332
Fond du Lac, WI 54936

Miss Debbie Davies
Designs & Signs
113 Apple Valley Road
Eden, WI 53013

Mrs. Jan Juckem
Jan's Leather Loft
76 First Street
Lomira, WI 54048

Ms. Amy Arnold
Kettle Valley Bank
12 Main Street
Eden, WI 53019

Mr. Gaardner Gumbly
Gamble & Gumbly
437 Third Street
Eden, WI 53019

Ms. Andrea Aronstein
Andrea's Auto Body
35 South Main
Allentown, WI 53002

Mr. Charles Cook
Cook's Ceramics
548 Carver Lane
Campellsport, WI 53010

Miss Susi Stachowicz
Spartica Sports
549 Wisconsin Avenue
Kewaskum, WI 53040

Ms. Signe Nelson
Nelson's Shrub Nursery
1338 South Oregon Street
North Fond du Lac, WI 54937

Miss Carla Covioux
Custom Catering
669 California Lane
New Holstein, WI 53061

Mr. Tony Condon
Condon, Condon, and Hill
              Investment Counseling
340 North Main
Eden, WI 53019

Please send this letter to all of these businesses. Use Eden chapter letterhead. Also, please arrange the businesses in alphabetic order (by business name) and print them in a list so we can use it at our meetings.

Oh yes — for the mailing, the businesses must be in ZIP code order. Is it easier to sort before you print?

Thanks!
Jica

Job 4 (continued)

Mr. Stevenson Sommers
Bank of Eden
42 North Main
Eden, WI 53019

Miss Francie Kraus
Speed King Mfg. Co.
3904 Apple Valley Road
Eden, WI 53019

Ms. Dinah Delwich
Delwich's Sandwiches
761 South Main
Eden, WI 53019

Mr. Joseph French
Columbia Crystal Works
1290 Oak Street
Oakfield, WI 53065

Ms. Marcy Missling
Proctor Pharmaceuticals
1408 Random Lake Lane
West Bend, WI 53095

Mrs. Jeanette Archer
Lionhart Leather Works
65 Limekiln Lane
West Bend, WI 53095

Mr. Phillip Pearson
Crockery Cookery
110 East Main Street
West Bend, WI 53095

Mrs. Jackie Jones
Moraine Pest Service
34 Third Avenue
Kewaskum, WI 53040

Dr. Donald Dudley
Dudley's Dude Ranch
446 Oakridge Road
Greenbush, WI 53026

Mrs. Paula Preston
Preston Press
568 Eighth Street
Eden, WI 53019

Miss Polly Peckham
Peckham Photography
43 Pilgrim Parkway
Plymouth, WI 53073

Ms. Georgie Gregg
Georgie's Greenhouses
667 Apple Valley Road
Eden, WI 53019

Mrs. Norma Steiner
Workers Health
3448 Shogun Road
DePere, WI 54115

Mr. Ramsey Hart
Rivermoor Paper Company
418 River Street
DePere, WI 54115

Job 5

AGENDA FOR OCTOBER
Spring Seminar Planning Committee

1. Approve arranged speakers - Becky
2. Approve AV checklist - Francis
3. approve location for seminar; reserve rooms - Francis
4. Determine size of mailing; get names - Rhonda
5. Discuss the CEU (5 hrs. of instruction = .5 CEU) - Rhonda
6. Plan brochure - Jacob
7. Discuss budget - Erv

Please put this agenda on Eden letterhead. At the bottom, include the names, committee responsibilities, and phone numbers of the committee members.

i.e.

Georgia Gates ..... Chairperson 555-3778

Erv has penciled the budget numbers into your dollar planner. They are shown on the next page. Print a copy of the planner. Write in the numbers. Then make a copy to attach to each member's copy of the agenda.

Thanks.

Georgia

Attachment: Budget

Job 5 (continued)

DOLLAR PLANNER

Revenue	Budget	Actual
Target Number of Attendees @ $40 each	4000	
Contributions from Corporate Sponsors	1500	
Target Profit	1000	

Expenses		

Speakers		
Keynote—fee and transportation	850	
Session Speakers—honorariums and transportation	400	
Lodging and meals	300	
Reproduction of speaker materials (consider who might donate this service)	25	
Communication expenses (calls, mailings, etc.)	50	
Complimentary registrations (actual costs)	50	

Publicity		
Advertising	50	
Brochure layout, printing, and mailing	300	
Door prizes (consider donations)	100	

Facilities		
Meeting room charges (check for hidden costs)	200	
AV equipment (rental or setup costs)	200	
Breaks	200	
Seminar luncheon	1000	
Executive committee dinner	200	

Participant Materials		
Printing of handouts	50	
Program	100	
Folders	100	
Name Tags	25	
Pencil & paper (may be provided by hotel)	?	

CEU Costs		
Certificates	15	15
$20 processing fee	20	20
Recording costs ($1.50 per person)	150	

Job 6

AUDIOVISUAL EQUIPMENT CHECKLIST

☐ 35 mm slide projector
___ no. carousels needed
___ remote control
___ extension cord
___ extra bulb

☐ screen
___ wall mount
___ portable
___ stage screen

☐ tape recorder

☐ videocassette player and monitor
___ ¾ inch
___ ½ inch

☐ flip chart
___ number of pads needed
___ markers

☐ easel

☐ board
___ whiteboard
___ markers
___ chalkboard
___ chalk
___ eraser

☐ pointer

☐ lectern with microphone

☐ podium with microphone

☐ lavalier microphone
___ 20-foot cord
___ 50-food cord

☐ standing microphone
___ number needed

☐ table microphones
___ number needed

☐ overhead projector
___ acetate roll needed
___ blank transparencies
___ water soluble markers
___ extension cord
___ extra bulb

☐ display panel
___ extension cord

move this section to the top of column 2

Fix this

make this section first

Add that statement at the bottom, please. Francis

Other: (please describe fully) _____

_____

_____

Please draw a diagram of the preferred room layout on the back of this page.

Job 7

Dear (speaker): , Wisconsin.

The members of the Eden Chapter of Professional Secretaries International are pleased that you have agreed to speak at the seminar to be held on Saturday, April 1, 19—, at the Adams Hotel in Eden. We expect about 100 secretaries with a wide range of experiences, backgrounds, and years in the office. Your presentation on (name of presentation in quotes) should be well received at this time. In the past few years, the profession has undergone some major changes. We hope you will be able to help us meet these challenges.   ℐ of these changes.
        the

Your session will begin promptly at (time) and will end at (time). As agreed upon, you will personalize your presentation for us and will provide handouts for participants. The Eden PSI Chapter will gladly reproduce the handouts if photo-ready copy is sent to me by February 15. Enclosed you will find a suggested format for the note-taking portion of your seminar handouts. Also enclosed is the seminar information that should appear at the top of the first page of your handouts or on a cover sheet.

Please send a vita and a brief description of your session within the next two weeks for the seminar brochure and program. Also, please return the enclosed AV checklist by October 31 and indicate your preferred room setup. PSI will handle securing the equipment and working with the hotel facilities staff.

        an honorarium of   agreeing
As agreed, (amount) will be paid to you immediately after the seminar. On behalf of the program committee, I would like to extend my thanks to you for arranging to be part of our seminar. I am looking forward to working with you. If you have any questions, please call me at 555-7812.
        414-

Sincerely,

Becky Brown, Program Committee

Enclosures

Please send this letter to the speakers on the attached list. I've noted the time for the presentation and the amount of the honorarium for each. Oh, yes — please make the corrections shown in the copy above. Thanks, Becky

Job 7 (continued)

Mrs. Marcia Carlson
Mt. Calvary College   11:00 - 12:15 $50.00
661 Third Street
Mt. Calvary, WI 53057
Presentation: "Beautiful Documents with Report Publisher"

Mr. Bret Bowers
The Humor Shoppe   11:00 - 12:15 $50.00
7839 Silver Spring
Milwaukee, WI 53229
Presentation: "Surviving the Workday with Humor"

Dr. Terry Lawrence
UW—Milwaukee
1266 Downer Street   11:00 - 12:15 $ 50.00
Milwaukee, WI 53228
Presentation: "Teamwork: Enhancing Office Productivity"

Mr. Roy St. Claire
Computer Heaven
88 South Main Street   1:15 - 2:30 $50.00
Eden, WI 53019
Presentation: "Perfect Documents with WordPerfect"

Miss Patricia K. Morin
PK Morin & Associates
12445 Bluemound Drive   1:15 - 2:30 $ 50.00
Milwaukee, WI 53226
Presentation: "Rightsizing: How It Could Affect Your Job!"

Ms. Lucia Lewin
Eden County Social
   Services Department   1:15 - 2:30 $50.00
481 Apple Valley Road
Eden, WI 53019
Presentation: "A Balancing Act: Home & Career"

Job 7 (continued)

(handwritten annotations top right:) top, Bottom, Left, Right margins - .5
Block Style
Mixed Punctuation
Put the date at the top
line' Date
QS
Address

Ms. Cassie Cavness
Cavness Training & Consulting
34 Casa Loma Lane
Los Carlos, CA 94337

DS

Dear Ms. Cavness:

, Wisconsin.

The members of the Eden Chapter of Professional Secretaries International are pleased that you have agreed to speak at the seminar to be held on Saturday, April 1, 19—, at the Adams Hotel in Eden. We expect about 100 secretaries with a wide range of experiences, backgrounds, and years in the office. Your presentations on (names of presentations in quotes) should be well received at this time. In the past few years, the profession has undergone some major changes. We know you will be able to help us meet ~~those~~ challenges *of these changes.*

p.m.

As agreed, you will speak to the entire group of seminar attendants from 9 a.m. to 10:30 and from 2:45 to 3:45. We have also scheduled you for two 1¼-hour breakout sessions beginning at 11:00 a.m. and 1:15 p.m. where you will work with smaller groups of participants. As agreed upon, you will personalize your presentation for us and will provide handouts for participants. The Eden PSI Chapter will gladly reproduce the handouts if photo-ready copy is sent to (name and address) by February 15. Enclosed you will find a suggested format for the note-taking portion of your seminar handouts. Also enclosed is the seminar information that should appear at the top of the first page of your handouts or on a cover sheet.

The Eden PSI Chapter will arrange for your round-trip flight between Los Carlos and Milwaukee. Please let us know your airline preference and your wishes regarding the time of travel as soon as possible so that tickets can be purchased. PSI will arrange for your ~~room~~ *& lodging.*

Please send a vita and a brief description of your session*s* within the next two weeks for the seminar brochure and program. Also, please return the enclosed AV checklist by October 31 and indicate your preferred room setup. PSI will handle securing the equipment and working with the hotel facilities staff.

Your fee of $500 will be paid to you immediately after the seminar. On behalf of the program committee, I welcome you to the Eden PSI Chapter seminar as a speaker and look forward to working with you. If you have any questions, please call me at 414-555-7812.

Sincerely,

~~Becky Brown, Program Committee~~

Enclosures

Job 7 (continued)

To appear on the cover sheet or on the first page of your handouts:

Eden Chapter
Professional Secretaries International
P.O. Box 77
Eden, WI 53019

Include somewhere near the beginning of the handout:

TITLE OF PRESENTATION or TOPIC

Objectives:
   1.
   2.
   3.
   4.
   5.

Possible format for note-taking forms:

(Statement of fact or discussion from your presentation.)

_____

_____

_____

(Another statement of fact or discussion from your presentation.)

_____

_____

_____

etc.

Job 8

Date

Ms. Eve Warren, Manager
Adams Hotel
276 Wisconsin Avenue
Eden, WI 53019

Dear Ms. Warren:

This letter is a ~~follow-up to~~ (confirmation of) our discussion last week regarding the use of the convention facilities at the Adams Hotel for the Professional Secretaries International seminar to be hosted by the Eden Chapter on Saturday, April 1, 19—.

Our group would like the Abel and Cain Ballrooms joined and set up with round tables for our opening session at 9:00 a.m. and the closing session at 2:45 p.m. We would also like lunch to be served in that conference area.

We will need four smaller meeting rooms (approximately 30 people each) for our concurrent sessions at 11:00 a.m. and 1:15 p.m. When registrations have been received, we will complete the function sheets for those rooms.

Our plan is to have a number of exhibits set up around the sides of the ballrooms. Exhibitors will want to have their exhibits in place by 8:00 a.m. so they are ready for the registration time. Exhibits will be removed while the ballrooms are being cleared after the luncheon.

Committee member Joanne Dahleen will contact you in January regarding food and beverages for the breaks and for the luncheon.

On behalf of the committee, we are looking forward to working with you for our spring seminar. If you have any questions, you can reach me weekdays at 555-0665.

Sincerely,

Francis Fiera, Program Committee

DOC CODE

Please make the corrections indicated and send this letter to Ms. Warren.

Thanks,
Francis

Job 9

Miss Kris Gehrke
28 W. Kamps Street
Eden, WI 53019

Mrs. Mattie Cavers
437 Henry Street
Theresa, WI 53091

Ms. Margot Christian
432 E. Forest Avenue
Oakfield, WI 53065

Mrs. Elyda Crisman
4391 Ann Street
Fond du Lac, WI 54935

Ms. Connie Erickson
4732 Henry Street
West Bend, WI 53095

Miss Nancy Thiex
4691 Apple Valley Road
Eden, WI 53019

Please add these people to the list that has
already been keyed. This is for the brochure
mailing.

Thanks! Rhonda

Job 10

Eden Chapter
professional Secretaries international.
presents . . .

a one-day spring educational seminar
at the Adams Hotel in Eden, Wisconsin

Saturday, April 1, 19—, from 8 am to 4 pm

Registration Cost:
    Non-Members $45
    PSI Members $40
    Early Registration $40
    (before Feb. 15)

Optional: PSI Discount Hotel Rate $49

.5 CEU for seminar attendance

Reservations are due by March 1, 19—.

Cancellation requests must be made in writing and postmarked no later than March 20 to qualify for a refund.

Secretaries & Administrative Assistants

Devote one day to becoming all that you can be!
Learn to have the right attitude and to do your work better
so that you feel better about yourself.
You can also increase your chances for advancement.

You are invited to come to the seminar . . .

Eden Chapter
Professional Secretaries International
P.O. Box 552
Eden, WI 53019

PSI SPRING SEMINAR SCHEDULE

8:00 am - 9:00 am   Registration; Continental Breakfast; Office Products Exhibits

9:00 am - 10:30 am   Keynote Speaker - Cassie Cavness **"Thriving in a Changing World"** Listen and learn as this well-known speaker presents ten techniques for meeting the challenges of today's office. Become an innovator rather than a follower as you develop career enhancement strategies made possible by your own personal development.

10:30 am - 11:00 am   Break; Office Products Exhibits

11:00 am - 12:15 pm   Concurrent Sessions

#1 Hands-on Workshop A*: **"Beautiful Documents with Report Publisher."** Join Marcia Carlson as you learn to use Report Publisher® to enhance the appearance and readability of the documents you create every day on the job—reports, letters, memos, contracts, and tabular material. (Two people per computer. Limited to the first 20 registrants.)

#2 **"Beyond the Office"** by Cassie Cavness. Get more tips from the keynote speaker about enhancing your life by extending the principles learned in the morning session into your daily life.

#3 **"Surviving the Workday with Humor"** by Bret Bowers, humor afficionado. Learn appropriate ways to apply the positive power of humor and creativity to some of the not-so-humorous things that happen in the course of the day's work.

#4 **"Teamwork: Enhancing Office Productivity"** by Terry Lawrence, Professor of Supervisory Management at the University of Wisconsin, Milwaukee. In this era of changes of office management, many companies have begun organizing workers into self-directed teams. Learn how can you you become a good team player without sacrificing productivity.

12:15 pm - 1:00 pm   Luncheon (included in cost of registration); Office Products Exhibits

1:15 pm - 2:30 pm   Concurrent Sessions

#1 Hands-on Workshop B*: **"Perfect Documents with WordPerfect."** Join Roy St. Claire as you learn to use WordPerfect® to enhance the appearance and readability of the documents you create every day on the job—reports, letters, contracts, and tabular material. (Two people per computer. Limited to the first 20 registrants.)

#2 **"Beyond the Office"** by Cassie Cavness. (This session is a repeat of Session #2 at 11 a.m.)

#3 **"Rightsizing: How It Could Affect Your Job!"** by Patricia K. Morin of PKMorin & Associates, Milwaukee. Ms. Morin has consulted with dozens of companies as they make changes in management style in an effort to keep costs in line with revenues. In this session you will learn how being prepared for management changes can actually give you an edge in getting the promotion for which you've been preparing.

#4 **"A Balancing Act: Home & Career"** by Lucia Lewin of the Eden County Social Services Department. Ms. Lewin has had extensive experience in working with families who are suffering from the problems that may be the result of mothers having to work. Learn techniques for dealing with children and/or spouse in making the home a place where everyone WANTS to return after a stressful day at work or in school.

2:30 pm - 2:45 pm   Break

2:45 pm - 4:00 pm   Closing Session by Cassie Cavness; Wrap-up and Evaluation; CEU Certificates; Door Prizes
*Computers and software graciously provided and set up by Computer Heaven of Eden, Wisconsin.

Spring Seminar Registration
Eden Chapter—Professional Secretaries International
Saturday, April 1, 19— Registration from 8 to 9 am at the Adams Hotel in Eden, Wisconsin

Name _____ Home Phone _____ PSI Member ID Number _____

Address_____City_____State_____ZIP_____

Social Security # (Required for CEU Credit) _____ Enclosed check or money order for $_____

Concurrent Sessions: Number your first and second choices (1 & 2) for the am sessions and the pm sessions.

Morning Concurrent Sessions		Afternoon Concurrent Sessions	
_____ #1 Report Publisher® _____ #3 Humor		_____ #5 WordPerfect® _____ #7 Rightsizing	
_____ #2 Beyond the Office _____ #4 Teamwork		_____ #6 Beyond the Office _____ #8 Balancing Home & Career	

Mail Registration form by March 1 with check made payable to:
Eden Chapter, Professional Secretaries International

%o Rhonda Evers, Program Committee
P.O. Box 552
Eden, WI 53019

Non-Member Resistration Fee $45
PSI Member Registration Fee $40
Non-Member Early-bird Fee $40
(postmarked by Feb. 15)

Job 11

AGENDA FOR NOVEMBER

1. Approve brochure (with corrections) - Jacob
2. Authorize printing of brochures - Georgia
3. Determine registration fee - Georgia
4. Discuss results from mailing to corporate sponsors - Tica
5. Review budget - Georgia

(Please prepare and distribute this agenda.)
It should be done like the October agenda
Thanks! Georgia

Our donations from corporate sponsors haave been wonderful! Workers Health is footing the entire bill for our keynote speaker because she's a St. Norbert alumni. A supporter who wishes to be anonymous has contribute d for advertising, and a couple of the local printing companys have donated there their services. What's more, Francis has convinced the manger of the Adams to provide pins and notepads for all seminar a participants. pens

I've filled in all of these figures on the attached dollar planner and marked the donations with an asterisk to be explained in the at the bottom of the form. Those amounts are included with the cash donations on the Contributions line at the top. Please key all figures into a dollar planner and distribute it with the November agenda.

Please forgive this mess. My typewriter at home is broken and I've lost my eraser.

Thanks!! Erv

Job 11 (continued)

DOLLAR PLANNER

Revenue	Budget	Actual
Target Number of Attendees @ $40 each	4000	
Contributions from Corporate Sponsors	1500	1485
Target Profit	1000	

Expenses

Speakers	Budget	Actual
Keynote—fee and transportation	850	850 ★
Session Speakers—honorariums and transportation	400	
Lodging and meals	300	
Reproduction of speaker materials (consider who might donate this service)	25	
Communication expenses (calls, mailings, etc.)	50	
Complimentary registrations (actual costs)	50	

Publicity		
Advertising	50	50 ★
Brochure layout, printing, and mailing	300	160 ★
Door prizes (consider donations)	100	

Facilities		
Meeting room charges (check for hidden costs)	200	
AV equipment (rental or setup costs)	200	
Breaks	200	
Seminar luncheon	1000	
Executive committee dinner	200	

Participant Materials		
Printing of handouts	50	50 ★
Program	100	
Folders	100	
Name Tags	25	
Pencil & paper (may be provided by hotel)	?	0

CEU Costs		
Certificates	15	15
$20 processing fee	20	20
Recording costs ($1.50 per person)	150	

★ Expense to be picked up by corporate sponsor

Job 12

The Eden Chapter of the Professional Secretaries International would like to extend its warmest appreciation to you and to (company name) for being a sponsor of our spring seminar that is coming up on April 1, 19—.

Your gift of (gift—you may need to adjust the sentence to fit the gift—cash, for example) will help the PSI chapter to provide seminar participants with something with which to remember the seminar as well as the good day they had in Eden. In addition, (company name) will be listed in the seminar program as a seminar sponsor.

The members of the Eden PSI chapter are fortunate indeed to live and work in a region where so many of the area businesses are supportive of its activities. Again, thank you for your participation.

Please send the letter above to the businesses on the list below thanking them for their donations. Insert the item donated in the blank at the beginning of Paragraph 2.   Thanks! Whitney

Andrea's Auto Body: a free lube and oil change
Columbia Crystal Works: a pair of crystal candle holders
Condon, Condon, and Hill Investment Counseling: $50
Cook Ceramics: 12 pots for centerpieces
Crockery Cookery: $100
Delwich's Sandwiches: two $5 gift certificates
Geohart Electronic Assembly: $50
Georgie's Greenhouses: a 25-percent discount on flowers
Jan's Leather Loft: two billfolds
Kettle Valley Bank: $25
Lionhart Leather Works: a 50-percent discount on a brief case
Paulus & Paulus, Inc.: $50
Peckham Photography: a free sitting for family portrait
Preston Press: free printing and folding of seminar brochures
    ($160)
Proctor Pharmaceuticals: $50
Speed King Mfg. Co.: $100
Sumner Publishing Company: free duplicating of handouts ($50)
Workers Health: your sponsorship of the keynote speaker
    (transportation and speaking fee) ($850)

Job 13

Please double-check the registration charges on the brochure. They should be $45, $40, and $40.

Also, we've decided to number the afternoon concurrent sessions as a continuation of the morning sessions. Change the afternoon sessions to #5, #6, #7, and #8 in both places on the brochure.

Thanks, Georgia

Attached is a letter to be sent along with the completed brochure to Mrs. Preston at Preston Press. Please get it out this week, if possible.

You may sign my name on the letter and put your initials beside the signature.

Thanks, Jacob

Job 13 (continued)

Enclosed is camera-ready copy of the brochure for the Eden PSI spring seminar to be held on April 1 at the Adams Hotel. As Whitney Woo, a member of our program committee, discussed with you several weeks ago, Preston Press has offered to print and fold our brochures at no charge as a donation to our seminar.

We would like 300 copies of the brochure printed on light green paper. The finished brochures should be folded in thirds so they can easily be prepared for mailing. We would like the printed brochures delivered by January 8 so that we can address them and have them in the mail by January 15.

As mentioned in an earlier letter, the Eden PSI Chapter appreciates the fine work done by your company as well as your willingness to support our efforts. Thank you!

Job 14

**Eden Chapter of
Professional Secretaries
International**

is sponsoring a
one-day seminar

**Thriving in a Changing
World**

Saturday, April 1, 19—
Adams Hotel
Eden

Call for information:
Jacob Jensen   555-2871
Georgia Gates   555-3778

Eden Daily Enquirer is donating space for a 2" by 3" advertisement for the seminar. Please prepare an ad that looks kind of like this.

Thanks!   Jacob

Job 15

Please prepare the labels for the brochure mailing and bring them to the next meeting. Thanks! Rhonda

Job 16

AGENDA FOR DECEMBER

1. Discuss flowers and/or table decorations - Joanne
2. Discuss the CEU application - Rhonda
3. Discuss the seminar printed program - Jacob
4. Discuss exhibits; list vendors to exhibit - Whitney
5. Discuss registration packets - Rhonda
6. Review budget - Georgia

Thanks ! Georgia

Our dollar planner needs to be amended because we decided to buy mailing labels preprinted with the names of local PSI members from PSI International. It was expensive, but we'll make up the extra dollars somewhere else.

Please add 2 lines under the Publicity section of the dollar planner and fix the line above the new lines so it looks like this:

Brochure layout and printing	300	160*
Paid to PSI for labels		140
Postage for mailings	90	

Thanks - Ev

Job 17

INVITATION TO MEMBERSHIP IN
PROFESSIONAL SECRETARIES INTERNATIONAL®

Are you an executive assistant who possesses a mastery of office skills, who demonstrates the ability to assume responsibility without direct supervision, who exercises initiative and judgment, and who makes decisions within the scope of assigned authority? If so, then you are eligible for membership in Professional Secretaries International.

Professional Secretaries International (PSI) is the world's leading organization for secretaries. Its aim is to elevate the secretarial standards and offer opportunities for professional and personal growth and development to achieve that goal. You, too, can achieve your goal by becoming associated with PSI. Membership affords the opportunity to become a better secretary through education and to share companionship with secretaries who have similar interests.

Would you like to become part of a professional association for secretaries? Then Professional Secretaries International is the association for YOU!

We invite you to check the following items for further information:

_____ I would like information on Professional Secretaries International.

_____ I would like information on the Certified Professional Secretary (CPS) program.

_____ I would like to attend a meeting of the Eden Chapter of PSI. Please let me know of future meeting dates.

Name # ← (Add a space) _____

Home Address # _____

Employer # _____

Telephone No. # _____

Please complete and leave this form on the table or mail it to:

Please put this on our letterhead and make it pretty. Thanks, Rhonda

Rhonda Evers CPS
Membership Chairman
Eden Chapter, PSI
P.O. Box 552
Eden, WI 53019

Job 18

Ms. Susan Fenner, PhD
Department of Education and Professional Development
Professional Secretaries International
10502 NW Ambassador Drive
P.O. Box 20404
Kansas City, MO 64195-0404

Dear Dr. Fenner:

Enclosed is the application for Continuing Education Units for the participants of our spring seminar on April 1, 19—. As you can see, we are expecting about 100 secretaries and administrative assistants to attend.

I am enclosing $15.00 for 100 blank certificates along with the required $20.00 processing fee. Also enclosed are brief biographical sketches on the keynote speaker as well as the six speakers for the concurrent sessions and a copy of the seminar brochure.

Plans are going well for our seminar. We are proud to be offering it with PSI endorsement since any affiliation with PSI adds credibility and substance to a seminar.

Sincerely,

Rhonda Evers, Program Committee

Required to be included:
Application (3 copies)
Biographical information on speaker(s)
Outline of program, topics to be covered, and time frames
$20.00 processing fee
Certificate cost

Please put this on Chapter letterhead, too, and make it look good. Prepare the attached forms. There is no special format for the speaker descriptions.

Rhonda

Job 18 (continued)

Speakers:

Keynote Speaker: Cassie Cavness   "Thriving in a Changing World"

Cassie Cavness is well known in the Midwest for her energetic and stimulating presentations regarding the frustrations faced by office workers in this changing world. Ms. Cavness discusses the transition from electric to electronic equipment and how it impacts everything that must be done in the office. She addresses international business and how office workers can arm themselves for the office of the future.

Ms. Cavness received her undergraduate training at St. Norbert College in DePere, Wisconsin. She has master's degrees in management and business from the University of Southern California. She is president of Cavness Consulting, Inc., in Los Carlos, California, a management consulting firm teaching leadership skills to administrative support staff.

Concurrent Sessions:

Marcia Carlson   "Beautiful Documents with Report Publisher"

An instructor in the office occupations department of Mt. Calvary College, Marcia Carlson has been teaching students how to design documents for a number of years. Her designs have won a number of national awards, and she is eager to pass on her skills to those who are in the business of document design.

Bret Bowers "Surviving the Workday with Humor"

Bret Bowers, owner and manager of The Humor Shoppe in Milwaukee, has a number of tried and true methods of salvaging a disastrous workday with humor. His tasteful presentations have helped office workers from coast to coast. Mr. Bowers has a degree in psychology from St. Olaf College, and he worked in management for a number of large companies in the Minneapolis-St. Paul area before moving to Milwaukee.

Terry Lawrence   "Teamwork: Enhancing Office Productivity"

Dr. Terry Lawrence is a graduate of the University of Wisconsin, Milwaukee, and she earned her PhD at Stanford University in California. In addition to teaching in the Supervisory Management program at the University of Wisconsin in Milwaukee, she has lectured widely in the area of Total Quality Management and is a firm believer in the power of work teams.

Job 18 (continued)

Roy St. Claire   "Perfect Documents with WordPerfect"

Roy St. Claire is trainer and instructor at Computer Heaven in Eden, Wisconsin. His degree in computer science from UW—Oshkosh provided him with a head start in computers. From there he was manager of information systems for ALP Insurance, Greenbush, in their home office for five years. He moved to the document design department for a change of scenery and discovered a love for the WordPerfect program and its seemingly endless features used in the design of attractive and readable documents.

Patricia K. Morin   "Rightsizing: How It Could Affect Your Job!"

Patricia K. Morin is owner and president of PKMorin & Associates, a management consulting firm in Milwaukee. A graduate of Marquette University with a degree in management, Ms. Morin's vocation and avocation is the study of downsizing and rightsizing in corporate America. In the process of studying the management changes being made by companies of all sizes, she has developed a plan for support staff members that helps them cope with the changes in their companies.

Lucia Lewin   "A Balancing Act: Home & Career"

With degrees in sociology and psychology, Lucia Lewin's job involves working with families and helping them to function as a happy family unit. Ms. Lewin's approach is that since it's the norm for both parents to be breadwinners in today's families, adjustments must be made so that all of the family members are happy, healthy, and involved in the business of being a family. In addition to working with individual families in Eden County, Ms. Lewin has lectured nationally regarding her strategies for helping families survive.

Job 18 (continued)

professional Secretaries international.
APPLICATION

Program Number
Assigned by HQ

Eden PSI Chapter   1234   0.5   100

Sponsor Name   Sponsor
ID Number   CEU Requested
(based on contact hours)   Number of Participants Expected

April 1, 19—   Five   One

Event Date(s)   Total Number of Contact Hours   Number of Meeting Days

Program Site Adams Hotel   Name of Instructor(s)

276 Wisconsin Ave.   Fill in all

Eden, WI 53019   seven names

here.

Title of Program Thriving in a Changing World

Program Objective (to be written on certificate) To provide workers with the
skills to improve their job satisfaction and their
chances for advancement.

Signature of PSI Sponsor President

Phone: Business 414-555-8213

Fax 414-555-8227

Residence 414-555-1967

Date _____

Signature of PSI Program Chairperson

Phone: Business 414-555-3778

Fax 414-555-3779

Residence 414-555-1653

Date _____

MAIL CORRESPONDENCE TO:
Name and Address

Ms. Rhonda Evers

P.O. Box 552

Eden, WI 53019

Number of Certificates Ordered:

Customized _____ Blank 100

FOR HEADQUARTERS USE ONLY

Application Received _____

Number of CEU Awarded _____

_____ _____
CEU Registrar   Date

Submit three (3) copies of application

Job 19

On Saturday, April 1, 19—, the Eden Chapter of Professional Secretaries International (PSI) is hosting a spring seminar at the Adams Hotel in beautiful downtown Eden. A number of speakers and seminar presenters will share information about working in today's office with PSI members as well as other secretaries and administrative assistants from the surrounding area. A copy of the seminar brochure is attached.

An important part of the plan for the day is for businesses like yours to be represented with an office products display in the ballroom, which will be the main meeting room. We are hoping for displays of office equipment, furniture, and supplies. While the primary purpose of the displays is not to sell products but to show seminar participants what is available, the sale of small office items will be allowed.

The seminar committee joins me in extending this invitation to you to participate in our PSI seminar. Please call me at 555-1357 by January 15 to tell me whether you can join us.

Mr. Hoan Nguyen
Eden Business Machines
4487 Apple Valley Road
Eden, WI 53019

Mrs. Phyllis Nagel
Micro & Office Supply
347 N. Main Street
Eden, WI 53019

Miss Lou VanDyke
Office Stop 'n Shop
111 Melrose Avenue
Mt. Calvary, WI 53057

Mr. Abe Williams
Computer Heaven
8933 Apple Valley Road
Eden, WI 53019

Ms. Maralyn Hankburg
Kettle Morraine
   Computers
1176 Saratoga Drive
West Bend, WI 53095

Mrs. Marilyn Munroe
The "Other" Office Store
333 Dexter Avenue
Fond du Lac, WI 54935

Mr. Ollie Dreyfus
Ollie's Office Supplies
437 Olive Street
Oostburg, WI 53070

Mr. Frederick Rivera
The Computer Tutor
27 Main Street
New Holstein, WI 53061

Mr. Paul Hamilton
Grafton Office Supply
290 First Street
Grafton, WI 53024

Ms. Lucille Caulkins
Copy-Quik, Inc.
211 West Pine Street
Juneau, WI 53039

Please send the letter above to these local businesses. Thanks, Whitney

Thriving in a Changing World

8:00 - 9:00 am
Registration .... Abel and Cain Ballrooms
Continental Breakfast, Office Products Exhibit

9:00-10:30 am
Cassie Cavness .... Abel and Cain Ballrooms
Thriving in a Changing World

10:30-11:00 am
Break, Office Products Exhibits .... Ballrooms

11:00-12:15 pm   Concurrent Sessions   (Tickets Required)
#1 **Report Publisher®**, Marcia Carlson .... Room C*
#2 **Beyond the Office**, Cassie Cavness .... Room A
#3 **Surviving with Humor**, Bret Bowers .... Room D
#4 **Teamwork**, Terry Lawrence .... Room E

12:15-1:00 pm
Luncheon .... Abel and Cain Ballrooms

1:15-2:30 pm   Concurrent Sessions   (Tickets Required)
#5 **WordPerfect®**, Roy St. Claire .... Room C*
#6 **Beyond the Office**, Cassie Cavness .... Room A
#7 **Rightsizing**, Patricia K. Morin .... Room E
#8 **Balancing Home & Career**, Lucia Lewin ...... Room D

2:30-2:45 pm
Break .... Abel and Cain Ballrooms

2:45-4:00 pm
Closing Session .... Abel and Cain Ballrooms
The Trip Home, Cassie Cavness
Wrap-up and Evaluation, CEU Certificates, Door Prizes

*Computers, software, and technical assistance for today's seminar graciously provided by Computer Heaven of Eden, Wisconsin.

Job 20   *About the Speakers . . .*

CASSIE CAVNESS holds degrees from St. Norbert College in DePere and UCLA. She is president of Cavness Consulting, Inc., in Los Carlos, California, a management consulting firm.

MARCIA CARLSON is an instructor in the Office Occupations Department at Mt. Calvary College. She has won numerous awards for her document designs.

BRET BOWERS has a degree in psychology from St. Olaf College and has held several management positions. He is currently owner of The Humor Shoppe in Milwaukee.

TERRY LAWRENCE teaches in the Supervisory Management program at UW-Milwaukee. She earned her PhD at Stanford University and is a trainer for Total Quality Management.

ROY ST. CLAIRE is a graduate of UW-Oshkosh with a degree in computer science. Currently he is a trainer and instructor at Computer Heaven in Eden.

PATRICIA K. MORIN is owner and president of PKMorin & Associates in Milwaukee. She is a graduate of Marquette University and a student of the downsizing and rightsizing theory of management.

LUCIA LEWIN is employed by the Eden County Department of Social Services, where she works with families to help them function as real families. She has degrees in sociology and psychology.

* * *

Thanks to the following Corporate Sponsors:

Andrea's Auto Body
Columbia Crystal Works
Condon, Condon, and Hill
   Investment Counseling
Cook Ceramics
Crockery Cookery
Delwich's Sandwiches
Geohart Electronic Assembly
Georgie's Greenhouses

Jan's Leather Loft
Kettle Valley Bank
Lionhart Leather Works
Paulus & Paulus, Inc.
Peckham Photography
Preston Press
Proctor Pharmaceuticals
Speed King Mfg. Co.
Workers Health

Thriving in a Changing World

sponsored by

Eden Chapter

Professional Secretaries International

April 1, 19—

Adams Hotel
Eden, Wisconsin

Make the commitment . . . to your profession
. . . to your career . . . to yourself

Membership in a professional association is evidence of your commitment to excellence as a team member with management. Whether you're an administrative assistant, executive secretary, word processing secretary, information specialist, office manager, or executive assistant, PSI can help you continue your career growth and assist in your personal and professional development.

By joining PSI, you will . . .

▲ Benefit from numerous personal and professional development programs that provide the opportunity to build management and leadership skills.

▲ Gain personal visibility and recognition while strengthening the image of the profession in the community.

▲ Network with colleagues who are experts in a variety of fields.

▲ Keep "up to date" on industry news and trends through association publications such as *The Secretary* magazine and *Vision* member newsletter, and through local, regional, and international conferences.

▲ Take advantage of reduced rates on educational materials and courses, and numerous other member benefits.

Our mission is to be the acknowledged, recognized leader of office professionals and to enhance their individual and collective value, image, competence, and influence.

The Eden Chapter . . .

The Eden PSI chapter meets the first Tuesday of every month at the Adams Hotel. Each meeting includes dinner and a program as well as the business meeting. You are encouraged to contact Rhonda Evers, CPS, who is membership chairman. She will provide any information you'd like about the Eden chapter of PSI or make a reservation for you for the next meeting.

Job 21

AGENDA FOR JANUARY

1. Discuss evaluation forms - Georgia
2. Approve flowers and decorations - Joanne & Francis
3. Discuss door prizes - Whitney
4. Discuss name tags - Rhonda
5. Discuss tickets for luncheon and concurrent sessions -
6. Revise seminar program - All   Rhonda
7. Assemble mailing of brochure - All
8. Review budget (There are no major changes in the budget since the last meeting.) - Erv

Job 22

Please draft an evaluation form for the seminar. A suggested format is attached.

Thanks, Georgia

Job 23

Because of registrations and room sizes, we must change the rooms of Concurrent Sessions 7 & 8. Session 7 will be in Room E and Session 8 will be in Room D. Please make these changes on the seminar program.

Thanks,
Rhonda & Francis

professional Secretaries international®

PARTICIPANT EVALUATION

| Program Number |
| Assigned by HQ |

Chapter/Division _____

Seminar Title _____

Seminar Date _____

	STRONGLY DISAGREE			NEUTRAL		STRONGLY AGREE	
PRESENTER/METHODS							
1. The presenter stated his/her objectives clearly.	1	2	3	4	5	6	7
2. The presenter was knowledgeable of the topic(s) covered.	1	2	3	4	5	6	7
3. The presenter taught the material in a way that made it seem practical or easily understood.	1	2	3	4	5	6	7
4. I am satisfied with the methods used to help me accomplish my learning objectives.	1	2	3	4	5	6	7
5. The audio/visual aids and other methods used to enhance my learning were effective.	1	2	3	4	5	6	7
SEMINAR CONTENT							
6. The seminar content matched the stated objectives.	1	2	3	4	5	6	7
7. The seminar content was relevant to my present or future work or personal life.	1	2	3	4	5	6	7
8. The content was arranged in a way that was conducive to my learning.	1	2	3	4	5	6	7
9. The skills and/or ideas taught in this seminar are relevant.	1	2	3	4	5	6	7
10. I can apply the skills and/or ideas I learned in this seminar.	1	2	3	4	5	6	7
PARTICIPANT BENEFITS							
11. The seminar met my expectations.	1	2	3	4	5	6	7
12. I learned new skills and/or ideas.	1	2	3	4	5	6	7
13. The quality of my work and/or life will be enhanced as a result of participating in this seminar.	1	2	3	4	5	6	7

PARTICIPANT BENEFITS (continued)

	STRONGLY DISAGREE			NEUTRAL		STRONGLY AGREE	
14. I will likely change my thinking and/or actions as a result of participating in this seminar.	1	2	3	4	5	6	7
15. The workbook/handouts or other materials obtained in the seminar will be useful in my work.	1	2	3	4	5	6	7

SEMINAR SETTING

16. The facilities used for this seminar were satisfactory.	1	2	3	4	5	6	7
17. The materials advertising the seminar stimulated my interest in attending.	1	2	3	4	5	6	7
18. I am satisfied with the greeting and orientation I received upon arrival.	1	2	3	4	5	6	7
19. I felt comfortable (physically) throughout the seminar.	1	2	3	4	5	6	7
20. The scheduling of the seminar was convenient.	1	2	3	4	5	6	7

OVERALL

21. Overall, I was satisfied with the seminar.	1	2	3	4	5	6	7

Comments _____

_____

_____

_____

Did you come to this seminar voluntarily?   Yes _____   No _____

Will there be barriers at work or home to prevent you from using what you learned in this seminar?
Yes _____   No _____   Not Applicable _____

Suggestions for speakers/topics you would like to see presented at future seminars. _____

_____

_____

Please complete and give this form to a PSI monitor at the end of the program or leave on your table.

THANK YOU FOR ATTENDING

Job 24

Please prepare 120 luncheon tickets that have the following information on them.

Thanks!

Joanne

"Thriving in a Changing World"
LUNCHEON
Saturday, April 1, 19—
12:15 - 1:00 p.m.
Adams Hotel Ballroom

1

Job 25

Please prepare 20 tickets each for Concurrent Sessions 1 & 5. Session 1 should look like this. Bold the name of the software.

Prepare 35 tickets for each of the other concurrent sessions.

Rhonda

Beautiful Documents With
Report Publisher ®
by
Marcia Carlson
11:00-12:15 in Room C

1

Job 26

Please prepare name tags with a LARGE first name, smaller last name, and an even smaller line with the city, state, and ZIP code.

Thanks,

Rhonda

RAFAEL
Zapata

Newburg, WI 53060

Job 27

AGENDA FOR FEBRUARY

1. Revise evaluation forms — Georgia
2. Approve name tags — Rhonda
3. Approve luncheon tickets — Rhonda
4. Approve concurrent session tickets — Rhonda
5. Approve seminar program — All
6. Review registrations — Rhonda
7. Review budget — Erv

Please attach the same budget as you attached in January. We'll work on the figures at the meeting.
Erv

Job 28

The evaluation forms are great. Good work!
Georgia

Job 29

The seminar program is wonderful!
The Committee

Job 30

The name tags are perfect!

Rhonda

Job 31

The luncheon and concurrent session tickets couldn't be better. Numbering them was a nice touch.

Thanks.   Rhonda

Job 32

AGENDA FOR MARCH

1. Review registrations and concurrent session requests — Rhonda
2. Double-check registrants for hands-on workshops — Rhonda
3. Review speaker AV requests — Becky
4. Determine room layouts — Francis
5. Review exhibitor requests — Whitney
6. Review budget — Erv

We're winding down. Keep up the wonderful work!

Georgia

Job 32 (continued)   DOLLAR PLANNER

Revenue	Budget	Actual
Target Number of Attendees @ $40 each (100)	4000	3970
Contributions from Corporate Sponsors	1500	1485
Target Profit	1000	

88 @ $40 and 10 @ $45

Expenses		
Speakers		
Keynote—fee and transportation	850	850*
Session Speakers—honorariums and transportation	400	
Lodging and meals	300	
Reproduction of speaker materials		
(consider who might donate this service)	25	0
Communication expenses (calls, mailings, etc.)	50	37
Complimentary registrations (actual costs)	50	70
Publicity		
Advertising	50	50*
Brochure layout and printing	300	160*
Paid to PSI for labels for mailings to PSI members		140
Postage for mailings	90	87
Door prizes (consider donations)	100	65
Facilities		
Meeting room charges (check for hidden costs)	200	200
AV equipment (rental or setup costs)	200	175
Breaks	200	225
Seminar luncheon	1000	984
Executive committee dinner	200	215
Participant Materials		
Printing of handouts	50	50*
Program	100	50
Folders	100	85
Name Tags	25	30
Pencil & paper (may be provided by hotel)	?	0
CEU Costs		
Certificates	15	15
$20 processing fee	20	20
Recording costs ($1.50 per person)	150	147

Please add the new line under Revenue and insert the new figures! Thanks! Erv

*Expense to be picked up by Corporate sponsor

Job 33

Concurrent Session 1 - Report Publisher

Natalia Krings
Adeline Gill
Floyd Smits
Vicky Smolaric
Linda Gauldon
Carol Reichelle
Elyda Crisman

Concurrent Session 5 - WordPerfect

Rafael Zapata
Beth Gnewuch
Jean H. Julsetz
Bea Brockman
Darcy Bork
Adeline Gill
Lisang Zheng
Tammy Sue Krause

Please send a letter to each of these people according to the session in which they have registered. Thanks, Rhonda

---

Dear (first name)

Congratulations! You were one of the 20 people who got their reservations to us in time to be included in the hands-on workshop "Beautiful Documents with Report Publisher."

That workshop is scheduled from 11:00 to 12:15 at the April 1 seminar in Room C. Please be prompt.

We are looking forward to seeing you at our PSI spring seminar. Your ticket for the workshop will be included in your registration packet.

Sincerely,

Rhonda Evers, Program Committee

Job 34

Concurrent Session 1 - Report Publisher

Cindysue Thiel   (Surviving)
Camille Yu   (Surviving)
Dawn Paterick   (Teamwork)
Sallie Wilke   (Beyond)

Concurrent Session 5 - WordPerfect

Debbie Gillmore   (Beyond)
Jessie DeSoto   (Rightsizing)
Star Zeske   (Balancing Act)
Bertie Eick   (Beyond)
Enoch Jacobchick   (Rightsizing)

These people had to be assigned to their second choice session. Please send them each a letter listing the session to which they were assigned.

Rhonda

Dear (first name)

Thank you for registering for our PSI spring seminar. I am sorry to inform you, however, that the hands-on workshop "Beautiful Documents with Report Publisher" was filled by the time your registration arrived.

Consequently, you are being scheduled for your second choice at that time which was (insert the full name of the second choice session). I trust that you will find this session educational and useful to you on your job.

We are looking forward to seeing you at our PSI spring seminar. Your ticket for the workshop will be included in your registration packet.

Sincerely,

Rhonda Evers, Program Committee

Job 35

Dear Ms. Cavness:

The time for our PSI spring seminar is rapidly approaching. Registrations are better than expected. It appears as though there will be nearly 100 seminar participants. The committee members have been working hard to assure that it will be a great seminar—one at which you will be proud to be a guest speaker.

Your room at the Adams Hotel has been reserved. The Adams is a luxury hotel with all of the comforts of home away from home—including a fully equipped exercise room, swimming pool, and whirlpool. We are certain you will enjoy your stay in Eden.

You are cordially invited to an executive committee dinner the evening before the seminar. Arrangement details will be provided to you when you check into the hotel. You may charge your breakfast to your room, and you are invited to attend the seminar luncheon at 12:15 p.m.

Your airline tickets are enclosed. As you can see from the itinerary, you will arrive in Milwaukee on United Flight #1270 at 3:10 p.m. on March 31. You will be met in the baggage claim area by Georgia Givins, who is a member of the Eden PSI Chapter. She has promised to wear a red coat and hat so you can pick her out of the crowd. Georgia will be available throughout your visit to help you set up your AV equipment, hand out materials, answer questions, or do whatever else is needed. She will also provide transportation to the airport for your return flight on April 1.

Again, we are looking forward to meeting you on March 31. If you should have any questions, please do not hestitate to contact me at 414-555-7812.

Sincerely,

Becky Brown, Program Committee

Enclosures

Please send this letter to Ms. Cavness. Thanks, Becky

Job 36

Dear (speaker)

The time for our PSI spring seminar is rapidly approaching. Registrations are better than expected. It appears as though there will be nearly 100 seminar participants. The committee members have been working hard to assure that it will be a great seminar—one at which you will be proud to be a guest speaker.

Eve Warren, manager of the Adams Hotel where the seminar will be held, has arranged for a block of rooms for seminar participants. PSI will arrange for your room if you wish to arrive the evening before the conference. The Adams hotel provides free parking for hotel guests as well as a health center complete with exercise equipment, a swimming pool, and whirlpool.

Please let me know if you wish to arrive on March 31. You are cordially invited to an executive committee dinner the evening before the seminar at 7:30 p.m. Arrangement details will be provided to you when you check into the hotel. A complimentary registration to the seminar is also being arranged for you, and you are invited to attend the seminar luncheon at 12:15 p.m.

Thank you for getting your handouts to us so promptly. They are currently being processed. You can expect about 30 people in your session at (time). Again, we are looking forward to your participation in our seminar. If you have any further questions, please don't hesitate to call me at 555-7812.

Sincerely,

Becky Brown, Program Committee

Please send this letter to all speakers except Ms. Cavness. Note that it verifies the time of their session.

Thanks, Becky

Job 37

Use 8½ x 11-inch paper to prepare a "poster" for each of the concurrent sessions to put outside of the door. Use _big_ bold letters - (one inch tall, if you can) and make them 'beautiful'!

Francis

> Room C
>
> BEAUTIFUL DOCUMENTS
> WITH
> REPORT PUBLISHER®
>
> Marcia Carlson, Speaker
> 11:00 - 12:15

Job 38

Please fill out the hotel function sheet for the hands-on session in Room C. Both speakers would like the room set up in classroom style.

Both speakers will use a demo computer (provided by Computer Heaven) attached to a display panel and an overhead projector. This requires extra extension cords. Make a note of that on the function sheet.

A lavalier microphone with a 20-foot cord is requested since the speakers will be moving between the lectern (better request one) and the demo computer. Also, a wall-mount screen will be best.

Water on a table outside of the room is requested. A one-time charge of $25 will be paid for room setup. No deposit is necessary.

Thanks, Francis

Job 39

I am pleased that you have agreed to represent your company at the Eden PSI chapter's spring seminar on April 1 at the Adams Hotel in Eden.

Registration begins at 8:00 a.m. on April 1, and participants will have until 9:00 a.m. to look at the exhibits. A 10:30 to 11:00 a.m. break time and the 12:15 to 1:00 p.m. lunch time will also afford participants an opportunity to check out your merchandise.

The hotel will have the ballroom open by 7 a.m. so you will have time to set up before the registration. You may remove your exhibits when the participants return to the concurrent sessions at 1 p.m.

You have been assigned to Table(s) (insert table number(s)). We are looking forward to seeing you at the seminar. If you have any questions, please call me at 555-1357.

The following exhibitors will be at the seminar. I've indicated their table numbers in parentheses. Please send them this letter.

Eden Bus. Machines (1 & 2)   The "Other" Office Store (5)
Micro & Office Supply (3)   Ollie's Office Supplies (6)
Computer Heaven (4)   The Computer Tutor (7)
                                      Copy-Quik, Inc. (8)

Whitney

Job 40

AGENDA FOR APRIL

1. Review seminar and make notes for next year - Georgia
2. Pay bills - Erv
3. Review the budget - Erv
4. Assemble information for the CEU - Rhonda
5. Tally the evaluations - Rhonda
6. Pat each other on the back for a job well done!
   (hopefully!!)

Job 41

professional Secretaries international.

WI 46 A 12
Program Number
Assigned by HQ

PARTICIPANT EVALUATION

Chapter/Division __Eden Chapter__

Seminar Title __Thriving in a Changing World__

Seminar Date __April 1, 19–__

PRESENTER/METHODS	STRONGLY DISAGREE				NEUTRAL			STRONGLY AGREE
1. The presenter stated his/her objectives clearly.	1	2	3	4	(12) 5	(45) 6	(41) 7	
2. The presenter was knowledgeable of the topic(s) covered.	1	2	3	4	(10) 5	(45) 6	(43) 7	
3. The presenter taught the material in a way that made it seem practical or easily understood.	1	2	3 (2)	4 (10)	5 (30)	6 (56)	7	
4. I am satisfied with the methods used to help me accomplish my learning objectives.	1	2	3 (1)	4	5 (7)	6 (40)	7 (50)	
5. The audio/visual aids and other methods used to enhance my learning were effective.	1	2	3	4 (2)	5 (5)	6 (34)	7 (53)	

SEMINAR CONTENT

6. The seminar content matched the stated objectives.	1	2	3 (5)	4	5 (17)	6 (14)	7 (62)	
7. The seminar content was relevant to my present or future work or personal life.	1	2 (1)	3 (7)	4 (4)	5 (29)	6 (47)	7 (20)	
8. The content was arranged in a way that was conducive to my learning.	1	2	3	4	5 (15)	6 (53)	7 (30)	
9. The skills and/or ideas taught in this seminar are relevant.	1	2 (10)	3	4 (3)	5 (27)	6 (10)	7 (48)	
10. I can apply the skills and/or ideas I learned in this seminar.	1	2 (8)	3 (5)	4	5 (30)	6 (37)	7 (18)	

PARTICIPANT BENEFITS

11. The seminar met my expectations.	1	2	3	4 (2)	5 (46)	6 (40)	7 (10)	
12. I learned new skills and/or ideas.	1	2	3	4 (11)	5 (30)	6 (48)	7 (9)	
13. The quality of my work and/or life will be enhanced as a result of participating in this seminar.	1 (3)	2	3 (7)	4 (14)	5 (29)	6 (21)	7 (24)	

PARTICIPANT BENEFITS (continued)

	STRONGLY DISAGREE			NEUTRAL			STRONGLY AGREE

14. I will likely change my thinking and/or actions as a result of participating in this seminar.

① (2) ② (1) ③ (8) ④ (13) ⑤ (24) ⑥ (26) ⑦ (24)

15. The workbook/handouts or other materials obtained in the seminar will be useful in my work.

① (14) ② (2) ③ (17) ④ (10) ⑤ (33) ⑥ (10) ⑦ (12)

SEMINAR SETTING

16. The facilities used for this seminar were satisfactory.

1   2   3   ④ (1) ⑤ (20) ⑥ (45) ⑦ (32)

17. The materials advertising the seminar stimulated my interest in attending.

1   2   3   ④ (5) ⑤ (14) ⑥ (48) ⑦ (31)

18. I am satisfied with the greeting and orientation I received upon arrival.

1   2   3   4   ⑤ (25) ⑥ (26) ⑦ (47)

19. I felt comfortable (physically) throughout the seminar.

1   2   3   4   5   ⑥ (49) ⑦ (49)

20. The scheduling of the seminar was convenient.

1   2   3   ④ (10) ⑤ (8) ⑥ (40) ⑦ (40)

OVERALL

21. Overall, I was satisfied with the seminar.

1   2   3   4   ⑤ (40) ⑥ (48) ⑦ (10)

Comments _____

_____

_____

_____

Did you come to this seminar voluntarily?   Yes _92_   No _6_

Will there be barriers at work or home to prevent you from using what you learned in this seminar?
Yes _9_   No _80_   Not Applicable _10_

Suggestions for speakers/topics you would like to see presented at future seminars. _____

_____

_____

Please complete and give this form to a PSI monitor at the end of the program or leave on your table.

THANK YOU FOR ATTENDING

Job 42

 professional Secretaries international ®

PARTICIPANT LIST

Include Full Names/Addresses and SSN (Canada SIN) or PSI-ID Number

PLEASE KEY INFORMATION TO INSURE ACCURACY

Name Judy Abdullah

Address: Home x or Work ____

Get the addresses from the mailing list!

SSN 333-44-8291

PSI-ID Number 4672

Name Delores Bartlein

Address: Home x or Work ____

SSN 443-34-5632

PSI-ID Number 4850

Name Kris Gehrke

Address: Home x or Work ____

SSN 532-76-4196

PSI-ID Number 4831

Name Kathleen Gillett

Address: Home x or Work ____

SSN 343-76-4904

PSI-ID Number 4673

Name Ricci Giordana

Address: Home x or Work ____

SSN 461-32-5196

PSI-ID Number 4692

Name Beth Gnewuch

Address: Home x or Work ____

SSN 398-72-5143

PSI-ID Number 4699

Job 43

 professional Secretaries international®

ATTENDANCE REPORT

Sponsor Name _____

Program Number Assigned
by Headquarters _____

CEU Granted
Each Participant _____

Event Date(s) _____

Total Number of Contact Hours _____

Number of Meeting Days _____

Program Site _____

Name of Instructor(s) _____

_____   _____

_____   _____

_____

_____

_____

Title of Program _____   _____

Number of Attendees: _____ x $1.50 = Amount Submitted $ _____

Signature of PSI Sponsor President _____

Signature of PSI Program Chairperson _____

Phone: Business _____

Phone: Business _____

　　　　Fax _____

　　　　Fax _____

　　　　Residence _____

　　　　Residence _____

Date _____

Date _____

Attach typed participant list and check for $1.50 per participant.

APPENDIX A
Formatting a Disk

Regardless of what kind of computer you use for your WordPerfect training, you probably need a disk for your work. When you buy new disks, most of them are not ready to be used in your computer. The majority of disks are prepared in a generic way so that they can be used by different kinds of computers—Apple, IBM, Compaq, Tandy, Zenith, Dell, Gateway, and others. The operating systems on computers vary, and when a disk is prepared to work in one brand of computer, it may not work in another brand.

Preparing a disk to use in your computer is called **formatting**. When you format a disk, you are setting it up to receive information in the language that your computer understands and is consistent with the disk drives and programs in your computer.

To format a disk, the disk operating system (DOS) must be present.

Hard Disk System

1. DOS will be installed on the hard drive.
2. Put the new disk to be formatted in Drive A.
3. Go to the C:\> prompt, key *format a:*, and strike **Enter**.
4. The message **Insert new diskette in Drive A and strike Enter when ready** will appear. Strike **Enter** again and your disk will be formatted.
5. After a time you will see the question **Format Another (Y/N)?** If you wish to format another disk, key **Y**, put a new disk in Drive A, and strike **Enter** to start the formatting.
6. If you don't want to format another disk, at the **Format Another (Y/N)?** question, key **N**. Formatting is complete and your disk is ready to use.

Dual Floppy System

1. Place the DOS disk in Drive A.
2. Put the new disk to be formatted in Drive B.
3. At the A:\> prompt, key *format b:*, and strike **Enter**.
4. The message **Insert new diskette in Drive B and strike Enter when ready** will appear. Strike **Enter** again and your disk will be formatted.
5. After a time you will see the question **Format Another (Y/N)?** If you wish to format another disk, key **Y**, put a new disk in Drive B, and strike **Enter** to start the formatting.

6. If you don't want to format another disk, at the **Format Another (Y/N)?** question, key **N**. Formatting is complete and your disk is ready to use.

A disk formatted for use on an IBM computer or compatible may be reformatted to use on a noncompatible computer. However, when you format a disk, you erase all of the information stored on that disk. Be certain you never accidentally format a disk containing information that you wish to keep.

APPENDIX B
Using a Mouse

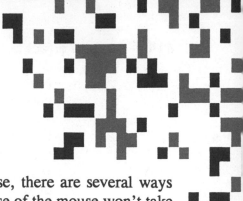

If your computer is equipped with a mouse, there are several ways you can use it in WordPerfect 5.1. While the use of the mouse won't take the place of the keys on the keyboard for most WordPerfect functions, its use can enhance your work with WordPerfect.

Hand Position

If you are left handed, many mouse programs enable you to switch the responses of the mouse buttons so that you can use the mouse with your left hand. Many people who are left handed use the mouse with their right hand with little adjustment because the actions of the fingers with the mouse are new, regardless of which hand you use.

When you position your hand on the mouse, the mouse should be held with the cord away from you. Your wrist and a portion of your forearm should rest comfortably behind the mouse. Most of the movement of the mouse will also involve the movement of your hand and forearm. Try to minimize the action of the wrist in moving the mouse to reduce the chance of repetitive motion injuries to your wrist.

Your thumb should be aligned on the left side of the mouse, and your ring finger and pinkie should be positioned on the right side of the mouse. Your index finger should rest above the left mouse button, and your big finger should rest above the right mouse button.

Clicking

As you move the mouse in your document, a colored spot will move on the screen. This colored spot is NOT your cursor. It is just an indicator or pointer. One of the more useful functions of the mouse is to position the cursor in a particular place in your document. This may be called "clicking an insertion point" because you can point to the desired location for the cursor and click the left mouse button once. Lesson 4 mentions positioning of the cursor by pointing and clicking.

Menus

The mouse can also be used for accessing the pull-down menus. You can choose to have the menu bar always displayed or you can choose to have it hidden. This choice is made by accessing Setup with **Shift-F1**, choosing **2 D**isplay and then **4 M**enu Options. The final choice in the

Menu Options menu is **8** Menu Bar Remains Visible, where you may choose Yes or No.

If you choose not to have the menu bar always visible, you can easily turn it on at will by clicking the right mouse button. Then you can use the mouse to point to the menu of choice and click the left mouse button to open that menu as well as choose items from the menu. The menu bar as well as the menu can be closed by either choosing an item from the menu or by clicking outside of the menu.

Blocking Text

Probably the most valuable use of the mouse in WordPerfect 5.1 is for blocking text. While text can be blocked by positioning the cursor, turning on Block, and moving the cursor to the end of the text to be blocked, it is much easier to use the mouse to drag across the text to be be blocked. With a little practice you can become skilled in the exact placement of the mouse pointer at the beginning and the end of the text being blocked, and in many cases it's considerably faster.

While many thousands of people successfully use WordPerfect 5.1 without the use of a mouse, many users find it useful and desirable. If you have a mouse and find its use awkward, practice. With a little practice, you will develop a skill that will serve you well. You will soon find that you'll like using the mouse for some tasks and the keyboard for other tasks.

APPENDIX C
Installing WordPerfect

For your WordPerfect work in this course, WordPerfect was already installed on the classroom computers. If you should own your own computer and wish to use WordPerfect on that computer, you must purchase the software and "install" the software on your computer.

When you purchase software, it comes on disks—either six 3½-inch disks or twelve 5¼-inch disks. These disks contain the software program in a compressed format. You cannot run WordPerfect from the disks that are in the package when you buy WordPerfect.

Hard Drive System. The install procedure for a hard drive system involves copying the information on the software disks into special directories that WordPerfect sets up on your hard drive.

Dual Floppy System. If you install on a dual floppy system, you must have a half dozen or so formatted disks handy. You will be asked to label the disks. Then you must follow the instructions in the install procedure to copy the appropriate files on the appropriate disks.

Network. If you are installing on a network, you will follow the same procedure. However, WordPerfect may not operate on the network until it is activated on your network server. Even after everything is set up on the server, you may need to make some adjustments in WordPerfect before it is used.

In any case, WordPerfect does all of the work for you. All you have to do is go to a DOS prompt, put the *Install/Learn/Utilities* disk into a floppy drive, and key the name of the drive followed by the word *install* (i.e., *a:install* or *b:install*). Then you must answer all of the questions asked during the installation and change disks when prompted. If you need to abort the installation at any time, you may do so by striking the **Esc** key.

Let's look at what some of those questions are and what you need to know in order do an educated job of installing WordPerfect.

1. Do you have a color monitor? A sample will show color on the screen so you can find out the answer to that even if you don't know. (It's not likely that you don't know!)
2. Are you installing to a hard drive, a dual floppy, or a network system?
   a. Dual Floppy. WordPerfect will tell you to prepare 10 disks. They should be formatted but blank, and they should be labeled with the list of labels that will show on the screen. Then you will continue the installation, putting the appropriate disks into the appropriate drives as directed.

b. Hard Drive. A large menu will appear that looks much like Figure A-1. Unless you are updating from an old release of the software or choosing a new printer driver, you'll probably choose **1 Basic**.

c. Network. The procedure here will be much like that for a hard drive system.

```
Installation

1 - Basic
2 - Custom
3 - Network
4 - Printer
5 - Update
6 - Copy Disks
7 - Minimal
8 - Exit
```

Figure C-1

3. Do you want the Utility Files? Answer **Yes**. These files make it possible for you to run the Speller and the Thesaurus.

4. Do you want the Learning Files? These files are prerecorded documents that are correlated with the lessons in the *WordPerfect Workbook*. If you have no intention of working through the *Workbook* lessons, you may answer **No**. (These files take up space on your hard drive.)

5. Do you want the Help Files? Answer **Yes**. The help files provide the WordPerfect on-line help.

6. Do you want the Keyboard Files? Answer **Yes**. The keyboard files allow you to choose different keyboard arrangements. They also make specialized macros available to you. The specialized macros will probably be more important to you than the keyboard files.

7. Do you want the Style Library? Answer either **Yes** or **No**. If you have lots of disk space available or if you are into legal work, you will definitely answer yes. The WordPerfect styles are interesting to look at and quite useful for some circumstances.

8. Do you want the Printer Test File? Answer **Yes**. This file should be retrieved and printed when you have your software installed and the correct printer chosen. It will show you much of what your printer is capable of doing.

9. Do you want the WordPerfect Program? Answer **Yes**. (This is a silly question. You wouldn't be installing WordPerfect if you didn't want to run the program!)

10. Do you want the Speller? Answer **Yes**. Even the best speller needs help once in a while.

11. Do you want the Thesaurus? Answer **Yes** or **No**. The thesaurus does take some disk space, but it is quite useful when you can't think of just the right word.

12. Do you want the PTR Program? Answer **No** unless you are a programming guru and feel capable of revising the programs that make the printer drivers work.

13. Do you want the Graphic Drivers? Answer **Yes**. These graphic drivers help WordPerfect work with your monitor. Without the graphic drivers, you wouldn't be able to see the miniature of your

document with Print Preview. Also, the graphic drivers make it possible for you to see the graphic images on the edit screen.

14. Do you want the Small .DRS file? Answer **Yes** if you are installing on a dual floppy system or if you didn't install the graphic drivers. Answer **No** if you are doing a basic installation to the hard drive.

15. Do you want the graphic images? Answer **Yes**. There are only 30 of them, but those graphic images make it possible for you to spruce up your work.

16. Check **config.sys**. WordPerfect checks the config.sys file to see if it contains the parameters necessary to run WordPerfect. If it isn't OK, WordPerfect will fix the file—with your permission.

17. Check **autoexec.bat**. WordPerfect checks the autoexec.bat file, too, to see if you can start WordPerfect from about any prompt. WordPerfect will fix the autoexec.bat file, too, with your permission.

18. Install Printers? Most likely you will have one or two printers that you will want to be using with your WordPerfect program. Answer to the affirmative. WordPerfect will prompt you to insert the Printer 1 disk, which contains the names of all 800 or 900 printers for which WordPerfect has printer drivers. (A "printer driver" is the WordPerfect program that enables WordPerfect to communicate through your computer to your printer.)

The printer names are listed alphabetically, and if you follow the prompt at the bottom of the screen, you can do a name search for the section that includes your printer. When you key the letter that makes your choice, you will be prompted to insert the disk that contains the desired printer driver.

That's about it for the installation. It wasn't so hard, was it? One other thing deserves mention. If the ONLY program you use is WordPerfect, you can set up the autoexec.bat file so that whenever you turn on your computer, it will take you directly into WordPerfect. You will probably want to ask someone who is knowledgeable about DOS commands to help you add one more line to the end of the autoexec.bat file. All that needs to be added is **wp**.

APPENDIX D
Working with DOS

Hiding behind the scenes when you're using WordPerfect is a program that enables your computer to communicate with the word processing program. This program is called the Disk Operating System (DOS). The disk operating system also enables you to do some housekeeping things that are not specifically word processing functions, like formatting disks (covered in Appendix A) and copying files from one disk to another.

The disk operating system that you must use on an IBM or IBM compatible computer is known as PC-DOS or MS-DOS. Although a good many operate with MS-DOS, some brands of computers use different operating systems. That's why a disk formatted for one computer may not work on another brand of computer.

DOS provides you with quite a number of capabilities. Those features, the commands that make them work, and a description of each can be found in the reference section of the DOS manual that comes with your computer. If you have a DOS manual handy, look at the reference section now so you know where to find it in case you should need it.

When you work with an application program such as WordPerfect, you can sift through the list of DOS commands and eliminate a good many of them as unnecessary because the same capabilities are included in the application program. In this appendix you will learn several of the most useful DOS commands. These include making backups of disks or files, erasing files from disks, and looking at directories of disks. While many of these functions are available inside WordPerfect, it is sometimes more convenient to use DOS to perform them.

If you are working on a hard disk system, all of the DOS commands are on the hard disk, perhaps in a directory named DOS. In addition, the filepath has probably been set up so that your computer can access all DOS commands from any DOS prompt whenever they are needed. WordPerfect 5.1 requires that you use the 2.1 version of DOS or a newer version.

If you're working on a dual floppy system, your WordPerfect program disk probably contains some of the DOS commands. These DOS commands are included in a file called COMMAND.COM that may have been installed on the WordPerfect disk when it was set up for your use. Having the COMMAND.COM file on the WordPerfect disk makes it possible for you to start the computer using the WordPerfect disk rather than having to first insert the DOS disk.

All of the DOS commands in the list below are available to all users of either hard disk or dual floppy systems. However, if you are using a dual floppy system, you must have the DOS disk to use some of the commands. This list divides the commands into *internal commands* (those for which a DOS disk isn't needed once the computer is displaying a DOS prompt) and *external commands* (those for which a DOS disk must be used).

INTERNAL COMMANDS

The DOS commands available on a dual floppy system once the system has been *booted* (started) are called *internal commands* because you may use them without using the DOS disk. The internal commands that will probably be most useful to you are listed below, along with a description of what the command can do and an example of what the command looks like when properly keyed at the A:\> or C:\> prompt.

1. **DIR**. This command is used to display the directory of the disk's contents. When keyed at the A:\> prompt, it will show a list of the files on the disk in Drive A. When keyed at the B:\> prompt, it will show a list of the files on the disk in Drive B. When keyed at the C:\> prompt—well, you can guess what it does here. The DIR command has several variations:

    - **dir** lists the files on the disk.

    - **dir/p** fills the screen with a list of files and pauses while you look at the files. You may strike any key to look at the next screenful of documents.

    - **dir/w** provides a list of files that shows in several columns across the screen. You can see more at one time than with the other **dir** commands. However, you can't see information about each file such as the size or the date and time of creation.

    - **dir *.com** displays all of the files with the extension COM. Of course, the extension asked for can be any extension, such as LTR for a letter, RPT for a report, or PRI for a primary file.

2. **ERASE** or **DEL**. Either of these commands are used to erase files from the disk. You can erase one file at a time or a group of files. Notice that in each option below, **a:** is included as part of the command. This is a precaution to remind you (and the computer) which disk drive you are using. If you are working from a hard disk, you would replace the **a:** with **c:**.

    - **erase a:filename.ext** erases the file called FILENAME with the extension EXT.

- **erase A:*.*** erases all files on the disk in Drive A.

- **erase a:*.ltr** erases all files with the extension LTR. (Always check your keying carefully when using the erase command so you erase exactly what you intend to erase.)

3. **COPY**. This command is used to copy files from one disk to another. Again, there are several variations:

   - **copy a:*.* b:** copies all files from the disk in Drive A to the disk in Drive B. The files are copied one at a time. The disk to which they are being copied must have been formatted previously. It may also already contain files. They will not be erased with this command unless they have the same name as the new files.

   - **copy a:filename.ext b:** copies the file called FILENAME with the extension EXT from Drive A to Drive B.

   - **copy a:oldfile b:newfile** copies a file from Drive A to Drive B and changes the name from OLDFILE to NEWFILE.

4. **MD**. The MD command is used to Make a Directory. Directories are like file folders. They help organize your work. To make a directory named *letters* on the disk in Drive A, key **md letters**. After you've created the directory, when you give the DIR command, you will see **LETTERS <DIR>** in your file list.

5. **CD**. Once the directory is created, you can move into that directory with the Change Directory command. Key **cd letters**. If the directory is on the disk in Drive A, after giving the Change Directory command, the filepath will read **A:\letters>**.

6. **RD**. If you no longer need a directory, it can be removed with the Remove Directory command. You may not be in the directory when you give the command, and the directory must be empty. If there are any files in the directory, you will get an error message when you key **rd letters** to remove the LETTERS directory.

EXTERNAL COMMANDS

External commands are those for which you need to use the DOS disk on a dual floppy system. The DOS disk should be placed in Drive A and the command keyed at the A:\> prompt. Three commonly used external commands are described below.

1. **FORMAT**. This command is discussed in Appendix A. There are several variations of the Format command:

- **A:\ > format b:** /s not only formats your disk but also installs the COMMAND > COM file on the disk. Thus it will boot the system and also allow you to use internal commands discussed above.

    NOTE: Some recent versions of DOS do not allow you to transfer the system in this way. Instead, you must first format the disk. Then you can transfer the system to the disk in Drive B by keying **A:\ > sys b:** followed by **A:\ > copy command.com b:**.

- **A:\ > format b:** /v enables you to give the disk a volume name of eleven characters or less. The volume name will show when you check the disk contents. Newer versions of DOS automatically ask for a version name when you format the disk, so this variation is not needed.

2. **DISKCOPY.** This command copies the contents of one disk to another disk, making them exactly alike. The command must be given with the DOS disk in Drive A. After giving the command, you will be prompted to put the *source disk* (the one from which you're copying) in Drive A and the *target disk* (the one to which you're copying) in Drive B and strike any key when ready.

   The Diskcopy command looks like this: **A:\ > diskcopy a: b:**. Be careful when you use this command. It formats the target disk at the same time that it copies. When a disk is being formatted, anything that is on the disk is erased.

3. **CHKDSK.** The CHKDSK command is used to check a disk to see if it has sustained damage or to see how much room remains on the disk. If there are damaged sectors on the disk, the CHKDSK command will report that fact.

   It is usually not a good idea to continue to use a disk that has been damaged. If you discover that you are working with a disk with damaged sectors, it would probably be a good idea to transfer any active files to another disk. The CHKDSK command is keyed at the A:\ > prompt with the DOS disk in Drive A. It is keyed like this: **A:\ > chkdsk b:**

   Both internal and external commands may seem a little foreign to you if you have never before used a computer. You will probably not get a great deal of experience using them because many of the same things can be accomplished from within WordPerfect. Be patient and try them out as you have need for them. The more you use the DOS commands, the more confidence you will develop in your ability to handle a computer.

GLOSSARY

Absolute Tabs   Tabs that are measured from the left edge of the paper as opposed to tabs that are measured from the left margin of a document. When you move the left margin of a document, absolute tabs remain in the same locations.

Alt Macro   A macro that can be started by holding the Alt key and striking one of the alphabetic keys. You may only have one Alt macro for each letter of the alphabet.

Archiving   Moving important but seldom-used documents to a safe, out-of-the-way place.

ASCII   American Standard Code for Information Interchange. This is a code where a document is unformatted and can usually be read by any word processing program.

Background Printing   The capability of a program to print a document while you are working on a different document.

Batch File   A file that may be set up to do a number of things automatically. For example, a batch file might start WordPerfect for you whenever you start your computer.

Block Protect   The feature that enables you to keep a block or section of text together on a page. You can adjust the size of the block to make soft page breaks fall in a desirable location.

Blocked   In word processing, referring to a section of text that has been selected or highlighted. You might block text to be moved, copied, or deleted. You might also block text to add a special kind of formatting, like bold, underline, or a new font.

Boilerplate   Prestored paragraphs or sentences or any amount of text (sometimes referred to as standard text) that is used in the assembly of documents.

Boot   To start a computer or program.

Byte   The computer measurement of storage—usually representing one character, space, or command such as Tab or Hard Return.

Case Sensitive   A feature, such as Search, where the results vary depending on whether the letters are uppercase or lowercase.

Codes   The hidden commands that cause your document to be formatted. In WordPerfect, you can use the Reveal Codes feature to see what codes are formatting your document and the location of those codes.

Concordance File   A concordance file is a listing of the words or terms to be included in an index. When a concordance file has been prepared, WordPerfect will search through the designated text, list the occurrences of the words in the concordance file, and arrange an index, complete with page numbers.

Context Sensitive   A feature that responds differently depending on what you are doing when you use it. In WordPerfect, the Help feature will go directly to the section on Outlining if you are working on an outline when you strike F3 for Help.

CPU   The working portion of the computer, known as the Central Processing Unit, that contains the processing and memory chips and the circuit boards that enable the computer to process your commands.

Database   A database is a collection of related information, such as a collection of names and addresses of a group of people or a collection of parts in an inventory. In WordPerfect 5.1, a database is referred to as a *secondary file*.

Default   A setting built into a program that takes effect unless some alternative setting is specified. For example, in WordPerfect 5.1, the default margin settings are one inch on all sides of the page.

Desktop   The opening screen in a graphic environment, where the user may start a program by choosing an icon representing the desired program.

DOS   The Disk Operating System (DOS) is software that enables your computer to communicate with your disk drives and your software. Commonly used DOS commands are discussed in Appendix D.

DOS Disk   A disk that contains the DOS commands. On a dual floppy system, you may need to use a DOS disk to start the computer.

Downloadable   Download means to transfer data from a mainframe computer or network to a smaller unit, like your computer. When referring to downloadable fonts, those fonts are being downloaded from the computer hard drive to the printer.

Dropped Cap   A large letter dropped below the line of writing used to call attention to the beginning of an article in a newsletter or magazine.

Dual Floppy   A computer system containing two floppy disk drives but no internal hard disk. Usually the user will put a disk containing the desired computer program in Drive A and a disk for saving documents in Drive B.

Endnotes   Endnotes are references to other works or publications. Endnotes are printed as a list on the final page of the document.

Extension   The part of a document name following the period when naming a document to save it on a disk. DOS restricts the extension portion of a document name to a maximum of three characters. In WordPerfect, it is not imperative that a document name include an extension. Exceptions are macros, style libraries, and graphics.

Field   A field is a single piece of information in a secondary file. Fields are separated by {END FIELD} codes and a hard return.

Filename   The first part of the name of a document to be saved on a disk. DOS restricts the filename to a maximum of eight characters.

Filepath   The route to where a document is stored on a disk. A filepath includes the use of different levels of directories. For example, a document named *whale* that is saved in a directory named *mammals* that is a subdirectory of a directory named *animals* on the hard drive of the computer would have the following filepath: *C:\animals\mammals\whale*

Font   A font is a set of all characters (letters, numbers, and symbols) in a particular typeface in a particular size. When you select a font (e.g., Times 12-point), you are specifying typeface and size.

Footers   Footers are pieces of information printed at the bottom of the pages of a multiple-page document to tie the document together. Footers might include page numbers, chapter or unit titles, the title of the publication, or the date, depending on the kind of document being prepared.

Footnotes   Footnotes are references to other publications or quotations taken from other publications. Footnotes are usually numbered and positioned at the bottom of the page on which the quoted or referenced text is mentioned.

Format (a disk)   To prepare a disk to be used in the computer. When you format a disk, you are setting up the disk so that it can communicate with the computer in which you will be using it. Instructions for formatting a disk can be found in Appendix A.

Function Keys   The set of 10 or 12 *F* keys on the keyboards of IBM and IBM compatible equipment are referred to as *function keys*. The function keys are used as an alternative to the menu system in choosing and executing WordPerfect features.

Global Search and Replace   Global Search and Replace is the ability to locate and change automatically the same word or phrase throughout a document or portion of a document.

GUI   Graphic user interface. An operating system or program where the documents appear in multiple windows, complete with menus, scroll bars, and icons, is considered a GUI. Popular examples of operating systems using a graphical user interface are Windows and OS/2.

Hanging Indent   Hanging indent is a paragraph format where the first line of the paragraph begins at the left margin and the remaining paragraph lines are indented to the level of the first tab stop.

Hard Copy   The printed copy of a document.

Hard Disk   The high-capacity storage device that is usually permanently affixed inside of the CPU of the computer. With a hard disk system, the computer programs such as WordPerfect are recorded on the hard disk for easy access.

Hard Hyphen   A hard hyphen is a kind of hyphen used between two word parts you don't want separated at the end of a line. Hard hyphens might be used as minus signs in formulas or between the parts of a telephone number. A hard hyphen is entered by holding Ctrl while striking the minus key.

Hard Page Break   A hard page break is one entered manually by the person preparing the document. Hard page breaks always stay in the same position in a document, regardless of text added or deleted. A hard page break is entered by holding Ctrl while striking Enter.

Hard Space   Hard spaces are used between two words or word parts you don't want separated at the end of the line, e.g., between the first name and the initial in Gail M. Weber. A hard space is entered by holding Ctrl while striking the space bar.

Headers   Headers are pieces of information printed at the top of the pages of a multiple-page document. Headers tie a document together and might include page numbers, chapter or unit titles, the title of the publication, or the date, depending on the kind of document being prepared.

Headwords   When working with the Thesaurus feature of WordPerfect, a headword is a word that is included in the thesaurus with its own set of synonyms and antonyms.

Icon   An icon is a miniature graphic representing a window, a document, or a program. Icons are most often used on the desktop.

Justification   Justification refers to the procedure of adding space between words to make the words at the end of the line end evenly with one another. The default in WordPerfect 5.1 is full justification (both right and left margins are justified). Other choices are left justification (only the left margin is justified), center justification (all lines are centered), and right justification (meaning the left margin is ragged).

Kerning   Kerning is adjusting the space between individual pairs of letters to make the text more visually appealing.

Keyboard Merge   A keyboard merge is when you merge a primary file with no secondary file. The variable information is keyed into the document by the user as the merge progresses. An {INPUT} code tells WordPerfect to stop for the user to key the required information.

Landscape   Landscape is the page orientation where the long edges of the paper are at the top and bottom of the page and the short edges are at the sides.

Leaders   Leaders are dots (periods) that direct (lead) your attention from one side of a line of text to the other.

Leading   Leading is a term used in page layout that refers to varying the amount of space between lines of type. In early years of printing, measured strips of lead were inserted between the rows of type when laying out a page.

Left-Text Area   The space to the left of the first tab stop in a problem where WordPerfect Math will be used. This area is not include in WordPerfect calculations.

Macro   A macro is a collection of keystrokes that are accumulated because they are used together frequently. Macros are used to simplify and automate repeated sets of commands.

Macro Chaining   Adding the command to start one macro to the end of another macro so that when the first macro is finished, the second macro will run.

Masthead   The large title and date section at the top of a newspaper or newsletter identifying the document, the volume or edition, and the date. Publishers use the same layout for the masthead with each edition so the reader feels comfortable with the look of the publication.

Menu Bar   The list of menus from which you can choose WordPerfect features. The menu bar can be set to always appear at the top of the WordPerfect screen, or the user can turn on the menu bar by striking either the right mouse button or the Alt-= key combination.

Merge Code   A merge code is used to organize the text appropriately when two files are combined. Merge (sometimes called mail-merge) is most useful for repetitive documents, i.e., in combining the names and addresses in a mailing list with a standard letter.

Mnemonics   Mnemonics are related letters used to simplify commands, like *b* for *bold* or *u* for *underline*. In WordPerfect menus, choices may be made by keying the underlined *mnemonic* letter.

Monospaced   The kind of spacing where each character takes up the same amount of space horizontally, regardless of the size of the letter. Courier 10cpi, the default in WordPerfect 5.1, is a monospaced font.

Named Macro   A macro that has a specific name. When a named macro is to be used in Word-Perfect, the command to start the macro is given, and the name of the macro must be keyed.

Network   A configuration of computers where they are all cabled together and one workstation is designated as the file server. In a networked environment, WordPerfect frequently is loaded on the file server only, and individual workstations access the program from the file server as needed.

No-Print Zone   An area around the outside edges of a sheet of paper where the printer is incapable of printing. The size of the no-print zone varies according to the kind of printer.

Orphan   An orphan is the last line of a paragraph that appears by itself at the top of a page of text.

OS/2   An operating system utilizing the graphical user interface where a user can have several documents or programs available at any one time and can move easily from one to another without having to exit from a program.

Point Size   Point size is the vertical size of a character of type. A 72-point character would be approximately an inch tall. A 12-point character would be approximately a sixth of an inch tall. The greater the number of points, the greater the size of a letter.

Pointing   Pointing is using the mouse to move the pointer on the screen. Normally when you have positioned the pointer at the desired location, either the left or right mouse button is used to position the cursor or make menu choices.

Portrait   Portrait is the page orientation where the short edges of the paper are at the top and bottom of the page and the long edges are at the sides.

Primary File   The file used in a merge that contains the standard text is normally referred to as the primary file.

Print Queue   The list of documents that are waiting to be printed.

Proportional   Proportional spacing is the method of printing where each printed character takes up only the space it needs rather than a fixed amount of space. In proportional spacing, for example, a *w* would take considerably more space than would an *i*.

RAM   Random Access Memory (RAM) is the temporary storage area or working space for the document you are creating and the program you are using. This storage area is emptied if the computer is turned off or the electricity supplying it is interrupted.

Record   A record is all of the information about a particular customer, client, or product in a secondary file. It is the complete collection of data about that individual.

Redline   A feature that enables you to mark text suggested for addition to a document so that a number of people can discuss the change to the text. Text marked with Redline is printed with a shaded background.

Relative Tab   WordPerfect relative tabs are designed to be in relation to the left margin. That is, if you move the margin, the tab will not remain in the original position but will move in relationship to the new margin.

Resident Fonts   Resident fonts are fonts that are built into the microcircuitry of your printer so you don't have to create the fonts or download them from your hard drive.

Sans Serif   Sans serif type is type without serifs. Letters have no feet or curves at the ends of the main strokes. Sans serif type is contrasted with serif type. Sans serif type is best used for headlines and text to which you wish to call attention.

Save (a document)   Transferring a document from the memory of the computer to a disk so that it is available at some future time.

Scanning   Using a scanner to convert a document on hard copy into a digital image.

Scrolling   Scrolling is moving through text or a list box using the arrow keys, the Home key, and the Page Up and Page Down keys.

Search   Search is a WordPerfect feature that enables you to key a unique string of characters and then tell WordPerfect to find that text string.

Secondary File   A secondary file is a collection of information to be merged with a primary file. Often the secondary file contains names, addresses, telephone numbers, etc., of customers or clients.

Serif   Serifs are the strokes or feet at the ends of the main strokes of letters. Serif type is contrasted with sans serif type where there are no strokes or feet on the letters. Serif type is easy to read in body text.

Soft Page Break   A page break that is automatically inserted by WordPerfect when a page is full.

Standard Text   Prestored paragraphs or sentences or any amount of text (sometimes referred to as boilerplate) that is used in the assembly of documents.

Strikeout   A feature that enables you to mark text suggested for deletion from a document so that a number of people can discuss the change to the text. Text marked with Strikeout is printed with a line drawn through it.

Style   A style is a master format for a particular kind of document or document part in WordPerfect. Styles are collections of keystrokes and menu choices to speed up the formatting of documents when working with the same formats repeatedly.

Subdocuments   The term used when working with the Master Document feature to describe the individual documents that are to be combined to make up the master document.

Submenu   A second menu that branches off from a WordPerfect menu. When looking at a WordPerfect menu, an arrow pointing to the right opposite one of the menu items indicates that the menu item has a submenu which provides more choices regarding the feature.

Subscript   Subscript is the term used to refer to the position of a character that is printed below the normal line of writing (the baseline). An example is the 2 in H_2O.

Superscript   Superscript is the term used to refer to the position of a character that is printed above the normal line of writing. An example is the 2 in x^2.

Suppress   A feature that tells WordPerfect not to include the header, footer, or page number on a specific page of a document.

Template   Depending on the situation, *template* might refer to a number of things. Here are some possibilities:
   a.   The printed strip of commands to be placed near the function keys on your keyboard. WordPerfect Corporation prepares these *function key templates* to help you remember which feature is accessed by which function keys.
   b.   The disk containing the prerecorded documents to accompany this WordPerfect 5.1 textbook. The *template disk* may be acquired from the textbook publishing company.

c.   A master format for a particular kind of document or document part in other brands of word processing software. In WordPerfect, this feature is known as a *style*.

Thumbnail   A thumbnail is a miniature view of a document. Thumbnails are useful to preview what a document will look like when printed.

Toggle Key   A key on the keyboard that you strike once to turn it on and again to turn it off. Examples are the Caps Lock and Insert keys, or F6 for bold and F8 for underlining.

Typeface   A typeface is one design of type. A typeface has a name, like Helvetica, Times, Swiss, and Univers. It includes all characters of all sizes in the matching design.

Typeface Family   A group of all related sizes and styles derived from a master typeface.

VDT   The term Video Display Terminal (VDT) is used to refer to the screen or monitor of the computer. It is on the VDT that you can watch your work with the computer.

Widow   A widow is the first line of a paragraph that appears by itself at the bottom of a page.

Windows   An operating system utilizing the graphical user interface where a user can have several documents or programs available at any one time and can move easily from one to another without having to exit from a program.

Word Wrap   The feature that causes a word that doesn't fit at the end of one line to drop to the beginning of the next line.

INDEX _____